THIRD MILLENNIUM SCHOOLS

THIRD MILLENNIUM SCHOOLS:

A World of Difference in Effectiveness and Improvement

EDITED BY

TONY TOWNSEND,
PAUL CLARKE
AND MEL AINSCOW

SWETS & ZEITLINGER
PUBLISHERS

| LISSE | ABINGDON | EXTON (PA) | TOKYO |

Library of Congress Cataloging-in-Publication Data

Third millennium schools : a world of difference in effectiveness and
    improvement / edited by Tony Townsend, Paul Clarke, and Mel Ainscow.
        p.   cm.
    The country reports of the 1998 International Congress for School
    Effectiveness and Improvement in Manchester.
    Includes bibliographical references and index.
    ISBN 9026515413
    1. Education--Evaluation--Cross--cultural studies--Congresses
2. School improvement programs-- Cross-cultural studies--Congresses.
3. Educational change--Cross-cultural studies--Congresses.
I. Townsend, Tony. II. Clarke, Paul, 1961- . III. Ainscow, Mel.
IV. International Congress for School Effectiveness and Improvement
(1998 : Manchester, England)
LB28. 75. T52   1999
370--dc21   98-31606
                                                                  CIP

Cover design: Paula van der Heijdt
Printed in The Netherlands by Krips, Meppel

ISBN 90 265 1541 3

Acknowledgments

This book has its origins in conversations that we had during our planning for the International Congress for School Effectiveness and Improvement (ICSEI) 1998 Conference in Manchester, an event which involved the three editors personally in planning sessions and in establishing links with colleagues from around the world to ensure a variety of input and thought-provoking debate. We felt that it was a timely thing to do to gather together a perspective on the state of the world within the disciplines of effectiveness and improvement, and with that in mind we suggested to Swets and Zeitlinger that it might be appropriate to produce a documented version of the country reports. The editors would like to acknowledge the support of Martin Scrivener from Swets, for without his support, this book could not have been published.

The Manchester ICSEI 98 conference was a good example of ICSEI at its best. It was a diverse group of people with a common interest and as such it reflected the unique character of ICSEI. ICSEI has developed over the years from a small group of interested researchers to an international
grouping of academics, practitioners and policy makers, many of whom take the lead in national developments, equally, many play a quieter but significant role in supporting, nurturing and helping people to learn across the globe.

We dedicate this book to all the people within the community of ICSEI for their sustained commitment to the cause and their willingness to challenge the present viewpoints. You are the making of third millennium schools.

Preface

In January 1988, a group of educators met in London for the first International Congress for Effective Schools (ICES). According to Judith Chapman's report in the first issue of the *Australian Network News* (1989: 1):

> *The initiative for ICES was taken by Dale Mann, former Chairperson (1976-85) of the Department of Educational Administration, Teachers' College, Columbia University, who served as the first Chairperson (1984-85) for the National Council for Effective Schools in the United States...[who] felt it timely to bring policy-makers, researchers and planners together.*

By mid-1987 eight countries, the USA, England, Wales, Scotland, Australia, Sweden, Canada and South Africa had shown sufficient interest for an international congress to be conducted in late 1987 or early 1988. 'The planning group at Columbia was interested in a Congress in two parts: (1) a conference on school effectiveness open to all with an interest and with papers presented in the normal fashion for such events, and (2) a decision-making meeting at which the organisation would be formally constituted and decisions made.' (Chapman, 1989:1)

In January 1988, the first Congress was held at the University of London. Policy makers, practitioners and scholars from fourteen countries, including the initial eight, together with Germany, Hungary, Ireland, Israel, the Netherlands and Norway, attended the Congress and adopted the name 'International Congress for School Effectiveness' (which later became International Congress for School Effectiveness and Improvement, when formally constituted in Israel in 1990.

Since that time conferences have been held all around the world, in Rotterdam, the Netherlands (1989); Jerusalem, Israel (1990); Cardiff, Wales (1991); Victoria, Canada (1992); Norrkoping, Sweden (1993); Melbourne, Australia (1994); Leeuwarden, the Netherlands (1995); Minsk, Belarus (1996); Memphis, USA (1997) and Manchester, UK (1998). In that ten year period in excess of 3000 people have attended, with perhaps 100 or so having attended most of them.

The country reports

Country reports have always been part of the development of ICSEI. At the first Congress of 1988 they formed a major part of the offerings. As Creemers and Osinga (1995: 1) indicate: 'The major studies (Brookover et al., Rutter et al., Motimore et al.) were well known but almost nobody had a full picture of the studies and the improvement projects going on in the field in all the countries participating in this first meeting.' A selection of the reports from this meeting was published in Reynolds, Creemers and Peters (1989).

The second meeting in Rotterdam in 1989 continued the tradition of having country reports and the publication by Creemers, Peters and Reynolds (1989) clearly demonstrated that the search for the more effective school was no longer just a tradition in North America and Europe. However, it also became clear that the time it took for research to turn into practice meant that it was not necessary to have country reports at ICSEI in every subsequent year. As it was, there was much new research and activity to report on in all parts of the world that needed to take precedence in the formative years of ICSEI.

Consequently, the next major attempt to collate a series of country reports was made for the Leeuwarden conference in 1995 where nine countries from Europe, North America, Asia, the Middle East and the Pacific region joined to become part of the ICSEI reporting network. The major theme of this conference was to try and establish the links between school effectiveness and school improvement. David Reynolds, Jaap Scheerens and Sam Stringfield were invited to comment on some of the developments that seemed to be happening on an international level. These opinions provided a context in which worldwide development in school effectiveness and school improvement, in the areas of research, policy and practice might be judged. Some of the country reports were subsequently published in *School Effectiveness and School Improvement* Volume 7 No 2 in 1996.

In 1998, with the support of the Manchester conference, with its theme of 'Reaching out to all learners' ICSEI country reports were reactivated, but with the special brief of trying to increase both the number and the diversity of the countries that provided a report. With the specific intent of trying to encourage educators in some new countries to consider development that might fall within the purview of school effectiveness and improvement, whilst maintaining contact with countries that had previously reported, people from around the world were contacted and asked to submit a report. The result is a total of twenty country reports, with twelve from countries not previously represented. New countries from Scandanavia, from the Pacific, from Asia, Africa and from South America are to be found in the current set.

Not only are we able to see what is happening to education in rich, developed western countries, where the school effectiveness research and school improvement policies and practices are well developed, although not necessarily well implemented, but we are now able to chart the progress of countries where the use of the school effectiveness research is comparatively new, countries that have to deal with issues such as making judgements about what effectiveness means when not every child attends school and countries that are struggling to come to grips with the aftermath of military or oppressive regimes.

Murphy has argued (1991:166-168) that there are four factors which can be considered as the legacy of school effectiveness. He suggests the most fundamental of the four is that 'given appropriate conditions, all children can learn.' The second product of the school effectiveness research stems from a rejection of the historical perspective that good schools and bad schools could be identified by the socio-economic status of the area in which they were located. School effectiveness examined student outcomes, not in absolute terms, but in terms of the value added to students' abilities by the school, rather than the outside-of-school factors. He further argued that school effectiveness researchers were the first to reject the philosophy that 'poor academic performance and deviant behaviour have been defined as problems of individual children or their families' (Cuban, 1989, in Murphy, 1991). School effectiveness helped to eliminate the practice of 'blaming the victim for the shortcomings of the school'. Finally, the research showed that 'the better schools are more tightly linked - structurally, symbolically and culturally - than the less effective ones'. There was a greater degree of consistency and co-ordination in terms of the curriculum, the teaching and the organisation within the school.

Substantial progress has been made from the early 1980s, when the five factor model of school effectiveness (leadership, instructional focus, climate conducive to learning, high expectations and consistent measurement of pupil achievement; Edmonds, 1979) was paramount, to the mid-1990s, when it is widely acknowledged that the effectiveness of any school must be considered within the context in which that school operates rather than simply on the various 'ingredients' that help to make up the school's operations.

A number of studies have suggested that the level of effectiveness of schools can vary on the basis of the social environment of the school's locality (Hallinger & Murphy, 1986), with the outcomes being measured (Mortimore et al., 1988), the stage of development the school has reached (Stringfield & Teddlie, 1991), the social class mix of the students (Blakey and Heath, 1992) or even the country in which the research is conducted (Scheerens and Creemers, 1989; Wildy and Dimmock, 1992). It has also been shown that total school performance, in terms of its effectiveness, can vary over time (Nuttall, 1992); that schools that are effective are not necessarily effective in all things; some might be effective academically, but not in terms of social outcomes, or vice-versa (Mortimore *et al*, 1988); nor are they necessarily effective for all students, since different school effects can occur for children from different groups within the same school (Nuttall, 1989).

Over the past twenty years, the research has clearly established that schools do make a difference, and that pupil achievement is not just a product of socio-economic background, even though this difference may be smaller (around 8-15 % of variation in pupil outcomes) than was first thought (Cuttance, 1985; Bosker and Scheerens, 1989; Daly, 1991).

The effective schools research seems to have had the underlying purpose of developing practical means for school improvement, but there are some important distinctions and relationships between school effectiveness and school improvement that can be identified. As Smink pointed out:

> *School effectiveness is concerned with results. Researchers try to describe certain variables for school success in measurable terms. On the other hand, school improvement places the accent on the process; here one finds a broad description of all the variables that play a role in a school improvement project. Both approaches need the other to successfully modernize the system.*

(Smink, 1991:3)

The current set of country reports clearly show how the linkages between effectiveness and improvement have grown in the past ten years and also demonstrate the substantial impact the research has had on educational policy, particularly with the world-wide reform movement with its particular focus on the self-managing school. If the purpose of the country reports is to provide a better understanding of what is happening in schools and school systems in different parts of the world, then the current set of reports provides a rich tapestry of information.

Tony Townsend, Paul Clarke and Mel Ainscow
Frankston, Australia, and Manchester, England,
August, 1998

References

Blakey, L. S., & Heath, A. F. (1992) 'Differences between comprehensive schools: Some preliminary findings.' In Reynolds, D. & Cuttance, P. *School Effectiveness: Research, Policy and Practice*, London, Cassell

Bosker, R. J. & Scheerens, J. (1989) 'Issues in the interpretation of the results of school effectiveness research.' *International Journal of Educational Research*, 13 (7), 741-51

Brookover, W., Beady,C., Flood, P., Schweitzer, J. & Wisenbaker, J. (1979) *School Social Systems and Student Achievement: Schools Can Make a Difference*, East Lansing, Institute for Research on Teaching, Michigan State University.

Chapman, J. (1989) 'Australian network grows from international beginning' in *Network News 1* (1), p 1.

Cuban, L. (1989) 'The "at-risk" label and the problem of school reform', *Phi Delta Kappan*, 71(8)

Creemers, B., Peters, T. & Reynolds, D.(1989) *School Effectiveness and School Improvement* , Amsterdam, Swets & Zeitlinger.

Creemers, B. & Osinga, N. (1995) *ICSEI Country Reports*, Leeuwarden, the Netherlands, GCO.

Cuttance, P. (1985) 'Frameworks for research on the effects of schooling' in Reynolds, D. *Studying School Effectiveness* Lewes, Falmer Press.

Daly, P. (1991) 'How large are secondary school effects in Northern Ireland?' *School Effectiveness and School Improvement*, 2(4), 305-323.

Edmonds, R. (1979) 'Some Schools Work and More Can', *Social Policy*, 9 (4), 28-32.

Hallinger, P. & Murphy, J. (1986) 'The social context of effective schools,' *American Journal of Education*, 94, 328-355.

Mortimore, P., Sammons, P., Stoll, L., Lewis, D. & Ecob, R. (1988) *School Matters*, Somerset, Open Books.

Murphy, J. (1991). *Restructuring schools: Capturing and assessing the phenomena*. New York: Teachers College Press.

Nuttall, D. (1989) 'How the Inner London Authority Approaches School Effectiveness' in Creemers, B., Peters, T. & Reynolds, D., (Eds) *School Effectiveness and School Improvement*, Amsterdam, Swets & Zeitlinger.

Nuttall, D. (1992) Letter to *The Independent*, 21 November.

Reynolds, D., Creemers, B.P.M. & Peters, T. (1989) (Eds), *School Effectiveness and Improvement: Proceedings of the First International Congress*, Groningen, Rion.

Rutter, M., Maughan, B., Mortimore, P. & Ouston, J. (1979) *Fifteen Thousand Hours: Secondary Schools and Effects on Children*, Boston, Harvard University Press.

Scheerens, J. & Creemers, B. (1989) 'Towards a More Comprehensive Conceptualization of School Effectiveness' in Creemers, B., Peters, T. & Reynolds, D. *School Effectiveness and School Improvement*, Amsterdam, Swets & Zeitlinger.

Smink, G. (1991) 'The Cardiff Conference, ICSEI 1991', *Network News International,* 1(3), 2-6.

Stringfield, S. & Teddlie, C. (1991) 'Schools as affectors of teacher effects.' In Waxman, H. & Walberg, H. *Effective teaching: Current research.* Berkeley, CA, McCutchan

Wildy, H. & Dimmock, C. (1992) Instructional Leadership in Western Australian Primary and Secondary Schools, Nedlands, University of Western Australia (photocopy).

Table of Contents

1.

Worlds of difference: an introduction to this book

Paul Clarke, Mel Ainscow and Tony Townsend

This chapter serves as a brief guide to the book, identifying some of the themes, and providing the reader with an overview before they begin to move on to the detail of each chapter. The book is structured around sections, starting with Europe, moving to North and South America, the Asian Pacific Region, concluding with the Middle East and Africa. In the last chapter we will draw together some of the themes and issues that are raised in the country reports and discuss prospects and problems for the field in the coming decades.

Europe

The United Kingdom

In Stoll and Riley's paper we are reminded of the relatively recent debates that examined the two disciplines of school effectiveness and improvement coming together and serving different but complementary purposes. They argue that it has been the practicalities of school development and improvement programs that has engaged practitioners and policy makers alike to seek appropriate intervention strategies in the English school environment. Primarily these have been legislative in nature, with the new labour administration being applied with an assumption that improvement will only occur through an increase in public accountability of schools in terms of performance and complementary national pressure.

A series of nationally driven initiatives is identified by Stoll and Riley. These include inspection, identification and intervention in failing schools, intervention in the methods to be adopted in teaching both literacy and numeracy, and an enhanced regulation and upgrade of the qualification route demanded for headteachers. As the authors indicate, all of these centrally developed initiatives frequently draw upon the effectiveness and improvement research community to inform and guide policy.

With such dramatic changes in the requirements being placed on schools it is hardly surprising that a number of themes are emerging in the English context that represent new challenges. Stoll and Riley include amongst these new developments the research interest in methodological approaches taken in both effectiveness and improvement to inform and sensitise the generic to the particularities of the school site, they also raise and applaud the research exploring pupil perceptions of improvement work, they note the LEA role, and the role that central government is playing in promoting school effectiveness and improvement knowledge.

Raising the critical issue of the place of this research in the enhancement of a school system they point to the growing critical body of research that is suggesting that the field is 'pandering' to policy makers. This is a dilemma that many researchers in the field have never previously been faced with, and the tensions that it raises are ones that will no doubt have their repercussions in both political and educational arenas.

A set of issues for future development concludes the Stoll and Riley chapter. The need for studies to take the long look, particularly in times of short term perspectives seems to be a necessary positional statement that indicates to the policy makers that some aspects of the debate are still very under researched and only sketched out. This is very true of their second issue, which calls for a focus on evaluation of the effectiveness of change strategies of schools situated in different contexts. The differential performance and differential intervention issues remain underdeveloped. To promote and disseminate knowledge we also face challenges in examining how to proceed best with professional development and how to create professional communities, Stoll and Riley weave together this and other issues to provide a cogent argument for future action.

Daly, Devine and Swan report from both Northern Ireland and the Republic of Ireland. In their chapter a central feature identifies efforts being made in both countries to consider the impact of differences identified in schools, in both pupil performance and in management activity. Following on from the identification of difference comes policy, and interventions in school improvement such as the 'Breaking the Cycle' initiative, taking place in the Republic, targets resources on those schools in which large numbers of pupils are considered to be at risk. The authors identify the place of new technology in facilitating this identification, and raise the need for more inter-country cooperation on ventures of this kind in the future.

From Scotland, John MacBeath reports the 'relative homogeneity' that is the Scottish system. The influential role of school effectiveness research on the development of policy is noted in Scottish Office Documents such as *Effective Secondary Schools* (SED 1989) where the salient features of the research are put into the hands of the teachers and school managers. This link of policy to practice has an empowering effect. Citing Hargreaves (1989) MacBeath suggests that this was 'an important step in helping teachers' to diagnose, commit and implement solutions that they formulated. The chapter proceeds to examine some of the contributing factors that are framing the present system-wide debate on change. These include the often negative impact that parental choice is having on school variance, the Scottish Schools Ethos Network, the importance of 'ownership' of change as an ingredient of success, and an interest in locally driven research such as the Grampian/Aberdeen study examining and reporting on policy initiatives arising from the Education Authority. In the case of the SOEID Improving School Effectiveness Project (ISEP) MacBeath notes that the ISEP provides confirmation of previous findings on differential effectiveness. The consequences of these findings, as well as lessons from the design and methodology have spawned further localised research initiatives that are focusing on careful feedback with support and challenge from critical friends.

The issue of findings informing practice is one that MacBeath returns to in his concluding section, where he suggests that 'the most significant development in school improvement has been to put the tools of self-evaluation into the hands of schools and teachers'. This raises new challenges, namely, for teachers and students to learn more about what is effective in their own classrooms, and in turn, to then disseminate what they learn to the wider community.

David Reynolds describes the changing demands of the market place and its impact on the Welsh education system. Reporting the considerable changes being made to the infrastructure of the Welsh system, Reynolds notes that whilst this changing organisational structure has been put in place to deliver alternative policies, the educational system itself is incorporated into the wider market-based solutions that have over the past few years applied to the English system. The assumed translation from one country to another of policies and practices is clearly not working in the Welsh context. Reynolds projects forward to the devolution of power to the Welsh Assembly as a venture likely to accentuate existing differences between Wales and England,

and as a possible forum for distinctly Welsh educational policy. It is here that Reynolds raises the significance of the local communities that Welsh culture so stoically emphasises, and maintains through its commitment to source language and to identity and belief. The defining feature for Reynolds of the emergent Welsh educational policy will be its ability to balance the transactions needed in contemporary personal life between the individual, the community and the state.

Mainland Europe

Moving onto the mainland continent of Europe, the system described by Zagoumennov in Belarus is one that is centralised, as there are government-based goals for both democratisation and economic reforms. Reporting that there is no formal system of evaluation of school effectiveness the author cites efforts from the Belarus Educational Centre for Leadership Development (BECLD) which, with Ministry support, is engaged in dialogue with educational stakeholders nationally to establish some school level basis of understanding of factors that can facilitate an effective system. Zagoumennov identifies leadership development as a primary focus of the Ministry of Education, along with new information technology developments and civic education. In developing these programs the Ministry seeks to enhance the system wide capacity of school leaders and teachers at the local level, to establish a systematic training program to do this, and to enhance the status of educational leaders in the Belarus society as they begin to demonstrate their improved performance. Zagoumennov suggests that these goals, and the BECLD faculty charged with developing the work have been challenged by factors that inhibit swift reform, in particular the values and beliefs of those at the school level were different to those advocating reform. When coupled with economic challenges, the progress that Zagoumennov reports has been slow, but he remains optimistic of the longer term success of the initiatives.

From Cyprus, Leonidas Kyriakides reports the significance of another centralised policy as a characteristic of the country approach to the effective improvement of schools. A prevailing factor in the impact of effective centre-periphery policy in Cyprus has been the maintenance and development of a skilled and professional teaching workforce. Kyriakides points out that school based curriculum development is a critically underdeveloped feature of the system. The link between curriculum reform and teacher development is identified as a vital means of enhancing school performance, but at present it is marred by the focus of accountability being on contractual responsibilities rather then on professional development and performance.

Kyriakides notes that there are interesting indicators, which are seeking to redefine the locus of control and influence on schools, noting that there have been four research studies concerned with parental involvement in Cyprus over the past five years. These projects reflect an uneasy tension between schools and parents, both having little power to influence practice, and with teachers that want a safe involvement of parents without challenging their authority and power.

In the final section of his chapter on Cyprus, Kyriakides reflects on the strategic direction of curriculum change, pointing out that policy makers cannot mandate change even in a small country like Cyprus. In stating this he raises a perennial issue about where to locate real reform in order to see it come to fruition. One interesting example given is of a new model curriculum being a blend of local and national material. In this way Kyriakides suggests that to meet the systemic needs for reform, a route has to be found to facilitate and preserve local activity and interest. This message resonates through many of the reports in this volume and has salience to every country engaged in educational improvement.

Reporting from France, Denis Meurat raises the ideological feature that has prevailed in the centralised French system where it was inconceivable that some schools could be more effective than others could. Meurat reports that the efforts to introduce change have been hindered because of a critical reception of the French educational research community who challenge the field on three main counts: that it is not theory based, that it is potentially useful and therefore an engineering rather then a scientific matter, and that it raises political interests and is therefore subject to a lack of critique.

The hostile reception from researchers does not mean that work has not been taking place in the field of school effectiveness and improvement in France. Meurat reports on a variety of school effects research in both the primary and secondary sectors but in conclusion remains tentative about the likely future of the school effectiveness agenda in the French arena. What is suggested however, is that activity within school more closely allied to teacher performance is gaining attention. In particular the impact of policy that is aimed at the teacher effect on pupil performance.

Scheerens reviews the state of the Netherlands research on effectiveness and improvement projects concluding on the latter that the targeted educational and instructional programs where there is school discretion on the focus for improvement is showing a positive benefit for school performance. In the Netherlands the development of fundamental as well as applied studies in effectiveness and improvement is seen as a beneficial move which should promote the connections between theory and practice. Scheerens maintains that the impact on educational policy initiatives is still modest, giving the example of current secondary school policy reform where school effectiveness literature has not been used to inform the reform.

Norway too is a country where the school effectiveness research tradition is not well established. Trond Eiliv Hauge indicates in his chapter how it has been only very recently that studies have begun to inform policy. However, the nineties have seen a plethora of national and international studies emerging, and Norway has participated and developed a 'more supportive climate for school effectiveness research' which in turn have gained ministerial support.

A major innovation has been the introduction of the National Curriculum through which studies have been conducted to examine the degree of readiness of practitioners to the desired changes. Hauge describes how such studies have underlined the dilemmas that policy makers' face when planning for change in a knowledge-driven society where there are tensions between the individual and the institution. This reflects sentiments expressed in earlier chapters reporting on the English, Welsh and Scottish systems. Hauge reports the research on innovations in planning, evaluation and reviewing of systems taking place and its attention to different layers of the system from school to local authority and to region and the ways that these layers interrelate. He suggests that such work is a means of empowering the local practitioner and improving democratic participation in schools.

The Americas

The American context comes in three reports, the first describing Canada from Larry Sackney, the second from Haroldo Quinteros in Chile, and the third from Janet Chrispeels and Gilbert Austin describing the USA scene.

Sackney outlines the key Canadian trends and emphasises that Canada does not have a national office of education. This means that Federal government has an influence on provincial and school activity but in a rather indirect way. At the provincial level, there has been a reduction in governing district boards, and the constitution of these boards is being restructured to facilitate ministerial advice on educational planning and standards of performance at provincial level.

Sackney describes a series of common features of reform in Canada and makes the point that school, district and provincial accountability is a salient feature of these reforms. In the research field Canada has been influential throughout the eighties and nineties in its work on school improvement and teacher development. Sackney illustrates a few of the many publications emerging from OISE in Toronto, a common ingredient of these being the close liaison between school, board and researchers. This partnership continues to produce outstanding and challenging material pertinent to the situation, but also raises questions for other systems to consider. Sackney concludes with one of those challenges, how to develop stakeholders in the school system so that they can relate to each other as a learning community, which is a challenge for all of us involved in the field.

From South America, Haroldo Quinteros reports on the system in Chile and describes a democratic centralised system that is still feeling the after effects of military government that ruled until 1990. Present reforms are taking place to overcome what he describes as the 'Chilean Educational Crisis'. These reforms address school overpopulation, poverty of materials, incomplete buildings, and obsolete methodologies, poorly trained and badly paid teachers who often work in two or three schools. Despite such challenging conditions Quinteros suggests that the future of Chilean education is promising and fundamental to his claim is that the reforms are taking place within a democratic framework. One noticeable feature of his report is the fact that teachers are directly involved in the research activity and experiment, a manifestation of the libertarian principle and of a nation searching for better solutions to persistent problems.

Moving to the United States of America, Janet Chrispeels and Gilbert Austin begin their report commenting on the 'extensive decentralisation of educational decision-making' in the country. This makes a 'country report' somewhat difficult as there is not necessarily a single picture of effective schools research and practice and there is a danger of masking the differences that make up the whole.

Their report deals extensively with activity taking place in the field, and it leads to five 'future trends' which they describe as being of significance 'if we are to advance the school effectiveness knowledge base and school practices in the twenty-first century'. These are:

- the relationship between district and school effectiveness,
- the link between classroom and school-wide effectiveness,
- the relationship between teacher professionalisation, empowerment, and student learning,
- the impact of decentralisation, and
- the development of valid and reliable assessment systems that accurately and authentically measure not only what students know, but also reflect growth and improvement.

Chrispeels and Austin conclude by indicating the need to develop understanding of these five trends, and importantly, to develop an understanding of the interrelationships between them. They suggest that research in this area will facilitate what Scheerens and Bosker (1997) called 'explanatory mechanisms' leading to a third generation of school effectiveness research and practice.

Asia and the Pacific

Section four of the volume addresses Asia and the Pacific region. Cuttance and Hill note that in the Australian context there is a long history of school effectiveness and improvement initiatives. They report that it is relatively recently that these have captured policy makers' attention, and similarly, have been systematised in a manner to be informative to policy. Perhaps the most noticeable dimensions of the reforms taking place in Australia are those taking place in Victoria and soon to be implemented in Queensland. In these examples the schools are grappling with 're-negotiation of the role of and relationships between schools, their communities and educational bureaucracies.' The chapter examines these tensions and indicates some of the structures that are emerging in response. The chapter has a strong resemblance in its themes to that of the first chapter by Stoll and Riley. There is an emphasis on accountability at a local level, a drive at the system level for high performance and a theme of continuous improvement prevailing as the means of achieving. Raising different issues to those identified in the English context, Cuttance and Hill describe the subtle yet politically significant differences in the quality assurance systems operating in different states. In their commentary they observe that policy remains ahead of the research evidence regarding the effectiveness of reform measures. They raise in their observations a critical challenge for researchers to establish methodological approaches that align more closely to practitioner needs and reform programs. And, taking this research to practice theme further, they make a similar point to John MacBeath in his chapter, by noting that the internalisation of school effectiveness and improvement at the school and classroom level is perhaps the most pressing agenda facing the system, and the effectiveness and improvement movement.

Wong Kam Cheung introduces the Hong Kong report with notification of the outcry on falling standards of education in general. Paradoxically, the Third International Mathematics and Science Study (TIMMS) placed Hong Kong fourth in the world. In a detailed discussion of the structure of the Hong Kong system Wong describes how the schools demonstrate characteristics of orderliness, discipline, attention to learning, testing and monitoring, and instructional leadership whilst at the same time emphasises basic skills in education and an important cultural emphasis on self-cultivation and a sense of equality. With the new government now in power there remains a concern for quality and improvement and a series of initiatives are reported that are designed to facilitate that process.

In the Malaysian report, Rahimah Haji Ahmad, Zulkifli Abdul Manaf and Charil Marzuki stress the importance that the education ministry places on the adoption of the philosophy and values of Islamic and moral education. Whilst there is a general consensus about the desire for high performing schools, the authors report that in-country research on school effectiveness and improvement is rather scarce. They suggest that the reason is a lack of agreed definition of school effectiveness and that the holistic concept of effectiveness is yet to make real sense. Studies have taken place in areas of leadership, teacher to student effect, use of resources and the development of profiles to examine the efficacy of the school climate. The authors conclude their report by stressing that education in Malaysia is an instrument to achieve national solidarity, and that efforts to improve the system aim towards that goal.

Peter Ramsay and Adrianne Affleck describe a New Zealand where education has undergone major reform in recent years. The thrust of these reforms is reported as being towards a devolved system with legislation designed to place the responsibility for performance at the school level, and subsequent legislation focused on curriculum design. Ramsay and Affleck describe in fascinating detail the research climate within which New Zealand education and policy has evolved. It is interesting to note how influential a role research has played in challenging assumed approaches and policies, in particular in the field of school culture and parental expectation. Commenting on government initiatives, they also raise the significance of the self-review process that seeks to facilitate school level consideration of what they are doing, where they are going, how they will get there and how they will know when they arrive. These considerations lead the report to the conclusions of 'where now?' and we are informed that longitudinal in-depth qualitative studies of success are one major point of future reference. A second point they identify concerns analysis of compensatory measures to address disadvantage and the third identifies matters of curriculum content. Ramsay and Affleck conclude by returning to an earlier theme, asking pointedly about what is valued as knowledge within schools, and how such values can, if left unquestioned, maintain and enhance inequalities.

Perhaps one of the most challenging and thought provoking contributions to the mainstream interpretations of effectiveness and improvement comes from the Pacific Islands reports. Tony Townsend and Asenaca Vakaotia introduce their report by suggesting that the desire to improve the education system has as much to do with improving the lives of people, as it has to do with economic competition. This perspective on improvement activity taking place across the Pacific region is then elaborated upon in a series of island reports and serves to illustrate the efforts that are being made to establish provision and equity for all students whilst maintaining an underlying sense of humanity and compassion for the needs of the people and environment within each of the islands. They report on the Basic Education and Life Skills program (BELS project) which has attracted donor funding focused on capacity building of staff and students across the region. In conclusion they report that the BELS project is increasing the awareness of the importance of literacy, the home school partnership and a search for interlinking of resources so as to improve the educational outcomes of the child.

The Middle East and Africa

Turning from the Pacific to the Middle East, Ass'ad Shibli's chapter describes the experience of the Arab sector in Israel. Whilst the system he describes is governed by compulsory and universal education law, he argues that it is characterised by division. The communal separation of Arabs and Jews in Israel means that each sector is drawing their content and resources from the same regulatory frame, but with very different administrative, organisation and implementation teams. This was initially quite favourably received by Israeli Arabs as it allowed them to be educated and to study in a familiar cultural environment. However, it has not led to an understanding of each culture, and ignorance and separation have led to hostility and strangeness between the two dominant communities. The separation of students is now a prevailing problem amplified by poor results in the Arab sector in comparison to the Jewish one, and raising questions about the inequality of education budgets.

Within this socio-political environment Shibli reports that the development of effective systems has been a struggle, and remains a contested issue. Some themes are emerging however that resonate with approaches occurring elsewhere. For example, the decentralisation of authority and the development of local responsibilities and shared approaches under the general banner of self-management echo other reports in this volume. One distinct feature of Shibli's report is the role that he sees improvement and effectiveness playing a conciliatory role promoting greater cooperation between the Israeli Arabs and the authority, with the hope that this will lead towards improvement in the general life possibilities of all the people in the region.

Finally we turn to South Africa and to a slightly revised version of the paper that the Deputy Minister for Education Father Smangaliso Mkhatshwa gave as a keynote at ICSEI 98. In his paper Smangaliso Mkhatshwa describes the principles that are guiding the new South African education reforms, identifying the spirit of renewal, remotivation and partnership as fundamentally important in the efforts to enhance the equity and engagement of all South African people under the new system. The stance taken by Smangaliso Mkhatshwa to school improvement and effectiveness is a critical one, raising the value laden nature of the two disciplines and suggesting that in the South African context much in this field is contested and represents part of the struggle to make sense of schools, and their contribution to everyday life in the region. In this sense Smangaliso Mkhatshwa is raising the profile of the emancipatory importance of education, a feature of school effectiveness and improvement which is relatively unexplored in the present literature. He notes how the national system is using the emancipatory understanding to forge new approaches to policy which will transform South African society from the legacy of apartheid to the new South Africa of tomorrow. In the paper he stresses the importance of the interconnectedness of systems as a means of achieving this, 'the challenge is to link macro social perspectives with the micro perspectives of individual schools' echoing a persistent theme we have heard across the chapters in this book. He emphasises the political point that there are limitations of policy to practice approaches, particularly in the area of quality assurance, and in response to this he reports the approach being taken in South Africa which seeks to encourage moral and political understanding in education policy and build both discipline and authority into the system at the national and local levels. It is in this final aspect of his paper that a real sense of the purpose of the South African approach is most impressive in its sense of urgency and agency. Smangaliso Mkhatshwa suggests that 'the task then, is to help schools identify the sorts of things they are able to tackle for themselves, and encourage them to take responsibility for doing so.' Perhaps of all the chapters in the book, it is this one that most powerfully brings together the sense of spirit in an emancipatory educational endeavour, with a practical sense of working through the troubled issues with a greater sense of a national goal to be achieved in the new millennium.

Conclusion

As we have constructed this chapter we have been very aware of the interpretive stance that editors, and authors in general, can and do take as they approach texts that might assume the reader is already aware of work in the same field. This 'taking for granted' aspect is prevalent in the literature of effectiveness and improvement as it is in many other genres, and it is this point that we wish to return to. As Stoll and Riley raise at the end of their chapter, 'how can we get the present effectiveness and improvement agenda out of the mindset of modernity, responding to problems, into one that is creatively posing new challenges?' We might reasonably ask, whose effectiveness and improvement agenda is the one that is most prevalent, for what reasons and what therefore are the implications of this viewpoint at both national levels as reported in these chapters, and when considering an international debate, what are the international repercussions of our locally, regionally and nationally developed interventions?

Traditionally the fields of effectiveness and improvement have not problematised their territory and not questioned in any substantial way the value base upon which they operate. Perhaps this lack of self-critical analysis has assisted the advancement of the two fields and has served the school audience well as it reflects the realities of school life, pragmatically dealing with the day to day and seldom investigating the underlying meaning and assumptions in favour of a clarity of purpose and direction.

If the time were ever right to stop and reflect on such matters it should be now. The complexity of the territory that our colleagues from around the world describe in these pages, and the contested nature of the appropriate directions for schools, districts, regions and nations to take in the face of the information age and a post industrial society and in many cases considerable political and economic challenges mean that the global as well as the local educational change agendas are increasingly prevalent in discussions we are having with schools and those who have the task of enhancing the effectiveness and improvement of the school system.

As you read these different chapters, and begin to form your own opinion on the state of the world, and whether the world is one of difference or similarity, or something of both, we would challenge you to begin to mentally start to construct the next set of country reports. As the process of translating the messages from these texts facilitates new lines of inquiry and new challenges at your place of work and eventually back to the meeting places we have around the world.

This current set of country reports clearly show how the linkages between effectiveness and improvement have grown in the past ten years. They also demonstrate the substantial impact that the research community is beginning to have on national educational policy. If the purpose of the country reports is to provide a better understanding of what is happening in schools and school systems in different parts of the world, then this current set of reports does that but it also challenges those who believe that there is a panacea for the effective improvement of systems. It colourfully reflects the spirit of diversity that are the people's of the world whilst underwriting the commonality of the human spirit seeking purpose, meaning and value through the educational endeavour.

SECTION ONE: EUROPE

Part One:
UNITED KINGDOM

2.

From infancy to adolescence: school effectiveness and school improvement in England since 1995

Louise Stoll and Kathryn Riley

Adolescence – 'a time of rapid change, immense uncertainty and acute self-reflection. The exhilaration and pain of growing up for many early adolescents resides in their having much less confidence in what they are moving towards than in what they have left behind.'

(Hargreaves et al, 1996).

Introduction

School effectiveness and school improvement in England led almost separate existences until the early 1990s. School effectiveness studies in the 1970s and 1980s focused on differences between more and less effective secondary schools (Rutter et al, 1979; Reynolds et al, 1987; Smith and Tomlinson, 1989) and the effectiveness of primary schools, as measured by a range of academic and social outcomes (Mortimore et al, 1988). Those studies identified characteristics associated with more effective schools. Other research in the 1980s and early 1990s included examination of differential effectiveness in relation to pupils' gender, pupils from different backgrounds, or of different abilities; consistency of effects on different outcomes and between subjects (departmental differences); the size of school effects; 'value added' comparisons of the academic outcomes of educational authorities; stability of school effects over time; context specificity of the 'characteristics of effectiveness'; and early work on conceptualising ineffective school and classroom processes.[1]

In the 1980s, school improvement, a more practitioner-oriented field, could be seen in the work of those involved in the 'teacher as researcher' (Elliott, 1980, 1981) and school self-evaluation and review movements (McMahon et al, 1984; Clift and Nuttall, 1987). The follow-up to review with a holistic organisational approach to change in schools could be seen in the Inner London Educational Authority's secondary report on improving schools (Hargreaves, 1984), its primary report (Thomas, 1988), and work of British participants in the International School Improvement Project (Hopkins, 1987).

The intellectual differences between the two fields have been charted (Reynolds et al, 1993), but since the early 1990s, a coming together has occurred, evidenced in improvement/development programs, that include 'Improving the Quality of Education for All' (IQEA) (Hopkins et al, 1994), the Lewisham School Improvement Project (Stoll and Thomson, 1995) and Hammersmith and Fulham's Schools Make a Difference Project (Myers, 1996). A previous review has described a plethora of development initiatives and networks throughout the country (Reynolds et al, 1996a).

Much has happened since that last review. There has been a burgeoning of activity in both school effectiveness and school improvement, (demonstrated in the response to a letter from us requesting information from colleagues working in these areas); further merging of the two communities; and the increasing prominence of a range of different players, including Local Education Authorities (LEAs).

In this chapter, we first examine the political and social context within which school effectiveness and school improvement reside, including a discussion of related national policy initiatives and the impact of the election of a Labour Government in 1997. School effectiveness and school improvement research projects and development initiatives are then described. The last few years have also seen increased sophistication of existing quantitative methodologies and development of a number of qualitative methodologies. These are also outlined. Perhaps most significant, however, for the current state and future potential of school effectiveness and improvement has been the unprecedented involvement of national policy makers and, in some ways related to this, a growing number of critiques, largely from outside, but also from within the field. After examining these critiques, we focus on issues and tensions for those working in the field, and conclude with future needs, if school effectiveness and school improvement are to maintain their momentum in a rapidly changing world.

The national and policy context

After 18 years of Conservative administrations, a Labour Government was elected in May 1997 and now seeks to make its own mark on education. It has inherited an education system in which schools in England have been brought increasingly into the front line of education reform. The message from successive governments – echoing that of many researchers – has been that schools matter, and they can make a difference. In some ways this message is an encouraging one for school reformers but it by no means represents unequivocal support for schools. Enshrined in legislation is an assumption that improvement will only be achieved through the twin pressures of increased accountability for performance (to national government and to parents), and through national direction.

Central features in the national framework include the inspection system led by the Office for Standards in Education (OFSTED), a national curriculum, and national testing through standards assessment tasks (SATs). As part of an accountability drive that characterises many aspects of the public sector, including education, information about school performance has now become public currency, and school league tables find themselves alongside health league tables. Politicians have argued that the publication of performance information will encourage public services to be more responsive to consumers, or users, and enhance the options for choice. The league tables of pupil performance (which include results on SATs and external examinations, as well as other information, such as attendance rates) now feature regularly in both national and local newspapers. The use of 'raw' information about school performance, unadjusted to take into account the intake of a school, has contributed to the debate about 'value added', discussed later in the chapter.

The national inspection system has begun to bite in several ways. By September 1997, 340 schools had been designated as having failed the (OFSTED) process, and as requiring 'special measures'. This figure represents some two per cent of primary and secondary schools and seven per cent of schools for children with special educational needs. Thirteen schools have subsequently been closed by local agreement, and one – Hackney Downs – by a government-appointed education association. Forty have been taken off special measures, and in February 1997, 85 per cent of the 'special measure' schools were described by OFSTED as 'improving' (Squires, 1997). In May 1997, the newly elected Labour Government 'named' 18 of these 'failing' schools as targets for radical action, including possible closure and reopening with new headteachers and staff.

While schools were brought into the reform frame, local education authorities (LEAs) were pushed out into the cold, a process begun by the 1988 Education Reform Act. LEAs were not to be abolished but it was assumed that as their responsibilities, resources and prestige diminished, they would wither on the vine. Over recent years, the relationship between central government and LEAs has remained uneasy, and that between schools and LEAs has been dependent on local circumstances and the nature of the local partnership (Cordingley and Kogan, 1993; Riley and Rowles, 1997a; Riley, 1998). In 1996, the Conservative Government introduced a White Paper which formed the basis of legislation in 1997. That White Paper set out national expectations about schools and supported a strong line of individual school autonomy:

> *The Government's priority is to foster the internal will and*
> *capacity of schools to generate their own improvement . . . staff*
> *and governors of every school should feel that it is directly for*
> *them to monitor the quality of the education they provide and*
> *improve schools.*

(Education White Paper, 1996:53)

The White Paper also acknowledged a role for the LEA: to offer advice and support services to schools, and provide performance data to help schools set their own improvement targets. This assistance was to be provided through: direct intervention where a school was found to have a major problem; working with schools in setting targets; and provision of services to help schools carry out their own improvement plans. LEAs were also encouraged to support networks of headteachers and governors, and develop new initiatives that would bring schools together, linking schools with other local agencies, such as Training and Enterprise Councils.

In 1997, the incoming Labour Government produced its own White Paper, 'Excellence in Schools', as a basis for legislation in 1998. Labour's White Paper presages a substantial increase in central government powers. Schools will be required to set improvement targets, and to introduce literacy and numeracy hours (in primary schools). Traditional teaching methods are emphasised and secondary schools are to be encouraged to 'set' pupils by ability. Mixed ability teaching will only be accepted where it can be shown to achieve above average results. The White Paper also envisages the introduction of compulsory home-school contracts (Barber, 1996) and promises additional school performance information to parents. National standards for teachers will be introduced (including an advanced skills teacher grade), and a General Teaching Council developed to 'regulate and promote' the profession. Aspiring headteachers will need to have completed the National Professional Qualification for Headship (NPQH) prior to appointment.

The White Paper also identifies a leadership role for the LEA in achieving many of these objectives. This role is dependent, however, on the ability of LEAs to win 'the trust and respect of schools' and champion' the value of education in its community for adults, as well as children' (White Paper, 1997: 69). For the future, each LEA will be required to draw up a development plan which should indicate how the LEA works with schools and how it will help them to establish 'robust mechanisms for self-evaluation' (DfEE, 1997). LEAs will also be subject to national inspection.

It is within this context that school effectiveness and school improvement research and development activity have operated.

Emerging themes and trends

In reviewing the broad field of school improvement and school effectiveness over recent years there are a number of striking features about who is involved in the work and how the work is being undertaken.

First, in terms of those involved, the number of academic institutions has grown considerably, new centres have been developed and several professorial posts have been created, in addition to the appointment of a coordinator for school effectiveness and school improvement research at the National Foundation for Education Research (NFER). The Government itself has expanded its School Effectiveness Division at the DfEE to create a new Effectiveness and Standards Unit, bringing in various academics to work in government, or closely with government-appointed committees, or agencies.

A *second* noticeable feature, has been the increase in the number of local education authorities that are focusing on the area, as exemplified in the advertisements for 'school development officers' and 'managers of school improvement' in the Times Educational Supplement. Birmingham LEA provides one interesting example of an LEA that has worked with its schools to develop its own school improvement culture and language (Birmingham City Council, 1996). Linked initiatives include, among others, The University of the First Age, offering extended learning activities (Farrar, 1998); 'butterflies', based on the new sciences, a collection of small initiatives taken by schools that have a disproportionate effect as a catalyst for improvement;

and 'guarantees', targets of input, process or experience and outcomes for the early years and secondary schooling.

A *third*, and related, feature is the strength and nature of the relationships which have developed between the academic institutions and schools and local education authorities.   Both research and development activities are increasingly carried out as joint partnerships, and as much of the research is rooted in practice, a strong link has been created which bridges the two worlds of research and practice (see also discussion on development work).

Recent developments in research on effectiveness and improvement

The research territory continues to expand. It is noticeable that while some research falls clearly within the boundaries of what have traditionally been known as school effectiveness or school improvement, other work draws on both. For this reason we have adopted a thematic approach to our description that reflects many of the contextual levels and key players influencing effectiveness and improvement.

1.   Developments in school effectiveness methodology across different phases of education

The last two years have seen further methodological developments in studying school effectiveness and appropriate assessments.   There is a strong and growing trend towards the establishment of accurate data sets that enable school effectiveness initiatives to be validated. Detailed studies continue on value added information in respect of school performance (Goldstein and Sammons, 1997). The National Foundation for Education Research (NFER), University of Durham and Institute of Education have also extended value added issues from schools to Further Education Colleges, the NFER carrying out a feasibility study of value added information for Advanced General National Vocational Qualification (GNVQ).   At the other end of the age range, one significant area of development has been that of baseline assessment of young pupils for the purposes of measuring value added in primary schools. The Curriculum, Evaluation and Management (CEM) Centre at the University of Durham has created base-line tests which include a multi-media, computer-adaptive test for 4 and 5 year olds (Tymms et al, 1997).   A large-scale, five-year longitudinal study of the progress and development of 2500 children in various types of pre-school and reception (kindergarten) classes, 'The Effective Provision of Pre-School Education Project', is also being carried out by researchers at London's Institute of

Education, the University of Oxford and University of Wales, Cardiff (Sammons et al., 1998).

  Further developments have occurred in multi-level modelling techniques to take account of cross-classification of data at different levels, for example, examining the influence of secondary and junior schools on GCSE results (Goldstein and Sammons, 1997) and missing identification of units (Hill and Goldstein, 1997). Research is also underway to identify and define the dimensions of secondary school effects across a range of outcomes and different educational policy contexts (Thomas and Smees, 1997).

2.   *Improving schools*

The school improvement focus continues to flourish. The Improving Schools Project (Hopkins et al 1996a; Reynolds et al, 1998) was a retrospective case study of 12 secondary schools (in 3 LEAs) that had demonstrated improvement, or decline in results over a period of years. These schools were situated in a variety of social contexts and were located at various points along the effectiveness continuum at the start of the project. Researchers interviewed senior managers, teachers, pupils, governors and non-teaching staff, as well as observing in classrooms (Reynolds et al, 1998). They found that while most schools used a number of 'tactics' to raise pupil performance, more rapidly improving schools showed greater evidence of strategic thinking.

  Two sets of case studies of improving schools have been carried out by the Institute of Education in London, one as part of a comparative study involving England, mainland China, Hong Kong and Singapore (Leo et al, 1997), the other examining schools that have been released from 'special measures', following their OFSTED inspection (see Government agency-commissioned research). The focus on school development planning as a strategy for improvement also continues (MacGilchrist and Mortimore, 1997; MacGilchrist, forthcoming).

3.   *Classrooms and departments*

An earlier analysis of developments in school effectiveness and school improvement expressed concern at the lack of classroom level research. While studies have examined effectiveness of secondary departments (Harris et al, 1995; Sammons et al, 1997) the focus on classrooms remains limited. The Centre for Successful Schools at Keele University has been investigating the school's view of good quality teaching and learning, while the Improving the Quality of Education for All (IQEA) team have examined the classroom conditions for school improvement (Beresford, 1995; Hopkins et al, 1998), and groups at the Institute of Education have summarised literature on effective learning (Watkins et al, 1996) and have considered links between school effectiveness, school improvement, teaching and learning (MacGilchrist et al, 1997). Other research has also explored the impact of extra curricular study support (Prince's Trust, 1997), and a recently started study at London's Institute of Education is examining grouping procedures.

4.   Pupils

There is a growing and significant focus on pupils. Researchers have examined pupil perceptions of their experience as learners in school (Rudduck et al, 1996; Rudduck et al, 1997; Beresford, 1997) to explore 'the agenda for school improvement that emerges from students... and the impact of taking such an agenda seriously on students' engagement with school and with learning' (Rudduck, personal communication). A two-year study by Homerton College, Cambridge and Keele University, 'Improving Learning: The Pupil Perspective', is currently exploring three issues in primary and secondary schools: catching up; school climates that present work as 'cool' – in other words, appealing and worthwhile; and pupils supporting each other in their learning. Pupil motivation, and its links to the teaching and learning process, has also been examined (Leo and Galloway, 1995), as has meta-cognition (Harris et al, 1995), and strategies to create an inclusive education system and to highlight the needs of marginalised groups have now begun to receive serious attention within the field (Booth and Ainscow, 1998).

5.   Local Education Authorities' role

A range of studies and evaluations have been undertaken on aspects of the local education authority role in supporting school improvement (Riley et al, 1995; Corbett et al, 1996; Southworth and Sebba, 1997). Staff at Manchester University, for example, have conducted reviews of the effectiveness of LEA school achievement projects, including a three-year evaluation of Bury's Celebrating and Extending Achievement initiative; London Institute of Education researchers have evaluated initiatives set up by a Library Board in Northern Ireland (Sammons and Taggart, 1998); while staff at Roehampton Institute are carrying out a major study of 17 LEAs that explores growing diversity between authorities; the degrees of their effectiveness; and their contribution to quality and school improvement (Coleman and Riley, 1995; Riley 1998). New unitary authorities are also being studied, to determine how they establish structures to promote, support and monitor school improvement (Joy et al, 1998).

6.   Other external contextual factors

Other related topics being examined by members of the research community include the implications of large scale reorganisation of schooling (closures, mergers, and change of age range) for school effectiveness and school improvement (at the University of Wales), issues of school autonomy and school improvement (Bush, 1996), and the cost effectiveness of different types of provision (Belfield et al, 1996).

7.   Comparative research

Several researchers in this country have also participated in cross-cultural studies and reviews of effectiveness (Teddlie and Reynolds, 1998; Reynolds and Farrell, 1996 – see Government agency-commissioned research); comparative case studies of improvement (Leo et al, 1997); reviews of international attempts to merge school effectiveness and school improvement (Reynolds et al, 1996b; Stoll and Reynolds, 1996); and assessment designs for school effectiveness research and school improvement in developing countries (Riddell, 1997). Concerns, however, have been expressed about the problems of comparative studies (see the later discussion on critiques).

8.   Government agency-commissioned research

Various Government agencies have also commissioned a number of research projects, literature reviews and evaluations of initiatives over this period, spanning a broad range of effectiveness- and improvement-related issues. Whilst many of these could be included in the preceding sections, we have listed them separately because they demonstrate the extent of Government involvement in and, some would argue, influence on the field at the present time. Contracts include:

- developing models for evaluating 'effective' schools and departments, using National Curriculum Key Stage 3 and GCSE data – University of Sheffield for the DfEE;

- baseline assessment (of young children on entry) and value added – University of Durham for SCAA (Tymms and Williams, 1996);

- the Value Added National Project (VANP), to investigate a design for a value added system for England – University of Durham for SCAA (Fitz-Gibbon, 1995; 1997);

- analysis of national GCSE and A level database – DfEE with the Institute of Education, University of London (O'Donoghue et al, 1997)

- Worlds Apart, a literature review for OFSTED, that looked at international achievement surveys and their implications for Britain – University of Newcastle for OFSTED (Reynolds and Farrell, 1996);

- case studies of schools that have come off 'special measures', carried out by the Institute of Education for the DfEE (Institute of Education and DfEE, 1997);

- a project examining post-inspection action planning and school improvement following inspection in special schools – University of Cambridge Institute of Education for OFSTED (Sebba et al, 1996);

- a study of effective teaching and learning in work-related contexts – Open University and University of Bath for DfEE (Harris et al, 1997);

- the influence of factors outside the formal school curriculum – Institute of Education for DfEE;

- School Development Planning for Student Achievement – Institute of Education and University of Nottingham for DfEE;

- a review of School Effectiveness Grants for Educational Support and Training (GEST) – School of Education, University of Cambridge and Homerton College for the DfEE;

- governing bodies and target setting – Institute of Education for DfEE;

- the Improving School Effectiveness Project – University of Strathclyde and Institute of Education for the Scottish Office Education and Industry Department (Robertson and Sammons, 1997; described in detail in the chapter on developments in Scotland).

Development work

Some projects underway at the time of the last review continue, most notably Improving the Quality of Education for All (IQEA), a network that has now expanded to several regions in the country (Hopkins and Sebba, 1995; Hopkins et al, 1996b). Development work in recent years can be summarised under three broad headings: development of techniques to assess, monitor and evaluate school effectiveness and school improvement; 'design' programs; and practitioner action research.

1.   Assessment, monitoring and evaluation of school effectiveness and improvement

The merger of school effectiveness and school improvement is seen clearly in the increasing number of higher education and research institutions that are working with LEAs, schools and further education (post age 16) colleges to help them interpret quantitative and qualitative data, and provide tools which will support improvement.   In particular, the last two years has seen an increase in the number of researchers who are developing value added frameworks for LEAs to analyse their primary pupils' progress (for example, Tymms, 1996, for Avon; Goldstein, 1997, for Hampshire; Sammons, 1997, for Surrey).

The Institute of Education has been working with Lancashire LEA to provide feedback data to secondary schools on a range of measures.   The National Foundation for Educational Research (NFER) also offers a Quantitative Analysis for Self-Evaluation (QUASE) subscription service for secondary schools, providing performance feedback to secondary schools at whole school and subject department levels, using value added analysis, particularly of GCSE results; and the University of Durham continues to offer its A Level, Year Eleven and Middle Years Information Systems.   The proliferation of studies on value added raises issues about dissemination, usage and resources.

In line with research developments related to pupil involvement, an increasing number of developmental projects now involve pupil surveys.   The often differing accounts of teachers, pupils and parents provide practical school self-evaluation opportunities and, when supported by clear guidance on interpretation, can lead to development strategies for school improvement (MacBeath et al, 1996).

There have also been several developments over the last couple of years in qualitative school improvement methodologies.   Most of those involved have designed instruments to help researchers and, importantly, practitioners 'map' various aspects of the change process in schools.   In Fielding's (1997: 147) words, 'the mapping techniques problematise important areas of school life about which school effectiveness has little or nothing to say', as well as: providing opportunities where those involved in change can 'make meaning' of it; acknowledging conflicts within the reality of schools; legitimating emotional aspects of experience; and involving pupils in the process of reflection on and development of schools.   Such techniques include a change response typology and change timelines (Clarke and Christie, 1997); typologies of school culture (Hargreaves, 1995; Stoll and Fink, 1996); cultural norms of different types of schools (Stoll and Fink, 1996; 1998); teacher surveys (Stoll, 1996) and a series of techniques developed in the

Cambridge Institute of Education, that focus on change timelines, the experience of change, the initiation of change, and the culture, structures and conditions of schools (Ainscow et al, 1995; Fielding et al, 1995)

2.   *Design programs*

A further example of links between effectiveness and improvement can be seen in the movement towards determining designs for effective school improvement programs (Reynolds et al, 1996b), and trialing and evaluation of new, revised or 'borrowed' design strategies, often with their origins in the United States, for example:

- the High Reliability Schools Project, a data-based improvement program in 20 schools, set up by the University of Newcastle, in association with Sam Stringfield of Johns Hopkins University in Baltimore;

- the Success for All Literacy Program, based on Success for All (Slavin et al, 1996) established by Nottingham University's Centre for School and Teacher Development, working with Nottingham schools.

3.   *Practitioner research and development and action research projects*

As noted earlier, a considerable number of development partnerships have been set up, involving schools, their LEAs and HE institutions. These development projects draw on school effectiveness and school improvement research findings and principles, but are collaboratively designed and tailored to fit the needs of the specific schools and LEAs. One project, the Essex Primary School Improvement Project, involves 24 schools. Schools are supported in a data-based focus on learning and teaching by cross-role teams of LEA staff, that involve educational psychologists and special needs support staff, as well as school development advisers, to bring a broader range of perspectives to the improvement process, and university staff are also involved (Lincoln and Southworth, 1996).

The many other LEA projects include, among others:

- the Quality Development Dialogue (Derbyshire LEA and Nottingham University); the Enfield School Improvement Project (with Cambridge University's Institute of Education; Beresford and Boyd, 1996);

- Hertfordshire LEA primary schools, who have worked with Cambridge University's Institute of Education on an analysis of the role of deputy heads and evaluation of value added analyses of school performance;

- Tameside LEA's Improving Standards in Schools, a phased project working with secondary schools, considering the nature of the learning community; and

- the Southwark Primary School Effectiveness Project and Raising Achievement in Island Schools on the Isle of Wight, both with the Institute of Education in London.

There are also a growing number of small school-based teacher/practitioner action research projects, carried out in conjunction with higher education institutions which look at a range of issues including: peer counselling, peer evaluation, assessment, pedagogy at different stages of the national curriculum, literacy, numeracy and gender (both girls and boys).

A number of new practical support materials for school improvement have also appeared in the last couple of years, largely in the form of training and activity guides (for example Harris et al, 1996; Hopkins et al, 1998), and new regionalised networks have appeared, notably the Sheffield Centre for School Improvement and North West Consortium for the Study of Effectiveness in Urban Schools.

Critiques of school effectiveness and school improvement

In the last couple of years there have been a number of critiques about what one educational journalist has described as the 'school effectiveness and improvement travelling circus' (Budge, 1996), culminating in two books that contain many of these critiques (White and Barber, 1997; Slee, Weiner and Tomlinson, 1998). Rejoinders have been made to several of these (Sammons, Mortimore and Hillman, 1996; Sammons and Reynolds, 1997; Mortimore and Sammons, 1997), although the debate continues. The criticisms can be broadly summarised as following:

- That assumptions are made about the purposes of schooling and what constitutes an effective education: whether it is an educational process (Elliott, 1996), whether it should include the achievement of moral aims (Winch, 1997) or involve critical thinking and creativity (Lauder et al, 1998). As Stoll and Fink (1996) and White (1997) point out, effectiveness is not value neutral.

- The second, and related, critique argues that those in the field are 'bedfellows' of neo-conservative politicians, 'peddling feel-good fictions' (Hamilton, 1995). Slee and colleagues (1998: 9) note that contributors to their book 'form a picture of the school effectiveness and improvement movement which is opportunistic and comfortable with a discourse of public policy which defines educational performance according to a narrow and fragmented set of test criteria'. Some believe that its very language appeals to governments who wish to control (Pring, 1995), and it has become 'the policy makers' tool' (Brown et al, 1995). Another critic suggests that there has been ideological appropriation of research by policy makers, and argues that in abstracting school performance indicators from the range of schools' possible outcomes, school effectiveness research is engaged in mission reductionism (Grace, 1998).

- A third area of criticism has been the apparent lack of recognition of the importance of the social and economic context on learning, and of the impact of policy changes on schools located in disadvantaged areas (Whitty, 1997; Slee et al, 1998). Critics argue that merely 'taking account' of background factors to 'level the playing field' in the assessment of the value added by schools is not the same as contextualised analysis of school effects. As Grace (1998) notes, Reynolds (1995: 59), a school effectiveness researcher, acknowledges:

we have been instrumental in creating a quite widespread popular view that schools do not just make a difference but that they make all the difference.

Others have argued that the claims that schools can make a significant difference are exaggerated, again pointing to the ideological use of research findings to deny the suggestion that schools might be limited by their context (Lauder et al, 1998). Recently, however, some within the field have also spoken out about context (Mortimore and Whitty, 1997), often directing their own critiques towards the system that has created such inequities (Myers and Goldstein, 1998).

- A further area of concern has been the damaging discourse of school failure, which some critics (eg Hamilton, 1995; Elliott, 1996) place at the door of school effectiveness research, because it offers 'apparent scientific legitimation' to those who wish to blame underachievement on failing schools and failing teachers. Some of those working in school effectiveness and school improvement have also questionned the policy context within which this discourse has flourished (Riley and Rowles, 1997; Stoll and Myers, 1998).

- School effectiveness research has also been viewed as promoting a managerialist and coercive view of schooling (Pring, 1995; Elliott, 1996; Hamilton, 1996), in which schools can be viewed as rational organisations where technical change (once its content has been agreed) is unproblematic (Ball, 1996; Fink and Stoll, 1998).

- The final area of criticism has focused on methodology. Methodological critiques have highlighted the lack of examination of curriculum factors in effectiveness studies (Scott, 1997); measurement confined to stable characteristics of schools (Brown et al, 1995); research frameworks and techniques that reflect researchers', rather than teachers' constructs (Brown et al, 1995: Elliott, 1996); ongoing debate about inference of causality (Hamilton, 1995; Scott, 1997); problems of engaging in international comparisons because of issues related to sampling, forms of reporting, curriculum match, and other factors including differences in cultural emphasis (Brown, 1998); and lack of theory, in particular concerning how school and classroom factors are related (Lauder et al, 1998).

Of all of the critiques, perhaps the one that is viewed as most unfair by many within school effectiveness and school improvement has been the suggestion that both researchers and those in the field are 'pandering' to policy makers. In reality, politicians and officials in government department and agencies 'cherry pick' findings to legitimate their policies (Goldstein and Myers, 1997). This leads us to some of the fundamental dilemmas which those working in the field, and attempting to use its findings, face.

Points of tension

The overview of developments in school effectiveness and improvement in this chapter suggests that there have been many successful initiatives and collaborations over recent years. However, national policies which have placed schools in competition with each other for 'clients' have worked against the development of professional networks, and against collaboration across schools, key elements of school improvement.

The national agenda raises many challenges and issues, and sets some boundaries about what can be achieved and how. The OFSTED framework has created a tension between evaluation and school improvement. Schools move forward, it has been argued, through a combination of pressure and support (Fullan, 1991). However, for this to happen there has to be a strong alignment between external evaluation and internal self-review. Evaluation strategies of whatever kind are only likely to be accepted where they appear to be beneficial (Russell and Reid, 1997).

The impact of OFSTED inspection has inevitably been a focus of considerable research interest (Ouston et al, 1996; Levacic and Glover, 1997; Riley and Rowles 1997a). But the assertion by OFSTED that inspection, of itself, creates improvement ('Improvement through inspection", OFSTED, 1993) has not gone unchallenged (Earley et al, 1996; Stoll and Fink, 1996; Wilcox and Gray, 1996; Riley and Rowles 1997b). While there is evidence to suggest that the OFSTED framework has created a sharper focus on many aspects of school life, particularly school management, the inspection process itself has been experienced by many teachers as an externally managed operation – a source of stress and deprofessionalisation to many (Jeffrey and Woods, 1996) – which has contributed little to their own professional understandings, or to the development of the school. Internal processes of self-review and reflection, sit uneasily with the current OFSTED model. Reforms may have taken place but the hearts and minds of teachers have not necessarily been engaged, and recent studies have emphasised the limited impact of structural change on classroom activities, and the growing distancing of management from practice (Bullock and Thomas, 1997; Thomas and Martin, 1996). Some school effectiveness researchers, among others, have become involved in the development of the (unofficial) Office for Standards in Inspection (OFSTIN), as a response to concerns about unvalidated methodology and the culture of blaming schools.

The combined impact of league tables and 'marketisation' of education creates another tension for those working in school reform. Schools have become far from equal in the resources they receive, and in the scale and range of difficulties that they face. There is considerable evidence to suggest that school choice (in reality the option for parents to express a preference) has reinforced social class segregation. As the education market has become more segmented, advantaged schools and advantaged parents have sought each other out (Ranson, 1993). Middle-class parents choose schools that other middle-class parents have already chosen (Ball, Bowe and Gerwitz, 1992).

For the advantaged schools, the task of reform and improvement remains challenging but achievable. For some increasingly disadvantaged schools, the weight of pressures can overwhelm staff. This is not a deterministic argument. Some schools do succeed against the odds (National Commission, 1996) but there are clear links between poverty and educational failure (Robinson 1997; Mortimore and Whitty, 1997), and there is evidence of how national policies have created greater polarisation in the education system (Bartlett, 1994; Catholic Education Service, 1997).

Finally, there are critical issues about the change process overall. Schools are now called to account publicly for their failures, as well as their successes. They are also expected to respond to the national framework and agenda. What they are to achieve, and how they are to achieve it, has become prescribed increasingly by central government. This creates a further tensions for those involved in school improvement initiatives: between professional autonomy and central direction.

Areas for future development

As we look forward, our analysis of developments over recent years suggests that there are a number of possible areas for future development, and we would like to highlight six, several of which are interrelated.

- There is a need for *further carefully controlled longitudinal studies that can lead to theory generation.* These studies would need to focus on school effectiveness and school improvement in the late 1990s, and would require three elements. The first would be the development of improved indicators of a broader range of outcomes that are relevant to being a member of society at the end of the 20th century and that are appropriate for a changing world. The second would require an examination of the influence and impact of different levels, for example classroom, school, local policy and government policy as well as societal issues, including deprivation. The third and final element would be to explore the connections between the various levels. Such research, of course, consumes resources and takes time, which is always problematic for those who seek simple solutions and quick fixes.

- A related issue for further study and development would be a *focus on examining and evaluating the effectiveness of different change strategies used by schools situated in different contexts and with variations in their initial change capacity* (Gray and Wilcox, 1996; Hopkins, 1996; Stoll and Fink, 1996; Ainscow and Clarke, 1997). Until more is known, through detailed case studies, as well as linked effectiveness and improvement studies with larger samples, and specifically focused and evaluated design programs, it is all too easy for blanket policy solutions to be advocated.

- The emphasis of a large number of research and development efforts on collection and analysis of increasingly sophisticated data and its use for target setting is significant. While value added information and school self-evaluation are obviously invaluable, it may be timely to question whether, in the drive for increased use of data for schools to measure their own performance and set targets, the essential emphasis on and resources for *the complex issue of change in teachers' practice* necessary to achieve these targets is insufficiently addressed. At a research level, this does not only mean determining 'what works' in terms of pedagogical practice: this would be simplistic. It means examining the link between pedagogy and curriculum, and understanding the sophisticated interplay between classrooms and schools: how school level conditions and school culture influence attempts to change pedagogical practice in different kinds of schools.

- Teacher learning is at the heart of this change. *Understanding professional development in the widest sense* – how schools become professional communities of learners (Stoll and Fink, 1996; Riley, 1998) and the types of professional development opportunities and networks which will support that learning – is essential. The extensive research base in the United States on professional development and professional community (Fullan and Hargreaves, 1991; Warren Little, 1993; Ball and Cohen, 1995; Louis, Kruse and Associates, 1995; Newman and Wehlage, 1995; Guskey and Huberman, 1996) and their links with standards, as well as a greater commitment to the teaching profession (Talbert and McLaughlin, 1994) could benefit further research and evaluation in England. While exploration has begun of teacher education partnership programs and their links to school improvement, the notion of a continuum of continuing professional development from pre-service to headship (principalship) and beyond in relation to school improvement and school effectiveness merits greater analysis.

  One specific aspect of professional development that could benefit greater study is an exploration of how schools use research findings and how they could be most valuably used. Without specific support, practitioners appear to view dissemination of research as imposed change (Wikeley, 1998).

- It may also be time to *broaden the scope of areas traditionally considered by school effectiveness and school improvement researchers and developers.* While, at different times, insights from psychology, sociology, management theory and, most recently the new sciences, among others, have found their way into projects, it is likely that more can be learnt from other disciplines, and from considering the ideas of futurist thinkers. This may help produce ideas for a different and wider range of development interventions than has previously been considered. Indeed, this may involve looking more closely at the types of learning experiences that occur beyond the school gates.

- The *careful evaluation over time of all improvement efforts must continue and be extended.* This may not sound like a new direction, but with a greater range of 'players' in school effectiveness and school improvement, it is worth emphasising that it cannot be assumed that implementing a specific change strategy will make a positive difference.

Conclusion

In considering the question, 'A positive difference to what?', we return to the first issue and one of the key critiques: *school effectiveness and school improvement for what purpose?* Ultimately, this is the key question to be considered by those involved in school effectiveness and school improvement in England, and indeed elsewhere, over the next few years. As we approach the new millennium, school effectiveness and school improvement in England face challenging and uncertain times ahead. A previous review began with the words, 'School effectiveness research in the United Kingdom has had a somewhat difficult infancy' (Reynolds et al, 1996a: 133), but we have now passed infancy and, indeed, childhood, and we must face up to a more complex and taxing agenda. The new Labour government has set its own educational agenda for the next few years. We also exist within a social context and an uncertain changing world that have significant ramifications for school effectiveness and school improvement. The challenges ahead lie in the way those in the field respond to these forces – whether we are controlled by them, or whether we can offer a unique and forward-looking perspective to schools that will support them in preparing their pupils for the 21st century. As one colleague mused: 'how can we get the present effectiveness and improvement agenda out of the mindset of modernity, responding to problems, into one that is creatively posing new challenges?' Perhaps some sort of answer can be provided by the authors of the next country review.

Acknowledgments

We would like to acknowledge with gratitude the help of the following colleagues in providing us with information for this chapter: Mel Ainscow, Michael Barber, John Beresford, Margaret Brown, Elisabeth Burridge, Tony Bush, Paul Clarke, Anthony Fielding, Carol Fitz-Gibbon, Harvey Goldstein, Alma Harris, David Hopkins, Dougal Hutchison, Ian Jamieson, David Jesson, Elisabeth Leo, Roy Long, Barbara MacGilchrist, Margaret Maden, Olwen McNamara, Peter Mortimore, David Reynolds, Jean Rudduck, Judy Sebba, Geoff Southworth, Hywel Thomas, Sally Thomas, Peter Tymms, Mike Wallace, Gaby Weiner, Felicity Wikeley, and Brian Wilcox. We, alone, are responsible for any interpretations, or misinterpretations, of their work! Special thanks to Felicity Wikeley for reading and commenting on a draft of the original report.

Note

1. For a more detailed discussion, see the last update on developments in school effectiveness and school improvement in England, which was presented at the International Congress for School Effectiveness and Improvement in Leeuwarden in 1995, and published in the following year in *School Effectiveness and School Improvement* (Reynolds, Sammons, Stoll, Barber and Hillman, 1996a).

References

Ainscow, M. and Clarke, P. (1997) *The Learning Network: Future Directions.* Unpublished discussion paper: University of Manchester.

Ainscow, M., Hargreaves, D. and Hopkins, D. (1995) 'Mapping the process of change in schools', *'School Effectiveness': Special Issue of Evaluation and Research in Education*, 9 (2), 75-90.

Ball, S. (1996) *Good School/Bad School.* Paper presented to the Annual Conference of the British Educational Research Association: Lancaster.

Ball, D. L and Cohen, D. K. (1995) *Developing Practice, Developing Practitioners.* Paper for the National Commission on Teaching and America's Future. School of Education and Institute of Public Studies: University of Michigan.

Ball, S., Bowe, R. and Gewirtz, S. (1992) *Circuits of Schooling: a Sociological Exploration of Parental Choice of School in Social Class Contexts.* Swindon: Economic and Social Research Council.

Barber, M. (1996) *The Learning Game: Arguments for an Education Revolution.* London: Gollancz.

Bartlett, W. (1994) 'Spoilt for choice', ESRC Research Briefing Note No. 9, British Education Research Association, *Research Intelligence*, 50, Midsummer, 16 + 21.

Belfield, C.R., Fielding, A. and Thomas, H.R. (1996) *The Cost Effectiveness of Post-16 Provision in Schools: Research Report for the Department for Education.* School of Education: University of Birmingham.

Beresford, J. (1995) *Classroom Conditions for School Improvement. A Literature Review.* Paper prepared for International School Effectiveness and Improvement Centre's Conference, 'Learning from Each Other'. London: Institute of Education, October.

Beresford, J. (1997) 'Ask the children', *Reading*, 31 (1), 17-18.

Beresford, J. and Boyd, E. (1996) 'Lessons from Enfield', *Managing Schools Today*, 5 (9), 36-38.

Birmingham City Council Education Department (1996) *Improving on Previous Best: An Overview of School Improvement Strategies in Birmingham.* Birmingham: Birmingham City Council Education Department.

Booth, T. and Ainscow, M. (1998) *From Them to Us: An International Study of Inclusion in Education.* London: Routledge.

Brown, M. (1998) The tyranny of the international horse race, in R. Slee, G. Weiner and S. Tomlinson (eds) *School Effectiveness for Whom? Challenges to the School Effectiveness and School Improvement Movements*, London: Falmer Press.

Brown, S., Duffield, J. and Riddell, S. (1995) 'School effectiveness research: the policy makers' tool for school improvement? *European Educational Research Association Bulletin*, 1 (1), 6-15.

Budge, D. (1996) Seafood is good for the brain, they say, but fortunately the best of Britain's researchers were not relying on the potted shrimps for inspiration last weekend. David Budge introduces a two page report from the annual BERA Conference, *TES*, (20th September 1996) page 16.

Bullock, A. and Thomas, H. (1997) *Schools at the Centre: A Study of Decentralisation.* London: Routledge.

Bush, T. (1996) School autonomy and school improvement in J. Gray, D. Reynolds, C. Fitz-Gibbon and Jesson, D. (eds) *Merging Traditions: The Future of Research on School Effectiveness and School Improvement*, London: Cassell.

Catholic Education Service (1997) *A Struggle for Excellence - Catholic Secondary Schools in Urban Poverty Areas.* London: CES.

Clarke, P. and Christie, T. (1997) 'Mapping changes in primary schools: what are we doing and where are we going?', *School Effectiveness and School Improvement*, 8 (3), 354-368.

Clift, P. and Nuttall, D. (1987) *Studies in School Self-evaluation.* Lewes: Falmer Press.

Coleman, P. and Riley, K.A. (1995) 'Accentuate the positive', *Education,* 186, 11 + 18.

Corbett, F., Fielding, M. and Kerfoot, S. (1996) *The Role of the Local Education Authorities in School Improvement in the Future: the Key Contribution of LEA Advisers. Reflections on the Role of LEA Staff in the First Year of the Essex Primary School Improvement and Research Program in partnership with the University of Cambridge Institute of Education.* Paper presented to the Annual Conference of the British Educational Research Association: Lancaster University.

Cordingley, P. and Kogan, M. (1993) *In Support of Education.* London: Jessica Kingsley.

DfEE (1997) *Framework for the Organisation of Schools: Technical Consultation Paper.* HMSO: Department for Education and Employment.

Earley, P., Fidler, B. and Ouston, J. (1996) *Improvement Through Inspection? Complementary Approaches to School Development.* London: David Fulton.

Elliott, J. (1996) 'School effectiveness research and its critics: alternative visions of schooling', *Cambridge Journal of Education,* 26 (2), 199-224.

Elliott, J. (1981) *School Accountability.* London: Grant McIntyre.

Elliott, J. (1980) Implications of classroom research for professional development, in E. Hoyle and J. Megarry (eds) *World Yearbook of Education 1980.* London: Kogan Page.

Farrar, M. (1998) *Accelerating Learning, Raising Potential: the Experience of the University of the First Age.* Paper presented to the Eleventh International Congress for School Effectiveness and School Improvement: Manchester.

Fielding, M. (1997) Beyond school effectiveness and school improvement: lighting the slow fuse of possibility, in J. White and M. Barber (eds) *Perspectives on School Effectiveness and School Improvement.* Bedford Way Papers, London: Institute of Education.

Fielding, M., Beresford, J. and West, M. (1995) *Using Mapping Techniques in IQEA Schools.* Paper presented at the Eighth International Congress for School Effectiveness and Improvement: Leeuwarden, the Netherlands.

Fink, D. and Stoll, L. (1998) Educational change: easier said than done, in A. Hargreaves, M. Fullan, A. Lieberman and D. Hopkins (eds) *International Handbook on Educational Change: Part 1.* Leuven: Kluwer.

Fitz-Gibbon, C.T. (1996) *Issues to be Considered in the Design of a National Value Added Project.* London: Schools Curriculum and Assessment Authority.

Fullan, M.G. (1991) *The New Meaning of Educational Change*. New York: Teachers College Press and London: Cassell.

Fullan, M.G. and Hargreaves, A. (1991) *What's Worth Fighting for? Working Together for Your School*. Toronto, Ontario Public School Teachers' Federation. Published as *What's Worth Fighting for in Your School (1992)*, Buckingham: Open University Press.

Goldstein, H. and Myers, K. (1997) *School Effectiveness Research: a Bandwagon, a Hi-jack or a Journey Towards Enlightenment?* Paper presented at the Annual Conference of the British Educational Research Association: York.

Goldstein, H. and Sammons, P. (1997) 'The influence of secondary and junior schools on sixteen year examination performance: a cross-classified multilevel analysis', *School Effectiveness and School Improvement*, 8 (2), 219-230.

Grace, G. (1998) Realising the mission: catholic approaches to school effectiveness, in R. Slee, G. Weiner and S. Tomlinson (eds) *School Effectiveness for Whom? Challenges to the School Effectiveness and School Improvement Movements*. London: Falmer Press.

Gray, J., Goldstein, H. and Jesson, D. (1996) 'Changes and improvements in schools' effectiveness: trends over five years', *Research Papers in Education*, 11, 35-51.

Gray, J. and Wilcox, B. (1995) *'Good School, Bad School.' Evaluating Performance and Encouraging Improvement*. Buckingham: Open University Press.

Guskey, T.R. and Huberman, M. (1995) *Professional Development in Education: New Paradigms and Practices*. New York, Teachers College Press.

Hamilton, D. (1996) *Fordism by Fiat (on the Disorganisation of Effective Schooling)*. Paper presented to the Annual Conference of the British Educational Research Association: Lancaster.

Hamilton, D. (1995) 'Peddling feel-good fictions', *Forum*, 38 (2), 54-56.

Hargreaves, A., Earl, L. and Ryan, J. (1996) *Schooling for Change: Reinventing Education for Early Adolescents*. London: Falmer Press.

Hargreaves, D. (1995) 'School culture, school effectiveness and school improvement, *School Effectiveness and School Improvement*, 6 (1), 23-46.

Hargreaves, D. H. (1984) *Improving Secondary Schools. Report of the Committee on the Curriculum and Organisation of Secondary Schools*. London: Inner London Education Authority.

Hargreaves, D.H. and Hopkins, D. (1991) *The Empowered School: the Management and Practice of Development Planning*. London: Cassell.

Harris, A., Jamieson I. and Russ J. (1996) *School Effectiveness and School Improvement: A Practical Guide*. London: Pitman Publishing.

Harris, A., Jamieson, I and Russ, J. (1995) 'A study of 'effective' departments in secondary schools', *School Organisation*, 15 (3), 283-299.

Harris, A., Jamieson I., Pearce, D. and Russ, J. (1997). *Equipping Young People for Working Life: Effective Teaching and Learning Through Work Related Contexts* London: DfEE Research Studies RS46, HMSO.

Harris, S., Wallace, G. and Rudduck, J. (1995) "It's not that I haven't learn't much. It's just that I don't really understand what I'm doing': metacognition and secondary school students', *Research Papers in Education*, 10 (2). 253-271.

Hill, P. W. and Goldstein, H. (1997) 'Multilevel modelling of educational data with cross classification and missing identification of units', *Journal of Educational and Behavioural Statistics*.

Hopkins, D. (1995) 'Towards effective school improvement', *School Effectiveness and School Improvement*, 6 (3), 265-274.

Hopkins, D. (1987) *Improving the Quality of Schooling*. Lewes: Falmer Press.

Hopkins, D., Reynolds, D. and Farrell, S. (1996a) *Moving on and Moving up: Confronting the Complexities of Improvement*. Paper presented at the Annual Conference of the British Educational Research Association: Lancaster University.

Hopkins, D., West, M. and Ainscow, M. (1996b) *Improving the Quality of Education for All: Progress and Change*. London: David Fulton.

Hopkins, D., Ainscow, M. and West, M. (1994) *School Improvement in an Era of Change*. London: Cassell.

Hopkins, D. and Sebba, J. (1995) *Improving Schools: An Overview of the Improving the Quality of Education for All Project*. Paper presented at the European Council for Educational Research Conference: Bath, September.

Hopkins, D., Harris, A., Ainscow, M., West, M. and Beresford, J. (1998) *Creating the Classroom Conditions for School Improvement*. London: David Fulton.

Independent Newspaper (1991)'A charter for schools', *The Independent editorial (5th June 1991)*. London.

Institute of Education and DfEE (1997) *The Road to Success: Four Case Studies of Schools Which No Longer Require Measures*. London: Institute of Education.

Jeffrey, B. and Woods, P. (1996) 'Feeling deprofessionalised: the social construction of emotions during an OFSTED inspection', *Cambridge Journal of Education*, 26 (3), 325-343.

Joy, B., Stoll, L. and Taggart, B. (1998) *School Improvement in the New LEA*. Paper presented to the Eleventh International Congress for School Effectiveness and School Improvement: Manchester.

Lauder, H., Jamieson, I. and Wikeley, F. (1998) Models of effective schools: limits and capabilities, in R. Slee, G. Weiner and S. Tomlinson (eds) *School Effectiveness for Whom? Challenges to the School Effectiveness and School Improvement Movements*. London: Falmer.

Leo, E. and Galloway, D. (1995) *Motivating the Difficult to Teach*. Paper presented to the Fourth International Special Education Congress: Birmingham.

Leo, E., Myers, K. and Stoll, L. (1997) *Improving Against the Odds: an Intercultural Study of School Improvement*. Paper presented to the Tenth International Congress for School Effectiveness and Improvement: Memphis, Tenenessee.

Levacic, R. and Glover, D. (1997) 'Value for money as a school improvement strategy: evidence from the new inspection system in England', *School Effectiveness and School Improvement*, 8 (2), 231-254.

Lincoln, P. and Southworth, G. (1996) 'Concerted efforts', *Education*, 187 (23), 8.

Little, J.W. (1993) 'Teachers' professional development in a climate of educational reform,' *Educational Evaluation and Policy Analysis*, 15 (2), 129-151.

Louis, K.S., Kruse, S.D. and Associates (1995) *Professionalism and Community: Perspectives on Reforming Urban Schools*. Thousand Oaks, CA: Corwin.

MacBeath, J., Boyd, B., Rand, J. and Bell, S. (1996) *Schools Speak for Themselves: Towards a Framework for Self-evaluation*. London: National Union of Teachers and University of Strathclyde.

MacGilchrist, B. (forthcoming) *Development Planning in Practice*. London: Paul Chapman.

MacGilchrist, B. and Mortimore, P. (1997) 'The impact of school development plans in primary schools', *School Effectiveness and Improvement*, 8, (2), 198-218.

MacGilchrist, B., Myers, K. and Reed, J. (1997) *The Intelligent School*. London: Paul Chapman.

McMahon, A., Bolam, R., Abbott, R. and Holly, P. (1984) *Guidelines for Review and Internal Development in Schools (Primary and Secondary Handbooks)*. York: Longman/Schools Council.

Mortimore, P. and Sammons. P. (1997) Endpiece: a welcome and a riposte to critics, in J. White and M. Barber (eds) *Perspectives on School Effectiveness and School Improvement*, London: Institute of Education.

Mortimore, P., Sammons, P., Stoll, L., Lewis, D. and Ecob, R. (1988) *School Matters: the Junior Years.* Somerset: Open Books. (Reprinted in 1994 by Paul Chapman: London.)

Mortimore, P. and Whitty, G. (1997) *Can School Improvement Overcome the Effects of Disadvantage?* Institute of Education Occasional Paper. London: Institute of Education.

Myers, K. (1996) *School Improvement in Practice: Schools Make A Difference Project.* London: Falmer Press.

Myers, K. and Goldstein, H. (1998) Who's failing?, in L. Stoll and K. Myers (eds) *No Quick Fixes: Perspectives on Schools in Difficulties.* London: Falmer Press.

National Commission on Education (1996) *Success Against the Odds: Effective Schools in Disadvantaged Areas.* London: Routledge.

Newman, F. and Wehlage, G. (1995) *Successful School Restructuring.* Madison, Wisconsin: Center on Organisation and Restructuring of Schools.

O'Donoghue, C., Thomas, S., Goldstein, H. and Knight, T. (1997) *1996 DfEE Study of Value Added for 16-18 Year Olds in England.* London, HMSO. (Available at http://www.ioe.ac.uk/hgoldstn/ key download)

OFSTED (1993) *Corporate Plan 1993-94 to 1995-96.* London: OFSTED.

Ouston, J., Fidler, B. and Earley, P. (eds) (1996) *OFSTED Inpsections: The Early Experience.* London: David Fulton.

Prince's Trust (1997) *A Breakthrough to Success - Study Support: a Review.* London: The Prince's Trust.

Pring, R. (1995) 'Educating persons: putting education back into educational research', *Scottish Educational Review,* 27 (2), 101-112.

Ranson, S. (1993) *Reviewing Education for Democracy.* Paper presented at the Institute of Public Policy Research Seminar on Alternative Education Policies, London: March.

Reynolds, D. (1995) 'The effective school: an inaugural lecture', *'School Effectiveness': Special Issue of Evaluation and Research in Education,* 9 (2), 57-73.

Reynolds, D., Gray, J. and Hopkins, D. (1998) *The Improving School Project.* Paper presented to the Eleventh International Congress for School Effectiveness and School Improvement: Manchester.

Reynolds, D., Hopkins, D. and Stoll, L. (1993) 'Linking school effectiveness and school improvement practice: towards a synergy', *School Effectiveness and School Improvement.* 4 (1), 37-58.

Reynolds, D., Sammons, P., Stoll, L., Barber, M. and Hillman, J. (1996a) 'School effectiveness and school improvement in the United Kingdom', *School effectiveness and school improvement,* 7 (2), 133-158.

Reynolds, D., Bollen, R., Creemers, B., Hopkins, D., Stoll, L. and Lagerwij, N. (1996b) *Making Good Schools: Linking School Effectiveness and School Improvement.* London: Routledge.

Reynolds, D. and Farrell, S. (1996) *Worlds Apart? A Review of International Surveys of Educational Achievement Involving England.* OFSTED Reviews of Research, London: HMSO.

Reynolds, D., Sullivan, M. and Murgatroyd, S. J. (1987) *The Comprehensive Experiment.* Lewes: Falmer Press.

Riddell, A. (1997) 'Assessing designs for school effectiveness research and school improvement in developing countries', *Comparative Education Review*, 41 (2), 178-204.

Riley, K.A. and Rowles, D. (1997a) 'Inspection and school improvement in England and Wales: national contexts and local realities', in T. Townsend (ed) *Restructuring, Quality and Effectiveness: Problems and Possibilities for Tomorrow's Schools.* London: Routledge.

Riley, K.A. and Rowles, D. (1997b) *From Intensive Care to Recovery: Schools Requiring Special Measures.* London: London Borough of Haringey.

Riley, K.A. (1998) *Whose School is it Anyway?* London: Falmer Press.

Robertson, P. and Sammons, P. (1997) *Improving School Effectiveness Project: Understanding Change in Schools.* Paper presented to the Annual Conference of the British Educational Research Association: University of York.

Robinson, P. (1997) *Literacy, Numeracy and Economic Performance.* London: London School of Economics.

Rudduck, J., Chaplain, R. and Wallace, G. (1996) *School Improvement: What Can Pupils Tell Us?* London: David Fulton.

Rudduck, J., Day, J. and Wallace, G. (1997) Students' perspectives on school improvement, in A. Hargreaves (ed) *Rethinking Educational Change with Heart and Mind (The 1997 ASCD Year Book)* Alexandria, VA: Association for Supervision and Curriculum Development.

Russell, S. and Reid, S. (1997) Managing evaluation, in B. Fidler, S. Russell and T. Simkins (eds) *Choices for Self-Managing Schools.* London: British Educational Management and Administration Society and Paul Chapman.

Rutter, M., Maughan, B., Mortimore, J. and Ouston, J. (1979) *Fifteen Thousand Hours: Secondary Schools and their Effects on Children.* London, Open Books.

Sammons, P. and Smee, R. (1997) *Using Baseline Screening Information to Examine Pupil Progress Across Years 1 and 2.* London, Institute of Education: Report prepared for Surrey Education Services.

Sammons, P., Sylva, K., Melhuish, T., Siraj-Blatchford, I. and Dixon, M. (1998) *Effective Provision of Pre-School Education: Applying Value*

Added Methods to Investigate Children's Attainment and Development Over Five Years. Paper presented to the Eleventh International Congress for School Effectiveness and School Improvement: Manchester.

Sammons, P., Thomas S. and Mortimore P. (1997) *Forging Links: Effective Schools and Effective Departments* London: Paul Chapman.

Sammons, P., Mortimore, P. and Hillman, J. (1996) 'A response to David Hamilton's reflections', *Forum*, 31 (3), 88-90.

Sammons, P. and Reynolds, D. (1997) 'A partisan evaluation - John Elliott on school effectiveness', *Cambridge Journal of Education*, 27 (1), 123-136.

Sammons, P. and Taggart, B. (1998) *Evaluating the Impact of the Raising School Standards Initiative in Belfast: The Pupils', Parents' and Teachers' Perspective.* Paper presented to the Eleventh International Congress for School Effectiveness and School Improvement: Manchester.

Scott, D. (1997) The missing hermeneutical dimension in mathematical modelling of school effectiveness, in J. White and M. Barber (eds) *Perspectives on School Effectiveness and School Improvement.* Bedford Way Papers. London: Institute of Education.

Sebba, J., Clarke, J. and Emery, B. (1996) *Enhancing School Improvement Through Inspection in Special Schools: Report of the Project on Post-Inspection Action Planning and School Improvement Following Inspection in Special Schools.* London: OFSTED, HMSO.

Slavin, R.E., Madden, N.A., Dolan, L. J., Wasik, B.A., Ross, S. and Smith, L. (1994) *Success for All: Longitudinal Effects of Systemic School-by-school Reform in Seven Districts.* Paper presented at the Annual Meeting of the American Educational Research Association: New Orleans.

Slee, R., Weiner, G. and Tomlinson, S. (eds) (1998) *School Effectiveness for Whom? Challenges to the School Effectiveness and School Improvement Movements.* London: Falmer Press.

Smith, D. and Tomlinson, S. (1989) *The School Effect: a Study of Multi-racial Comprehensives.* London: Policy Studies Institute.

Southworth, G. and Sebba, J. (1997) *Increasing the LEA's Capacity to Support Schools as They Seek to Improve.* Paper presented to the Annual Conference of the British Educational Research Association: York.

Squires, R. (1997) Robin Squires, Minister of State for Education, speaking at the Newcastle LEA 'SCOPE' Conference: 7th February.

Stoll, L. and Fink, D. (1998) The cruising school: the unidentified ineffective school, in L. Stoll and K. Myers (eds) *No Quick Fixes: Perspectives on Schools in Difficulties.* London: Falmer Press.

Stoll, L. and Myers, K. (1998) No quick fixes: an introduction, in L. Stoll and K. Myers (eds) *No Quick Fixes: Perspectives on Schools in Difficulties.* London: Falmer Press.

Stoll, L. and Reynolds, D. (1996) Connecting school effectiveness and school improvement: what have we learnt in the last ten years? in T. Townsend (ed) *Restructuring and Quality: issues for tomorrow's schools.* London: Routledge.

Stoll, L. and Thomson, M. (1996) Moving together: a partnership approach to improvement, in P. Earley, B. Fidler and J. Ouston (eds) *Improvement Through Inspection? Complementary Approaches to School Development.* London: David Fulton.

Talbert, J.E. and McLaughlin, W. (1994) 'Teacher professionalism in local school contexts', *American Journal of Education*, 102 (2), 123-153.

Teddlie, C. and Reynolds, D. (1998) *The International Handbook of School Effectiveness Research* London: Falmer Press.

Thomas, N. (1985) *Improving Primary Schools: Report of the Committee on Primary Education (The Thomas Report).* London: ILEA.

Thomas, H. and Martin, J. (1996) *Managing Resources for School Improvement: Creating a cost-effective school.* London: Routledge.

Thomas, S. and Smees, R. (1997) *Dimensions of Effectiveness: Comparative Analyses Across Regions.* Paper presented at the Tenth International Congress for School Effectiveness and Improvement: Memphis, Tennessee.

Tymms, P.B. (1996) *The Value Added National Project: Technical Report Primary 2: An Analysis of the 1991 Key Stage 1 Data Linked to the KS2 Data provided by Avon LEA.* London: Schools Curriculum and Assessment Authority.

Tymms, P., Merrell C. and Henderson, B. (1997) 'The first year at school: a quantitative investigation of attainment and progress of pupils', *Educational Research and Evaluation* 3 (2), 101-118.

Tymms, P. and Williams, D. (1996) *Baseline Assessment and Value-added*, London: Schools Curriculum and Assessment Authority.

Watkins, C., Carnell, E., Lodge, C. and Whalley, C. (1996) *Effective Learning.* Research Matters No. 5, London Institute of Education, School Improvement Network. (Available at http://www.ioe.ac.uk/iseic/sin/ key download)

White, J. (1997) Philosophical perspectives on school effectiveness and school improvement, in J. White and M. Barber (eds) *Perspectives on School Effectiveness and School Improvement.* Bedford Way Papers. London: Institute of Education.

White, J. and Barber, M. (1997) *Perspectives on School Effectiveness and School Improvement.* Bedford Way Papers. London: Institute of Education.

Whitty, G. (1997) *Social Theory and Education Policy: The Karl Mannheim Memorial Lecture,* London: Institute of Education, January.

Wikeley, F. (1998) 'Dissemination of research as a tool for school improvement?' *School Leadership and Management*, 18 (10), 59-73.

Wilcox, B. and Gray, J. (1996) *Inspecting Schools: Holding Schools to Account and Helping Schools to Improve*. Buckingham: Open University Press.

Winch, C. (1997) Accountability, controversy and school effectiveness research, in J. White and M. Barber (eds) *Perspectives on School Effectiveness and School Improvement*. Bedford Way Papers. London: Institute of Education.

The (Education) White Paper (1996). London: HMSO.

The White Paper (1997) Excellence in Schools. London: HMSO.

3.

School effectiveness and school improvement in a changing Ireland

Peter Daly, Dympna Devine, and Desmond Swan

Ireland comprises Northern Ireland (which forms part of the United Kingdom) with a population of about 1.6 million people and the Irish Republic with a population of some 3.6 million. A recent OECD Report (1996) referred to Ireland as a 'peripheral island in north western Europe' - a sobering reminder, perhaps, of its relative significance. The Education system is made up, for the most part, of voluntary schools which are supported by the state Department of Education which states its mission to be to ensure that a comprehensive cost effective and accessible education system of the highest quality is provided.

Education in Northern Ireland

Partly like Scotland, Northern Ireland has a regional educational administrative system, featuring the Department of Education and Science, Northern Ireland (DENI) and five local Education and Library Boards (ELBs), unelected local authorities, under the overall control of the Secretary of State for Northern Ireland, answerable to parliament at Westminster. A minister of state has particular responsibility for education. At present, Northern Ireland has retained a number of features of the British school system more characteristic of its early post-war development notably selection for academic grammar school places on completion of primary school. The widespread involvement of church authorities in the management of schools is a distinguishing feature, as is the large-scale provision of single-sex secondary schools.

Integrated education

Since the 1970s, a small integrated school sector has been slowly emerging. Some three percent of pupils are currently enrolled in integrated schools. Although set up under varying types of managerial arrangements, most schools already are or expect to be state financed. These schools draw pupils and staff from the two main ethno-religious groups in the region. They are subject to the same central curricular and assessment arrangements as mainstream schools, in exchange for state financial support. Secondary integrated schools do not select pupils on academic grounds. (See Cairns, Dunn and Giles 1993).

School effectiveness studies

Recent changes reflect the influence of the Education Reform (Northern Ireland) Order, 1989, which brought Northern Ireland largely into line with the provisions of the 1988 Education Act for England and Wales, notably in regard to the delivery of a 'national' curriculum and related assessment arrangements. Such changes reflect a growing adoption by the State of market principles in relation to the education service.

In terms of Scheerens' (1993) distinction among types of school effectiveness studies, most studies of school effectiveness in Northern Ireland have been applied studies. However Daly's (1991) study had a 'fundamental' aspect featuring an investigation of secondary school effect size. Given the considerable variation in secondary school type, related mainly to selection and management differences, it was considered appropriate to investigate this issue in the light of studies of school effect size elsewhere. In a re-analysis of data from two school surveys in the 1980s, involving random samples and taking advantage of recent advances in multilevel modelling techniques, it was concluded that there were significant school effects on pupil performance in public examinations at the end of the period of statutory schooling - ie for pupils completing five years of secondary schooling. Using prior performance and family background measures and adjusting for school type differences, residual school variance component estimates ranged from five to nine per cent depending on the pupils' academic performance outcome measured - findings, still largely in line with international studies (see

Sammons, 1996). A further finding of Daly's (1991) study related to the impact on performance of attendance at a selective (grammar) school. Impact estimates appeared to be relatively constant, after adjustment, ranging from a quarter to a half of a standard deviation on four outcome measures namely English, Mathematics, Chemistry and an overall weighted performance measure. Unfortunately there were no measures of non-cognitive outcomes available for analysis.

These findings are worth considering today as a new Labour government at Westminster is linked to a political party which has, historically, promoted non-selective (comprehensive) secondary schooling in England, Scotland and Wales. The Secretary of State is now subjecting the Northern Ireland school system to greater scrutiny. However Daly's (1991) findings may be largely a reflection of the impact of historical advantages, such as superior state funding arrangements originally in place, contextual effects in terms of pupil-composition (social and academic mix) and unmeasured teacher effects.

In a more recent study Daly (1995a) considered the impact of management differences on pupils' performance in public examinations taken, typically, at the end of the period of compulsory schooling with particular reference to Catholic Schools. A multilevel value-added approach was taken. Catholic pupils form approximately half of the school-going population. Government statistics have consistently demonstrated the superior academic achievement of pupils attending non-Catholic schools - ie pupils attending voluntary Protestant schools or state schools infrequently attended by Catholic pupils. [See Cormack and Osborne (eds.) 1992]. Daly's (1995a) study suggested that, after adjusting for pupil-intake differences and for school-type differences (selective/non-selective) there wasn't evidence of a significant academic advantage conferred on pupils attending non-Catholic schools. It is important to realise also that this finding relates to a Northern Ireland population where Catholics represent an economically disadvantaged group relative to non-Catholics in terms of economic indicators such as employment status and dependence on state benefits [Cormack and Osborne (eds.) 1992; Shuttleworth, 1995]. However, Daly's (1995a) findings were based on a re-analysis of data from surveys carried out in the 1980s.

Because earlier studies had not revealed much in the way of school-type differences related to gender composition, Daly (1996) studied the girls in the two 1980s surveys mentioned above with particular reference to the impact of attendance at single-sex schools on academic achievement, compared to attendance at co-educational schools. Performances in English, Mathematics and on an overall weighted performance measure were treated as outcomes. Results did not indicate a single incidence of a significant single-sex school advantage for girls in either survey although the six estimates were negative. Drawing attention to the inconclusive nature of the research literature on the theme of single-sex versus co-educational schools, in terms of their academic impact, this Northern Ireland study added further weight to the view that the case for single-sex schools was not yet convincingly demonstrated even if the economic argument, which hastened the decline of single-sex secondary schools in many industrialised countries, could be countered. These Northern Ireland findings were broadly in line with findings from Steedman's (1985) study of English and Welsh secondary schools. They were also broadly in line with Marsh's (1989) re-analysis of American Catholic schools data and with the Gill (1993) and Yates (1993) reports on Australian school studies.

In a related study Daly (1995b) examined pupil gender and school gender differences in science course enrolment and in attainment in science in public examinations. The analysis of the data from the earlier survey indicated that girls were less likely than boys to enrol for science courses and were significantly behind them in terms of attainment. However this pattern appeared to have significantly changed by the late 1980s with girls holding their own with boys in terms of enrolment and attainment. The earlier survey analysis revealed no significant school gender type effect but the second survey indicated a superior co-educational school effect, perhaps, reflecting greater availability of resources. However, Shuttleworth and Daly (1997), in a later study of the uptake of 'hard science' defined as physics, chemistry and technology courses in relation to the General Certificate of Secondary Education (GCSE) suggested that religious and gender inequalities in 'science' course participation continued in Northern Ireland. The findings were, cautiously, interpreted as indicating possible restrictions on educational and occupational opportunities for Catholics and for girls irrespective of religious background. Again, single-sex schools did not confer significant advantages over mixed schools. A further study of public examination entry and attainment in regard to mathematics Daly and Shuttleworth (1997) suggested that girls were moving ahead of boys on these measures related to gender differences after five years of secondary schooling. This study included data from a third survey carried out in the early 1990s - by which time girls were significantly ahead of boys in mathematics attainment. No significant school-gender type differences were found, however.

Caul (1994) in a study of secondary schools in Northern Ireland, looked at differences in academic outcomes of public examinations, controlling for the percentage of pupils taking free school meals, (an indicator of social disadvantage). A qualitative study of four of the samples fourteen schools was also carried out. While it was noted that the pattern of differential performance was not particularly surprising, given the selective nature of the school system, an important issue was raised about the possibly poor prognosis for school improvement in schools where the academic balance of pupil-intake was particularly uneven, with low attaining pupils dominating.

In particular it was suggested that some schools, as a result of the 'creaming-off' effect of grammar schools and of apparently more successful non-grammar schools in a neighbourhood, could find it very difficult to achieve a 'turn-around' in improvement terms. The importance of attention to academic-balance in regard to pupil-intake had been noted, for example, by Rutter et al (1979), by Willms (1985) and by Daly (1987).

School improvement in Northern Ireland

The Education Reform (Northern Ireland) Order (1989) radically changed the state's approach to the funding and management of schools. The local authority bodies, the Education and Library Boards, experienced a reduction in their control of schools in line with the position of local education authorities in Great Britain. These changes, government argued, gave an enhanced role to school governors and to parents seen as clients (see McKeown, 1993 for a discussion of these changes). It is worth recalling, however, Caldwell's (1988: 303) statement about this type of school management change then emerging in many countries.

The decentralisation is administrative rather than political, with decisions at the school level being made within a framework of district, state or national policies and guidelines. The school remains accountable ... for the manner in which resources are allocated

As in the rest of the United Kingdom, a state presumption that competition among schools promotes quality assurance is reflected in the statutory publication of schools' public examination and test results, unadjusted for pupil intake differences.

School improvement initiatives

There have been two major school improvement initiatives - one associated with the Targeting Social Need Program (TSN) and the other associated with the Raising School Standards Initiative (RSSI). The TSN program originated as an initiative across all government departments in 1991. In regard to educational expenditure the TSN program approached £32 million for 1995-1996 - representing about 5 per cent of the 'notional' schools' budget. Money is dispersed across schools according to a varied and somewhat controversial formula related to the Local Management of Schools (LMS) funding. Emphasis is on support for the 'most needy' schools including voluntary grammar schools. The initiative has been criticised in the House of Commons

Northern Ireland Affairs Committee Report (1997) as requiring better management and greater accountability - giving rise to a more streamlined relationship to the other major project initiative, the RSSI.

The latter program is directed at some 33 secondary schools across Northern Ireland and their main feeder primary schools, typically, two or three per secondary school since 1995. Originally only four low achieving Belfast secondary schools and their ten feeder primary schools were involved as part of a larger industrial regeneration project (Making Belfast Work). The initiative, now funded by DENI, has a budget of £17 million to carry it through to 1997-98. Schools are closely monitored by DENI inspectors in relation to raising achievement levels while receiving extra professional support. However the House of Commons Northern Ireland Affairs Committee Report (1997) has been somewhat critical of the limited time scale and of the less than clear rationale for inclusion in the program. In order to ensure participation and thereby secure the extra funding, schools had to submit whole school development plans, complete with costings, and be subject to additional inspection by DENI. The Committee took exception to what it regarded as a hidden strategy to spread resources equitably across denominational and Board area lines rather than in terms of 'absolute' appropriateness. This initiative is also the subject of a research study being carried out by a team from the University of London Institute of Education providing 'value added' information for government and for the schools concerned. The report will be made available at a later stage.

There has been a revival of interest in researching aspects of selection for secondary schooling - especially in the context of changes which are associated with a national curriculum for the United Kingdom with relatively minor adaptations for Northern Ireland. Over the past ten years, a number of leading researchers have drawn attention to limitations, technical difficulties and demonstrable inequities associated with the implementation of varying procedures devised by government to allocate state-funded grammar school places (see Bunting, Saris and McCormack 1987; Sutherland and Gallagher, 1987; Gallagher, 1988; Sutherland, 1993). A new Labour administration at Westminster, while distancing itself from any major change in policy in relation to the remaining grammar school provision in England and Wales, is coming under pressure to review this policy in relation to Northern Ireland (see House of Commons Northern Ireland Affairs Committee, Second Report 1997).

Academic selection of pupils for attendance at state financed grammar schools, whether this takes place, typically, at age eleven or at age fourteen in the Craigavon area, will continue to generate much public debate, as well as private anguish for the rejected majority. (Alexander, J. et al. 1998). Commenting on a study by Gallagher et al (1997) funded by the Northern

Ireland Economic Council, the Council noted the view expressed in that study that the education system in the United Kingdom had over-emphasised the 'needs of the academically most able' while not giving sufficient consideration to less able pupils.   In a foreword to the study the Council remarked (Gallagher et al, 1997: vii) 'There is little doubt that a similar conclusion applies to Northern Ireland, particularly in view of the Transfer Procedure and the division of post-primary schooling into grammar and secondary schools'.

Education in the Republic of Ireland

The education system in the Republic of Ireland is one of the most centralised in Western Europe in so far as there is no regional or local tier of government for either primary or second level schools. Traditionally the system has been an 'aided' one with the Churches, private bodies or individuals taking the initiative in setting up schools which, provided certain minimum criteria were met would be recognised and largely funded by the state. The system is primarily denominational in character, although in recent years a growing number of multi-denominational primary schools have been established. While the state owns few schools it wields considerable power at all levels, determining the primary curriculum in some detail and monitoring its implementation through the Inspectorate. It also dictates minimum standards for teacher qualifications, determines (through negotiation with the unions) teacher salary levels, the kind and level of school support service and establishes rules for the management and maintenance of schools. Overall the system amounts to a partnership - sometimes a power struggle - between the teacher unions, Churches, and Government with parents emerging as another power bloc.

Following the establishment of the State (in 1922), on the crest of a wave of cultural and political nationalism, primary schooling was used principally for the revival of the Irish language, but otherwise a policy vacuum existed up until the 1960's and later. The rapid expansion of the second and third level systems took place toward the end of the 1960's in line with government policy directed toward the modernising and industrialising of the Irish economy. Soaring demand for schooling, the declining influence of the Churches, and an increasingly complex and pluralistic society all make increasing demands for new policies and approaches coming up to the millennium. The 1990's has been a period of major evaluation of the educational system reflected in the publication of a Green Paper on education 1992 (Education for a Changing World), the convening of an independent national Education Convention in 1994, which consulted widely with all the education partners and produced its own report (Coolahan, 1994) and the White paper 1995 (Charting our Education Future) which took on board many of the recommendations arising from the national convention. The most contentious proposals for reform related to the establishment of an intermediate administrative tier at regional level in the form of Regional Education Councils. Included in the Education Bill 1997 (No 1), following the fall of the then coalition government, this proposal was subsequently dropped by the incoming government which drafted a second bill (Education Bill 1997, No 2) in November of the same year. The Bill, currently at committee stage, is significant in placing the education system on a legislative footing for the first time since the foundation of the state, detailing rights and duties in respect of education. The Bill has implications for increasing accountability overall within the system, with the school inspectorate specifically geared toward the monitoring of standards through whole school evaluation, including the quality of teaching and effectiveness of individual teachers.

School effectiveness studies

Apart from the early fundamental research on school effectiveness using curriculum-sensitive outcome measures (Madaus, Kellaghan, Rakow and King, 1979) the bulk of school effectiveness studies has been 'applied', using Scheerens' (1993) term. An interest in pupil and school gender issues was heightened by the publication of a study by Hanafin and Charthaigh (1993). Based on a sample of 17 post-primary schools in the Limerick area, the study raised a number of important issues related to claims about the academic and other advantages for girls, of attending single-sex schools. Their findings appeared to support some popular demands for the continuation of single-sex secondary school provision, where this already existed, despite an earlier government indication of a desire to move more towards co-educational school provision. The government responded to public interest in the study by commissioning a large-scale investigation of schooling and gender equality. The first report of a research team based at Dublin's Economic and Social Research Institute (Hannan et al) appeared in 1996. This report's main focus was on co-education. The report was based on a random sample of some 116 post-primary schools and 10,000 pupils. The use of a multilevel design placed the investigation in the mainstream of recent school effectiveness research studies. Cognitive and non-cognitive outcomes were considered. In the first report, the research team concluded that co-education had no significant impact on average performance in the main public examination taken by school leavers - the Leaving Certificate Examination. Co-education, however, had a negative impact on the attainment of girls and boys in mathematics.

In regard to non-cognitive outcomes, co-educational school pupils viewed the impact of their schools on their personal and social development more favourably than pupils in single-sex schools. Furthermore, a majority of pupils in all schools expressed a preference for co-educational schools. Nevertheless, co-education did not have much impact on specific measures of pupil development or on stress levels. The research team is now looking in more detail at case studies of selected schools.

School effectiveness research has made many advances both methodologically and conceptually since its foundation in the 1960s. A recent study into school effectiveness in Irish primary schools (Devine and Swan 1997) forms part of a larger international study, the International School Effectiveness Research Project (ISERP), which seeks to build on the advances made to date, by investigating a wide range of attributes of school achievement and analysing them according to levels of influence related to the individual, the class, the school and the broader national context. In so doing the study draws on a range of theoretical and methodological advancements which have come from those working within the field of school effectiveness and school improvement. In particular, the use of qualitative data gathering techniques and the explicit focus on process indicators of school effects, coupled with a standardisation of research instruments in the nine countries participating in the project (United States of America, Canada, Hong Kong, Taiwan, Australia, The Netherlands, The United Kingdom, The Republic of Ireland and Norway), are considered to be among the strengths of the study. Cross-cultural studies of this kind are important not only in highlighting cultural influences on student achievement, but also the transferability or otherwise of factors which have been identified as important in specific cultural contexts.

To ensure comparability across countries in the ISERP project, in each country 'effective', 'typical' and 'ineffective' schools were chosen. Within each group of schools a distinction was made between low SES and middle SES schools. For each of these categories there was at least one school. In total at least six classes were included in the study beginning with children aged 7/8 years. The study began therefore with children who had just commenced second grade and continued through until they reached the end of third class.

In the Irish study six schools in all were chosen with one class in each school, except for one school which had two classes at each grade level. Therefore the Irish study had a student sample from seven classes in all. However, two of the classes selected had a mixed age group - comprised of two grade levels - second class and third class. This accounts for the small sample of students selected in Riverdale and Church Avenue. In each instance only those children in the second grade were chosen for the study. The schools, with their coded names, social classification and student sample, are indicated in Table 1 below.

Table 1: Sample in the Irish study by student number,
school and social classification

School	Social Classification	Student Numbers	Number of Classes
Country Lane	middle class	34	1
Cherry Orchard	middle class	37	1
Riverdale	middle class	13	1
Secret Garden	disadvantaged	46	2
Church Avenue	disadvantaged	12	1
Tower View	disadvantaged	23	1
Totals		165	7

Data collection took place over a two year period and incorporated the four levels identified by Creemers (1994) and Stringfield (1994) at the individual student level, class level (observation of practice using standardised ISERP instruments, interviews with teachers), school level (interviews with principals and observation of school life) and national/local community level. The main focus of the study was on student outcomes in the area of mathematics achievement, and social outcomes, involving areas such as self concept in mathematics, attitude towards school, locus of control and democratic attitudes. Mathematics was chosen as the key academic outcome, given that it is the most uniform subject internationally in terms of knowledge content, and also the subject where there is the greatest evidence of school effects (Reynolds *et al*, 1994). However data was also collected with respect to reading achievement over the two years in the six schools, using a national standardised reading achievement test. The main findings of the Irish study may be summarised as follows:

Student academic achievement

- Differences were identified among the six schools in cognitive outcomes but many of these were mediated by individual level factors such as student social class, gender and ability. The school level effect appeared to be more pronounced in this study with respect to reading achievement rather than mathematics performance.

- Class-level factors identified as important in influencing achievement included a tendency toward organised, focused teaching, with review and practice, as well as the creation of a positive learning climate for students. Social class of the student body was shown to be an important factor mediating class/school level practice, with a particular emphasis on the maintenance of appropriate classroom behaviour as well as the above, in the more effective schools in the designated disadvantaged sample.

Student social development

A significant school effect was recorded with respect to student self-concept and perception of democracy within the classroom, but not in relation to attitude towards school, or locus of control. Direct correlations between these measures and cognitive achievement were, in general, inconclusive, and a more substantial study would be required to ascertain their precise effect on student performance in school. An inter-relationship between class and school-level factors is considered to be central to the realisation of high self concept scores among students in the more effective schools, in particular a clear articulation of the importance of promoting self-esteem amongst children by both principals and teachers in these schools and a willingness to emphasise this in classroom practice. In relation to perceptions of democracy within the classroom, it was noted that in general children in the more middle class schools had a more positive perception of democratic practices within their classrooms than did those in the designated disadvantaged schools. This was explained by the tendency toward greater efficiency and organisation in the delivery of lessons in schools serving a lower socio-economic student body and a tighter control over children's behaviour in the practice of teachers in these schools.

Interrelationships between the variables

- Schools which are effective in one area may not necessarily be so in another. While this applies within the area of mathematics itself (ie schools found to be high achievers in applications were not necessarily so in relation to computations), it also relates to cognitive and non-cognitive areas of development. In many instances the absence of a significant school effect could be attributed to class-level factors, such as within-school differences in teaching practice, as much as to individual-level factors such as student social class or gender. This raises questions as to the definition of effectiveness and whether it is appropriate to classify a school as either effective or ineffective. For this reason this study utilised the term 'more' or 'less' effective to accord with the view (Hargreaves 1995) that schools may vary in their degree of effectiveness along a continuum that is open to change.

- A related issue concerns the role of social class in mediating the effectiveness levels of particular schools. In this study the contrast between schools in the lower socio-economic environment was much more evident than in those serving a middle class population. This has been noted by other researchers in the field (Teddlie 1995). The suggestion is made that middle class parents, with their greater access to economic and cultural resources (Boudieu 1986), will intervene more directly in their children's education, than will those from a predominantly lower socio-economic background. Where parents are actively encouraged and facilitated in becoming involved in the school life of their children, the outcomes, as reflected in Secret Garden in this study, are very positive. This provides a very identifiable school-level effect which was not evident in the less effective Tower View.

- At the school level case study data revealed considerable differences between schools in a number of different areas. While all children attending Iris primary school are exposed to the same curriculum this does not imply that their overall experience of school will be similar. Data in this study, relating in particular to classroom procedures, as well as the measurement of non-cognitive outcomes confirms this view. The influence of school-level factors should be borne in mind in considering overall differences in children's experience of school. Specifically as noted in this study, these relate to the influence of the principal in promoting a particular ethos/vision for the school, an emphasis on positive staff relations, care and maintenance of school buildings, and the facilitation of open communication and contact with the parent body. Differences in relation to these areas were particularly pertinent in comparing the more and less effective schools in the lower socio-economic group sample.

School improvement initiatives

A variety of school-improvement programs to address problems associated with educational disadvantage have been developed in the Republic of Ireland since the 1960s. In light of the relationship between home background and children's school performance, several of the programs had as an area of concern the role of parents in their children's education. In recognition of the view that children are likely to suffer in their scholastic progress when home and school differ in their approaches to life and learning, special efforts were made to promote home-school collaboration in pursuance of the shared objectives of the two institutions in fostering children's development (see Kellaghan, Sloane, Alvarez, & Bloom, 1993).

In a recent (1990) initiative, the Department of Education of the Irish government launched the Home-School-Community Liaison (HSCL) Scheme which was designed to use school-based personnel to increase the involvement of parents in their children's learning. By 1992, 80 primary schools and 26 post-primary schools in disadvantaged areas were participating in the scheme. A consideration of the state of affairs relating to home-school relationships that existed in schools before the commencement of the Scheme indicated a need for schools to adopt a more proactive role in promoting such relationships. Three major approaches seemed appropriate. First, the variety and quantity of home-school contacts would need to be increased. Secondly, the quality of the contacts should be improved. In particular, parents should be assisted to play a more central and active role in their children's education. Thirdly, there was a need to ensure that as great a number of parents as possible would be involved in home-school activities. Special efforts would be required to target parents whose involvement in the formal aspects of schooling seemed slight (Ryan, 1995).

An evaluation of HSCL programs in schools over a three-year period indicated that a considerable amount of activity had been generated, thus meeting a major objective of the Scheme to promote active co-operation between home and school. Schools provided a wide range of courses for parents (mostly mothers), including self-development courses, parenting courses, classes in the primary-school curriculum, and leisure courses. Homes were visited and opportunities were provided in schools for parents to meet socially. Parents became involved in a variety of school activities, both in the classroom and outside it. There also was some evidence that movement had occurred towards the achievement of a second objective of the Scheme - to raise awareness in parents of their own capacities to enhance their children's educational progress and to assist them in developing relevant skills. This conclusion may be inferred from observations that parents had increased in self-confidence, knew more about what was happening in school, and had learned how to help their children with school work (Ryan, 1995).

It was anticipated that effects on pupil achievement of a scheme directed primarily at parents would be likely to be long-term rather than short-term. It was nevertheless decided to obtain data on pupil achievement at an early stage. A quasi-experimental design was employed in which data were obtained on the literacy and numeracy achievements of pupils in first, third, and fifth grades in six schools in the first term of the first year of the scheme. These achievements could be regarded as those that might be expected in the absence of a home-school-community program of activities. When the Scheme had been in operation for four years, the literacy and numeracy achievements of pupils in the same grades in the same schools were again assessed. Any differences between the performance of pupils at the Scheme's inception (who might be regarded as constituting a control group) and the performance of pupils when the Scheme had been in operation for four years (the experimental group) might reasonably be attributed to participation in the Scheme.

Analysis of pupil achievement data indicated that following the implementation of the HSCL scheme, pupils performed significantly better on literacy tests at grades 1 and 3. Differences between the groups on numeracy tests were not significant at grades 1 or 3. At grade 5, the control group outperformed the experimental group in both literacy and numeracy (Ryan, 1996). The results are neither clear-cut nor readily interpretable. However, insofar as they indicate an impact on pupil achievement of a program targeted primarily on parents, and in operation for a relatively short period of time, they suggest that in the longer term stronger pupil effects may be anticipated.

A more recent initiative (in 1996) by the Department of Education to address problems associated with disadvantage, known as 'Breaking the Cycle', involves more intensive targeting of resources on a relatively small number of schools in which large numbers of pupils are considered to be at risk of educational failure. Schools in the scheme have access to special grant assistance for the purchase of books, teaching materials, and equipment. An enhanced capitation grant and in-career development for school staff are also provided, while class size in junior grades (up to and including second grade) has been reduced to about 15 pupils (see Kellaghan, Weir, ó hUallacháin, & Morgan, 1996). An evaluation of the scheme is underway.

In conclusion the existence of a state-of-the-art data base for the study of secondary schooling in the Irish Republic (Hannan et al 1996) is a very valuable asset. The new primary school study (Devine and Swan 1997) has indicated the range of data that might be collected in setting up a comparable data base for the study of primary schools. New data sets of a similar nature, related to primary and secondary schools, are urgently required in Northern Ireland.

Well designed school improvement studies in the Irish Republic will be of growing interest to people in Northern Ireland. Data on economic aspects of schooling eg local financial management of schools (site-based management), in Northern Ireland, (McKeown et al. 1997) should be of considerable value to a wide range of interested parties in the Irish Republic as the state considers moving towards a policy of increasing local financial management of schools despite the absence of a regional administrative tier.

Ireland appears to be on the verge of a new era rooted in a peace initiative which, if successful, will change the political relationship between Northern Ireland and the Irish Republic as well as relationships between both and Great

Britain. The growing importance of building on the economic and cultural ties between all three requires greater attention to the educational systems which contribute to overall political stability and cultural developments. Accountability of state and state supported schools to the citisens who sustain them and in whose name they are sustained is a concern likely to grow rapidly in this context.

Acknowledgements
Peter Daly would like to thank Tony Gallagher, Tom Kellaghan, Seamus McGuinness and Emer Smyth with whom he discussed some aspects of this report. Tom Kellaghan also provided additional material. They are not responsible, however, for any views expressed here. The authors are particularly grateful to Karen Wylie for her skill and patience at the word processor.

References

Alexander, J., Daly, P., Gallagher, A., Gray, C. and Sutherland, A. (1998) *An Evaluation of the Criagavon Two-tier System* Graduate School of Education, Queen's University of Belfast. Report commissioned by DENI

Bourdieu, P. (1986) 'The Forms of Capital' in J. Richardson (ed.): *Handbook of Theory and Research for the Sociology of Education*, New York, Greenwood

Bunting, B., Saris, W. E. and McCormack, J. (1987) A second order factor analysis of the reliabililty and validity of the 11 plus examination in Northern Ireland, *The Economic and Social Review 18*, 3, 137 - 147

Cairns, E., Donn, S. and Giles, Mezanie (1993) Surveys of integrated education in Northern Ireland: A review. In *After the Reforms: Education and Policy in Northern Ireland.* eds. Osborne, R., Cormack, R. and Gallagher, A. Aldershot. Avebury.

Caldwell, B. (1988) Towards a new paradigm in the governance of public education: The contribution of effective schools research. In: Reynolds, D., Creemers, B. P. M. and Peters, T. (eds.) *School Effectiveness and School Improvement* University of Wales College of Cardiff and Groningen Institute for Educational Research

Caul, L. (1994) *School Effectiveness in Northern Ireland: Illustration and practice.* Report of the Standing Advisory Commission on Human Rights. London: HMSO

Coolahan, J. (ed.) 1994 *Report on the National Education Convention* Dublin The National Convention Secretariat

Cormack, R. J. and Osborne, R. D. (eds.) (1991) *Discrimination and Public Policy in Northern Ireland*, Oxford: Clarendon Press

Creemers, B. The History, Value and Purpose of School Effectiveness Studies, in Reynolds, D. *et al*: *Advances in School Effectiveness Research and Practice*, Oxford: Pergamon Press, 1994

Creemers, B., Reynolds, D. and Swint, F. (1995) 'The International School Effectiveness Research Programme: Results of the Quantitative Study', Paper presented at the Annual Meeting of the American Educational Research Association, San Francisco, April 1995

Daly, P. (1987) 'School Effectiveness and Pupils' Examination Performance in Northern Ireland.' In *After the Reforms: Education and Policy in Northern Ireland.* eds. Osborne, R., Cormack, R. and Gallagher, A. Aldershot. Avebury.

Daly, P. (1991) How large are secondary school effects in Northern Ireland? *School Effectiveness and School Improvement, 2, 4*, 305 - 323

Daly, P. (1995a) Public accountability and academic effectiveness of grant-aided Catholic Schools, *School Effectiveness and School Improvement 6, 4*, 367 - 379

Daly, P. (1995b) Science course participation and science achievement in single-sex and coeducational schools. *Evaluation and Research in Education, 9*, 2 91 – 98

Daly, P. (1996) The effects of single-sex and coeducational secondary schooling on girls' achievement, *Research Papers in Education, 11, 3*, 289-306

Daly, P. and Shuttleworth, I. (1997) Determinants of public examination entry and attainment in mathematics: Evidence on gender and gender-type of school from the 1980s and the 1990s in Northern Ireland. *Evaluation and Research in Education, 11, 2*, 91 - 101

Department of Education (1995) *Charting our Education Future.* Dublin: The Stationery Office

Devine, D. and Swan, D. (1997) *The International School Effectiveness Research Project – The Irish Study* Report to the Department of Education and Science. Dublin. Department of Education , University College Dublin

Gallagher, A. M. (1988). *Transfer pupils at Sixteen.* Belfast: Northern Ireland Council for Educational Research.

Gallagher, T., Shuttleworth, I and Gray, C. (1997). *Educational Achievement in Northern Ireland: Patterns and Prospects* Belfast. Northern Ireland Economic Council

Gill, J. (1993) Rephrasing the question about single-sex schooling. In: Reid, A. and Johnston, B. (eds.) *Critical Issues in Australian Education in the 1990s.* Adelaide: Painters Press

Hanafin, J. and N' Charthaigh, D. (1993). *Co-education and Attainment.* Limerick: University of Limerick

Hannan, D. F., Smyth, E., McCullagh, J., O'Leary, R. and McMahon, D. 1996 *Co-education and Gender Equality: Exam Performance, Stress and Personal Development.* Dublin: Oak Tree Press in association with the Economic and Social Research Institute

Hargreaves, D. (1995) School Culture, School Effectiveness and School Improvement, *School Effectiveness and Improvement, 6,* No 1, pp 23 - 46

House of Commons Northern Ireland Affairs Committee Report (1997) *Underachievement in Northern Ireland Secondary Schools.* London: The Stationery Office

Kellaghan, T., Sloane, K., Alvarez, B., & Bloom, B. S. (1993). *The home environment and school learning. Promoting parental involvement in the education of children.* San Francisco: Jossey Bass.

Kellaghan, T., Weir, S., ó hUallacháin, S., & Morgan, M. (1996). *Educational disadvantage in Ireland.* Dublin: Department of Education/Combat Poverty Agency/Educational Research Centre.

Madaus, G. F., Kellaghan, T., Rakow, E.A., and King, D.J. (1979) The sensitivity of measures of school effectiveness. *Harvard Educational Review, 49,* 207 - 230

Marsh, H. W. 1989. The effects of attending single-sex and co-educational high schools on achievement, attitudes and behaviours and on sex differences. *Journal of Educational Psychology, 81,* 651 - 653

McKeown, P. (1993) The introduction of formula funding and local management of schools in Northern Ireland. In: Obborne, R., Cormack, R. and Gallagher, A. (eds.) *After the reforms: Education and policy in Northern Ireland.* Aldershot: Avebury

McKeown, P., Byrne, G. and Barnet, R. with Fee, R. and Leith, H. (1997) *An Initial Analysis of the Impact of formula Funding and Local Management of Schools on the Management of Northern Ireland Schools: A Schools' Perspective.* Bangor. Department of Education. Northern Ireland.

OECD. (1996) *Education at a Glance: OECD Indicators.* Paris: OECD

Osborne, R. D., Cormack, R. J. and Miller, R. L. (eds.) (1987) *Education and Policy in Northern Ireland Belfast:* Policy Research Institute

Programme for a partnership government, 1993 - 1997 (1993) Dublin: Fianna Fáil and Labour Parties

Reynolds, D. *et al* (1994) School Effectiveness - The Need for an International Perspective in Reynolds, D. *et al: Advances in School Effectiveness Research and Practice,* Oxford: Pergamon Press

Reynolds, D., Creemers, B. P. M. and Peters, T. (eds.) *School Effectiveness and School Improvement* (1989) University of Wales College of Cardiff and Groningen Institute for Educational Research

Rutter, M., Maughan, B., Mortimore, P. and Ouston, J. (1979) *Fifteen thousand hours: Secondary schools and their effects on children* London: Open Books

Ryan, S. (1995). *The Home-School-Community Liaison Scheme. Summary Evaluation report.* Dublin: Educational Research Centre

Ryan, S. (1996). 'Evaluation of Home-School-Community Liaison (HSCL)\Scheme. Achievements of first, third and fifth class students: Initial and follow-up assessments'. Unpublished paper. Educational Research Centre, Dublin

Sammons, P. (1996) Complexities in the Judgement of School Effectiveness, *Educational Research and Evaluation* 2, 2, 113 - 149

Scheerens, J. (1993). Basic school effectiveness research: Items for a research agenda. *School Effectiveness and School Improvements, 4*, 17 - 36

Shuttleworth, I. (1995). The relationship between social deprivation as measured by free school meals eligibility, and educational attainment in Northern Ireland: A preliminary investigation. *British Research Journal, 21*, 4, 487 - 504

Shuttleworth, I. and Daly, P. (1997) Inequalities in the uptake of science at GCSE: Evidence from Northern Ireland. *Research Papers in Education, 12*, 2, 143 - 155

Steedman, J. (1985). Examination results in mixed and single-sex secondary schools. In: Reynolds, D. (ed.) *Studying School Effectiveness.* London: Falmer

Sutherland, A. E (1993) The transfer procedure reformed? In: Osborne, R., Cormack, R. and Gallagher, A. (eds.). *After the Reforms: Education and Policy in Northern Ireland.* Aldershot: Avebury

Sutherland, A. E. and Gallagher, A. M. (1987). *Pupils in the border land.* Belfast: Northern Ireland Council for Educational Research

Teddlie, C. (1995) *ISERP Case Studies, USA Sites, Comparison of Four Differentially Effective Schools*, Louisiana State University College of Education

The Education Reform (Northern Ireland) Order (1989). Belfast, HMSO

Willms, J. D. (1985). The balance thesis: Contextual effects of ability on pupils' O-grade examination results. *Oxford Review of Education, 13*, 211 - 232

Yates, L. (1993). *The Education of girls: Policy research and the question of gender.* Victoria: The Australian Council for Educational Research

4.

Visiting the secret gardens: The Scottish system

John MacBeath

The Scottish system is in some ways a unique and happy hunting ground for school effects research. It does not have the wide variety of school types as in England, for example, nor is there the same wide variation among education authorities. It does not have the large private school population of many other countries and parents are much more likely than in many other countries to send their child to the local school. 97% or so of the pupil population attend all-through comprehensive schools from the age of 5 to18. There is no national curriculum nor national testing but there are curricular guidelines and Scottish Certificate Examinations at the of fourth, fifth/sixth years of secondary school (Standard Grade and Higher Grade). These constrain teaching and learning within quite tight content boundaries and give secondary subject classrooms a somewhat familiar feel no matter where they are in the country, the Highlands, Islands, Lowlands, or in the inner-city.

This relative homogeneity is reinforced by a tradition for teachers to be appointed by authorities not individual schools, with the effect that there is less differential from school to school in the quality, qualifications and experience of teachers. In general it is true to say that 'good' or 'effective' teachers are just as likely to be found in highly disadvantaged schools as in more privileged schools. The 'vertical partnership' (Raab, 1992) of Scottish Office Education and Industry Department (SOEID), authorities and schools is still a significant one, despite redrawing of authority boundaries under the Conservative Government. This 'vertical partnership' ensures a much greater homogeneity among schools than would be found in England or countries in which there is a greater degree of decentralisation. OECD statistics (1992) showed much less between-school variance in Scottish than in English schools in Mathematics achievement. In Scotland it was 16% and in England 63%.

The Scottish figure is much closer to France (highly centralised) while the English figure is closer to the Swiss (highly decentralised).

Her Majesty's Inspectorate (HMI) have taken a different path from their English equivalent, OFSTED, and the debate about failing schools has not been a Scottish one. Although it is abundantly clear from HMI reports that the quality of schools and of school leadership is variable, the mechanisms for addressing these issues comes more through concerted action by HMI, authorities and the school rather than by market-driven mechanisms. Because of this intervention, and due to a relatively healthy teacher supply, schools are not allowed to deteriorate to the point where 'special measures' or closure are advocated. So, for effectiveness researchers, Scotland provides a more even playing field with fewer variables to control than in many other school systems.

A tradition of school effectiveness

School effectiveness research has played a significant role in the development of education policy in Scotland. Through the 1980s and 1990s there was an ongoing relationship between policy-makers and researchers. This is reflected in Scottish Office documents 'Effective Secondary Schools' (Scottish Education Department, 1988), followed a year later by 'Effective Primary Schools' (SED, 1989). These documents were designed to distil the essence of school effectiveness research and put into the hands of teachers and school management, issues that had previously been only the province of researchers. In the words of David Hargreaves this was an important step in helping teachers 'take ownership of their diagnosis of the school and develop a commitment to implementing the solutions they themselves formulate.' (Scottish Educational Research Association keynote address,1989, p12.)

These documents provided the basis for policy initiatives on school development planning, seen as the mechanism through which greater school effectiveness would be delivered. In 1991 the SOED circulated to all schools a publication entitled 'The Role of School Development Plans in Managing School Effectiveness.' The publication of the school self-evaluation guidelines in the following year (SOED 1992) signalled a sea change in thinking about how schools improve. Her Majesty's Inspectorate moved their criteria for evaluating school quality and effectiveness out of the secret gardens of the Official Secrets Act into the public domain, a paradigmatic shift in philosophy. The three sets of guidelines were:

- A set of qualitative indicators based on criteria used by HMI in inspections;
- Relative Ratings, giving secondary schools formulae for calculating the differential effectiveness of subject departments;
- Ethos indicators, providing schools with techniques for gauging the more subjective aspects of school life from the perspectives of pupils, teachers and parents.

The research base

Through the 1980s the Centre for Educational Sociology in Edinburgh (C.E.S.) produced a substantial and influential body of work (for example, Gray, McPherson and Raffe 1983, Cuttance 1988, McPherson, 1992, Paterson, 1992) Their data confirmed the very powerful effects of factors beyond the control of schools but also demonstrated that individual schools could make a significant difference at the margins. Much of this work drew on the Scottish School Leavers Study, a large database on successive cohorts of school leavers. Attainment and attitudinal data were used in conjunction with analysis of the schools which those students had attended. Gray and his colleagues showed that when background factors were applied to exam league tables a significant re-ordering of the ranking among schools took place, leading them to the conclusion that if parents chose schools on the basis of examination results alone 'they would very often choose the wrong school.' They concluded that being in school A as against school B could make one or more O grades of a difference. It also suggested that schools could be effective along different dimensions in respect of attitude, attendance or attainment.

Drawing further on the school leavers data Willms (1985) found that if you were a pupil of average ability your chances of exam success were better in schools where your peers were of high ability than in schools where they were of low ability -evidence of the 'contextual' or 'peer group' effect, which has been rediscovered in many subsequent studies.

Parental choice

The substantial and continuing stream of work on parental choice has been important at both a policy and research level, illustrating clearly the effects of choice policies on increasing school variance and inequality and impinging directly on the 'contextual effect' - one of the key factors by which parents choose or reject a particular school for their children.

Recent studies are a continuation and re-analysis of a 1989 study by Adler and his colleagues which provided evidence that parents used negative criteria in their choice of school, avoiding schools on the basis of perceived indiscipline and community reputation. A follow-up study in 1992 (Willms and Echols) reported that parents who exercised their rights to choose tended to be more highly educated and of higher socio-economic status than those who didn't. This meant that the schools which their children left became more socially homogeneous, depriving them not only of those pupils but of parents with expertise and potential influence. A 1995 revisiting of the Adler data by Echols and Willms, reaffirmed that is was less the 'pull' of quality than the push of undesirable schools. In 1996 Willms reported these conclusions:

- There is strong evidence that parental choice has contributed to an increase in between-school segregation leading to greater inequalities in attainment.
- Policy-makers should give attention to effects on the whole school community. A school's performance is contingent on the type of pupil attending. Without safeguards to ensure equality disparities will continue to increase.
- While a small minority benefit from parental choice the costs for others and for the system as a whole are high.

As that stream of research showed, social class factors, denominational factors and geographical factors exercise a peculiar and powerful influence in the Scottish context. Advantaged and disadvantaged areas tend to be highly concentrated, a hangover from peripheral housing estates policies of the 1950s onwards, contrasting sharply with relatively homogeneous middle-class enclaves. The disparities were highlighted in successive reports by Strathclyde's Chief Executive Department (1984, 1994). Their data allowed comparisons of two school catchments less than a mile apart from one another. In the council estate, compared to the owner-occupied suburb, there were:

- five times more babies under 2.5kg at birth;
- four times higher rate of prenatal mortality;
- twenty-five times more mothers under the age of 20;
- thirty times more births to unmarried mothers;
- five times the number of mothers booking in for ante natal care in
- one area compared with the other;
- a twenty times lower rate of adult illiteracy;
- six times higher rate of unemployment;

- average life expectancy 30% below average in one area and 30% above in the other.

    (Social Strategy for the Eighties, 1984 and Social Strategy for the Nineties, 1994, Strathclyde Regional Council)

Ethos effects

The extent to which schools are able to counter the socio-economic effects so graphically illustrated by the Strathclyde statistics has been the central question in effectiveness studies since Coleman (1966). The power and influence of school ethos has had a high policy profile by the SOEID, arising from effectiveness studies in which it has been found to be a consistent factor in more effective schools internationally (Scheerens and Bosker, 1997). This prompted a recent study of ethos and its relation to attainment and social class (Croxford, McPherson, Munn, Paterson, forthcoming). Researchers collected data on teachers' and headteachers' perceptions with those of pupils and to measure variations in and between schools. Data on socio-economic status (11 measures of pupils SES) were collected together with teacher perceptions of pupils' SES and ability. The research team reported that:

- Social and economic structures of the society have a much more pervasive and enduring influence on pupil attainment than school ethos.
- The social composition of the school and teachers' and pupils' expectations which derive from that are the most salient aspect of the school.
- Low SES is more closely linked to truancy than low attainment. Truancy causes low attainment rather than the other way around.
- Pupils have more in common generally than as pupils of particular schools.
- 90% of variation in attainment lies at pupil level and only 10% at school level. Teacher perceptions matter but that individual SES and the contextual effect matter more.

Such findings are in line with mainstream effectiveness research on the school effect, generally found to be around ten percent plus or minus (Scheerens and Bosker 1997). From a policy viewpoint the relatively weak impact of ethos might be seen as depressing but it has not impeded the progress of a singularly promising Government initiative, the establishment of a Scottish Schools Ethos Network, as of 1998 with 500 member schools exchanging views, good practice on a national basis and persisting in the belief that effective schools can change attitudes of teachers, pupils and parents as well as raising attainment.

Effectiveness in question

'Although sweeping claims have been made for the importance of school effectiveness findings, on closer scrutiny they may appear somewhat disappointing' concluded Brown, Riddell and Duffield (1996). Their study took the form of a close scrutiny of four schools high and low in SES and high and low in effectiveness. They used classroom observation, post-lesson teacher interviews and interviews with pupils and senior management to get different perspectives on school culture. One of the early conclusions of the study was that the factors associated with high effectiveness was the history of the school as perceived by parents and staff. These expectations, they said, are mediated by social class which in turn influences support, policy, involvement. A second more tentative finding was the collegiality of the school, the morale of teachers and the incorporation of pupils into the culture, in other words 'ownership' as an important ingredient of success.   Six propositional points for school effectiveness research more generally are suggested:

- How teachers conceptualise pupil progress is of more significance than the more easily measurable achievement, management structures or broad brush judgements of teaching methodology.
- Advances will only be made when researcher frameworks take account of teachers' implicit theories.
- Strategies for improvement are likely to be highly dependent on the social class of the school.
- Lists of effectiveness characteristics are unlikely to help low SES schools where self esteem and motivation to learn are low.
- There is no evidence that management innovations such as school development planning are improving school effectiveness.
- Value-added measures are seen as irrelevant by low SES schools and are not seen as having meaning for parents. Norm-referenced measures do not provide an incentive for reform.

Papers generated by the project have been critical of the effectiveness-policy relationship both at national U.K. level where the Secretary of State's enthusiasm for better teaching methods is seen as simplistic (Duffield, 1998), and at the level of Scottish policy-making (Brown, Duffield, Riddell, 1995) where the SOEID is criticised for embracing a top-down model of school improvement focusing on whole school management rather than on the critical area for insight and professional development - the individual classroom.

Effectiveness - an authority level study - Grampian/Aberdeen

From 1991 to the present a series of studies have been conducted in Grampian Region and with its successor Aberdeen City Council Education Authority (Croxford and Cowie 1996, Croxford and Robertson 1996). The main features of the Grampian research were postal questionnaires, value-added analysis of attainment in the Scottish Certificate of Education (SCE), development of indicators of school ethos and confidential feedback of results to schools.

While the study found, in line with previous work, marked inequalities from school to school, the differences were largely attributed to intake factors. The main value of the study was seen less as comparing schools, or providing yet another research report, but as an improvement project for schools in the authority. The feedback of data to schools provided a valuable source of monitoring as well as tools and data for gauging consumer satisfaction. These were helpful to schools in target setting. The policy initiatives at local authority level which have been fed by this study are described by Aberdeen Education Authority (March 1998) as including:

- Development and use of performance indicators for systematic use of audit in the school improvement process;
- school development planning;
- target setting;
- Quality Initiative in Scottish Schools - reports on Standards and Quality as part of wider national initiative;
- Support for material for teachers on self-evaluation - production of CDi for national use 'How Good are we?'
- School Improvement Professional Development Program for Headteachers;
- Best Value Initiative - part of a Government initiative to inform strategic planning aimed at using data most effectively for improvement purposes.

Improving school effectiveness

Many of the themes in the Grampian/Aberdeen projects reflect those of a
larger national study commissioned in 1995 by the SOEID. The Improving
School Effectiveness Project (ISEP) was asked to evaluate the impact of
policy initiatives such as ethos indicators, development planning, and learning
and teaching. The central purposes of the study, however, were to help
develop a national framework for value-added interpretations, and to shed
light on the causal relationship between school processes and outcomes.

The project, bringing together teams from the University of Strathclyde
and the Institute of Education in London (MacBeath and Mortimore 1995),
worked with 80 schools across Scotland over a two year period. The schools
involved had to make a substantial commitment in terms of data gathering at
the outset of the project and again two years down the line - 14 background
factors on each pupil in the primary 4 and secondary 2 cohort, four
attainment tests in Mathematics and English, pupil attitude questionnaires,
teacher questionnaires and parent questionnaires. In addition, in the 24 case
study schools (an in-depth sub-sample of the 80) 11 qualitative instruments
were used to gather information on ethos, development planning, the
management of change, teaching and learning.

The case study schools had the benefit of two members of the research
team to assist with the collection, interpretation and feedback of data to staff.
One, the critical friend, worked alongside teachers and management to plan
and implement change while the other member of the team, the researcher,
had the task of documenting the process and evaluating the role and influence
of the critical friend (MacBeath and Mortimore, 1998).

Many of the findings confirm previous studies of differential effectiveness.
Socio-economic disadvantage was shown to have a strong positive
relationship with attainment at Primary 4 (age 8-9) and Primary 6 and at
Secondary 2 (age 13-14)   although background factors weighed less in
mathematics than in reading. School effects were also stronger at primary
than at secondary level. As in previous studies there was a 'contextual' or
'peer group' effect, significant for reading but not for Mathematics. Pupils
young for their year group performed significantly less well at all levels than
their older peers (Sammons et al 1988).

Attitude measures showed significant variations among schools on two
measures - 'engagement with school' and 'pupil culture'. These were related,
but only weakly, to social class and varied among schools to a lesser extent
than did attainment measures. On the attitudinal measure 'self-efficacy' girls
were less positive than boys. Attitudes of primary teachers were consistently
and markedly more positive than their secondary colleagues but at both
primary and secondary level there was a consistently wide gap between

teachers' view of their schools as they were and what they saw as the characteristics of the effective school. (Thomas et al.1998)

Many of these are classic school effects findings. The more innovative aspect of the project was the feedback and use of data by the school itself. Data was processed and returned to schools confidentially together with aggregated data for all the schools in the project. Schools were then able to compare their own attainment and attitudes to those of other schools. Much of the interpretive work occurred, therefore, at school and teacher level, with support from the critical friend (Robertson, 1998).

While feedback of attainment data gave a focus for target setting and re-prioritising of teaching and learning, it was the attitudinal data that provided the most powerful lever for change. Results from the teacher questionnaire (54 questions and two independent scales, one asking for teachers' judgements on the school as they saw it at that moment, the other asking for a rating of the same items by their importance in creating an effective school) appeared to penetrate deepest into the belief system of the school and exposed its strengths as well as its frailties. Responses provided a kaleidoscope of perceptions of the school as it was and as staff thought it should be, revealing some of the learning disabilities of schools but also showing how schools can learn through a process of feedback with support and challenge from a critical friend (Stoll and Smith 1996, MacBeath and Jardine, 1996). The design and methodology of the ISEP study has been used in a number of follow-up studies.

Raising achievement in Glasgow

A smaller version of the ISE project has been used in Glasgow to address the issue of transition between primary and secondary schools. The research team is working with two secondary schools and their associated primaries, gathering data at primary 6 (11 year olds) and following that cohort through primaries 6 and 7 and into first and second year secondary. In preparation for the arrival of these cohorts of pupils into the secondary schools, critical friend work is ongoing in order to help the receiving schools to sustain the continuity and progression of children's learning.

Base line assessment for all primary 6 children included assessments in reading, mathematics, attitudes to school, self-confidence/self-esteem. This data was fed back to schools as a basis for diagnostic and formative assessment by teachers. The ISEP teacher questionnaire and change profile were also used to explore staff attitudes and morale and as a basis for future planning.

Qualitative data from teacher, pupil and parent interviews will also be used to illuminate the study, focusing specifically on learning and teaching.

National evaluation of study support

Methodology and instruments from the ISE Project are being used in a national research project (Myers, MacBeath, Robertson 1988) examining value-added in out-of-school 'study support', that is centres where students can go in their own time to do homework, study or pursue interests beyond the curriculum. The question is 'how effective are these centres in enhancing achievement? motivation? self esteem? Answers are being explored through a cohort study of around 10,000 students, following them from 1997 to the year 2000. Baseline measures of student attainment and attitudes have been taken along with background data such as gender and ethnic background.

By taking measures of all pupils in a school cohort it will be possible to compare those who make use of study support and those who don't, and to differentiate by types of study support- breakfast clubs, after school classes, residential schools or summer universities. As well as measures of student attainment and attitudes use has been made of the ISEP teacher attitude scales to provide some whole school measures of ethos, morale, communication, and attitudes to learning, for example. The improvement dimension of the study comes through the feedback of the data to the participating schools and study centres so that they can themselves address issues of quality and effectiveness.

One of the offshoots of this project has been the development of a software program which students and teachers can use to enter their responses on two scales - the school now (or study support now) and the effective school (or effective study support). This is an interesting breakthrough in that it saves the intermediate data processing and analysis stage. Aggregation and disaggregation of data is performed by the program and teachers, or students, can interrogate the data and get an immediate read out on question such as the difference between attitudes of boys and girls, differences between teachers and students, the gap between what teachers believe is important for study support (or the school) and current performance.

The baseline data in the Trust's National Project will be used as a starting point for an action-based improvement project to build effective bridges between the two key sites of learning - school and classroom, home and community, furnishing the outlines for a national code of good practice.

The purpose of study support is to build the confidence of young people so that they are lifetime learners, able to go on learning when the teacher is no longer there and they have moved beyond curriculum. Hopefully the study will be able to shed some light on this question. There has, however, been relatively little work on how students manage in the years after school in work or in higher education or whether school effects carry over. There is one Scottish study (MacPherson and Robertson, 1998) which followed two cohorts of students, one into Edinburgh University, the other to Strathclyde University in Glasgow, measuring attainment at first class exams. The evidence was equivocal about the school effect, essentially reporting little or no school effect once other factors had been taken into account. The study does suggest, however, that any effect is differential and is more likely to be found in Science and Engineering than in Arts subjects.

Reflections on past, present and future

In Scotland it is six years since the first guidelines on self-evaluation were published by the then Scottish Education Department. Building on those six years of experience policy documents have been slimmed down, made more user-friendly and widely welcomed by schools. 'How Good is our School?' (SOEID, 1996), developed in collaboration with teachers and researchers, sets out 33 criteria of the 'good' school but presents them not as definitive criteria but as a starting point for schools to explore their own quality and 'effectiveness'. There has been a groundswell of interest and growth in expertise at school level and teachers and students from primary, secondary and special schools have spoken at national conferences and led workshops in Scotland and further afield.

It was to Scotland that the National Union of Teachers (NUT) in England and Wales turned for help in developing a national framework for self-evaluation. The study published as Schools Speak for Themselves (MacBeath, Boyd, Rand, Bell, 1995, NUT) became a central plank of union policy and has been widely used not only in England and Wales but in many other countries. Its success has been ascribed by the Union leadership to the resonance that it has had with classroom teachers because it has built on their understanding from the bottom up and met them half them way down with the overarching theory.

The most significant development in school improvement has been to put the tools of self-evaluation into the hands of schools and teachers, and a start has been made on including school students as experts and key sources of evidence on school quality and effectiveness. As outside critical friends we have, in the last year or so sat around the table with headteachers, teachers, and school students openly exploring the quality of learning and teaching in their schools.

We have learned that evaluating quality cannot be a one-off exercise. It does not come about through audit or inspections. It is a process through which schools get to know themselves, use evidence, build on strengths, acknowledge and attend to the warts. In this process students, both at primary and secondary level, have an incisive and vital part to play.

As successive effectiveness studies have shown it is at classroom level, in the daily transactions between pupils and teachers that self-evaluation comes truly into its own. When they ask the question 'How good is learning in our school?' they open the doors into the learning, which leads from soft to hard data and from the teaching organisation to the learning organisation. For parents it may also spark the same aggressive curiosity, prompting the question 'How good is learning in the home and in the community?'. When young people begin to ask themselves the question 'How effective a learner am I?' the self-evaluation question comes full circle and the contribution of school effectiveness research is put to the test.

The challenge to school effectiveness and improvement for the immediate future is to engage teachers and students in studying effectiveness in their own classrooms, using quantitative tools more routinely and confidently, looking at learning with more rigorous qualitative measures.

References

Brown, S. Riddell, S. and Duffield, J. (1996) Responding to Pressures: a study of four secondary schools in Woods, D. (Ed.) *Contemporary Issues in Teaching and Learning*, London and New York, Routledge

Brown, S. Riddell S. (1996) 'School Effectiveness and School Improvement: The Ways Forward'. Paper delivered to the CES Conference, Department of Education, University of Stirling, February

Centre for Educational Research and Innovation (1995), *Education at a Glance.* Paris: OECD

Croxford, L. (1996) *The Effectiveness of Grampian Secondary Schools.* Grampian Regional Council, Centre for Educational Sociology, Edinburgh

Cuttance, P. McPherson, A., Raffe, D., Willms, D (1988) *Secondary School Effectiveness, Report to the Scottish Education Department*, Centre for Educational Sociology, University of Edinburgh, August

Duffield, J. (1998) Learning Experiences, effective schools and social context, *British Journal of Learning support. 13*, No. 1 February

Echols, F.H. and Wilmms, J.D. (1986) *Reasons for School Choice in Scotland*, Center for Educational sociology, University of Edinburgh

Gray, J., McPherson, A. and Raffe, D . (1983) *Reconstructions of Secondary Education*, London, Routledge and Kegan Paul

MacBeath J. and Mortimore P. (1994). 'Improving School Effectiveness: a Scottish Approach'. Paper presented at British Educational Research Association, Oxford, September.

MacBeath J. and Mortimore P. (1997). 'School Effectiveness: is it improving?', Paper presented at the Tenth International Conference on School Effectiveness and School Improvement, Memphis, January

MacBeath, J. (1998) 'The Coming Age of School Effectiveness', Keynote Address to the 11th Annual Congress of School Effectiveness and School Improvement, January

McGlynn, A & Stalker, H (1995) Recent Developments in the Scottish Process of School Inspection, *Cambridge Journal of Education, 25*, (1): 13-21

McPherson, A. and Robertson, (forthcoming) *School Effects on Attainment in University*, ESRC

McPherson, A (1992) 'Measuring added value in schools', *National Commission on Education Briefing No 1*, February 1992, London, National Commission on Education.

Myers, K. MacBeath, Roberston, I. (1998) 'Changing your life through Study Support: How will we know if it makes a difference?' Paper presneted to American Educational Research Association, San Diego, April

Paterson, L (1992) Social Class in Scottish Education in Brown, S & Riddell, S (Eds), *Class, Race and Gender in Schools: A New Agenda for Policy and Practice in Scottish Education*, Glasgow: Scottish Council for Research in Education

Raab, C. (1992) In Munn, P. *Parents and Schools*. London, Routledge

Riddell, S. and Brown, S. (Eds), *School Effectiveness Research: Its Messages for School Improvement*, Edinburgh, HMSO.

Roberstson, P. (1998) *Improving School Effectiveness*: summary paper presented to the Scottish Office Education and Industry Department, February

Sammons, P., Thomas, S. Mortimore, P. (1997) *Forging Links*. London, Paul Chapman

Thomas, S., Smees, R., MacBeath, J. Sammons, P. Robertson, P. (1998) *Creating a Value-added Framework for Scottish Schools*, Institue of Education, University of Strathclyde

Scheerens, J and Bosker, R. (1997) *The Foundations of Educational Effectiveness* London, Pergamon.

Scottish Education Department (1988) *Effective Secondary Schools*, Edinburgh, HMS0

Scottish Education Department (1989)   *Effective Primary Schools*
    Edinburgh, HMS0

Scottish Office Education Department (1991) *Management of Educational
    Resources: 5, The Role of School Development Plans in Managing
    School Effectiveness*, HM Inspector of Schools, Education Department

Scottish Office Education Department (1991) *Using Examination Results in
    School Self-evaluation: Relative Ratings and National Comparison
    Factors*, Edinburgh, HMSO

Scottish Office Education Department (1992) *Using Performance Indicators
    in Primary School Self-evaluation*, Edinburgh, HMSO

Scottish Office Education Department (1992) *Using Performance Indicators
    in Secondary School Self-evaluation*, Edinburgh, HMSO

Scottish Office Education Department (1992b) *Using Ethos Indicators in
    Primary School Self-Evaluation: Taking Account of the Views of Pupils,
    Parents and Teachers*, HM Inspectors of Schools., Edinburgh, HMSO

Scottish Office Education Department (1996) *How Good is our School?*
    Audit Unit, HM Inspectors of Schools, Edinburgh, HMSO

Stoll, L. and Smith, I. (1996) 'Closing the Gap: what teachers expect and
    what they get', Paper presented at British Research Associaiton
    Conference, Lancaster, September

Willms, J.D. and Cuttance, P. (1985) School Effects in Scottish Secondary
    Schools, *British Journal of Sociology of Education, 6,* No. 3.

5.

School effectiveness and school improvement in Wales: the end of the beginning?

David Reynolds

Introduction

The education system in Wales is subject currently to a variety of economic and social pressures, some in common with the rest of the United Kingdom and some distinctive. First, economic pressures from developed Pacific Rim or 'Tiger' economies and also from developing societies mean that the assembly line work that has formed the basis of the inward investment into Wales of the last two decades can be relocated elsewhere. It is notable that these emerging economies have considerably higher levels of educational achievement than Wales (Reynolds and Farrell, 1996) and there are historic concerns about the levels of achievement of schools in Wales by comparison with England (Reynolds, 1990 and 1995).

Second, there are the pressures from the new Labour government to improve educational achievement generally and particular pressures to improve the achievement levels of primary (or elementary) schools.

Third, the 'outputs' of the Welsh educational system continue to be distinctive, involving a high proportion of graduates being in humanities and social science and proceeding into non-scientific/technological employment.

Explanations for this phenomenon range from the nature of Welsh language culture, to the historical desire of those representatives of what might be called 'Old Labour' to generate non-scientific school outputs to avoid any possibility of their directly creating wealth.

A Welsh educational market place?

There have been in Wales, historically, signs at various times that the distinctive problems of Welsh education were being recognised. The Welsh 'Education Debate' of the early to mid 1980s spawned a variety of interventions from the Schools Council Committee for Wales and a variety of publications from the Welsh Inspectorate. Indeed, the Curriculum in Action initiative of 1983, involving each local education authority in Wales selecting a named 'under performing' school and encouraging the school to review and improve its internal functioning and outcomes had no British equivalent at the time, and indeed was probably three to five years ahead of the thinking within the English school improvement community of the time.

However, this acknowledgement of Welsh distinctiveness had largely vanished by the mid to late 1980s, when Wales was incorporated with England in the debate about education that generated the 1988 Education Reform Act. Only in the distinctive curriculum status given to Welsh as a 'core' subject in approximately a quarter of Welsh secondary schools and in the different curriculum content for some other subjects was there any acknowledgement of Welsh 'difference', although the years since the passage of the Act have seen in fact the generation of a distinctive Welsh set of administrative and organisational arrangements to deliver different educational policies if they could be designed.

This infrastructure involving a separate curriculum and assessment authority, a separate Welsh Office department, a separate schools inspectorate/Chief Inspector, separate Higher and Further Education Funding Councils, a separate Research, Statistics and Intelligence branch, separate arrangements to the English Teacher Training Agency and the historically separate examination board and University represents a substantial administrative and organisational entity. In no sense, though, has this infrastructure been used to generate distinctive educational policies for Wales (other than in the area of the Welsh language) or to generate research on what the public policies might be (the Welsh Office educational research budget has customarily been swallowed up in support of the England and Wales wide projects on pupil assessment and curriculum development, and the specific needs of the Welsh language: it is also important to note that the budget itself has been severely reduced in the last three years).

At a time when the organisational structure has been in place to deliver alternative policies, the educational system itself has been incorporated into the same market-based solutions as England in an attempt to 'lever up' educational standards. These policies, though, are no guarantee of higher educational standards in Wales (nor in England for that matter), because of the distinctively different Welsh context. Specifically:

- The notion that choice of school by parents will lead to competition between schools and thereby raise educational standards is untenable in Wales, where perhaps 40% of parents have no real choice of school because of the substantial distances between schools, particularly at secondary stage. The historically low levels of involvement of parents in Wales also noted in many studies would mitigate against any policies that use 'outside system' factors as quality monitors.
- The use of the Assisted Places scheme to aid independent school competition with the State sector is irrelevant in Wales, where the independent sector has been small and unpopular.
- The notion that the standards of Welsh nursery education will be improved by the 'bidding in' of extra supply from the private sector, which underpinned the last Conservative government's nursery vouchers scheme, was particularly irrelevant in a Welsh context where state nurseries are almost the exclusive provision, reaching over 90% of all four year olds and where private provision is mostly small scale voluntary initiatives rather than the commercial undertakings prevalent in England.
- The notion that a substantial grant maintained or 'opted out' sector could be a further form of competition to improve Welsh state schools has been clearly invalidated by the very small proportion of Welsh schools that have changed status, a marked contrast with England where over 25% of secondary age pupils now attend the grant maintained sector.

The unintended consequences of educational change

The match between the educational rhetoric about the beneficial operation of educational markets and the reality of the Welsh societal context has been intensified by the unintended consequences of the last government's range of policies. Specifically:

- All schools in Wales have one more subject to be taught to their pupils than schools in England: either Welsh to pupils in 'Anglicised' areas or English to pupils in Welsh speaking areas/schools. The programs of study for all other subjects are very similar for the Welsh school curriculum, though, as compared to the English. Crucially, the standards of attainment expected at the various age levels and the examinations to be taken by children at age fourteen are the same in Wales as in England, despite the increased Welsh curricular range.

- All pupils in schools in Wales have the experience of learning a second language, whether it be pupils from English speaking homes learning Welsh for the first time or pupils from Welsh speaking homes learning English. Given this clear difference in linguistic experience, one would have expected that the programs of study for modern foreign languages in Wales would have built on, and incorporated, this clear Welsh distinctiveness, and the skills in linguistic acquisition of its pupils. Instead, Wales has identical programs of study for modern foreign languages to those of England.

The end of the beginning

There are more recent signs, however, that a set of distinctively Welsh policies appropriate to a distinctively Welsh context are beginning to emerge. Distinctiveness is shown in:

- The absence of any publication of primary school performance tables for Wales, by comparison with the annual publication of performance data for the 18,000 English primary schools in national newspapers and the like.

- The adoption of different targets for primary school children's performance (England has targets of 75% of children performing at level four in the national educational assessments in Mathematics and 80% in English, whereas Wales has set similar targets but across the three subjects of English, Mathematics and Science).

- Educational policies within Wales have been notably more conciliatory and shorn of the harsh rhetoric about the quality of teaching and schools that have marked public pronouncements from Her Majesty's Chief Inspector of Schools in England, Chris Woodhead. The Welsh Inspectorate have consistently stressed, by contrast, the need for schools to conduct self review and self analysis to improve educational quality and outcomes, rather than be improved by the 'pressure through parental judgement' which has been the preferred mechanism of the English Chief Inspector of Schools.

- The forthcoming devolution of power in the area of education to the Welsh Assembly, due to begin operation from the Autumn of 1999, is highly likely to further accentuate existing differences between countries, since the Assembly will have the power both to vary the amount of money spent on each area of public policy within the total of the 'block grant' allocated to it by the British Treasury and to vary the organisational arrangements for education in Wales within the context of the primary legislative authority which would still remain at Westminster.

In this situation, the absence of more than very preliminary formulations about what distinctive Welsh educational policies should be (Reynolds, Bellin and Osmond, 1995) is much to be regretted, although a recent grant from the Joseph Rowntree Foundation to the Institute of Welsh Affairs to develop thinking about appropriate policies in a wide variety of public policy areas including education is likely to improve matters. Nevertheless, Wales enters the era of devolved power with a distinctive absence of the creative thinking from 'think tanks' and the like that has in England been associated with the generation of new Labour's educational policies.

Research in effectiveness, improvement and related areas

Further concerns relate to the absence of much work in the general disciplinary area of effectiveness and improvement that can resource the much needed re-thinking of educational policy. The early work of Reynolds and associates (1976, 1985) was conducted in the Welsh valleys, but since then there has been little further school effectiveness research of note and rather little piloting of school improvement programs either.

There are indications of considerable growth of interest in matters of educational policy within Wales, with issues such as school choice (Gorard, 1997a and b), and the relative academic performance of the Welsh system by comparison with England (Gorard, 1998) attracting interest. More general curriculum issues and theorising is also well established (Daugherty, 1995, 1996, 1997; Jones, 1994; Phillips, 1996) as are surveys of bilingual issues (Baker, 1992, 1996). The high levels of social disadvantage within Wales have also spawned considerable interest in educational indicators to assess the impact of such disadvantage upon schools (Bellin et al, 1996; Higgs et al, 1997). Other strong Welsh traditions of enquiry are shown in the history of education (Jones, 1997).

However, research and practice in the area of effectiveness and improvement as we noted above remains partial and parlous, with the exception of research conducted utilising the school effectiveness 'input-process-output' paradigm into the bilingual sector of education, which has grown rapidly in recent years.

This sector takes a very high proportion of pupils in its primary and secondary schools in some areas - close on 20% of an age cohort in the Welsh valleys area for example - and usually takes between 5% and 10% of total pupils across most of South Wales.

It has been clear for some time that the Welsh medium secondary schools have historically been highly successful institutions in their examination results, and much the same has been said to apply to the primary sector too, although the absence of published information in Wales about the 'SATs' and achievement levels at Key Stage 2 makes this assertion a difficult one to prove. However, it has often been said that the reason for the success of the bilingual secondary schools is that they simply have more 'middle class' or 'advantaged' intakes, rather than being that historically rather elusive phenomenon, an effective Welsh educational system.

Research conducted last year casts doubt on these customary 'input' explanations for the sectors' success. Using the conventional methods of school effectiveness research in which schools' outcomes are related to their intakes to allow the predicted school effectiveness level to be shown, it is clear that Welsh medium schools achieve at least as well as predicted and in some years better than predicted, but in no years worse than predicted (Reynolds and Bellin, 1996).

If, as seems highly likely from these figures, the success of the Welsh medium sector is due in part to the effectiveness of the provision, what factors seem likely to explain its success? And - crucially - how could the non-bilingual sector of Wales make use of this authentic Welsh success story?

First, there may of course be 'interaction effects' caused by children having two first languages as it were. The majority of the children in these schools come from English speaking homes and acquire in their schools a second language. Perhaps the patterns of thought linked with the two languages set up interesting cognitive interactions that are more potent than the thought processes of monolingual children.

Second, it may well be that the Welsh medium sector possesses that most beloved factor of contemporary management theorists - clarity of goals, or 'mission'. In contrast to the non-Welsh sector where goals are clearly more and more numerous, more confusing and often downright contradictory, the Welsh medium schools by contrast have simple, straightforward and easily measurable goals related to the prospering of Welsh identity.

Third, the range of activities for pupils within the bilingual schools seem to be considerably wider than that offered within the non-Welsh sector. The cultural activities that spread into lunch times and Saturday mornings, the wide variety of cultural and linguistic clubs and societies that exist in most Welsh medium primary and secondary schools and the musical involvements, all seem notable.   These activities provide the possibility of informal relationships between children and teachers, they increase the amount of time in which children are 'chaperoned' away from peer group influences, and they also seem likely to generate amongst children a firmer social identity than would have existed without them.

Fourth, the staff in the schools are likely to be highly motivated. At the most basic level of all, they will all have made the positive decision to teach in the specific type of school, thus indicating considerable commitment. The groups of staff themselves are likely to be cohesive, reflecting the communality of their commitment and backgrounds.

Overall, what seems noticeable about the bilingual sector is the degree of congruence between the various partners in education. Children come from homes committed to the schools and meet teachers who have firm ideas as to their mission. The system itself is deeply imbued with messages, moral and social, that generate strong social identity and high levels of academic achievement that result from secure children. Parents, teachers, schools and the children form an interlocking, overlapping community of interest.

Education and the future of Wales

Ultimately, though, the nature of the research and policy agenda that is needed within Wales is dependent upon beliefs as to the nature of the Wales that its people want. In a world where increasingly the individual relates more and more directly to the central State, and where the salience of the community level in people's lives is increasingly emasculated and destroyed by central State actions and interventions, Welsh history and culture have always emphasised the importance of community as the third dimension upon which societies must rest. If one wishes for a three dimensional society in which the individual, the local community and the State (whether British or European) interact and produce the three dimensional human beings whose heads and whose hearts are developed by means of handling the complex interactions between the three organisational levels, then in Welsh educational policies too there must be an attempt to retain a 'middle' third tier that would build upon what local authorities have done historically.

More generally, attitudes to the Welsh educational policies that are necessary must be determined by our Welsh attitudes to issues of human and social identity. In a world where increasing internationalisation removes cultural barriers and where 'culture' flows freely to make all increasingly similar and homogenised, the recent rediscovery within many countries and settings like Wales of the importance of the local, the ethnic, the minority and the specific, all suggest a widespread felt need for individuals to retain distinctive identities in the face of global homogeneity. Somehow, one needs to use the local, the community and the Welsh location not to minimise outside influences but to create a strong identity from which individuals can draw as they look outwards. The Welsh need is not to build walls to protect identity but instead to use a strong identity as a support whilst people look outward for new ideas and experiences. Using the Welsh educational system to build that firm identity which facilitates children then taking the most useful and excellent knowledge from outside of its boundaries is something that Wales may have a chance of doing but which many other societies have lost their chance of doing. If Wales can balance individuals' social needs for identity and security with their intellectual need for exploration, and if Wales can create citisens that are mature enough to handle the transactions between the three levels of individual, community and State, then it may well be that we will have accomplished something which has great utility and great importance for others outside of our own boundaries.

References

Baker, C. (1992), *Attitudes and Language*, Clevedon: Multilingual Matters.

Baker, C. (1996), *Foundations of Bilingual Education and Bilingualism.* (Second edition.) Clevedon: Multilingual Matters.

Bellin, W., Farrell, S., Higgs, G. and White, S. (1996), 'A strategy for using census information in comparison of school performance', *Welsh Journal of Education, 5* (2), 3-25.

Daugherty, R. (1995), *National Curriculum Assessment: A review of policy 1987-1994*, London: Falmer.

Daugherty, R. (1996), 'In search of teacher assessment ñ its place in the National Curriculum assessment system of England and Wales', *The Curriculum Journal, 7* (2), 137-152.

Daugherty, R. (1997), 'National Curriculum Assessment: The experience of England and Wales', *Educational Administration Quarterly, 33* (2), 198-218.

Gorard, S. (1997a), 'Paying for a Little England: School choice and the Welsh Language', *Welsh Journal of Education, 6* (1).

Gorard, S. (1997b), *School Choice in an Established Market: Families and Fee-paying Schools*, Aldershot: Avebury Press.

Gorard, S. (1998), 'Schooled to fail? Revisiting the Welsh School-Effect', *Journal of Education Policy, 13* (1), 115-124.

Higgs, G., Bellin, W., Farrell, S. and White, S. (1997), 'Educational attainment and social disadvantage: contextualising school league tables', *Regional Studies, 31* (8).

Jones, G. (1994), 'Which nation's curriculum? - the case of Wales', *The Curriculum Journal, 5* (1), 5-16.

Jones, G.E. (1997), *The Education of a Nation*, Cardiff: University of Wales Press.

Phillips, R. (1996), 'History teaching, cultural restorationism and national identity in England and Wales', *Curriculum Studies, 4* (3), 385-399.

Reynolds, D. (1976), 'The Delinquent School', in P. Woods (Ed), *The Education of a Nation*, Cardiff: University of Wales Press.

Reynolds, D. (1985), *Studying on School Effectiveness*. Cowes: Falmer Press.

Reynolds, D. (1990), 'The Great Welsh Education Debate, 1980-1990', in *History of Education, 19* (3), 251-260.

Reynolds, D. (1995), 'Creating an Educational System for Wales', *The Welsh Journal of Education, 4* (2), 4-12.

Reynolds, D., Bellin, W. and Osmond, J. (1995), *An Introduction Policy for Wales*, Cardiff: Institute for Welsh Affairs.

Reynolds, D. and Bellin, W. (1996), 'Welsh-medium schools. Why they are better', *Welsh Agenda*, (The Journal of The Institute for Welsh Affairs), Summer, 19-20.

Reynolds, D. and Farrell, S. (1996), *Worlds Apart? - A Review of International Studies of Educational Achievement Involving England*, London: HMSO for OFSTED.

SECTION ONE: EUROPE

Part Two:

MAINLAND EUROPE

6.

School effectiveness and school improvement in the Republic of Belarus

Iouri Zagoumennov

Background

In 1996 there were over 1.5 million students in Belarus, with 142,000 teachers in 5000 schools. Seventeen per cent of the schools were elementary, 23% are basic schools (elementary and middle) 58% are secondary schools (elementary, middle and high) and 2% are gymnasia, lyceums and colleges (university oriented specialised secondary schools).

In recent times there has been a continuing decline in the birthrate due to the economic 'crisis' the country has been in since the middle of the 80s. Since 1985 the birthrate has dropped by 35%. Some 52% of Belarus families with children have only one child, 40% have two children, 6% have three children and 2% have four or more children. Some 12% of these families have a single parent.

The educational system of Belarus stays centralised. This reflects the general policy of the government and is based on the assumption that the country cannot advance economic and democratic reforms simultaneously. Within this concept 'democratisation' and 'decentralisation' are viewed only as strategic goals.

School effectiveness research

Academic achievement (exams, international competitions)

The 'soviet school model' that Belarus school system still belongs to has both strong and weak points. Its major goal is to prepare every student to enter a university. This policy leads to a centralised curriculum with high academic standards. In this respect 'school effectiveness' is viewed as meeting the academic requirements set by the central government. It's true that Belarus students have high academic achievements, particularly in science, which was confirmed by special research carried out by UNESCO in 1991, and their continuous victories at prestigious international academic competitions.

The weak points are interrelated with the strong ones. High academic pressure in schools, and unrealistic academic standards, have led to the success of a limited number of talented students while the majority of 'average' students are failing to meet the requirements set by the Ministry of Education. However there is no formal system of evaluation of school effectiveness in Belarus. The one that used to be in practice in the former Soviet Union was eliminated in the 80s due to the mass falsification of data.

The only information on academic achievement held by the central ministry of education currently is the number of students who get unsatisfactory grades in more than two academic subjects and have to repeat the courses. According to official data in 1996 some 1% of Belarus students fell in this category. However a study which involved over 200 headteachers from 5 administrative regions of Belarus (Minsk, Brest, Vitebsk, Mogilev and Gomel) conducted in 1996 showed that this data cannot be trusted as an indicator of school effectiveness. In its recent documents and publications the Ministry of Education also acknowledges that 'the majority of Belarus students are not able to succeed in all academic subjects'.

Student health

Another drawback, which is only beginning to be officially recognised by the educational authorities in Belarus as an indicator of 'school effectiveness', is the damage high academic pressure has produced on students' health. According to Belarus law the weekly limit for adult working hours is 40 hours. Meanwhile students of 13-14 have to study some 60 hours weekly (even more in colleges, gymnasium, lyceums and other specialised schools). As a result some 70% of school graduates have problems with physical development or suffer from chronic diseases (Volodko, 1996).

According to the data of the Belarus Ministry of Education, between 1995 and 1996 the number of students who had to attend special health rehabilitation classes in secondary schools increased by 63%, the number of disabled students increased by 43% and the number of mentally and physically handicapped students by 33%.

Indicators of school effectiveness, introduced by the Belarus Educational Centre for Leadership Development (BECLD)

Belarus Educational Centre for Leadership Development has developed and tested a new approach to evaluation of school effectiveness. The research was focused on the basic assumption about effective schooling held by educators, school leaders, parents, students and other educational stakeholders in Belarus as compared to the official approach currently exercised in the country (Zagoumennov, 1994-96). Through the research eight assumptions were identified and discussed with the education stakeholders all over the country:

1. *Each student is capable and will be successful if the educational environment is fitted to the student's needs, interests, and personality.*
This first assumption is based upon the belief that every student has the potential to learn. Every student will succeed in learning if the education environment, which includes school and non-school settings, is designed to build on the natural interest of the student to learn. The learning style of the student needs to fit with the teaching style of the education environment. The curriculum should reflect a balance between what the individual student needs and wants to learn with what the society needs to transmit in order for its preservation.

The assumption has an implication for evaluation of school effectiveness. Not just standardised achievements need to be taken into account but the progress each individual makes in school.

2. *Secondary education needs to strike a balance between the twin goals of quality and equity; equality of opportunity to receive a quality education should be the basis of educational policy and decisions.*
High expectations for the quality of education in terms of achievement outcomes for each student is imperative to effective education. Those high expectations should meld with the individual student's strengths and interests. To meet those high expectations educational resources should be equitably distributed according to the needs of each student so that all students have an equal opportunity to maximise their potential.

This assumption is based on the need to find and evaluate a reasonable balance between quality and equity; both academic achievements (standardised and individual) and people's feelings are 'ends' for an effective school. There are many ways of enabling 'elite' and 'non-elite' students to grow together, such as co-operative learning teams, and at the same time achieve excellent academic results.

3.   *The development of skills and attitudes to pursue lifelong learning in order to be able to function successfully in a world of changing information and scientific progress should be the focus of the curriculum.*

The focus of education should not be mainly on the mastery of encyclopaedic knowledge. In a world where information is expanding geometrically, mastery is an impossible goal. Instead, each student needs to develop a desire for continuous learning and the skills to master new information as it is created. Higher order thinking skills which allow students to evaluate the worth of new ideas should be a major goal of the curriculum.

There are many educators in Belarus who understand the importance of teaching not just facts, but higher-order thinking skills as well. School teachers and administrators think that it is the fault of educational authorities that 'encyclopaedia' knowledge is still a priority in evaluation of school effectiveness in Belarus because the tests authorised by district, city, regional, and governmental officials are overly focused on this kind of knowledge. In turn, educational authorities are concerned about the ability and expertise of the currently practising teachers to adopt and use a new paradigm that emphasises teaching higher order thinking skills. Obviously, better assessment instruments and techniques that measure higher order learning and teacher retraining are needed for this belief to be realised.

4. *The socialisation of students, the formation of their relations with the surrounding world, should be based on a balance between the best interests of the students and the usefulness of those interests to the society providing the education.*

To be 'interesting' to other people individuals are supposed to have 'interests' and develop them in a way that benefit both the individual and other people. If you like to sing, try to become skilful enough so that other people enjoy your singing. Do something for you class, school, and/or community based on your best interests. Every student could develop these interests and become good or even the best at doing something. The group could then benefit from the excellence achieved by individuals in the group sharing their expertise. The tasks of the teachers are to diagnose students' best interests, support them, make other students aware of the strengths of their classmates, and provide an opportunity for students to pursue and use their best interests for the common good. This parameter of school effectiveness needs to be monitored and to be taken into account.

5.   *Education should be concerned with the total health of the student.*
Schools focus on preventative health care rather than treatment of illnesses. Good personal cleanliness, physical fitness, immunisation, and interpersonal relations are a mark of a well educated person. Teachers are also supposed to be aware of each individual student's health problems as well as the methodology of dealing with this student while teaching not to damage his/her health.

According to the opinions of parents, students and school administrators in most cases Belarus teachers are not concerned with students' health problems because of their ignorance and lack of motivation. Educators strongly object to caring about students' health as their responsibility and to taking it into account as a parameter of school effectiveness. They would rather blame health care institutions for doing nothing.

Some schools, especially university oriented ones, advance entrance health requirements that make it possible only for students with very good health to enter these schools. High academic pressure in these schools often leads to health problems and initially healthy students have to leave school later on as well.

6.   *The metaphor of a good family should be the basis for school practice.*
In a good family each child is loved for who that child is, not what they should be. Caring for the individual requires a balance between the meeting the requirements for being part of the family and the growth of the individual.

In the 1500s Machiavelli wrote his famous Prince in which he described two basic methods of making people do what you want them to do: love and fear. He was absolutely convinced that fear is the most powerful means to achieve success. Machiavelli has his followers in Belarus today. There are many people in schools who base their leadership and teaching style in dealing with students on Machiavellian assumptions, with devastating results.

Almost in every Belarus school you will find a teacher who would strongly object to being evaluated by students, parents and educational authorities based on the criterion of 'caring'. These teachers are convinced that any technique is good when dealing with students as long as the technique leads to improved academic achievement. This type of teacher expects long term appreciation to replace short term hatred when the student understands that the teacher used some unpopular means for the students' sake.

7.   *There should be an atmosphere of collaboration among students, parents, teachers, administrators, staff, community, higher education,*

and government policy makers for the common good of each student and the school.

This assumption implies that there is enough 'space' for everybody in school to be successful and to be praised. It also implies that success of a particular individual in school depends on the success of other individuals (group, class, school) so that individuals are motivated to support each other and share in the success of their colleague rather than be successful because of the failure of others.

The metaphor of being in one boat could be used to illustrate the assumption above. The boat is supposed to reach the desired destination (common goals, objectives). Everyone has individual responsibilities in the boat. The success of the voyage depends on how effective each individual is. It is quite common in schools, though, for successful students and/or teachers not to be favoured by their peers, especially after being praised by authorities. An effective school in this respect is the one that has developed a culture that respects collaboration and cooperation for the common good.

8. All parties that are impacted by the school should have input into the design of the education of that school.

The principle of consensus should govern the input of the eight stakeholders: students, parents, teachers, administrators, staff, community, higher education, and government policy makers. School leaders need to build this consensus by their actions and words. Where consensus conflicts with laws or professional standards, legality and professionalism should be paramount in the decision.

The research shows that the majority of school administrators and teachers in Belarus (over 80%) strongly object to parent, community, student or other stakeholder involvement in decision-making. The objection used as a means to not involve these stakeholders is that their competence to make decisions is not as good as is that of teachers. Interestingly, district administrators (over 75%) in turn are reluctant to share their decision-making power with school building administrators and teachers for the same reason; they doubt that building administrators and teachers have enough competence. In turn regional superintendents doubt the competence of district administrators and so on.

This assumption provides the basis for a mechanism that would enable school self-development. The transformation and on-going development of a school could be initiated either from the top down or the bottom up. To reach the balance of interests of all the stakeholders both top-down and bottom-up modes should be set. The degree of the autonomy and decision-making power are to be determined based on school effectiveness as perceived by all the stakeholders.

The identified assumptions influence the type of school, the goals and objectives of the school, its priorities, the activities that lead to the accomplishment of the goals and objectives, its structure, the criteria and indicators of success made by the school, and the corresponding system of evaluation of school effectiveness.

All the assumptions above are interrelated and are both ends and means for an effective school. Thus socialisation of students based on their best interests requires new approaches to academic achievements, the balance of equity and quality, and caring. To succeed a school needs to fit the educational environment to each student's interests, needs and personality, to find the right balance between equity and quality, to introduce a new approach in both academic areas and socialisation, to centre its interests on student's health, to develop collaboration and empower all those who are impacted by the school.

Innovative programs of evaluation of school effectiveness

The assumptions developed by the BECLD laid the foundation for a new system of evaluation of teachers' effectiveness which was introduced nation-wide in the 90s by the Ministry of Education. The new system of merit pay made the salary and benefits of Belarus teachers dependent on their qualification and effectiveness. Accordingly four categories of teachers were differentiated based on qualification and effectiveness criteria. The qualification was tested through the exams teachers may volunteer to take. As for the effectiveness the guidelines were developed (Zagoumennov, 1995) and each school was supposed to develop its own methodology based on eight assumptions about an effective school. They were also free to develop their own assumptions as soon as they are supported by their stakeholders and educational authorities.

This approach has led to a great degree of progress in schools with strong leadership and progressive educational communities. However little progress has been made in schools where headteachers were reluctant to take the initiative and the communities were not influential enough to impact the school. With no pressure from the central and local educational authorities who preferred the initiative to stay voluntary it was quite possible for schools to ignore the effectiveness criteria and base their teachers' merit pay mostly on the results of qualification exams. It's also true that the difference in payment between the categories was not enough to motivate teachers to improve their work.

Another initiative based on the same assumptions about effective schooling was developed by the BECLD in co-operation with the Ministry of Education and regional departments of education. It was aimed at identification of the most effective schools at the local, regional and national levels through the nationally televised contests 'Educational Leaders of the Year' which were launched in 1995 and 1996. The contest promoted co-operation between schools, business and communities. Schools which volunteered to compete conducted self-evaluations and were also assessed by independent evaluators. Publicity of the contest and involvement of the communities and business secured the objectiveness of the evaluation results.

The shift from the traditional approach to school effectiveness (academic achievements) to the new one was quite evident in schools that took part in the finals (especially in 1996). However, our further research (1997) showed that in the majority of Belarus schools there was little progress. The traditional approach most schools are used to is still exercised.

School improvement initiatives

Curriculum reform (Ministry of Education)

A new curriculum reform was launched in the country in 1997 and will last for 10 years. The new secondary school will comprise 12 years (compulsory - 10 years). There is supposed to be more stress on study and high-order thinking skills in the curriculum and more attention will be drawn to students' physical development. Students will not have classes on Saturdays.

Elementary school will include 4 years. It will have two major goals: the development of positive attitudes to learning (currently only some 14% of students are happy with the schools they attend) and functional competence (students will get more understanding about the usefulness of acquired knowledge for their lives).

The basic compulsory school will include 6 years. Its major goal will be 'preparation to life' as opposed to the preparation to the university. The concept of an academic subject is changing dramatically. It's no longer the summary of a particular science - chemistry, for example but much more practice oriented - for example, chemistry in people's life. Optional courses will comprise some 25-30% of the curriculum.

University preparatory school - lyceum includes 2 years of study. The lyceum may have the following profiles: general, humanitarian (gymnasium), natural science, arts, politechnic. The curriculum will be focused on the basics of science. Some 40-45% of the graduates of the compulsory school are expected to continue their education in the 11th and 12th grades.

It is planned to change the system of evaluation of students' academic achievements. However, the government is reluctant to use western methodology to measure students' progress as in the neighbouring Ukraine the government has failed to implement nation-wide the USA testing system because of the mass falsification of data. In Belarus the graduation exams are likely to be eliminated while the university entrance exams will stay unchanged.

Educational leadership development at BECLD

Background.

This project which was developed and run by the NGO Belarus Educational Centre for Leadership Development in co-operation with the Ministry of Education and addressed the need to support educational reform in the Republic of Belarus by empowering school leaders, educational local governments, civil servants and public educational organisations through management training, networking, dissemination of information and enhancing the development of educational leadership in the country.

While most of the countries of the former Soviet Block have succeeded in their decentralisation reforms the Belarus educational system is still centralised and top-down. There were two basic reasons for this:

- The central government and its institutions remained the monopolists in education and were reluctant to share power with other stakeholders. The monopolism hindered the reforms and the bottom-up initiatives in the country.
- The central government was not pushing the decentralisation reform because to its mind there was not enough managerial and educational expertise at the community, school, district, city and regional levels.

The project activities were focused on activity in both directions, destroying the monopolism, collaboration with all stakeholders, developing bottom-up initiatives, providing alternatives in training, research and information networking.

In 1994 - 1996 the financial support for the project was provided by the Institute for Local Government and Public Services (Budapest, Hungary). Since 1997 it has been carried out in co-operation with the Minsk Regional Department of Education.

Goals and objectives of the project:

Goal 1.   Dissemination of information relevant to the development of educational leadership and decision-making for secondary and vocational school leaders, district, city and regional superintendents, other public administrators dealing with educational issues, people from business and public organisations interested in educational reform in Belarus. A number of objectives have been addressed.

Objectives: 1.   Publication of the quarterly journal *Educational Leadership and Management*. It deals with organisational theory, human resource management, educational legislative policy, educational finance management and effective leadership practice both in Belarus and abroad. It also contains the teaching material to be used in training educational leaders. An electronic copy of the journal is available via the Internet.

2.   Information exchange on the issues of educational reform between Belarus educational leaders and their foreign counterparts has been initiated. As a result Belarus educational leaders have up-to-date information on leadership development abroad and the international educational community become aware of the changes taking place in the Belarus educational system.

Goal 2.   Development of a system of leadership and management training for educational leaders.

Objectives: 1.   Curricula, teaching materials have been developed and pre-service training for educational leaders has been provided. All of the graduates of these pilot courses have been promoted and obtained leading positions at the school, district, regional and national levels.

2.   A group of the trainers from the regions were trained to use educational leadership curricula, teaching materials and methodology (train the trainers model).

Goal 3.   Promotion of educational leaders' status and prestige in the society.

Objectives: 1.   National awards for the most effective school leader, public administrator and businessman involved in educational restructuring in Belarus were established and nationally televised contest 'Educational Leaders of the Year' was launched.

2.   A new NGO - the Association of Secondary Education Administrators was initiated and   continuous support has been provided to the National   Association   of Secondary School Principals.

The evaluation of the project was been carried out using the following criteria:

- The quality of the informational and educational services provided,
- The number of people receiving information and training.
- The quality of the teaching materials (software, hand-outs, video simulations, case studies, etc.).

The data also included detailed reports on the leadership training programs.   Students were encouraged to rate the proposed seminars and information service. The observers from the funding organisation, Ministry of Education and western experts were invited to express their opinion concerning the instruction, printed and e-mailed instructional and informational materials.

Bimonthly reports on the progress of the project have been sent to the ILGPS. Samples of the journal, newsletter, teaching and other materials developed by the BECLD were included.

Analysis of change.

The project has been challenged by three major factors:

- the educational values and beliefs of most Belarus school administrators turned out to be difficult to change and required much effort and skills by the BECLD faculty;
- the tax policy of the Belarus government has not been favourable for non-profit initiatives;
- some national and regional educational institutions funded by the government strongly opposed the BECLD initiatives which were destroying their monopolism in the sector. First they did their best to stop these initiatives but finally ended with the duplication of the BECLD programs. The government organisations started publication of a journal for educational managers. They also launched pre-service courses for educational administrators.

They also initiated the national contest to nominate the most effective school of the year. What is important is that all these programs are now funded by the government. This was exactly what the BECLD, being an NGO, was aiming at, since one cannot rely only on western support to reform a national educational system.

Strategy design.

Having introduced the basic elements of a self-development mechanism into the educational system nation-wide the team focuses its attention on the development of a regional infrastructure. For this purpose it has selected the largest administrative region in Belarus - the Minsk region which comprises 30 school districts and over 1000 schools.

New information technology development

Background.

The education information network that used to exist in the former Soviet Union is completely destroyed. Schools have no budgets to subscribe to foreign educational editions. On their school improvement efforts Belarus school leaders can benefit neither from the experience of their western counterparts nor from the experience of each other since there has never been any national school improvement networks in these countries since leadership was not required in centralised systems of education.

One possible solution of the problem is the development of new technologies. Telecommunications may become one of the major tools in this field. Four objectives are to be achieved for this purpose:

- An school improvement telecommunication database (WWW) needs to be created to serve the needs of school leaders in the countries moving from centralised educational systems to decentralised ones. It should contain both western and eastern leadership theories and methodologies as well as experiences in effective educational leadership transformation efforts.

- The school improvement telecommunication network is to be developed so that school leaders from Belarus can communicate with each other and their western counterparts on an everyday basis, co-ordinate their transformation activities, develop joint projects and thus benefit from each other's experience.

- School leaders need to be trained to understand the importance of new technologies and to use them for professional development and for managing their schools.

- School leaders need to be trained to initiate the use of the new technologies at the classroom level and for the professional development of teachers.

The group of Belarus experts led by L.Shelkovich (Institute for Educational ᵥAdministration, SCAF-Belarus, BECLD, Minsk Regional Department of Education) has been working in all these directions. It started in 1993 with 5 pilot schools that represented 4 educational regions of Belarus. It was initially suggested that each school team consist of a headteacher as team leader, a teacher of information technologies responsible for the technical part of the activities and finally - a teacher of English to facilitate the communication with counterparts abroad. Later the teams were joined by other teachers, students and parents who volunteered to participate in the project. The project was supported by the USA that purchased the modems for the schools, paid the telecommunication costs and involved several western experts (New York University) to assist their Belarus colleagues.

Analysis of change.

The first experience proved that success of the project depends on three major factors:

- the motivation of educational leaders and their ability to select and lead the team of teachers, students and parents;

- the opportunities experts can provide for educational leaders to access school improvement databases. Since most of the Belarus educators don't know English and thus cannot use western databases, it was very important to create one in Russian.;

- the opportunities the experts can provide for educational leaders to communicate with each other and their counterparts abroad.

The next stage of the project was aimed at strengthening these three factors. This stage was aimed at involving more school teams in the project, development of the leadership WWW and educational telecommunication network. It was supported by the Eurasia Foundation.

A non-profit telecommunication network - EcldNet was developed, the technical part of which includes a server running the latest Linux system with 32 Mb RAM, 1.5 GB disk, 3 modems and 14 PC work stations; the connection to the Internet was established through a 19.2 Kbps leased digital line.

In general, the EcldNet WWW which is run both in English and Russian is a depository of Belarus scholarship which is available to relevant scholarly communities in Belarus and world-wide. The EcldNet WWW is a resource for school leaders and universities in Belarus for school effectiveness and school improvement efforts.

A system of training for educators to use the network information technologies and their further involvement in the international educational network has been developed. Even more important, the system of 'training the trainers' has led to a 'chain reaction' when the trainees are already providing training for their own students and faculty as well as other educators in their region (Grodno school-gymnasium #30 which later received a grant for this purpose from the Eurasia Foundation is a good example).

The experts developed the structure for school districts and schools' WWW home pages and taught them to create their web pages which are located either on the EcldNet server or their own WWW servers. The second stage of the project resulted in the following:

- The databases relevant to educational reform are now available for the Belarus students and educators. Since they were developed both in Russian and English they have naturally become a part of the international (Internet) educational database.

- The education information network has been initiated in Belarus gradually involving all schools and universities in using telecommunication as a powerful means of educational reform.

- Belarus educators and students are becoming aware of the benefits provided by the EcldNet educational network, WWW and other information resources and become motivated and skilled to enter the Internet community.

Strategy design.

As soon as the innovation was initiated nation-wide the 'torch' was passed to the regional teams and the team of experts led by L.Shelkovich focused its efforts on one of the regions - Minsk - which is the largest in the country. In co-operation with the Minsk Regional Department of Education it has launched a new project aimed at involving each school district and each school in the telecommunication network and training educational leaders, teachers and students to use this modern technology on a daily basis. The assumption is that local governments, in spite of the current economic crisis, will contribute to the project. It's important that through the joint efforts of the Ministry of Education, the Open Society Institute and several other foundations, a new Internet node has been just built in Minsk that provides free access to the Internet for educational and other non-profit organisations in Belarus.

MATRA-program 'Civics Education in Belarus' (1996-1998)

The objective of the Matra-program (Dutch Ministry of Foreign Affairs) is to contribute to the social transformation process in a number of countries in Central and Eastern Europe. This project in Belarus is based on the same perspectives as the Matra-program: that government and educational actors are supported in the process of social change.

The project is being carried out by the Belarus Ministry of Education, Minsk Regional Department of Education, BECLD and Educaplan (the Netherlands). The short term aims of the project are as follows:

- Creating and strengthening an educational network for civic education in Belarus
- Developing a new curriculum (guidelines) and methodologies (technologies)
- Developing and executing a training program for Belarus teacher trainers in civic education.

Project design.
According to the wishes and needs of the Belarus partners the project design has 4 phases. In each phase Dutch experts with different backgrounds and experience (curriculum development, methodology, teacher training and implementation) support the Belarus experts in the development and implementation process:

1. Preparation

In this first project phase (1996-1997) Belarus and Dutch experts collected and investigated the existing (revised) curricula, methodologies and training programs on civics education in Belarus and other countries. Special attention was paid to recent related developments and results of similar educational projects in other Central and Eastern European countries.

2. Project execution

Based on the revision recommendations for curricula and Civics Education Programs on different levels (phase 1), training workshops were provided for educational managers, teachers of primary schools, secondary school teachers in social studies and staff members of several teacher training institutions. During these workshops participants developed curricula for primary and secondary education, and related pre- and in-service training programs (1997).

3. Implementation

The curricula and experimental classroom materials for Civics Education (phase 2) will be tested and assessed within the participating pilot schools (1997-1998). School teachers register the results on special evaluation forms. Based on these forms Belarus experts will write an Assessment Report, containing recommendations for the revision of curricula and classroom materials. This report will be the input for an implementation conference (1998).

4. Revision and evaluation

The draft version of the curricula, programs and classroom materials (phase 3) will be readjusted and adapted according to the recommendations of the implementation conference. These readjusted (final) versions, including training programs for pre- and in-service education will be presented during a Dissemination Conference with key decision-makers (national and regional level). Finally the project will be evaluated by all project participants.

The Dalton methodology based on the principles of *freedom, self-activity, co-operation and social education* is also being tested and implemented in Belarus schools through this Matra-program.

Conclusions

We have outlined in this report some of the major initiatives in school effectiveness and improvement in the Republic of Belarus. Whilst it is evident that Belarus schools are advancing in educational reform, it is also clear that the progress could have been much better. The main obstacles are not just the economic problems the country is currently facing but the educational values which most of the Belarus educators and educational policy-makers still have. Changing values is a slow process. However we stay optimistic and hope that school effectiveness and improvement programs will continue and contribute to the integration of the Belarus education system into the European and global educational communities.

References

Ministry of Education (1996) *General Secondary Education in the Republic of Belarus* (Statistic Data), Ministry of Education of the Republic of Belarus, Minsk (in Russian).

Ministry of Education (1996) *Program of Realisation of School Reform in the Republic of Belarus*, Ministry of Education of the Republic of Belarus (in Russian).

Selischev, V. (1996) 'The Conditions for Change in the Educational System in Belarus' in *Global Perspectives on School Leadership*, Nova Southeastern University, USA - Uppsala University, Sweden, 81.

Shelkovich, L. (1996) 'New Technologies in Educational Leadership in Eastern Europe' in *Global Perspectives on School Leadership*, Nova Southeastern University, USA - Uppsala University, Sweden, 80.

Volodko, V. (1996) *The Content of School Reform in Belarus*, Ministry of Education of the Republic of Belarus (in Russian).

Zagoumennov, I. (1996) 'Educational Leadership Development in Belarus' in *Global Perspectives on School Leadership*, Nova Southeastern University, USA - Uppsala University, Sweden, 83.

Zagoumennov, I. (1993) 'Shifting to a New Paradigm: School Reform in the Republic of Belarus' in *International Journal of Educational Reform, 1*, 36-40.

Zagoumennov, I. (1997) *Development of Civic Education in the Republic of Belarus*, Ministry of Education of the Republic of Belarus (in Russian).

Zagoumennov, I. and Shelkovich, L. (1995) 'School Culture' in the *Journal of Educational Leadership and Management, 2*, Minsk, 9-14 (in Russian).

Zagoumennov, I. (1995) *Guidelines for Evaluation of School Effectiveness*, Ministry of Education of the Republic of Belarus, Minsk (in Russian).

7.

The management of curriculum improvement in Cyprus: a critique of a 'centre-periphery' model in a centralised system

Leonidas Kyriakides

Introduction

One of the main characteristics of the educational system in Cyprus is that its administration is centralised and both primary and secondary schools are considered as government, and not as community, institutions. The maintenance of the centralised system has historical and political origins (Kyriakides 1994) but also a decentralised system in a small country like Cyprus would be very demanding in manpower. With 380 primary schools and 120 secondary schools, it has the same administrative range as a large local educational authority in England. It is, also, much smaller than an administrative region for education in France.

Pre-primary, primary and secondary education are under the authority of the Ministry of Education which is responsible for the educational policy making, the administration of education and the enforcement of educational laws. In addition, teachers' appointments, secondments, transfers, and promotions are the responsibility of the Educational Service Commission, an independent five-member body, which is appointed by the President of the Republic. There are local school committees which are responsible for the

construction, maintenance and equipping of school buildings but they have no
say in purely educational matters.

The next section of this paper is concerned with the process of curriculum
change in Cyprus and examines five important aspects of the management of
change. They illustrate the reasons for the limited effectiveness of introducing
curriculum change at the school level in Cyprus. The importance of exploring
teachers' perceptions of curriculum reform is raised in the third section.
Teachers' meaningful involvement in the formation and evaluation of
curriculum policy is supported. It is also argued that neither the state nor the
teachers can be the sole definers, arbiters and guardians of curriculum policy.
Thus, the last section presents a strategic direction for curriculum change in
Cyprus which might be used in order to create shared visions between
teachers and policy-makers. A more appropriate model of curriculum change
than the existing one is, therefore, presented. Finally, the difficulties of
introducing this model are taken into account and a short-term strategy is
provided.

Some conceptual issues of the management of curriculum improvement in Cyprus

Curriculum improvement has not proved easy to effect in many countries. Its
success is not dependent on its content only (Fullan 1991). Thus, five
dimensions of the process of change in Cyprus are presented in this section.
The first is concerned with the process of designing and diffusing curriculum
change whereas the other four deal with some further issues indirectly related
to the process of change.

The process of curriculum change

A 'centre-periphery' model in a centralised system

The process followed for the design and diffusion of curriculum change in
Cyprus has been a 'centre-periphery' model (Schon 1971), operating in what
is a highly centralised system. The design of both the curriculum of 1981 and
the new curriculum were almost completely controlled by government
inspectors and did not establish any mechanism for consulting teachers.
Inspectors have also the responsibility for monitoring the implementation of
the curriculum by the teachers. They are required to give guidance to the
teachers but at the same time, to evaluate their work by giving marks, which
play a decisive role in teachers' career development. Their role as assessors
creates a climate of mistrust which tends to undermine their principal role in

curriculum and school improvement (Karagiorgis 1986). Thus, inspectors control the design of the curriculum, the implementation through provision of guidelines and advice to teachers for problems with implementing the curriculum policy and the evaluation by being responsible for teachers' appraisal

Beside the creation of the curriculum which the Ministry of Education sent to schools, textbooks are also given to teachers, together with advice on how to implement the national curriculum. It is assumed that these textbooks will help teachers to implement innovations designed by the Ministry so that the implementation of curriculum policy can be assured. Thus, textbooks are used to ensure the implementation of curriculum reform. However, it is not enough to offer teachers better books and packaged pedagogies. Although good materials and advice do matter, it is the quality of teachers themselves and their generative role in the curriculum change which determines the quality of teaching and therefore the effectiveness of any curriculum change (MacDonald 1991). Even in Cyprus the curriculum is not teacher-proof. From a position of political strength it has been no easy matter for the Ministry of Education to operationalise a centre-periphery curriculum reform process as has been found elsewhere (Sutherland 1981).

School Based Curriculum Development (SBCD)

SBCD is very weak in Cyprus and is also a consequence of high central control that does not allow for much differentiation among the schools. Cypriot teachers struggle with their problems and anxieties privately, spending most of their time apart from their colleagues. There is very rarely interaction concerned with professional issues among the staff of schools (Kyriakides 1994). The need for promoting SBCD emerges from the failure of the process of change in Cyprus, arising from the idea that the officers of the Ministry of Education can be the sole definers, arbiters and guardians of good practice. This idea has encouraged professional dependency. Against this, SBCD implies that teachers should be involved in the policy formation and evaluation. Thus, the new role of teachers will encourage both professional autonomy and self-motivated development that have been seen as significant sources of curriculum change. This is because SBCD is a process requiring collaboration by teachers able to interpret general curricular assumptions into a specific curriculum practice. It has been shown elsewhere that curriculum co-ordinators and heads play a decisive role for the development of a collegial school which is the ideal type of management for a school attempting to develop its own curriculum policy (Campbell 1985).

The need for professional interaction which is crucial for developing collaborative culture, was provided by the symposium of the council for cultural co-operation about 'The Management of Innovation in Primary Education' (Council of Europe 1984). Cyprus participated in this symposium and shared the idea that increased internal communication positively influenced the implementation of an innovation. It was argued that teachers should have the opportunity to share ideas about pupils' reactions, about the use of materials and about teaching strategies. However, the promotion of co-operation among the staff has been difficult to realise in practice in Cypriot schools; the system has never encouraged co-operation among teachers.

Although some primary schools and most of the secondary schools have curriculum co-ordinators, the role of these co-ordinators is restricted to giving advice informally to the few teachers who ask them for it from time to time, and they do not have time free of class contact in order to prepare guidelines, materials and learning resources or to work alongside their colleagues. In addition, they may not have a higher level of subject knowledge than other teachers.

Curriculum reform and teacher development in Cyprus

The difficulties of the 'centre-periphery' model of curriculum change has also to do with the fact that the quality of teachers determines to some extent the implementation of curriculum policy. The need for a strong link between curriculum reform and teacher development is also reflected in theories of curriculum change (Fullan and Hargreaves 1992). This raises questions on links between teacher's professional development and curriculum reform in Cyprus. It is argued that there is no link between curriculum reform and teacher development and attributes that to the process of curriculum change followed in Cyprus that implies a limited role for teachers.

Initial teacher training (ITT)

Cypriot pre-primary and primary student teachers are nowadays trained through courses equivalent to a four year bachelor degree in education rather than three years of a teachers' training college. However, the fact that neither Pedagogical Academy of Cyprus previously nor the department of education at the University of Cyprus currently offered any compulsory course on curriculum development suggests that policy makers do not consider it appropriate for teachers to study curriculum development.

Moreover, in Cyprus, to become a secondary teacher you have to obtain a University degree related to the specific subject you teach. For instance, a Mathematics teacher must be a holder of a university degree, equivalent to a BSc in Mathematics. Recruitment of secondary teachers, therefore, does not depend on teaching competences and does not require any initial teacher training.

In-service training (INSET)

Analysing the provision of INSET, similar conclusions can be drawn. The INSET of primary and secondary school teachers is the task of the Pedagogical Institute (PI). There is no school-based in-service training in Cyprus. Although it was argued that 'school-based in-service training will be widely used during the above five-year period (1990-95)' (Ministry of Education 1990, para 1.4.9.2), there is nothing to suggest that the centre is going to bring about any change in the kind of INSET provided in Cyprus.

Optional courses provided by PI are the main kind of INSET offered to Cypriot teachers. Apart from the negative effect on teachers' professional development by the lack of other kinds of INSET, the fact that INSET in Cyprus is mainly based on optional seminars which are held in the afternoon means that most teachers can not attend them easily. Moreover, the decision to attend any of these courses is purely individual and does not relate to the defined needs of the school. This seems to support the argument provided above that there is a lack of coherent educational planning in each school.

It is also important to indicate that all secondary teachers must undergo in-service training during the first year of their probationary period. This compulsory training is provided by the PI. It involves two days per week with reduction in teaching hours to accommodate it. Thus, the newly-appointed teacher receives 'sandwich course' training between the PI and the school in which she/he is serving. The content seems well balanced between general pedagogical considerations and subject teaching (UNESCO 1997). However, there is nothing on the process of curriculum change or on the current policy for curriculum reform. Moreover, topics like school effectiveness and school improvement are not offered to the newly appointed teachers. It can be therefore argued that Cypriot policy makers should explore the possibilities of developing a link between policy on teachers' professional development and policy on curriculum reform. A particular concern should be on teachers' role in the process of curriculum change.

Contractual and professional accountability

It can be argued that when a government brings in curriculum reform it can call upon two different kinds of accountability. It can call upon the obligations that teachers have to their employers who lay down certain things that they have to do (Contractual accountability). Thus, policy documents can be seen as part of the contract which teachers have accepted when they become employed. The state can also call upon teachers' professional accountability to bring in reform. This implies that teachers should be involved in the process of curriculum change so that their professional values and ideology are taken into account. In that case policy-makers have to ensure that reforms are compatible with, or take account of, teachers' perceptions. These two kinds of accountability have been frequently in conflict in the reform process of Cyprus.

Where Cypriot teachers are enthusiastic in applying innovations it is mainly because their appraisal depends on it (Kyriakides 1994); the underlying model of change management is based on contractual rather than professional accountability. It has been already mentioned that inspectors control both the design of the curriculum and the evaluation. The result is that many teachers may agree uncritically and superficially with curriculum policy because they feel that this is what they are expected to do. Thus, the weakness in policy of curriculum reform in Cyprus lies in the way curriculum change is brought about which encourages a belief that getting on is mainly a matter of saying and doing what significant others (ie inspectors) wish to hear and see. As a consequence, teachers fail to develop their professionalism through this process of unthinking conformity.

Fullan (1993) suggests that neither centralisation nor decentralisation works. Centralisation errs on the side of overcontrol, decentralisation errs towards chaos. Cypriot teachers are neither free to decide what to teach nor how to teach. It can be argued that there is a need for encouraging teachers' involvement in both policy formation and evaluation. Teachers' role in relation to curriculum policy should be to treat policy critically and to find ways of communicating their views to inspectors. Teachers might move from passively receiving material from the inspectors to treating it critically and being responsive to it by providing their views and judgements for it. In addition, there is a need for both primary and secondary schools in Cyprus to be able to develop their own school policy which could be based on the ideology promoted by the national curriculum and the special needs of the school. Thus, the current attempt to change curriculum practice is very likely to fail to improve curriculum practice since it has not been combined with the professional development of teachers through new school-based collaborative cultures (Kyriakides 1996). The lesson has not been learnt that developing the curriculum requires developing the teachers also.

Partnership in Cyprus: parental involvement and pupil involvement

The aims of the education service in Cyprus are set out in various government publications and policy documents. By analysing these aims one can identify an attempt to link education to the historical, social, moral, cultural, economic and political context of Cyprus (Kyriakides 1994, UNESCO 1997). However, the aims say little about the concept of partnership that is now given high priority in many countries. It can be argued that policy documents do not encourage the idea that schools should take account not only of policy decisions of government and inspectors, but also of the expectations of parents, employers and community at large. Neither official policy documents nor any non-statutory guidance suggests that the development of the curriculum at the local level should be seen in terms of pupils' and parents' role. Thus, this part is concerned with the concept of partnership that seems to be a crucial issue for any attempt to bring about change at both national and local level.

Yet even within this highly centralised system there is some opportunity for parental participation. The relationships between family and schools in Cyprus can be formal or informal. Formal are the relations that the school personnel have with the elected members of the central committee of Parents' Association (PA) and informal are the relations that parents as individuals have with the school. As far as the role of PA, it can be argued that their role is basically to raise money through the organisation of various events and to support school programs financially. They have no say in purely educational matters. However, the national assembly of the PA is a powerful pressure group and policy makers take PA seriously into account. Regarding the informal relations of parents with schools, parents visit the school as an invited audience at school performances. They are also invited to be informed about their children's achievement and behaviour at school.

Although there is lack of systematic research in the field of education in Cyprus, during the last five years four research studies concerned with parental involvement have been conducted. The main findings of these studies are presented below. First, research into sources of influences upon Cypriot teachers (Kyriakides 1997a) revealed that parents had the weakest power to influence practice. Second, research into teachers' perceptions of parental involvement (Georgiou 1996: 41) showed that 'teachers want the parents to become involved but at a safe distance and only without challenging or questioning their authority'. Third, investigations concerned with the climate of schools concerning parental involvement revealed that although teachers in theory are in favour of a co-operation between school and home, when this co-operation becomes specific educators are concerned about possible threats to their professionalism (Phtiaka 1996). Moreover, there was no national policy about parents' participation in primary schools of Cyprus because neither parents influenced teachers nor teachers wanted them to influence their classroom practice (Kyriakides 1994). Furthermore, although Cypriot teachers did not want parents to influence their practice, they complained at the same time that parents did not visit schools to discuss their pupils' progress. This seems to be in line with the results of other studies conducted in different cultures internationally. Rosenholtz (1989a: 109) argues that 'the more teachers complain about uncooperative parents, the more they tend to believe there is little to do'.

The advantages of involving parents in the process of curriculum development can be identified not only in the findings of a current study undertaken in Cyprus (Kyriakides 1997b) but also in research findings conducted in different cultures internationally (Rosenholtz 1989a, Mortimore et al 1988) showing that involving parents in instructional tasks has positive effects on learning. It can be, therefore, claimed that there is a need for finding ways of fostering more effective home-school collaboration in Cyprus. Fullan (1991) argues that such collaboration is essential since no one group can make all the difference on its own. This argument is supported by research showing that teachers working with parents may come to understand better their pupils, bring about unique rather than routine solutions to classroom problems and reach to a shared understanding (Epstein 1986, 1987). Thus, a more explicit policy on collaboration between school and home should be developed in Cyprus. The lack of such policy in Cyprus is in contrast to the fact that the state has been interventionist on issues of teaching methods which might be thought as the professional responsibility of teachers.

There is also the issue of pupils' involvement. There are Pupils' Councils in each school. However, the Pupils' Councils work almost as parallel organisations rather than being integrated into the school consultative process. There is no coherent structure of formal consultative meetings with school management. It has been also shown that Cypriot pupils do not significantly influence classroom practice (Kyriakides 1997a). Nevertheless, policy makers have taken steps towards an imaginative and progressively focused policy but there is a need to take some more decisions and encourage teachers in order to integrate the policy for pupils' involvement into a coherent structure in which all the elements are brought together to focus on the aims of the service. Finally, there is also a danger of 'politicisation' of such organisation and this appears to be the case to some extent in Cyprus. In such cases the Pupils' Councils may become pressure groups rather than elements in a coherent policy for partnership in education.

Cypriot teachers should consider the curriculum as a 'social policy' designed to satisfy pupils' needs and should think of children as participants in the process of curriculum change. Torrance (1989) illustrates a dialogue between teachers and pupils which can be seen as a reflection on the process of learning. It can be claimed that such dialogue may be used by teachers to identify their pupils' needs, interests, plans and ambitions. Information gathered from this dialogue may be also used to guide curriculum development. In addition, pupils may develop a sense of ownership and investment in what they are doing which provides motivation for learning. It is therefore an effective strategy in the process of change to involve parents and pupils and to find out about their expectations and the help which they are able to provide in the process of improving the pupils' learning and the curriculum.

Curriculum evaluation and research into school effectiveness and improvement

One of the key aims of the educational system of Cyprus is to enable all Cypriots pupils to develop to their fullest potential and gain knowledge, skills and values that will allow them to lead productive lives as citizens and workers. To address this aim the Ministry of Education should create mechanisms that will provide systematic information about the conditions of schooling, educational processes and educational outcomes for all grades and subjects. The generation of this information is work that requires the application of scientific educational research in order to monitor progress towards the goals that have been defined for the education system. However, research studies undertaken in Cyprus are mainly small-scale and uncoordinated (UNESCO 1997). There is only one research project that has some policy potential for the Ministry of Education. This is concerned with the introduction of the new curriculum in primary Science and the effectiveness of the new series of textbooks in primary Science published by the Ministry of Education (Pedagogical Institute 1996a). Nevertheless, the few research studies into curriculum policy conducted in Cyprus did not influence policy-making. Thus, the lack of systematic research into curriculum policy affects the way in which curriculum evaluation is conducted in Cyprus. Karagiorgis (1986: 89) argued that:

> *a weak point of education development is that no systematic scientific evaluation has been applied to new procedures and methods accepted and implemented in schools*

Another important implication from the lack of any research for the evaluation of curriculum change is that no innovation has been designed for the specific conditions of Cyprus. The role of research is very restricted and has no impact either on policy formation or on pedagogical debate. This implies that there is lack of serious consideration of the complex process of change that should be based on a diagnosis of the need for change from participants. In addition, there is no arena for professional criticism of either curriculum policy or the centralised system. The lack of such criticism supports people's perceptions of inspectors as experts of curriculum change and of teachers as those who have merely to deliver the curriculum. Thus, the educational system in Cyprus remains highly centralised and matches with what Schon (1971) has described as a 'stable state'. The Ministry of Education in 1974 accepted that:

> *research is needed for the evaluation of the programs which will lead to a scientific approach, which will be a more costly approach, but less costly in the long run in the effective running of the educational system.*

>   (Council of Europe 1974: 35)

However, since then nothing has been done which suggests an unwillingness to change that situation. Nevertheless, it is important for the Ministry of Education to proceed to the establishment of a national educational research unit (UNESCO 1997) responsible for conducting research into curriculum policy and able to influence decision-making.

On the other hand, schools should be organised in such a way that all pupils will be held to high standards and given the means to achieve them. This implies that existing schools should be 'transformed' and revitalised the teaching and learning processes by incorporating high standards and inspiring high performance. However, research findings reveal that most schools in Cyprus need help in the ongoing process of improvement both from inspectors and administrators within the education system and from specialists in teaching and learning each subject (Kyriakides 1994). Since the culture of schools varies, it is extremely unlikely that all schools should choose an identical process of growth and change. For this reason, an optional INSET course was organised last year at Pedagogical Institute (Pedagogical Institute 1996b). Teachers had the opportunity to explore different designs for the improvement of their school. Teachers of each school worked as a team and made their own whole-school design. Three case studies arising from this program are currently being conducted in order to examine the implementation of the design of three different schools and whether this process will contribute in the improvement of these three schools. This research aims to provide an answer to the question whether school-based curriculum development can be developed in a highly centralised system such as the one in Cyprus. These projects may also contribute in the development of local curricula and in the creation of an interaction between national and local curricula.

Finally, a study concerned with educators' perceptions about headteachers' role for school effectiveness has been conducted (Kyriakides 1998). This can be seen as the first systematic attempt of a national agency to deal with the concept of school effectiveness which seems to be neglected in Cyprus. However, there is a lot to be done both at the national and school level in order to support the transformation process of a large number of schools in Cyprus. A continued focus on changing the school environment, would give the opportunity for Cypriot pupils to learn in exciting and effective school environments.

Teachers' perceptions of curriculum reform and the process of change

The teacher's role in the process of curriculum change can be seen not only in terms of the abilities to implement curriculum policy but also in terms of the importance of their perceptions of curriculum reform for its implementation. This is an issue derived from theories of curriculum change which reveal that the exploration of teachers' perceptions should be considered as a main aspect of any attempt to evaluate curriculum change. This issue is clarified in this section by drawing from theories about the process of curriculum change (Part A), studies concerned with teachers' status and professionalism (Part B), and research into teachers' thinking (Part C) to illustrate the importance of teachers' perceptions for the process of curriculum change.

Teachers' perceptions and models of curriculum change

Fullan (1991: 94) argues that the reasons for the failure of most educational reforms goes far beyond the identification of specific technical problems. He supports Wise's (1977 and 1979: 96) argument that policy-makers are frequently 'hyper-rational' and points out that:

> *innovators need to be open to the realities of others: sometimes because the ideas of others will lead to alterations for the better in the direction of change, and sometimes because the others' realities will expose the problems of implementation that must be addressed and at the very least will indicate where one should start.*

Thus, the need for exploring teachers' perceptions of curriculum policy is important since research into these perceptions might contribute to teachers' meaningful involvement in the formation and evaluation of curriculum policy. The need for such involvement is supported by an attempt to evaluate the models of curriculum change used in Cyprus presented above. The failure of centre-periphery model in Cyprus can be attributed to the fact that teachers' perceptions were inadequately considered at two important stages; the adoption, ie the teachers' decision to use an innovation, and the implementation, ie its realisation. As far as School Based Curriculum Development is concerned, Shipman's (1973: 53) conclusion about the critical factors in its effectiveness included teachers' perceptions. Even the role of head is considered in terms of a school ethos which promotes teachers' involvement. Similar findings were derived from other studies focused on the implementation of SBCD (eg Campbell 1985, Shipman 1974).

Teachers' perceptions, professionalism and curriculum change

The need for exploring teachers' perceptions can not be identified only in studies focused on the process of change but also in studies focused on teachers' role and job satisfaction and particularly in terms of the notion of 'psychic rewards' identified by Lortie (1975). This has been linked with the notion of change by Rosenholtz (1989b: 421) who indicates that:

> *Of the many resources required by schools, the most vital are the contributions − of effort, commitment and involvement - from teachers ... Central to a school's academic success, then, is its ability to motivate teachers to make meaningful contributions to it.*

This requirement for teachers' productive commitment to schools is not only able to provide that 'psychic reward' to teachers but is also crucial for school effectiveness. It can be, therefore, argued that both formation and implementation of curriculum policy should be based at teachers' meaningful involvement in it. Teachers' meaningful involvement in the process of curriculum change may have implications for the political ideology in the structure of the educational system. Skilbeck (1990) suggests that a sharp and uncompromising distinction between centralised and decentralised systems is clearly inadequate in the situations most of the countries are now addressing. He indicates that it presupposes a simple dichotomy which does not represent the reality of various educational system. He also supports the need for sharing roles and responsibilities. Thus, exploration of Cypriot teachers' perceptions of curriculum policy may contribute to the development of a system based on sharing roles and responsibilities for the process of curriculum change. This exploration may also have significant implications for teachers' role and professionalism.

Research into teachers' thinking

The importance of teachers' perceptions is also supported by research on teachers' thinking (Yaxley 1991, Zeichner et al 1987). Although such research does not provide us with a comprehensive and theoretical framework for thinking about teaching, it does provide us with an insight into the process of curriculum change. Calderhead (1987:17) points out that research into teachers' thinking shows:

> *how unrealistic it is to conceive of innovation as a set of pre-formulated ideas or principles to be implemented by teachers. Innovative ideas are interpreted and reinterpreted by teachers over a period of time and translated into practice in a process that involves teachers drawing upon several different knowledge bases and interpreting and manipulating various interests.*

It can be therefore claimed that policy on curriculum change should treat teachers as 'reflective practitioners' (Schon 1983). Research on teachers' thinking reveals that teachers possess a body of specialised knowledge acquired through training and experience related to teaching methods, subject matter and child behaviour together with other information resulting from their experience of working with children in numerous contexts (Calderhead 1987). Thus, not only teachers' perceptions should be examined but also factors that influence them.

In addition, Doyle (1986) argues that teachers deal with complex and ambiguous problems and have to make professional judgements and decisions. Thus, policy-makers should find out ways to enable teachers to disclose their 'knowledge in action' (Schon 1983) verbally which can contribute to the development of curriculum policy. This argument implies that Cypriot policy makers should explore teachers' perceptions at the stage of both formation and evaluation of any curriculum reform.

The above brief analysis of theories of curriculum change from three different perspectives reveals that teachers' perceptions of curriculum policy needed to be taken into account. But even if Cypriot policy makers have claimed that they are interested in teachers' professional involvement in the revision and updating of curriculum policy (Sophianos 1978), they never attempted to explore teachers' perceptions of curriculum policy. As it has been shown above, Cypriot teachers have to decide how to organise rather than create the new national curriculum. It can be claimed that there is a hidden agenda of hierarchical and bureaucratic decision-making in the process of curriculum change in Cyprus and this provides the basis for a significant criticism of policy makers' attempts to manage curriculum improvement.

A strategic direction for curriculum change in Cyprus

The last part of this section is an attempt to present a strategic direction for curriculum change in Cyprus. Policy makers can not mandate change even in a small country with a highly centralised system like that of Cyprus. This is partly due to the different needs that exist between and within schools. As it has been mentioned above, the failure of the current model of curriculum change has also to do with the fact that teachers' perceptions are not taken into account. Moreover, research studies concerned with factors influencing Cypriot teachers' perceptions and their implications for the process of change (Kyriakides 1997a) raise doubts on whether either the state or teachers can be the sole definers, arbiters and guardians of curriculum policy. This implies that educational change can be achieved when people's attitudes change. However, this is not an easy task. People's beliefs are part of a deeply rooted belief system based on perceptions of their role and which extends to social and political concerns. Thus, curriculum reform is complex (Fullan 1993) and a flexible approach to strategic planning might be used to create shared visions between teachers and policy-makers. A new model of curriculum change should be adopted. Curriculum change has to be based on a two-way relationship of pressure and support and continuous negotiation between the centre and the periphery which will amount to both 'top-down and bottom-up influences' (Fullan 1993; Turnbull 1985). It can be also claimed that both educational theory and teachers' perceptions should be taken into account by policy makers when they attempt to design and/or evaluate the national curriculum. Thus, the adoption of this model may diminish any authoritarian dimension of the educational system.

The new model of curriculum change should also advocate the need for both national and local curricula. As it has been shown above, each school should be able to develop its own school policy which might be based on both the special needs of the school and the ideology promoted by the national curriculum. Moreover, pupils and parents have to play a significant role in the process of change. Policy makers should support the idea that curriculum change at the local level should not depend only on educators' perceptions but also on the joint efforts of families, pupils and schools.

Finally, it has been mentioned that a close relationship between initial and in-service training with curriculum policy does not exist in Cyprus. Such relationship is required. Curriculum policy should be taken into account by those who are responsible for designing the University courses and those who are responsible for the INSET courses in Cyprus. Finally, there is a need for an interaction between INSET and local curricula. INSET may be organised in order to influence local curriculum and at the same time to get feedback from the local curriculum about curriculum policy. Thus, evaluation of curriculum reform should be provided through the interactions which should exist between the national and local curricula, and the interactions of each kind of the curriculum with teachers' perceptions and professional training.

Shipman (1985) points out that there are many obstacles for research and educational theory to influence policy-making. This is particularly true for the suggestions made in this paper about the introduction of a new model of curriculum change in Cyprus since they have to do with changes in teachers' culture. It is very unlikely that Cypriot teachers will be ready to accept the new model of curriculum change since it implies a reconceptualisation of their role and suggests that they take on further job responsibilities, which they are reluctant to do as relevant research studies have shown (Kyriakides 1994, 1997a). Similarly, policy-makers may not accept that they should take into account teachers' perceptions of curriculum policy since this might raise questions about policy makers' expertise. For this reason, a short-term strategy of curriculum change is provided below.

The short-term strategy supported in this paper is based on Adams and Cohen's (1981) suggestion that in the process of change it is convenient to start with the smallest element first. This strategy is also based on the assumption that we should regard each individual teacher as a discrete unit upon which change of beliefs should take place. Thus, individual teachers should be involved in the business of reform and be encouraged to share ideas in order to develop a collaborative culture. This could be done through establishing professional associations. Teachers, on a voluntary basis, could share their experiences about the implementation of the curriculum policy and develop their own goals and strategies. Thus, the main effort of this strategy should be concentrated not on how to persuade teachers to use materials which have been produced by a central team but on how to persuade them to share experiences. If teachers share experiences they will be able to define their own needs. This strategy may be a first step towards developing a collaborative culture among teachers. Moreover, these associations may contribute to the educational debate. This might be done through a circulation of the ideas which will be generated to the government and to the teachers' trade union. Thus, the assumption that inspectors are responsible for producing curriculum policy and teachers for implementing this policy may be questioned.

Obviously, this suggestion is mainly based on using a network model and can be criticised as a broadly unsystematic approach for curriculum change (Boyd 1984: 108) with too much reliance on the voluntary participation of teachers. It can be also argued that this strategy assumes that the teacher-members of the association will influence their colleagues' perceptions. However, this is an assumption that needs to be tested empirically. Nevertheless, this is only a short-term strategy which attempts to generate opportunities for reflective professionalism that can form a comprehensive vision. But this attempt depends on those few teachers who despite the system will try to change the structure of the system and contribute to the change of teachers' culture.

In conclusion, this paper may provide Cypriot teachers, heads, inspectors, and researchers with suggestions on how they could work, individually and together, for a reconceptualisation of the process of curriculum change in Cyprus. Change is not an easy task since it is a matter of changing culture but there are only two ways to respond to the challenge of change. We could either adopt the requirements of the system passively or attempt to take charge, despite the dominant perceptions about how the 'system' should operate. Thus, the improvement of schools depends on those individuals who will be persuaded that they should choose the latter rather than the former mode and attempt to become collaborative change agents.

References

Adams, S.R. and Cohen, D. (1981). *The process of educational innovation: An international Perspective.* London, Kogan Press/ Paris, The UNESCO Press.

Boyd, J. (1984). *Understanding in Primary Curriculum.* London, Hutchinson.

Calderhead, J. (1987). (Ed) *Exploring Teachers Thinking.* London, Cassell.

Campbell, R.J. (1985). *Developing the Primary School Curriculum.* London, Holt Rinehart and Winston.

Council of Europe (1984). *Symposium in the Management of Innovation in Primary Education.* Strasbourg, Council for Cultural Co-operation.

Council of Europe (1974). *Educational Research Policy in European Countries: 1973 Survey.* Strasbourg, Documentation Centre for Education in Europe.

Doyle, W. (1986). 'Classroom Organisation and Management' In M.C. Wittrock (Ed) *Handbook of Research on Teaching, 3rd Edition* New York, MacMillan.

Epstein, J.L. (1986). 'Parents' Reaction to Teacher Practices of Parent Involvement' *The Elementary School Journal, 86* (3), 277-294.

Epstein, J.L.(1987) 'Parent Involvement: What research says to administrators *Education and Urban Society 19*, 119-36.

Fullan, M. (1991) *The New Meaning of Educational Change.* London, Cassell.

Fullan, M. (1993). *Change Forces / Probing the Depths of Educational Reform.* London, The Falmer Press.

Fullan, M. and Hargreaves, A. (Eds) (1992). *Teacher Development and Educational Change.* London, The Falmer Press.

Georgiou, S. N. (1996). Parental Involvement in Cyprus *International Journal of Educational Research, 25* (1) 33-43.

Karagiorgis, A.G. (1986). *Education Development in Cyprus 1960-1977* Nicosia.

Kyriakides, L. (1994). *Primary Teachers' Perceptions of Policy for Curriculum Reform in Cyprus with Special Reference to Mathematics.* Unpublished doctoral dissertation, University of Warwick, Coventry.

Kyriakides, L. (1996). 'Reforming' Primary Education in Cyprus *Education 3-13, 24* (2), 46-50.

Kyriakides, L. (1997a). Influences on Primary Teachers' Practice: some problems for curriculum change theory *British Educational Research Journal, 23* (1), 39-46.

Kyriakides, L. (1997b). *School Based Curriculum Development in Primary Schools of Cyprus: Implications for curriculum change theory.* Nicosia, Pedagogical Institute.

Kyriakides, L. (1998). 'Teachers' and headteachers' perceptions about headteachers' role for school effectiveness' Proceedings of the 7th National Conference of the Association of Cypriot Primary Headteachers (pp 61-87) Nicosia.

Lortie, D.C. (1975). *Schoolteacher.* Chicago, University of Chicago Press.

MacDonald, B. (1991) 'Critical Introduction From Innovation to Reform - A Framework for Analysing Change' In J. Rudduck (Ed) *Innovation and Change: Developing Involvement and Understanding* Milton Keynes, Open University Press.

Ministry of Education (1990). *Development of Education:1988-90 National Report* Presented in International Conference on Education 42nd Session, Geneva.

Mortimore, P.; Sammons, P.; Stoll, L.; Lewis,D. and Ecob, R. (1988). *School Matters: The Junior Years.* London, Open Books.

Pedagogical Institute (1996a). *Evaluation of the New Curriculum in Primary Science.* Nicosia, Pedagogical Institute.

Pedagogical Institute (1996b). *Seminaria epimorfosis (INSET Optional Courses of P.I.)*. Nicosia, Pedagogical Institute.

Phtiaka, H. (1996). Each to his own? Home-school relations in Cyprus *Forum of Education, 51* (1), 47 - 59.

Rosenholtz, S.J. (1989a). *Teachers' Workplace: The Social Organisation of Schools*. New York, Longman..

Rosenholtz, S.J. (1989b) 'Workplace Conditions that Afffect Teacher Quality and Commitment: Implications for Teacher Induction Programs' *The Elementary School Journal, 89* (4), 421-439.

Schon, D.A. (1971). *Beyond the Stable State*. Harmondsworth, Penguin.

Schon, D.A. (1983). *The Reflective Practitioner* London, Temple Smith.

Shipman, M.D. (1973). 'The Impact of a Curriculum Project' *Journal of Curriculum Studies, 5* (2), 47-56.

Shipman, M.D. with Bolam, D. and Jenkins, D. (1974). *Inside a Curriculum Project*. London, Methuen.

Shipman, M.D. (1985). 'Ethnography and Educational Policy- Making' In R.G. Burgess (Ed.) *Field Methods in the Study of Education*. London, The Falmer Press.

Skilbeck, M. (1990). *Curriculum Reform: An Overview of Trends* Paris, OECD.

Sophianos, C. (1978). *Basic Issues of Educational Policy* Nicosia, Ministry of Education.

Sutherland, A. (1981). *Curriculum Projects in Primary Schools: An Investigation of Project Adoption and Implementation in 185 Northern Ireland Schools*. Northern Ireland Council for Educational Research.

Torrance, H. (1989). 'Theory, Practice and Politics in the Development of Assessment' *Cambridge Journal of Education, 19* (2), 183-191.

Turnbull, B.J. (1985) 'Using Governance and support systems to advance school improvement' *The Elementary School Journal, 85* (3), 337-351.

UNESCO (1997). *Appraisal Study on the Cyprus Education System*. Paris, IIEP.

Wise, A. (1977). 'Why Educational Policies Often Fail: The Hyperrationalisation Hypothesis' *Curriculum Studies, 9* (1), 43-57.

Wise, A. (1979). *Legislated Learning*. Berkeley, University of California Press.

Yaxley, B.G. (1991) Developing Teachers' Theories of Teaching: A Touchstone Approach London, The Falmer Press.

Zeichner, K.M.; Tabachnick, R.B.; and Densmore, K. (1987). 'Individual, Institutional, and Cultural Influences on the development of teachers' craft knowledge' In Calderhead, J. (Ed) *Exploring Teachers Thinking* London, Cassell.

8.

Inequality and school effects: school effectiveness research in France

Denis Meurat

The political and social context of educational effectiveness in France

For a long time, the political environment was not favourable to school effectiveness research, but important changes have happened recently. Until about 1980, the idea that some schools could be more effective than others appeared to be almost impossible in a centralised system like the French one. The school level was simply not relevant. Since the eighties, however, through a growing consciousness that uniformity did not guarantee either effectiveness or equity, the autonomy of schools increased in such a way that, today, the proportion of decisions which are taken at the school level in the public system is about the same as in US and German public schools (OCDE, 1995)[1]. In some areas, it is possible, under certain limitations, to choose one's school (Ballion, 1991) while, for some time, middle class parents have developed a consumer's attitude towards schooling (Ballion, 1982).

Moreover, as elsewhere, the idea has spread that educational effectiveness had to increase in order to enhance both economic productivity in a more competitive environment and social cohesion in a situation of high unemployment and growing social inequalities. Schools were seen by educational decision-makers as an important level in that perspective. Concrete decisions were taken to increase autonomy at the school level, and also to develop the culture of evaluation. For instance, France is, as far as the author knows, the only country (with Scotland) where all secondary schools are provided with indicators allowing schools to compare themselves with the regional and national means and with other schools. Among these indicators are some kinds of 'value added' indicators (Emin, 1995).

However, incentives for schools to be more effective remained weak: Inspection addresses almost exclusively individual teachers. Inspections at the school level are exceptional. The possibility for parents and pupils to be listened to at this level is limited.

Moreover, while the state transferred some prerogatives to the schools, teachers picked these up to a far lesser degree. Teaching remained an individual activity. Only a small proportion of teachers found the action at the school level relevant. Therefore, the practice of self evaluation and planning is rather weak at this level, regardless of the indicators provided by the administration.

These are strong factors for limiting evaluation and planning at the school level, and, as a consequence, limiting school effectiveness research.

Another hindrance to the development of research into school effectiveness - or educational effectiveness in general - comes from the intellectual climate, especially among educational researchers. School effectiveness research has, in their eyes, three main handicaps:

- it is not grounded on a theory, which makes it a low level intellectual activity.

- it is potentially useful, which makes it closer to engineering than to scientific research.

- Governments (left or right) are interested in its results. Therefore research is susceptible to losing its 'critical' dimension.

In fact, with the notable exception of IREDU (Institut de recherche en économie de l'éducation, Dijon), few centers of educational research are able to reach international standards in quantitative research on educational effectiveness. For that reason, a lot of the bibliography of this account will be composed of studies published by the Ministry of Education, in which the Direction de l'Evaluation et de la Prospective [2] makes many efforts to promote a culture of evaluation (Thélot, 1994).

For that reason also, research related to educational effectiveness has often been done by sociologists (Dubet et al, 1989; Ballion et al, 1991; Cousin et Guillemet, 1992[3]) or by economists (Direction de l'Evaluation et de la Prospective, 1994), or even by foreign educational researchers (Grisay,1990, 1993, 1997), more than by French educational researchers. As we will see, however, this situation also gives French research on school effectiveness its singularity (more focused on the production of inequalities, for example), which may be of some interest to the international school effectiveness movement.

Brief history of the research on schools and school effects in France

The research on schools in France is less a cumulative process than a succession of attempts, coming from different theoretical frameworks, to explain school functioning.

When researchers began to be interested in schools, their first question was not their effectiveness but their singularity. How can the schools be so different, if they share the same national curriculum and teachers with the same training?

The Sociology of Organisations, a field where Michel Crozier is a leading figure in France, was the first to try to answer this question. The study of Dominique Paty (1980) is the main example. She studied twelve middle schools, and discovered in each of them a prominent feature that, according to her, gave the whole functioning of the school its singularity and its coherence.

Ballion et al (1991) had a more ethnological approach. The co-authors were specialists in the enthnography of the company, and their work was a comparison between schools and more traditional forms of productive organisations. They insisted on the artisanal and individual character of the process of production in schools, the non-cumulative aspect of the teaching time (every school year is a new period), the weakness of what would look like the planning or method function in a company, and more generally, on the small number of occasions where the school was really the relevant level of decision-making: sharing of some resources, orientation of the students inside the school, and almost nothing else.

This study was a useful response to ideological discourses promoting the idea that schools were like the other businesses, but, instead of discovering what kind of organisations the schools were, it led to the conclusion that schools were more or less non-organisations, or, if any, more like the Mintzberg 'professional bureaucracy' than anything else.

Derouet's (1987, 1989) work comes from a more specific theory, a political sociology which aimed at explaining the process through which actors reach the kind of agreement which allows them to work together (Boltanski et Thévenot, 1987). Derouet argues that the time when all teachers share the same values is finished. Several 'principles of justice' can now help actors to give a sense to their task, and, he argues, the school is the place where actors, referring to diverse principles have to find compromises, or agreements of other kinds (for example, ignoring each others' view), in order to work and live together. He studies how some events become tests for compromise or agreement and are the occasion for some changes in them.

For researchers like Derouet, this kind of comprehension of the school process without regard to its outcomes is necessary to deal (on valid theoretical bases) with the question of the effectiveness of the school. To look for what are the schools' real purposes (or objectives) is, of course, prior to the measurement of effectiveness. For them, 'effectiveness', as used in the school effectiveness research, means only the ability to reach certain kinds of objectives, measurable through quantitative methods, and has only an appearance of generality and neutrality. In reality, the effectiveness approach is embedded in one particular principle of justice, which Derouet calls 'industrial', and which is characterised by quantitative measurement of school performances.

It is probably unavoidable that the research on schools should be shared by two antagonistic camps, one of which takes into account what the official objectives of schools might be (to make children learn, for example) and one which tries to show that the rationality of schools is not the official one. It is true that the ethical and political relevance of school effectiveness research cannot be greater than the objectives it assumes for schools. It is true also that research with no reference to what society expects from education, research which considers as equivalent all objectives that the actors could have, is in risk of futility.

However, this kind of research has some interest for school effectiveness. For instance, although French educational authorities and most of the anglo-saxon research insist on the coherence of teaching practices, the sharing of the same goals, the same 'spirit', and the like, we find in Chauveau (1995) and especially in Grisay (1993), the idea that most, or at least some, effective schools are not warm teams sharing the same enthusiasm for the same goals, but places where peaceful and positive agreements of limited scope have been found between teachers. In other words, Mintzberg's adhocracy[4], which is often proposed to schools as an alternative model to 'professional bureaucracy', appears to be not fully in coherence with the real conditions of work inside schools.

Not all research on schools share this view on school outcomes. The first French studies on school effects were Liensol et Meuret (1987), Duru et Mingat (1987, 1988), and Dubet et al (1989).

Liensol and Meuret calculated performances of 210 senior high schools with value added indicators[5] The objective was less to measure school effects, than to show that 'league tables' (which were published by newspapers on the basis of simply the rate of success to the baccalauréat) were misleading indexes for the effectiveness of schools in preparation for the baccalauréat. Results also showed that the performances of a third of the schools were dramatically different from one year to the other, and that differences between schools were substantive, although they were less important than when measured by the rate of success.

Duru and Mingat's concern was also not directly school effectiveness, but more a contribution to the sociology of social inequities in school careers. Duru and Mingat wanted to investigate the specific role of classrooms and schools in the production of these inequalities. During the period of the study, pupils at the end of grade 7 either passed to grade 8, repeated, or were oriented towards vocational schooling. The object of the study was to consider the predictors of the probability of passing into grade 8. A sample of 2500 pupils attending grade 7 in 1982-83 was studied. Some fundamental results were obtained:

- Among pupils with the same achievement level, as measured by test, high SES pupils had better marks and more chances to enter grade 8. Among pupils with the same marks, again high SES pupils had more chances to pass. The inequality of probability to pass between high and low SES pupils was explained more by this kind of bias than by the differences in achievement between the two groups.

- Among the pupils of a given school, this bias disappears almost completely. It appears to result from differences between schools regarding:
    (i)   marking,
    (ii) severity of orientation among pupils with the same marks, and
    (iii) different weighting of the criteria implicitly used to select those pupils who would pass among the number admitted to pass.

- The part of variance explained by the inclusion of schools or classrooms in the models, after considering the individual characteristics of the pupils was different regarding progression of achievement, marking and orientation. Classroom characteristics figured higher for the progression of achievement, but school characteristics figured higher for the orientation. School and classrooms added about the same quantity of explanation for marking.

Significantly, Duru and Mingat chose to investigate how the differences of orientation, and not of progression, were produced.

However, regarding marking, they proposed the interesting result that, among the mark gap of 2.2 points between children of workers and of executives, 1 point is explained by differences in knowledge acquisition during grades 6 and 7, 0.5 is explained by a marking bias in favour of executive children and only the remaining is explained by differences of achievement during the primary schooling.

For pupils with the same age and marks, the probability to pass is higher for pupils attending large schools, with a high mean achievement level of the student body. It is lower for schools with a high proportion of low SES pupils; for pupils of mean age and marks, and for a given SES, the probability to pass may vary from 48% to 95%.

Dubet and al. (1989) studied three middle schools with rather the same student body. One is very dynamic, with innovative teachers, with a little team of teachers around the school leader that defines the school 'spirit'. The second is more traditional, with a bureaucratic school leader, where little happens at school level, but with teachers very engaged in their individual tasks. Pupils felt good when in classrooms, but very bad in other places of the school. The third college is shared between two groups of staff which did not share the same pedagogical values, it is a peaceful, dynamic, warm place outside classrooms, and is harsh and highly hierarchical inside the classrooms. Although they are aware of the weakness of their measures of school outcomes, the authors propose as a conclusion that the effect of the collective mobilisation is probably low on global effectiveness, but probably important for the progression of low SES children, which may be seen as in line with Grisay (1990) results.

What might be called true school effectiveness studies, that is, dealing directly with the questions related to whether some schools are more effective, and why, and presenting standard quality samples, measurements and analysis, only came about in the 1990s.

The French school effectiveness studies

Primary schools: the Bressoux study

This study (Bressoux, 1993) is on school and classroom effectiveness for reading improvement between grade 2 and grade 5, that is, after the main phase of learning in reading which occurs in grade 1. The first phase was between grade 2 and grade 5, from January 1989 to March 1990. A sample of 60 schools and 2486 pupils was considered. The second phase was between grade 3 and 5, from March 1990 to May 1991, in the same schools (2512 pupils). Validity of the tests was satisfactory (KR > 0.87). The independent variables which were related to classrooms and school effectiveness were defined *a priori*.

No relationship was found between classroom effectiveness and classroom size, student body (mean achievement, percent of low achievers, low SES, minority pupils, heterogeneity of the initial score in reading), gender of the teacher, time devoted to the learning of reading, teaching in small groups or in front of the whole class, relations with parents. Three variables appeared to have an impact: school leaders (who in French primary schools teach in a classroom) are more effective than other teachers, teachers' expectations, and numbers of grades in the same classroom, with classrooms having two or three grades being more effective.

It was found that classroom 'equity' - a smaller gap between progressions of low and high achievers - increased with the time devoted to oral learning and the absence of grouping according to the reading level, all being favourable to equity. A high proportion of low SES pupils is related to inequity.

School effects appear to be less important than classroom effects: 4% (versus 11%) of the variance of the final score is due to classroom effects in a model where the school level (the classroom level) is introduced after the initial score and the social characteristics of the pupils. Regarding school effectiveness, the main findings were:

- Effective schools appear to be generally also more equitable. This result was also found by Grisay (1993) for the first two years of secondary schooling.

- There is a moderate correlation between the effectiveness of same schools in the two phases (r = 0.31).

- There is no link between effectiveness and the size of the school, the school student body[6], the stability of the staff, and whether or not the school leader is in charge of a classroom.

Unhappily, other dimensions of the schooling process were not available.

Another study on primary schools is Chauveau and Rogovas-Chauveau (1995). They studied twelve effective primary schools in ZEP (Zones d'éducation prioritaire, Educational priority areas). This study presents strong methodological weaknesses, as the authors themselves recognise, including: there is no control group; the indications on school process were gathered only through a small number of interviews with teachers, directors, inspectors; no investigation was made of pupils' opinions, and no real longitudinal approach of effectiveness was made. However, results are in line with major trends of the school effectiveness research, although they probably stress too much exclusively on the relations between teachers, as a result of the investigation method.

Main characteristics of these schools are: a peaceful climate, focus on academic areas, especially on reading, no strong pedagogical ideology shared by all teachers, but agreement on coexistence of different pedagogical approaches, teachers are in the school for several years and do not want to leave it, a good and collaborative climate between teachers, a good judgement on the school leader by teachers and inspectors, teachers do not dislike their pupils and have positive expectations for them.

Secondary schools: the Grisay studies

The first school effectiveness study in France was completed by A. Grisay (Service de Pédagogie expérimentale, Université de Liége, Belgique) in 1990. It was a secondary analysis of data gathered in 60 middle schools for the evaluation of a national sample of pupils from 1980 to 1984. The number of process variables was reduced by the type of data available. An index of effectiveness was calculated by regression of a final test (Mathematics and French) on an initial one. The final test occurred two years after the initial one. The results of this study were:

- Middle schools with high SES pupils are generally more effective than those with low SES pupils. However, some low SES schools are fairly effective. This result was found again in the second - and main - Grisay study (see below).

- Predictors of effectiveness are not the same depending on the student body. In high SES effective schools, the discipline is rigorous, the climate is rather impersonal, the homework is important, opportunity to learn is especially high in mathematics.

  In the rare high SES ineffective schools, the pupils as well as the school leader describe the climate as really bad (noise, aggressiveness, robberies, although the discipline is strong), the initial achievement of the pupils is heterogeneous, parents are rather severe, but are said by their children not to help them at home. Good pupils often leave these schools after one or two years.

- Low SES effective schools have a heterogeneous student body - they are not uniquely attended by low SES or underachieving pupils, a rather small number of pupils, teachers are young and demanding, opportunity to learn is high, climate is peaceful and warm, teachers have rather friendly relations with pupils and frequent relations with parents.

- Low SES ineffective schools are characterised by low requirements and by what Grisay calls an 'impression of distance' between pupils and their teachers, pupils and parents, teachers and the parents. Such a distinction between factors of effectiveness in low and high SES schools, however, did not appear so clearly in the second Grisay study.

In 1988, The Direction de l' Evaluation et de la Prospective asked Aletta Grisay to lead a longitudinal study on school effectiveness in French middle schools. The designing of the sample, of the instruments, and the gathering of the information was made in collaboration with the SPE and the Direction de l'Evaluation et de la Prospective. Some inspectors, teachers and principals participated in the design of the instruments. This study is notable for:

- The size of the sample (100 schools, with, in each school, a random sample of 80 pupils entering grade 6). In the course of the four years, most pupils left these schools. As far as possible, other pupils, whose characteristics were the same as those who left, were included in the sample in order to maintain a high number of individuals. The size of the sample allowed a lot of analysis involving sub samples (rural schools, deprived area schools, see below).

- The wide range of outcomes on which schools were assessed: French and mathematics, but also: locus of control, study skills, civic attitudes, self perception, motivation, inclination towards cooperation, towards competition, sociability.

- The collection of a wide range of data on school processes, and classroom processes through questionnaires answered by pupils, teachers and school principals.

- The quality of the constructs: All of them came from data analysis, and their alpha reliability is generally high.

- The attempt to look for joint effects of process and inputs. In other words, the value added by the school is calculated by regression only on the initial test, and the residual is shared in three parts: one which is related to the process of schooling, one which is related to the SES status of the pupils and their age when entering the school, and one which is related to the fact that, presumably, best/high SES students are placed in better conditions of work. The idea is that, when regressing on both SES and initial level, it is assumed that the SES is only an external factor. If high SES students perform better also because they are in better schools, then this traditional method underestimates the schools effects [7].

A diagnosis of the school has been returned to each of the hundred schools involved in the study, and explained during six meetings held in six regions, with roughly a dozen school leaders or/and teachers attending these meetings. They showed great interest in the diagnosis, which means probably that schools would consider with interest the possibility of calculating for themselves indicators issued from the school effectiveness research.

The first phase of the study (Grisay, 1993) ran from 1990 to 1992 and covered the first two years of secondary schooling. A second phase ran on the same cohort during the following two years, with minor changes in the questionnaires (more concern about civic knowledge and attitudes, and on the role of the principal (see Sacré, 1997). Grisay (1997) is an account of both phases. Regarding school effectiveness, main findings of the study are:

- While the students' two year progress is significant in mother language and mathematics, as documented by the anchor items, only a little improvement appears in civics and no improvement at all in study skills. The pupils' attitude towards school seems to deteriorate: a negative evolution is observed in the interest in school, locus of control, motivation, and verbal aggression.

- The between school variance, as well as the school effect (4% of the variance), appear to be moderate for academic achievement, and even less for all the cross curriculum criteria. However, the second phase of the study, which put more emphasis on the classroom level through multi-linear modelling, found that the between classrooms variance for academic achievement was rather high for schools which are supposed to be comprehensive.

- Some variables appear to have a positive effect on both academic and several attitude scores: good climate (pupils need to be treated with consideration and fairness, they express a positive judgement on their teachers attitude and skills, they see their teachers as willing to help all pupils to learn, even the weakest), little time is lost through truancy, lateness or behavioural problems, pupils do know the rules of the school, and there is extensive opportunity to learn. But these variables are highly correlated with high SES student bodies. In fact, it appears that almost all the student body effect belong to the joint variance, that is: almost all the supposed external effect appears to be an internal one.

- Only few variables which are directly under the control of policy decisions at the school level appear to have an impact on academic effectiveness: knowledge of the school rules by the pupils, the principal often comes into the classrooms, remedial structures of diverse kinds exist in the school (methodology courses, help for pupils with difficulty), careful monitoring of truancy.

- Curiously enough, it was found in the first phase of the study that, while the human climate was a predictor of academic effectiveness, some characteristics of the academic process were predictors of effectiveness for some cross-curriculum scores. For instance, structured instruction was a predictor of better progress for study skills and locus of control scores.

- The variance of the answers of the teachers is almost as high inside each school than for the whole sample of teachers. Teaching appears to be a very individual activity. Therefore, it is no surprise to see that, often, innovative teaching practices are associated with a lack of coherence in the teaching practices. In this case, innovation is not associated with effectiveness. However, in some effective schools, innovative practices are associated with coherence of practices.
- Homogeneous grouping is negatively related to school equity.
- Parental interventions seem also to be important, especially for study skills and interest in school and especially for pupils with academic difficulty when they enter the school.

Many secondary analyses were made of the data constructed by A. Grisay including those by Meuret (1994); Trancart (1994); Meuret (1995); Trancart (1995); Meuret and Marivain (1997); Sacré (1997).

Meuret (1994) used LISREL modelling to assess the effectiveness of the ZEP policy. Using, unlike Grisay, regression on both initial achievement and SES, he found that, ten years after the beginning of the policy, the ZEP schools were still less effective than non ZEP schools regarding academic achievement, and that the gap between ZEP and non ZEP was higher for low SES pupils than for middle SES ones, for pupils with low initial scores than for the others, for foreign pupils than for French ones. However, he found no significant difference in effectiveness between ZEP and non ZEP schools regarding study skills, motivation, sociability, civic attitudes. He found also that some ZEP schools were highly effective academically, and therefore advocated in favour of a monitoring of the policy focusing on the results obtained inside each school.

Meuret and Marivain (1997a,b) studied the inequality of well-being among pupils, using again LISREL, to study the factors of well-being. They define well being as a tridimensional construct: feeling of success, happiness, status. Predictors of well-being are, by decreasing order of importance, judgements on the personal and professional quality of the teachers; support, expectations, and confidence from the home; then, with less importance, rights and responsibilities in school life, absence of delinquency, then, with still less importance, the initial level of the pupils in Mathematics and French, and, with strictly no influence, the merit or the effort of the pupil, of which the residual of their academic progression was taken as an index.

They found significant inequalities of well-being between individuals, smaller inequalities between categories of pupils (with low SES pupils feeling

worse than high or middle SES, boys feeling worse than girls), and little
school variance between schools, as well as little school effects on well-being,
except for low SES children. Children generally feel better in schools where
cooperation is praised more than competition. However, some other
predictors of school effects appear to be dependent on the pupil SES. Low
SES children feel better in schools where positive relations exist with their
parents and which are effective regarding motivation. High and middle SES
children feel better in schools where press for achievement is not too high. If
one considers that equity calls for equality of well-being between pupils, as
well as if one considers that equity calls for proportionality between effort and
well-being, the distribution of well-being among pupils appears to be
inequitable.

Sacré (1997) uses the data gathered in the Grisay study to investigate the
link between school leadership and effectiveness. Main results are:

- When teachers describe their school centres of interest, interest for the
  work of the pupils comes last in the list, after for instance human
  relations management, and looking for the coherence of the objectives.
  When school leaders themselves rank their activities, interest for the
  work of pupils also comes last.

- Answers from school leaders on their own activities present a strong
  bias for desirability. Therefore, when trying to look for relations
  between school leader behaviour and the characteristics of school
  functioning, Sacré relied only on the description of this behaviour by
  the teachers.

- Using these answers, the difference which appears between school
  leaders is linear: some appear to have positive behaviour (19 schools),
  others negative (18 schools) but the majority has a balanced judgement
  (59 schools).

- There appears to be some differences between schools from the
  'positive' and the 'negative' group. In the former, opportunity to learn
  is high, pupils receive more structured teaching, have a more positive
  judgement on their teachers, and feel better; they have a strong sense
  of competence, they felt they were treated with more justice and with
  more consideration.

- However, no significant relationship appears between 'positive',
  'negative' and 'lambda' groups regarding effectiveness, be it with
  regard to academic effectiveness (progress in French and mathematics),
  to the development of working skills, to the inclination to cooperation,
  to civics attitude, or to sociability.

The results of this study are interestingly diverse from most Anglo Saxon results, since school leadership frequently appears as one of the main effectiveness factors. According to the author, the main reason for that is probably not that school leaders would have less autonomy in France than in other countries (see OCDE, 1995), but the fact that they have perhaps less influence on the teachers, are less involved in pedagogical domain and are perhaps less in contact with students. For instance, only 18% indicated they assist sometimes in courses, and only 18% indicated that he/she sometimes invited pupils into his/her office to congratulate them.

Trancart's (1993) study is about children who appear to be in a difficult situation when beginning middle school (with both low achievements and former repetitions). During their first year of secondary schooling, the level in mathematics and French of these pupils makes some progress, which is not the case for their behaviour and attitude towards schooling. At the end of their second year of secondary schooling one in five of these pupils may be considered to be not in difficulty any more. The relation between the progress of the pupils with difficulty and school processes has been studied with multivariate modelling (HLM). School effect accounts for about 8% of the variance. The well-being of the pupils, their rights and responsibilities in school life and discipline decisions, have positive effects on achievement. Delinquency rate and teachers thinking that pupils' failure is the fault of the pupils themselves have negative links with achievement.

Trancart (1995) found no difference between urban and rural middle schools regarding effectiveness in French, study skills and civic attitudes. Rural middle schools appeared to be slightly more effective for mathematics. Low SES children had better progression in rural schools than in urban middle schools, perhaps because the SES is in fact not exactly the same or because rural schools are more effective for them. This result is true for mathematics, French, study skills and motivation. High SES pupils have a lower self image in rural middle schools than in urban ones.

Conclusion

It is difficult to predict the future of school effectiveness research in France. There is no centre of research for which it would be an important part of the activity. There is a growing interest in France for educational effectiveness, but the main institutions in the field are more interested in the teacher or policy level than in the school one. Results of school effectiveness studies themselves have somewhat been interpreted as showing that school effects were weak. Moreover a cultural gap remains between the institution mainly in charge of evaluation (The 'inspection générale') and the culture of teachers on the one hand and the school effectiveness approach on the other.

Opportunity could be given by the perspective of an international research activity or if some new prerogatives were given to schools. But, as far as the author knows, there is no such perspective in the current political agenda.

What could be the specific French contribution to the school effectiveness research? Perhaps this. We can distinguish two kinds of school effects: compositional effects, which are a direct consequence of the school student body, and policy effects which are the effects of malleable variables. The Grisay study shows that the school process is highly dependent from the student body. Therefore, the distinction between compositional and policy effect is not so clear, and this appears to play a major role in generating inequalities of achievement among pupils or among categories of pupils.

Most effectiveness predictors appear more easily in schools with high achieving/high SES pupils. Moreover, most of them seem to belong to a kind of snowball process, or to improvement cycles, such as having a good initial level of effectiveness, leading to easier teaching, more opportunity to learn, greater expectations, greater well-being, better judgement of teachers, less discipline problems, which in turn leads to more effectiveness, then better levels, and so on. Only four variables from the Grisay study can be considered as escaping from this kind of cycle and are true malleable variables.

This is a rather disappointing idea. If effective school processes do occur mainly when some conditions regarding the student body are met, it is not so easy to transfer the processes of effective schools to non-effective schools. This, however, can be considered as an indication for the need for further research.

One hypothesis could be: If effectiveness appears to be essentially a kind of indirect effect of the student body, it is precisely because effectiveness is not, as a matter of fact, the objective of most schools. It could therefore be interesting to design an effectiveness study on a sample of schools really deciding to look for effectiveness, with standardised tests being used in the normal process of schooling, and careful monitoring of the progress of all pupils.

Attention has to be paid to what can initiate improvement cycles, that is, the order of appearance of the variables in a dynamic perspective. This is perhaps an interesting kind of link between the school effectiveness and school improvement approaches.

Notes

1   About 20% of the pupils attend private (but granted by the state) schools. All studies reported here, however, deal only with public schools, with the exception of Liensol and Meuret (1987b), which showed no mean differences between the effectiveness of private and public senior high schools for the preparation to the baccalauréat, but that private schools were over-represented among very effective as well among very ineffective schools. Public senior high schools appeared to be more effective for low SES students, and private schools for high SES and high achieving students. However, this study was conducted only on 50 public and 39 private schools, from a unique region of France (Lorraine), without national representativity.

2   In December 1997, the Direction de l'Evaluation et de la Prospective was suppressed as such, and its former tasks were attributed to a 'Direction de la Programation et du développement'. Should this modification enhance the place of evaluation in the educational system is unlikely.

3   This study was a comparison of senior high schools with glowing performances with schools with decreasing performances, measured by 'valued added' indicators. The school functioning was analysed from interviews with teachers and school leaders.

4   'adhocratie' is an organisation where people are deeply engaged in the same, well identified 'project'. The NASA of the Apollo project is the paradigm of adhocratie.

5   This study did not use regression of a final test on an initial one but the calculation of an expected proportion of students passing the baccalauréat on the basis of the age and SES of pupils in this school. Then, the observed rate was compared to the expected one. The current indicators which are provided to schools (Emin, 1995) do use this method.

6   This result is not in line with Grisay's ones for secondary schooling be it because primary schooling is more egalitarian than the secondary, or because Bressoux models includes the SES as an external factor. (See discussion of this point here after).

7   See Bosker and Witziers, 1995, for a discussion on how to measure
      school effects.

References

Ballion, R. (1982), *Les consommateurs d'école*, Stock, Paris.
Ballion, R., Bayart, D. et Meyer,D. (1991) Le fonctionnement des lycées,
      étude de cas, *Dossier Education et Formations, 10*, Ministère de
      L'éducation nationale-Direction de l'Evaluation et de la Prospective. (All
      documents edited by Ministère de L'éducation nationale; Direction de
      L'Evaluation et de la Prospective may be ordered at Ministère de
      L'éducation nationale. Direction de L'Evaluation et de la Prospective,
      DEPA2, 58 Boulevard du lycée 92170 Vanves, France, Fax: 33 1 40 65
      72 29)
Ballion, R. *La bonne école*, Hatier, 1991.
Boltanski, C and Thévenot, L. (1987) *Les économies de la grandeur,
      Cahiers du centre d'études de l'emploi*, PUF.
Bosker, R and Witziers, B. (1995) 'School effects: problems, solutions and a
      meta analysis', Paper for the 1995 ICSEI congress in Leeuwarden.
Bressoux, P. (1993) 'Les performances des écoles et des classes', *Dossier
      Education et Formations, 30*, Ministère de L'éducation nationale-
      Direction de l'Evaluation et de la Prospective.
Bressoux, P. (1994) 'Les recherches sur les effets maîtres et les effets écoles',
      Revue Française de pédagogie, 108.
Bressoux, P. et al. (1996) *Aplication de l'analyse multiniveau à l'évaluation
      des politiques publiques en éducation, rapport de recherche pour le
      Commissariat général du Plan*, Paris.
Chauveau, G. et Rogovas Chauveau, E. (1995) Douze écoles efficaces, in
      l'Ecole efficace, Armand Colin, Paris.
Cousin, O. et Guillemet, J.P.(1992) 'Variations des performances scolaires et
      effet établissement', *Education et Formations, 35*, Ministère de
      L'éducation nationale- Direction de l'Evaluation et de la Prospective.
Derouet, J.L.(1987) 'Approches ethnographiques en sociologie de
      l'éducation : l'école, la communauté, l'établissement scolaire, la classe',
      Revue Française de pédagogie, 78.
Derouet, J.L. (1989) *L'établissement scolaire comme entreprise composite.
      Programme pour une sociologie des établissements scolaires, in Justesse
      et justice dans le travail*, Cahiers du centre d'études de l'emploi, PUF.
Dubet, F. et al. (1989) Mobilisation des collèges et performances scolaires,
      Revue Française de Sociologie, 30,n°2.

Duru-Bellat, M. et Mingat, A. (1987) Facteurs institutionnels de la diversité des carrières scolaires, revue française de sociologie, vol 28-1.

Duru- Bellat, M. et Mingat, A.(1988) 'Le déroulement de la scolarité au collège : le contexte ' fait des différences ', *Revue Française de Sociologie, 29*-4.

Duru-Bellat, M. et Mingat, A. (1993) *Pour une approche analytique du fonctionnement du système éducatif,* PUF, Paris.

Duru- Bellat, M. (1996) 'Social inequalities in french secondary schools : from figures to theories', *British Journal of sociology of education, 17,* 3.

Emin, J.C. (1995) *La mise en place d'un dispositif d'indicateurs pour le pilotage des établissements secondaires français, in Measuring the quality of schools,* OCDE-CERI.

Grisay, A. (1988) *Du mythe de la bonne école à la réalité (fuyante) de l'école efficace, Notes de recherche sur les performances des établissements scolaires,* Doc. ron., Service de Pédagogie expérimentale, Liège (Belgique).

Grisay, A.(1990) 'Des indicateurs d'efficacité pour les établissements scolaires', *Education et Formations, 22,* Ministère de l'éducation nationale- Direction de l'Evaluation et de la Prospective.

Grisay, A. (1993) 'Le fonctionnement des collèges et ses effets sur les élèves de sixième et de cinquième', *Dossiers Education et Formations, 32,* Ministère de l'éducation nationale- Direction de l'Evaluation et de la Prospective.

Grisay, A. (1995) 'Effective and less effective junior schools in France', Paper for the ICSEI congress in Leeuwarden, january 1995. (This paper is available at A. Grisay, Université de Liège, Service de Pédagogie expérimentale, 5 Bd du rectorat, Sart Tilman B4000 Liège Belgique).

Grisay, A. (1997) 'Evolution des acquis cognitifs et socio-affectifs des élèves au cours des années de collège', *Dossiers Education et Formations, 88,* Ministère de l'éducation nationale- Direction de l'Evaluation et de la Prospective.

Liensol, B. et Meuret,D. (1987a) 'Les performances des lycées pour la préparation au baccalauréat', *Education et formations 11* Ministère de l'éducation nationale- Direction de l'Evaluation et de la Prospective.

Liensol, B. et Meuret,D. (1987b) 'Les performances des lycées publics et privés pour la préparation au baccalauréat', *Education et formations 12,* Ministère de l'éducation nationale- Direction de l'Evaluation et de la Prospective.

Meuret, D. (1994) 'L'efficacité de la politique des zones prioritaires au début du collège', *revue Française de pédagogie, 109,* Paris.

Meuret, D. (1995) 'Schools and the production of inequalities, the case of French junior secondary schools', Paper for the ICSEI congress in

Leeuwarden, January 1995. (This paper and those following are available from D. Meuret, IUFM de Bretagne, 153, rue St Malo, 35000, Rennes).

Meuret, D. and Marivain, T. (1997a) 'Inequalities and conditions of well being in French junior secondary schools', Paper for the ICSEI congress in Memphis, January 1995

Meuret, D. et Marivain, T. (1997b) 'Inégalités de bien-être au début du collège', *Dossiers Education et Formations, 89*, Ministère de l'éducation nationale- Direction de l'Evaluation et de la Prospective.

Mintzberg, H. (1979) *The structuring of organisations : a synthesis of the research,* Prentice Hall.

Paty, D. (1980) *Douze collèges en France*, La documentation française, Paris.

Sacré, A. (1997) 'Une approche du rôle de la direction dans l'efficacité des collèges', *Education et Formations, 49*, Men-Direction de l'Evaluation et de la Prospective.

Thélot, C. (1994) *L'évaluation du système éducatif*, Nathan, Paris.

Trancart, D. (1993) 'Progrès cognitifs et non cognitifs et effet de l'établissement pour les élèves en difficulté au début du collège', *Education et Formations, 36*, Ministère de l'éducation nationale- Direction de l'Evaluation et de la Prospective.

Trancart, D. (1995) 'Performances et progression des élèves ruraux : Acquis cognitifs et non cognitifs', *Education et Formations, 43*, Ministère de l'éducation nationale- Direction de l'Evaluation et de la Prospective.

Direction de l'Evaluation et de la Prospective (1994), 'L'investissement éducatif et son efficacité', *Dossiers Education et Formations, 47*.

OCDE- CERI (1995) *Les processus de décision dans quatorze systèmes éducatifs de l'OCDE*, Paris.

9.

Recent developments in school effectiveness research in the Netherlands

Jaap Scheerens

Introduction

In their review of school effectiveness in the Netherlands, Scheerens and Creemers (1995: 192) concluded that enhancing school effectiveness did not rank high on the agenda of educational policy in the Netherlands.

Despite this relative lack of interest from policy makers they discerned a growing number of university-based studies on educational effectiveness issues. The outcomes of the studies conducted between roughly 1980 and 1994, which they reviewed, appeared to be disappointing in the sense that confirmation of conditions which appeared to be effectiveness-enhancing in other countries was quite inconsistent. Furthermore they noted several school improvement projects in which the knowledge base on educational effectiveness was well-integrated and used, the so called 'Friesland Project' in particular.

With the increased attention on assessment and monitoring they saw opportunities for empirical effectiveness research, because of the increase in availability of data sets which contain both outcome and relevant process and input variables.

In the current overview, some of the recent policy considerations, together with recently completed and initiated studies in school effectiveness and improvement will be described. Again some relevant parts of the political and societal context of effectiveness thinking and research will be addressed. This will lead to a re-assessment of the state of educational effectiveness in the final section.

Key trends in policy

In primary education there are five major policy initiatives, all emanating from the central level:

- The ongoing program to support schools in less advantaged areas, the so called educational priority policy.

- The program aimed at a stronger integration of 'regular' education and special education. The operational aim of this policy is to reduce the percentage of pupils in special schools.

- An almost accomplished policy of 'scaling up' primary schools. In many cases this means that originally separate schools in a local community become part of a network of schools with a common management and board.

- A fairly recent policy initiative to reduce class-size, particularly in the lower grades of the primary school. Currently the average class-size in primary schools in the Netherlands is among the highest in Western Europe.

- A policy aimed at the stimulation of 'quality care' and school self-evaluation.

In secondary education (upper level) the main policy initiative is major curricular reform emphasising general learning skills (learning to learn) and independent learning. This policy initiative also has its consequences for the lower secondary level, particularly in the sense of regrouping subject matter areas and a growing orientation towards independent learning.

Despite years of attempts by various coalition governments to make lower secondary education more comprehensive, the categorisation of the system has been preserved and is even sharpened in the sense that pupils' crucial school career decisions show a tendency of being taken at a fairly early age. An interesting new development in secondary education is the fact that the results of secondary schools (eg. the exam results) are now published in a newspaper. The Ministry has reacted by promising a more detailed 'school report' on each school that will be made public by the inspectorate.

Many of these policy decisions have been based, or are based, upon the need to improve the effectiveness of education within the Netherlands. A review of the research into effectiveness thus becomes critical to understanding many of these moves.

The state of effectiveness research

Interim results of the Twente research program

In their book 'The Foundations of School Effectiveness' Scheerens and Bosker (1997) present the results of a four-year study, subsidised by the (now abolished) Foundation for Educational Research (SVO). The study summarises the results of the ongoing research program on school effectiveness of the Department of Educational Organisation of the University of Twente. This program includes conceptual studies, development of models and theories, so called 'foundational' studies into various consistency issues (eg. stability over time) in educational effectiveness, review studies, meta-analyses and international comparative studies.

In spelling out the conceptual map of schooling the authors consider a broad range of possible *effects*, a set of points of impact or actions to attain particular effects, referred to as the *modes* of schooling (goals, organisational structure and procedures - including management, culture, environment and the technology of the primary process) and *functions or underlying mechanisms* that explain why actions impinged on certain modes lead to effect attainment. The rest of the book summarises results in terms of impact of the most frequently assessed modes on the predominant effectiveness criterion (productivity) and provides hints with respect to underlying principles.

According to Scheerens and Bosker alternative ways of modelling cross-level relationships (eg. between school organisational and instructional conditions) is the most promising direction for improvement and specifications of school effectiveness models. They give examples of multi-level analyses and applications of system dynamics as useful methodological approaches to bring this about.

With respect to the overall issue of consistency in school effectiveness their conclusion is that schools appear to be stable in effectiveness as long as the time interval is tight and if effectiveness is assessed at the formal end of a period of schooling. There is less stability in case of a longer time interval and when effects are measured in the beginning or in the middle of a certain level of schooling.

Considerable inconsistency in effectiveness measures when different subjects are assessed suggests that, particularly at the secondary level, *teacher* effects appear to dominate over *school* effects. With respect to differential school effects, i.e. differential for different groups of students, the conclusion is that schools matter most for underprivileged and/or initially low-achieving students.

An in-depth analysis of instruments used in school effectiveness and school self-evaluation studies leads to the conclusion that the operational definitions of the most common concepts are quite divergent. The following factors are considered: achievement orientation and high expectations, educational leadership, consensus and cohesion among staff, curriculum quality/opportunity to learn, school climate, evaluative potential, parental involvement, classroom climate, effective learning time, structured instruction, independent learning, differentiation, reinforcement and feedback.

In reviewing three major reviews (those by Levine & Lezotte (1990), Sammons, Hillman & Mortimore (1995) and Cotton (1995) Scheerens and Bosker conclude that there is a lot of consensus on the factors at school and classroom level that are considered to enhance effectiveness. This optimistic conclusion comes under fire when the results of empirical meta-analyses are brought into the picture. From their own meta-analysis the authors conclude that the impact of school organisational conditions like achievement orientation, leadership, monitoring/evaluation, cooperation among staff and parental involvement appears to be rather modest.

Results of re-analyses of an international assessment study (the IEA Reading Literacy study) show even weaker effects.

In the final chapters of the book the authors explore theory-embedded principles and a more theory-driven redirection of educational effectiveness research. According to their views a synoptic rational-planning proactive approach on the one hand and an evaluation feedback-oriented retro-active approach are the most promising effectiveness-enhancing mechanisms. In their own research program this has led to an increased emphasis on studying evaluation feedback mechanisms, for example within the context of school self-evaluation.

Dissertations

Since 1995 three doctoral theses in the domain of school effectiveness were published: Van der Velden, 1996; Heyl, 1996 and Lam, 1996. The central research question in Van der Velden's dissertation focused on the impact of the educational mission of primary schools on the achievement results of pupils from disadvantaged backgrounds (ethnicity and low SES). He re-analysed data from the national evaluation study on the impact of the so called Educational Priority Program. This is a policy program that provides schools with a high proportion of disadvantaged pupils with extra resources.

Achievement results in the domains of language and arithmetic were used as the effect variables, which were adjusted by taking into account scholastic aptitude and prior achievement. The added-value effect scores were related to school and classroom characteristics of 203 primary schools. Results were analysed by means of linear structural equations modelling (LISREL), in order to investigate direct and more indirect causal links between school and classroom factors on the one hand and achievement on the other.

The results show that there are significant differences between schools in overall school mission. A subject matter oriented perspective was contrasted with a 'reform pedagogic' pupil-oriented perspective.

The hypothesis that differences between these two types of school missions had an impact on teaching strategies was not supported by the data. School and classroom variables selected from the literature on school and instructional effectiveness showed, in general, no associations with the effect variables. Positive exceptions were small effects of systematic monitoring of student achievement and use of a particular differentiation model in the domain of arithmetic.

In his discussion of the results the author is critical about the validity of the school effectiveness model, among other things, because of the correlational nature of his own and most other studies. He recommends methodological refinements in future studies such as improved instrumentation and experimental designs.

Heyl's dissertation study looked into the functioning and impact of teachers' networks in secondary schools. His two central research aims were as follows:

- to check whether similarity in instructional behaviour of teachers is related to the intensity of their informal contacts;
- to explore the informal organisation of schools.

In this study consensus and cohesion in teaching behaviour was taken as an effectiveness-enhancing characteristic, an assumption that was not directly studied. Heyl applied an advanced methodology of studying social networks. Relationships between teachers were investigated by means of a crossed multilevel model. In this model the highest level consisted of schools, in combination with sender and receiver effects of teachers, while the second level consisted of the directed relationship between two teachers. The lowest level represented the level of the individual teacher.

Among schools there appeared to be important differences in the structure and intensity of contacts between teachers. Individual characteristics of teachers (eg. age, gender) as well as the subject matter area that was taught were factors that were associated with different patterns of interrelationships.

For example, there was more exchange among teachers in subjects like languages and social science on didactic approaches than among teachers in the domain of art and crafts. Principals and deputy principals appeared to be quite important in informal social networks. The question of whether lack of formal cooperation was compensated for by informal communication had to be rejected. There were at least as many instances where formal and informal communication appeared to be mutually reinforcing.

Some evidence was found for the thesis that the social and personal behaviour of teachers becomes influenced by social contacts with their colleagues. Several network characteristics appeared to be positively associated with the degree to which teachers showed friendly and understanding behaviour towards their pupils; which in its turn has been shown to be positively associated with pupils' achievement.

The third dissertation by Lam (1996) had instrument development with respect to 'time at school' as its main objective. A set of instruments for specific use by the inspectorate of primary education was developed and validated. Data concerning time to learn was collected by means of two logs titled 'educational time at school level' and 'educational time at classroom level' and by means of documentary analysis of school activity plans. Data concerning teacher behaviour and time on task was collected by means of classroom observations and interviews with teachers, with instruments that were titled 'quality of teaching' and 'time on task' respectively.

Various types of reliability and indices of congruent and construct validity were computed on pilot instruments, yielding at last instruments that met acceptable standards of psychometric quality.

On the assumption that several of the constructs that were operationally defined and instrumented in this study should show a positive association with achievement, a LISREL analysis was conducted to check this assumption; an investigation that in the context of this study was seen as a contribution to determining construct validity, but which in a different setting would be seen as a common school effectiveness study.

The results of the LISREL analysis showed acceptable fit of the model. The educational processes and the average SES-score of the school explained 28% of the variance in school average achievement. No significant effect of net learning time (time on task) could be shown.

Two more dissertations, one from GION (Van der Tuin) and one from the University of Twente (De Vos) are forthcoming. In Van der Tuin's dissertation both multi-level and structural modeling techniques are used to connect variables at pupil, classroom, department and school level, in a study directed at mathematics achievement in secondary schools. De Vos' dissertation titled 'Educational effects: A simulation-based analysis' uses system dynamics and simulation techniques to model multi-level and non-recursive relationships between school, classroom and pupil level variables.

Evaluations of school improvement projects

There are two currently ongoing school improvement programs in which the school effectiveness knowledge base is the main guiding principle in the shaping of improvement-oriented actions. The first is the National School Improvement Project, which is an extension of the 'Friesland-project referred to in Scheerens & Creemers' 1995 review, in which 28 primary schools participate. The aims of this project are:

- To implement an achievement-oriented school policy, focused on specific objectives in the domain of technical reading.
- To increase the evaluative potential of schools (i.e. stimulate the use of pupil monitoring systems and assessing the content that is covered during lessons).

Apart from these objectives that relate to the school level, the following sub-objectives at the teacher level were specified:

- The introduction of systematic planning approach to technical reading.
- Teacher training aimed at optimising effective learning time and direct instruction.
- Specific training in domain-specific didactics concerning technical reading.

(Houtveen, Booy, De Jong & Van de Grift, 1996: 8).

The project was evaluated over a three-year period, using a quasi-experimental research design. The evaluation results indicated that teachers had made substantial progress in the practice of efficient use of time and direct instruction approaches. At the level of group three project schools scored significantly higher, on average, than control schools on a technical reading test. At the level of grade four, this significant difference had disappeared, however. After this first evaluation follow-up programs have started in the domain of arithmetic, mathematics and reading comprehension.

A second ongoing school improvement project is a project in the city of Rotterdam aimed at fighting the lagging behind of disadvantaged learners. It takes place in schools with large percentages of ethnic minority pupils. It is aimed at improving achievement of this category of pupils in the domains of arithmetic/mathematics and language. The 'classical' five factor model of school effectiveness (strong educational leadership, high expectations of pupils' progress, basic skills emphasis, a safe and orderly climate and frequent monitoring of pupils' achievement) is used as the basic rationale for the improvement program.

In its actual implementation the use of 'direct instruction', geared to efficient classroom management increasing net learning time and frequent diagnostic testing appear to be the cornerstones of the program.

Existing textbooks and methods are enforced by means of a more detailed pre-structuring of the subject matter and an intensive and direct from of teacher counselling (so called classroom consultation). The first evaluation results are positive, both with respect to improved teacher behaviour and improved learning achievement (Hogendijk and Wolfgram, 1995).

Not so much a large-scale school improvement project but rather a national policy program is the 'educational priority policy', which provides schools in areas with a large proportion of ethnic minority and low SES pupils with extra resources and support. Attached to this policy program is a program evaluation in which achievement in language and reading is tested regularly and background characteristics of pupils, schools and classrooms are measured. The school effectiveness literature has strongly influenced the choice of school and classroom/ teaching variables so that the evaluation results are quite relevant for this line of empirical educational research.

Sontag and Meijnen (1995) looked for effects at the lowest grade of primary education, in a study that involved 28 schools, 35 teachers and 250 pupils. Pupils were tested twice for non-verbal intelligence and passive vocabulary knowledge. School-level variables included in the study were: staff consensus, teacher expectations and educational leadership. At the classroom level classroom climate, frequency of performance evaluation, emphasis on basic skills and age composition of classes were measured.

Multi-level analyses with test scores adjusted for SES, ethnicity, gender and pre-test scores, indicated that staff consensus was the only variable that had a significant positive association with achievement. The authors concluded that high staff consensus may contribute to a more favourable climate in the school as it leaves teachers more time and energy for educational activities (Note: the summary of this study is based on Van der Werf, 1995: 78-79).

Studies aimed at the higher grades of the primary school were constructed with respect to achievement data collected in 1988, 1990 and 1992 (Van der Werf, 1995). Multi-level analyses were carried out to determine whether schools differed from each other, after controlling for pupils' background characteristics, such as SES, ethnicity and intelligence. The between school variance ranged from 6 to 16% depending on the year of measurement and the subject matter area (with greater variance for arithmetic than for language).

The patterns of association of school and classroom characteristics with the effect variables are not convincingly supporting the factors that are known from the school effectiveness literature. For the 1988 data 'incidental' positive associations were found for whole-class instruction, the use of minimum objectives and homework, with the amount of homework showing the relatively largest effect. 'Incidental' in this sense means that effects were found only for a particular category of schools and not for all categories of schools and only for one, instead of both subject matter domains.

A telling blow for the effect of the policy program was the conclusion that the 'one thing that did not work' were the extra resources given to schools (Van der Werf, 1995: 80), which is in fact the heart of the educational priority program. Analyses of the 1990 and 1992 data roughly continued this picture. More in-depth study of schools with a majority of pupils from ethnic minority backgrounds indicated that the more effective schools created better opportunity to learn and effective learning time. More effective schools also appeared to have a more positive classroom climate, placed a stronger emphasis on reading comprehension and placed more emphasis on basic skills.

At the lower secondary level it was found that at this level the margins to improve the achievement of disadvantaged target groups are much smaller than at the primary level. School variables that appeared to matter at this level were: achievement-oriented policy and pupil guidance policy. The most effective instructional variables were: emphasis on basic skills and amount of homework; for ethnic minority pupils high expectations and high academic standards appeared to be particularly effective (Van der Werf, 1995: 91).

From the overview of the two improvement projects on the one hand and the national 'Educational Priority Program' on the other it can be concluded that targeted educational and instructional interventions show better results than more general, resources-oriented, stimulation programs where the actual educational improvement is more or less left to the discretion of individual schools, or community-based groups of schools.

Ongoing and recently started studies

Since 1993 the Dutch Foundation for Educational Research (SVO) funds a research program 'Educational Effectiveness' coordinated by Bert Creemers and Jaap Scheerens. The overall aim of this research program is to specify and empirically test integrated multi-level educational effectiveness models. Four sub-projects are currently in progress.

The first project explicitly addresses the combination of school and instructional effectiveness. The project, conducted by De Jong, develops a model about the relationship between effectiveness enhancing at the school and at the classroom level. The model builds upon the well-known Carroll model of school learning (Carroll, 1963). This model is revised and enlarged with factors at the school level in such a way that factors at the higher level are seen as conditions for factors at the lower level. The model was tested in 28 schools with 2 teachers in each school. Variables measured at the pupil level are: prior knowledge, intelligence, general and subject motivation, mathematics marks, time on task and mathematics achievement after one year of education. Teacher variables related to 'opportunity to learn' are measured by means of logs. The quality of instruction is assessed by trained observers. Interviews concerning cooperation among teachers and school organisational variables were administered to teachers. Multi-level analyses techniques are used to analyse the results.

In the second project, titled 'Alternative causal specifications of school effectiveness models' two partial studies have been conducted with respect to the consistency of effectiveness over subjects and grade levels and the stability of effectiveness over time. The project leader, Hans Luyten, found considerable differences within schools between subject matter areas and grade levels. Differences between teachers who teach the same grade to parallel classes are considerably smaller. With respect to stability over time for primary school effectiveness, a fair amount of stability, even over a five-year period, was found.

The third partial study makes a comparison between Dutch and Flemish mathematics results. Considering the fact that Dutch mathematics education is strongly influenced by constructivist views of mathematics teaching and Flemish mathematics education is more traditional, this comparison is meant to shed light on the comparative effectiveness of constructivist versus more traditional teaching practices.

The third project, conducted by Rispens and Lesemans, addresses effective instruction and stimulation of development in the preliminary education (the nursery grades of primary schools) in relationship to characteristics of the family.

The central research question of this study concerns the effect of teaching on the cognitive and social-emotional development of young children. Sub-questions refer to the impact of teacher and curriculum characteristics on these outcomes. The study has a longitudinal design (three measurement points) and comprises close monitoring of pupils for a period of one year. The methods of data collection in this study are: interviews with parents and teachers, testing of pupils and video recordings of social and instructive interactions in the classroom.

The fourth and last study of the educational effectiveness research program, conducted by Wubbels, Brekelmans and Brok, focuses on the role of the teacher in educational effectiveness. In-depth observation of teaching behaviour and classroom interaction is the methodological core of this study. Grade three English language lessons at the lower secondary level are studied. Communication is conceptualised in terms of an interpersonal and a learning-action perspective. The effect of these different types of interaction on English language achievement will be assessed. The results will be compared with those of an earlier study which involved science teachers. Finally differential effects with respect to gender and ethnicity will be investigated.

In 1996/1997 an important structural change took place in the available funding mechanisms for educational research in the Netherlands. For a period of 25 years SVO, the Foundation of Educational Research was the main founding agency. In 1996 SVO was abolished. Part of the budget (50% to be exact) was transferred to the Dutch Foundation of Scientific Research (NWO). Among the many implications of this change, there was a slight shift in the emphasis in applied versus fundamental research. Most SVO-grants were made available for applied studies, whereas NWO is more oriented towards fundamental research.

A first (yearly) research program from the NWO content was developed in early 1997, and four studies dealing with school effectiveness issues were granted (two from the University of Twente, one from GION (Groningen) and one from ITS, an institute that is part of the Catholic University of Nijmegen.

The first study from the University of Twente (Bosker/Scheerens) is aimed at further exploration of alternative models of facilitation across levels, eg. the way school organisational conditions interact with instructional conditions in affecting educational outcomes.

The second study from the University of Twente (Scheerens, Moonen) is conducted in cooperation with the Foundation of Economic Research (SEO) from the University of Amsterdam (Van Praag). The aim of this study is an integration of school effectiveness modeling and application of micro-economic theory to educational settings. Problem areas that are investigated are the impact of reducing class size, applications of econometric modeling and system dynamics, and the implementation of applications of communication and information technology in education.

The study from GION (Creemers, Jansen) looks into the integration of effectiveness and educational attainment research at the secondary level. In this study two types of outcomes are used: value-added achievement test scores, and indicators of educational attainment, such as the percentage of students that pass the final examination, the level of education reached after a fixed period of time, etc. The project aims at an integral application of value-added test score-based and attainment indicators.

A third study that was funded as part of the NWO-1987 research program is a study by Jungbluth (ITS, University of Nijmegen) which focuses on teacher expectations of pupils' achievement, which are determined by the socio-economic background of the pupils.

University-based research programs

In two universities, Groningen and Twente, with the respective institutes GION and OCTO, educational effectiveness is a central research theme. The two institutes and research groups have a lot in common and co-operate on several projects.

The GION program is titled 'Educational evaluation and effectiveness', focuses on large-scale program evaluations (the evaluation of the Educational Priority Program and the Cohort Research Study VOCL in secondary education, which is carried out together with OCTO), model-driven studies and some international studies, including a study on effective school improvement which was recently funded by the European Union.

The GION effectiveness program has a clear focus on instructional effectiveness at the classroom level, although organisational and environmental conditions are also included.

The research program of the group Educational Organisation and Management and OCTO of the University of Twente is titled 'School Effectiveness' and has a stronger focus at the school organisational level. The main areas of research within this program are:

* conceptual and theoretical development and so called 'foundational studies' (eg. meta-analyses and studies into consistency aspects of educational effectiveness);

* international comparative studies (the research group is strongly involved in the OECD indicator project and leads an EU-funded network on educational assessment, effectiveness and innovation);

* methodological refinements in testing multi-level conceptual modes on school effectiveness;

* extension of research activities in sectors like corporate training, vocational education and adult education.

Effectiveness-oriented studies at SCO of the University of Amsterdam focus on pre-school education and effectiveness in the lower grades of primary education (eg. Sontag & Meijnen, 1995).

Researchers from ITS, University of Nijmegen (Jungbluth, Dekkers) have carried out studies which look into the impact of the socio-economic background of pupils on educational effectiveness (Jungbluth, 1997) and differential effectiveness.

These four research groups are also represented in one of the research divisions, titled 'Educational Evaluation and Effectiveness' of ICO, the Interuniversity Center for Educational Research. ICO is a so called research school in which nine universities participate in collaborative research and post-graduate training.

Aspects of the political and societal context

An interesting structural phenomenon of the Dutch educational system, which partly explains the fact that school effectiveness research, to a considerable extent, exists as fundamental, 'academic' research, is the existence of a rather elaborate educational support structure. The guidance of schools and school improvement resides with the support institutes, while there is only a limited integration of their work with that of educational researchers.

A more culturally embedded feature of the Dutch educational system is the peculiar mixture of centralisation and decentralisation tendencies. Most reform initiatives come from the central level. In fact, for years schools and critics have complained about an overabundance of central policy initiatives. The fact that there has traditionally been a lot of influence from educational pressure groups and the constitution forbids 'state education' has acted as a strong counterbalance, so that quite a few of the many policy initiatives only result in partial implementation.

In their 1995 review Scheerens and Creemers said that 'the current hobbies' in educational policy, namely creating bigger schools and delegating some decision-making authority to lower administrative levels, appeared to be demanding most of the energy available for innovation. This situation, where there was a strong emphasis on structural reform, as compared to efforts to improve the educational 'primary process', changed somewhat over the last couple of years. This will be illustrated by means of two policy initiatives, one at the primary school and one at the secondary school level.

At the primary school level, after an advisory committee had studied the pro's and con's of reducing class size, a new policy initiative was launched in 1997 under the heading of 'Class size and quality'. Over the period 1997-1999 a yearly budget of 320 million Dutch guilders is provided to schools to reduce class size in the four lower grades of the primary school. Next to the reduction of class size, accompanying measures to improve the quality and the outcomes of primary school education are being taken. These policy measures were inspired by the recommendation of an Evaluation Committee in 1993 to stimulate 'result-oriented' thinking and by a review of the school effectiveness research literature by Scheerens (1997). The actual policy measures are to stimulate adaptive teaching, to strengthen educational leadership, to provide more curricular structure by specifying middle range objectives (next to the already available 'end terms') to stimulate school self-evaluation and the use of pupil-monitoring systems, to stimulate school responsiveness vis à vis parents and to make better use of communication and information technology.

Clearly these new policy initiatives can be seen as an example of the incorporation of school effectiveness inspired thinking in educational policy.

In secondary education too, although less pronounced, there is a tendency to focus more strongly on the quality of educational outcomes. In the Autumn of 1997 a newspaper published the results of all secondary schools, which were rendered in marks (1-10) based upon average exam grades, retention rates and an indicator of the ethnic composition of the school. Evidently this initiative provoked a greater interest and awareness of existing quality differences between schools. A research project, initiated by the inspectorate, was launched to improve the outcome indicator.

A second, more encompassing, development in secondary education, in particular the upper grades of secondary education, is focused at innovations regarding the teaching and learning process. The policy concerned is labelled as changing the school into a 'Study House', expressing the idea that learning processes should receive primary attention and teaching processes should be seen as 'merely' supportive.

Van den Akker (1996: 4) summarises the aims and methods of this innovatory policy, which is to be implemented by the Summer of 1998, as follows:

aims: a stronger focus on the development of learning skills, with 'learning to learn' as an overarching principle, and a strong interest in information, communication, problem-solving and investigative skills;

methods: a stronger emphasis on active and independent learning, learning in groups and a more flexible and varied learning environment.

Since the 'Study House' ideas focus on processes rather than outcomes it appears to be somewhat at odds with the also present increased interest in the quality of outcomes. A second interesting phenomenon is that the didactic approach is strongly inspired by constructivist views on learning. In this sense the new policy can be seen as a challenge to the instructional effectiveness knowledge base, which has demonstrated the effectiveness of structured, direct teaching approaches.

The - briefly sketched - developments in educational policy create a climate for school effectiveness research and school improvement that appears to be more supportive than in previous years. As stated in the above the innovations at the primary school level are close to school effectiveness thinking. Expected developments with respect to result-oriented school leadership, curricular structuring and the use of school self-evaluation and pupil monitoring, form an interesting setting for school effectiveness research.

The developments in secondary education, the 'Study House' in particular, have inspired researchers to think of studies in which constructivist-inspired learning environments will be contrasted with direct-teaching approaches. Again this provides a context for effectiveness-oriented research that is more stimulating than was the case in the period when educational policy was strongly focused on structural and administrative changes.

Conclusion

From the overview of educational effectiveness research and related studies on school improvement the conclusion is warranted that the field is very much 'alive' in the Netherlands.

The newly existent framework for financing educational research stimulates a tendency towards fundamental, rather than applied studies. Hopefully these funding arrangements in conjunction with the relative importance of 'free' university-based research programs on educational effectiveness will further stimulate theory and model-driven studies, that already mark the position of Dutch contributions to the international state of the field.

The policy climate for effectiveness-oriented research has improved over the last two or three years, in the sense that the re-found interest in improving the primary processes of learning in instruction, create new challenges and opportunities. A major challenge for effectiveness researchers is to integrate the individual efforts more in order to tackle the remaining uncertainties on what 'really' works in Dutch education.

Although there is a distinct influence of school effectiveness oriented thinking and knowledge, the impact on educational policy initiatives is still modest. In applied, evaluation-oriented policy research programs, two major cohort-studies in particular, the choice of variables has clearly been inspired by the school effectiveness research literature. In their efforts to enhance the effects of class-size reduction by additional measures to improve quality, the present administration partly bases accompanying measures on school effectiveness findings.

It is quite noteworthy, however, that the major policy-reform in secondary education has been developed without taking the school effectiveness literature into consideration.

Seen from an international perspective educational effectiveness research in the Netherlands is strong for its fundamental nature: several studies aimed at foundational issues like consistency, meta-analyses, theory and conceptual development and model-building. The growing interest in school self-evaluation offers a new opportunity to integrate foundational and applied work.

References

Akker, J.J.H. van den (1996). *Het Studiehuis: ook een leeromgeving voor docenten?* Amsterdam: Vrije Universiteit, oratie.

Carroll, J.B. (1963). A model of school learning. *Teachers College Record, 64,* 722-733

Cotton, K. (1995). *Effective schooling practices: A research synthesis.* 1995 Update. School Improvement Research Series. Northwest Regional Educational Laboratory.

Heyl, E. (1996). *Het docentennetwerk. Structuur en invloed van collegiale contacten binnen scholen.* Enschede: Universiteit Twente.

Hogendijk,W. & Wolfgram, P. (1995). *KEA halverwege.* Projectverslag schooljaar 1994/1995. Rotterdam: CED.

Houtveen, A.A.M., Booy, N., Jong, R. de, & Grift, W. van de (1996). *Effecten van adaptief onderwijs.* Evaluatie van het Landelijk Project Schoolverbetering.

Lam, J.F. (1996). *Tijd en kwaliteit in het basisonderwijs.* Enschede: Universiteit Twente.

Levine, D.U., & Lezotte, L.W. (1990). *Unusually effective schools: A review and analysis of research and practice.* Madison, WI: National Center for Effective Schools Research and Development.

Sammons, P., Hillman, J., & Mortimore, P. (1995). *Key characteristics of effective schools: A review of school effectiveness research.* London: OFSTED.

Scheerens, J. (1997). *De bevordering van schooleffectiviteit in het basisonderwijs.* Enschede: Universiteit Twente, OCTO.

Scheerens, J., & Bosker, R.J. (1997). *The foundations of educational research.* Oxford: Elsevier Science Ltd.

Scheerens , J., & Creemers, B.P.M. (1995). School effectiveness in the Netherlands; research, policy and practice. In B.P.M. Creemers & N.

Osinga (Eds), *Country Reports ICSEI 1995* 81-106. Leeuwarden: Gemeenschappelijk Centrum voor Onderwijsbegelei-ding.

Sontag, L., & Meijnen, G.W. (1995). De invloed van school- en klaskenmerken op de cognitieve en linguistische vaardigheden van kleuters. *Pedagogische Studi'n, 72*(4), 258-272.

Velden, L.F.J. van der (1996). *Context, visie, aanpak en effectiviteit.* Groningen: GION.

Werf, M.P.C. van der (1995). *The educational priority policy in the Netherlands. Content, implementation and outcomes.* The Hague: SVO.

10.

Research and policy developments in school effectiveness and improvement in Norway

Trond Eiliv Hauge

Reforms in the nineties

The Norwegian education system has undergone extensive changes in the nineties. All education levels in the system, and the governing system as well, have been reformed. It started in 1993 with a huge reorganisation of higher education institutions, melting 129 individual institutions at regional level into 26 administrative units. In this process regional teacher education colleges lost their long-lasting autonomous positions; they were departmentalised and subordinated in a common administrative structure covering a variety of professional education offerings. One year later, in 1994, upper secondary schools underwent a large reorganisation process: the main courses at grade level one were dramatically reduced to thirteen, the differences between vocational and academic studies were reduced and a set of national target oriented curricula were introduced at all grade levels. In 1997 the nine year comprehensive school (comprising primary and lower secondary school) expanded to ten years by including six year old children. At the same time a new national target-oriented curriculum was introduced.

The management system for primary and secondary education went through an extensive decentralisation process in the last part of the eighties with the deregulation of a rather strict economy transaction system between national, regional and local government levels. This process was followed up in the nineties by moving more power to the individual school and the principal for finances, staff relations and school management in general. Parallel to these changes new internal and external school evaluation systems have developed, which may be looked upon as a means of compensating for what national educational authorities were losing through the decentralisation process

The question of school effectiveness is set under pressure during the reforms in the nineties. There are several reasons for this situation: the reforms in primary and secondary education are challenging common opinions and expectations of education among people in general, the reforms are focusing on student assessments and school based evaluations to a larger extent than before, and the demands for quality control and enhancement have been strengthened as a management principle in school. At the same time political support for giving more power to parents and students to choose schools on their own is growing, which in turn has stimulated the development of student assessment as a means for measuring school effectiveness.

Research on school effectiveness and school improvement in retrospect

Research on the effectiveness of schools, defined by Mortimore (1993:297) as: 'One in which students progress further than can be expected from a consideration of intake', has a weak research tradition in Norway. Up to the nineties there were few studies which really focused on student outcomes related to intake and school level variables (Hauge 1994, Reynolds et al. 1994). The main research model for school effectiveness was concentrated on students' outcomes in relation to home, social background and classroom variables. Variables at the school level were mostly looked upon as selection criteria making representative sample of classrooms (for example, see Solheim et al. 1984).

A large number of 'effectiveness' studies may be classified as follow-up studies of reforms and changes in the education system, and focusing on student choice, recruitment, attitudes and achievements. Variables like student grouping, streaming, teaching methods, team-teaching, teacher roles, school-parent relationship, the school's local curricula orientation, school climate and the organisation of special education have been illuminated. However, studies in these categories are weak regarding interactional effects between student learning and school level dimensions. Multi-level analyses based on data from individual students, classroom and school conditions are missing (Hauge 1994).

The history of research on school effectiveness in the seventies and eighties seems to reflect a dominant trend in national education policy, focusing on organisational structures and content matter (written curricula) as the main strategies for changes to student learning. Research funds and interest have, to a large extent, been directed to investigations of school developmental problems, initiated from the national government. As a consequence school effectiveness and improvement purposes are often being blended in one and the same study.

Recent research on school effectiveness and improvement

School effectiveness research has grown to be more visible and significant in the nineties for several reasons. One reason is its connection to a set of profound changes in the national school management system, which have forced school principals and local authorities to plan and evaluate their work according to national and local goals of education. 'Management by objectives' has became the overall management philosophy, comprising curriculum matters as well. The principles are explicated in several white papers to the Parliament (see St. meld. 37 (1990-91), St. meld. 29 (1994-95), St. meld. 47 (1995-96)). At the same time national efforts to illuminate and undertake follow-up studies of students' learning outcomes have been strengthened, pushed forward by an OECD-evaluation of Norwegian educational policy in 1987 (KUF 1989), a large commissioned work on quality control and improvement some years later (Granheim et.al. 1990, Granheim & Lundgren 1990) and by a new commissioned work on national school evaluation (Ministry of Education 1997). The nineties may also be characterised by transferring more freedom to parents and students in choosing schools, which to a certain extent has put pressure on schools to document their work and publish student results. In concluding this brief overview, we are inclined to believe that there is a far more supportive political climate for school effectiveness research in the nineties than in the decades before.

Visible manifestations of this change are Norwegian participation in three large scale international school effectiveness studies funded by the Ministry of Education: the TIMSS study, the IEA study of Language and the ISERP study (see below). Also the Ministerial work on educational indicators (cf. OECD 1995) and initiatives to do follow-up studies in the TIMSS area and in other school subjects, together with the government interest and support to effect studies based on economic resource perspectives (Bonesrönning & Rattsöe 1994, Birkemo & Bonesrönning et.al.1997) are contributing to this manifestation. However, at the same time we are noticing how more traditional follow-up studies of reforms and innovations still are of central concern, just as they were in the seventies and eighties. Various research studies contributing to the understanding of school effectiveness and improvement in the nineties are described below.

International studies on student learning outcomes

Student learning outcomes are focused upon in three large scale studies. Two of them are development products of research studies in the seventies and eighties and are not focusing on the single school as the entity for change, they are first and foremost directed to the study of teaching and learning in specific subjects. The third one is grounded in premises given in the dominant school effectiveness research analysing effects at school level (cf. Mortimore 1993, Reynolds et.al 1994).

The TIMSS study: the Third International Mathematics and Science Study

This study, involving about 50 countries, is focusing on mathematics and science teaching in primary, lower and upper secondary schools by investigating various aspects of intended, implemented and experienced curricula in these subjects. The characteristics of teaching at system level, classroom level and student level are investigated, trying to answer the following questions: What are students expected to learn? Who delivers the instruction and how is instruction organised? What have students learned? The main question to be answered through the international comparisons is what factors are promoting learning in the selected subjects. Norwegian students aged nine and thirteen in primary and lower secondary school, and students in last grade of upper secondary schools were sampled in the study. Information from classroom teachers and students was gathered in 1995. The study is mainly quantitative in its orientation, but includes a small qualitative classroom observation study.

The TIMMS study follows on from the Second International Mathematics Study (SIMS) and the Second International Science Study (SISS) of the eighties, where Norway was participating.

A cross-national investigation of curricular intentions in school mathematics has been published by Schmidt *et al.* (1997). An investigation based on classroom observations in six countries, Norway included, was been reported by Schmidt *et al.* (1996), and the preliminary results of nine and thirteen year old students' achievements and attitudes to mathematics and science in Norway are reported by Kjaernsli & Lie (1996) and Lie, Kjaernsli & Brekke (1997).

The study has so far produced valuable knowledge with respect to Norwegian students' achievements compared to students in other countries. The relative influence of variables at different study levels on student achievement has so far not been reported upon. The lessons concerning system and classroom effects is still therefore limited. According to the chosen research model, effects at school level are not possible to account.

The IEA study of Reading Literacy: the International Studies of Educational Achievement

This is a study which to some extent fits into the comparative model of the TIMSS project, however it does not include information at the system level. It involved 32 countries. Reading literacy was tested in 1990-91 for a group of 2,500 Norwegian students at age nine and fourteen in primary and lower secondary schools. Further information was gathered on students' home background and characteristics of the schools they belonged to, (i.e. hours of instruction, school and class size, student/teacher ratio, teachers' education, ways of teaching, library functions, special reading programs and parental co-operation - Elley, 1994). The 1990-91 Reading Literacy Study is the second study of reading achievement undertaken by IEA. The first one was conducted in 1970-71. The study is completely quantitative in design.

The international findings from the study are thoroughly reported by Elley (1994), the Norwegian ones are documented by Tönnessen (1995, 1996a, 1996b), Höien *et al.* (1993) and Lundberg *et al.* (1994). The reports trace differences in reading abilities at class level back to students' home background and the characteristics of teachers and their teaching. Small class sizes, amount of instruction time and female teachers all seem to contribute to better reading achievements. The relative influence of different home background variables, school resources and instructional variables on students' reading achievement are measured in the international population as a whole, but are not yet disaggregated and reported for the Norwegian case. However, the general findings underline, among other things, the positive interaction between a strong literacy tradition in society, access to library and books in school, parental co-operation for the school's goals in literacy and students' high reading achievements. Teachers who emphasise the enjoyment in reading clearly seem to evoke better achievements in their classes (Elly, 1994: 229-31).

The ISERP study: the International School Effectiveness Research Study

In contrast to the TIMSS and IEA Language study the ISERP study has a multi-level approach to the assessment of school effectiveness. It is designed to measure the relative influence of a wide range of variables at school level, classroom level and contextual level on student learning outcomes. Nine countries are participating in the study: Australia, Canada, Hong Kong,

Ireland, the Netherlands, Norway. Taiwan, the United Kingdom and the United States.

The ISERP study is a two years follow-up study of students from first to second grade in primary schools (age 7-9), and involves only a small sample of about six schools in each participating country. Schools were chosen to represent effective, average effective (typical school) and ineffective schools, and within each group of schools a distinction is made between low SES and middle SES schools. Two classes in each school were included and followed up during the school years 1992-93 and 1993-94. In Norway, due to the organisation of the project, nine schools were involved, six in Oslo and three in Trondheim. To make an international comparison moderately difficult student mathematics achievements were chosen as an academic outcome measure.

The study consisted of both quantitative and qualitative parts. The qualitative part included case studies within countries and comparisons of these across countries. The quantitative part comprised a wide range of information; eg. student background, achievements in academic and social areas, classroom observation, curriculum and organisation of teaching at class level, school leadership and collaborative culture at school level and contextual data.

Results from the international study are preliminary and offer no firm conclusions on what makes schools more effective in one country compared to others. From the Norwegian point of view the study has revealed the importance of analysing cultural differences between countries when international comparisons are done. The concept of school effectiveness in this context has to be seen not only as a technical term, but as a value-loaded term affecting basic goals and principles of learning in school (Hauge 1997a). So far this study has resulted in the development of more elaborated models and a number of ideas about 'what makes a difference' instead of providing a firm empirical basis for educational indicators (Creemers & Reynolds 1997). Reports from the Norwegian research team are given by Birkemo, Gröterud, Hauge, Knutsen & Nilsen (1994), Birkemo (1996), Gröterud & Nilsen (1997) and Hauge (1997a). The international study is reported by Reynolds et.al (1994).

National studies on students' learning outcomes

The vast majority of national research studies on student learning outcomes are either survey or cross-sectional studies, characterised by poor descriptions of school level variables. In this respect they are in line with the majority of effectiveness studies in the seventies and eighties. We do not find many other studies, apart from the ISERP study, that are designed to look at deviation scores by intake and output measures and interaction effects between school and classroom variables.

Thematically one main part of the studies may be looked upon as following earlier studies that focused on student behaviour in school, their well-being, social and academic competencies and differences in achievements due to grade level and school structure (cf. Hauge 1994). Studies by Bru, Boyesen, Munthe & Roland (1997), Sandberg & Vibe (1996), Ogden (1995), Roland (1993), Olweus (1993) are part of this tradition, however they have accommodated to new societal challenges. The study of Ogden (1995) is an exception because it focused on what happened to students in schools over a period of three years. This study, located in schools in a single municipality and not yet completed, is in some respect able to trace effects back to school and classroom levels.

The study of Engen, Kulbrandstad & Sand (1996) represents a new and growing research branch in Norwegian educational research. It looked at the learning outcomes of students from linguistic and cultural minorities in lower secondary school. This study shows that minority students, as a group, obtained results in mathematics and Norwegian that were inferior to those of the majority students. Other studies by Sörlie & Nordahl (1997) and Lödding (1996) confirm these tendencies.

School effectiveness research may comprise a wide variety of research areas, if we move beyond the traditional definition of this research (such as that by Mortimore, 1993: 297). This is surely demonstrated by Kvalsund (1994) who investigated students' social relations in schools located in typical rural and coast-line districts. Some of the schools were working with less than 50 students and had to practice a non-grading system. This intensive study of 19 small schools reveals clear differences between graded and non-graded schools with respect to networking between students in classroom and out-door activities. Collective play and age integrated student relations characterised the non-graded schools far more than in the graded schools.

School effectiveness research based on economy perspectives

The emphasis on economic accountability in the education system is a growing trend in government initiatives and supports school effectiveness research in the nineties. From belonging on a side-track, school effectiveness is now moving into the main stream on the research agenda when looking into the 1997-2003 national research program on education recently commenced (Norges Forskningsraad 1997). Managerial and economic resource perspectives are dominating themes when questions of quality and effectiveness in education are discussed in this program. The development of quality indicators and ensuring systems are given high priority when research funds are allocated.

Some research studies in this area have already been published resulting in lively and defensive debates in educational research communities (Monsen & Tiller 1991). However, the new six year national education research program seems to express an ideological change in what will count as interesting education research questions in the future.

What are the contributions from the social economists points of view on school effectiveness so far? Studies done by Bonesrönning (1996), Bonesrönning & Rattsö (1994) Friestad & Johnsen (1992) and Robertsen & Friestad (1991) are pointing to findings that resource inputs per student regarding class sizes and teacher/student ratio, do not effect student achievements at all or at the best very little. Research models are used which is well known in social economy theories applied to the public sector (Jacobsen, Johnsen & Robertson 1995). Bonesrönning (1996) underlines through highly sophisticated analyses of student progress from lower secondary to higher secondary schools that schools are offering students with equal achievement levels quite different learning opportunities. Student achievement gains vary substantially between efficient schools of different size and different student body compositions.

Questions raised above are now bring followed up by a cross-disciplinary research group (Birkemo & Bonesrönning *et al.* 1997) in a large national study focusing on the interaction of resource inputs and achievement in schools, the equality of teaching offered in different regions and the quality of teaching. The project is funded by the Norwegian Research Council for the years 1997-2002.

Studies of reforms and innovations

The review of school effectiveness research in the seventies and eighties by Hauge (1994) documented how this research follows reforms and innovations in the education system. A review of research on teachers and teacher education in Scandinavia since the sixties confirms this tendency (Hauge 1997b). In the recent review this follow-up research on reforms and innovations comprises an important part of the total body of studies. However, its main contribution to the understanding of school effectiveness is first and foremost connected to conditions of teaching and learning in schools, eg. curriculum implementation at school level, improving teachers' work and teaching, planning and evaluation in schools. Effects at the student level are being assessed indirectly.

The implementation of national curricula

In this group of studies we include first of all a large composite group of ongoing studies focusing on the implementation of the secondary school reform 1994, and three extensive studies of how central principles of education are realised in basic schools.

Reform 1994, the large scale upper secondary school reform activity, was the catalyst for a broad variety of evaluation research studies in secondary education that are still going on at the end of 1998. Findings from different parts of the research are collected in two recently edited volumes by Blichfeldt *et al.* (1996) and Lödding & Tornes (1997), and underline the difficulties in implementing the equalising intentions in the reform, due to very complex aspects of the reform itself, and attitudes and readiness of people outside schools to support joint integrated school and work-place programs. Studies of how cultures in schools are reluctant to internalise the intentions and procedures of autonomous and responsible learning among students also illuminate the barriers to implementing the reform. The evaluation studies underline dilemmas in planning for change in a modern knowledge driven society, where power relations between individuals and educational institutions are changing.

Solstad (1994) looked at the implementation of the national curriculum plan of 1987 in primary and lower secondary schools in one Norwegian county, Nordland, a sparsely populated coastal region in the northern part of the country. His intention was to provide an account of a national development initiative, while assisting schools in the transformation according to the plan. This extensive research study, named 'Equity at Risk', was based on a comprehensive follow-up study of 300 schools, and is an outstanding documentation of school improvement efforts both at school and system level, and underlines the need to plan for change in a systematic way if success is expected. It provides an account of the in-service strategies and initiatives undertaken to assist schools in their struggle to approach equitable education. The study is a reminder of how the new Reform 1997 in primary and lower secondary schools is going to be implemented.

The question of how individual student's learning needs are taken care of in basic schools was focused upon by Nilsen (1993), who studied teachers' values, attitudes and teaching practices concerning integrated and inclusive education and the caring for students with special learning needs in mixed ability classes. This is a quite extensive and representative study among teachers in a large school district near Oslo. Nilsen's findings were that students' rights to get teaching according to their learning needs and competencies, which are at the heart of the national curriculum plan of 1987, were only to a certain extent fulfilled in practice. Whole class instruction is the dominant approach by teachers, however the patterns of teaching vary according to teacher attitudes towards inclusive education and the caring for students as individual learners. Teacher conceptions of contextual frame factors facilitating their work in classroom also influence their way of teaching.

The work of Imsen (1996) highlighted the gender equity question and the implementation of this central education principle in schools. This was a nation wide representative study among teachers and students in grade five and eight, sampled by the class unit. This survey study underlined the finding that Norwegian schools still fail to implement this principle in their daily work. This includes, for example, aims and content matter of teaching, working methods in the classroom and promoting expected attitudes among students.

Research on innovations in school

Five groups of studies illustrate experiences from innovations in Norwegian settings. The first two studies illuminate the problems arising when schools are adapting new models of organisational planning, evaluation and collective work time for teachers, imposed by national or regional educational authorities. The third one tells the story of a grass-roots movement in language teaching, influencing curriculum thinking and assessment procedures. The fourth one looks at how information technology is used in schools, and the fifth one looks into a single school's attempt at school-based development work.

Eilertsen (1994) and Eilertsen & Hansen (1993) studied the effects of development planning, a model which all Norwegian schools, primary and secondary, have been forced to undertake in the nineties, in nine upper secondary schools in the Northern part of Norway. The planning model, very much inspired by the 'management by objectives' philosophy, has been imposed by regional and local authorities to enhance teachers' collective thinking and work in schools, but is also looked upon as a continuous feedback system between schools and educational authorities. Effects on the organisational level and classroom work were investigated through interviews with principals, department heads, teachers and students. Schools are changeable; this is the lesson drawn from the project when looking at the roles of middle managers, the department heads, who experienced a strengthening of their roles as educational leaders. The collective planning model also seems to be a constructive means to improve democratic behaviour in teaching. However, the studies confirm what is underlined by Fullan (1993) that neither top-down nor bottom-up models are the ultimate solution for change in schools. Pressure and support from above was an important factor getting schools to improve their work in Eilertsen's studies, however the feelings of ownership of the development planning processes both at school and classroom level appeared to be necessary conditions for long-lasting effects.

During the last four to five years many schools have adopted models for school-based evaluation and are evaluating their work on a regular basis, sometimes initiated on their own, sometimes by local or regional educational authorities. This organisational enterprise is now, from 1997 onwards, an activity for every school, imposed by central regulations. Intentions and work models are described in various governmental documents (Underveis 1994, St.meld. 47). This type of school-based evaluation has been studied by various research groups (Alfredsen, Harsvik & Haarvik 1997, Aalvik 1994, Hauge 1991). The main experience corresponds with international research on school improvement. Long-lasting effects can be expected when institutionalising innovation policy is adhered to and the principal of the school is personally involved in the improvement work and signals to teachers that he is seriously interested in that work. An important condition for success appears to be that school-based evaluation projects have to be planned and implemented as development work inside schools. At the same time the studies confirm what is underlined by Eilertsen (1994) that school improvement efforts need to be supported externally to avoid 'floppy' organisational happenings.

The story of teachers' reactions to changes in work-time schedule and work-time agreements for teachers in primary and lower secondary schools is reported by Klette (1997). With the new work-time agreement implemented in 1994, the teachers' work is divided into three different components:

- weekly hours spent on education,
- organised collaborative work with colleagues, meetings etc, and
- time for homework/working preparation.

The controversial part of the agreement is the regulation of organised collaborative work. Klette especially focused on this part. One of the most challenging findings in this investigation, covering data from 2,400 teachers, is the extensive and comprehensive discontent with the collaborative work-time schedule in schools. Many teachers felt the schedule was an imposed regulation having no meaning for their daily work. Klette raises the issue of teachers' feelings of de-professionalisation as a consequence of the change. The study illuminates the change problem in schools when top-down decisions are imposed on teachers' work.

The philosophy and methods in process oriented writing have been quite influential for teacher education, for pre-service, as well as for in-service education, during the last ten years. In a study of teaching in lower and upper secondary schools supervised by Hertzberg, the implementation of these ideas was investigated by Helstad & Roe (1996) and Grötan (1997). They asked a random sample of mother tongue teachers about their methods and attitudes in teaching writing. In addition they also made a case study of three schools. In both types of schools they found that the vast majority of teachers were familiar with process oriented writing, although teachers in lower secondary schools used process oriented writing in one form or another somewhat more than teachers in upper secondary schools. However, when we look at teachers using the whole package of ideas in this approach and teachers using only part of the ideas, only fifteen percent were high users of all the elements. Another finding was that elements in the writing process which did not challenge the traditional concept of teaching were among the easiest ones to be adopted. These case studies gave evidence of the complicated improvement processes arising in schools when innovations are initiated by individual teachers.

A study by Klette (1994) focusing on one single school culture and change strategies is in accordance with the findings described above. It illuminated how school-based development work influences the daily work of teachers, and how traditional and modernistic approaches live side by side in complex social patterns. It is difficult to foresee how and when these patterns become powerful enough to move schools into paradigmatic shifts in practice, including teachers' knowledge base and the organisation of teaching and learning in school. Lessons to be learned from this study as compared to studies of imposed innovations mentioned above, are how top-down or externally initiated innovations have to fight with deep-rooted knowledge structures and cultures in schools.

The question of the effects of new information technology on learning and teaching in school is and should be of high interest when school effectiveness and improvement is discussed. Despite strong efforts from the national government to enhance the access to and the use of computer technology in schools (see St. meld. 24, 1993-94, IT i norsk utdanning 1996), these efforts are not followed up by extensive effectiveness research to any extent. Only one small study by Holmbo (1997), which followed on from the TIMSS study, offered some insight in this respect. The main conclusion was that few teachers are really able to integrate this technology in their teaching, either because of poor access to hardware and/or software, or because schools have no overall philosophy for the use of technology or because teachers are not well enough qualified. However, the number of computers and how these are integrated in daily teaching vary extensively between schools and districts (SSB 1997).

Conclusions

The whole education system in Norway has been and is still going through extensive changes during the nineties, for a wide variety of reasons. Reforms in primary, lower and upper secondary education have resulted in changed school structures, new roles for teachers and principals and new curriculum guidelines as well. Simultaneously the educational management system has been changed through decentralisation processes.

The demands on school and system effectiveness have significantly increased during the reform period. These demands are expressed through movements and discussions about educational accountability, ensuring quality, student testing and school inspection. The 1997 commission report on the development of a national school evaluation system (Ministry of Education, 1997) underlines the importance of these issues. The new national education research program for the years 1997-2002, also contributes to this agenda by inviting and focusing on school effectiveness research driven by resource perspectives. However, how far the national government wants to go concerning implementing new models of school evaluation by the use of extensive testing and inspection systems is still open.

The present review has shown that school effectiveness research has become a growing domain in the nineties. It includes a wide variety of studies focusing on impacts of reforms and innovations on teachers' work and organisational behaviours in school, as well as studies on resource effectiveness and student learning outcomes. However, there are few studies focusing on effectiveness at the school level or on multi-level effects. The review has revealed that it is somewhat difficult to differentiate between studies of school effectiveness and studies of school improvement.

Just as school effectiveness research in the seventies and eighties has been very much concerned about students' social development and well-being in school, so is the research in the nineties. The balanced view of students' social and academic outcomes seems to be a significant feature of the Norwegian research studies.

Compared to what happens in other countries in the Western world Norway has for many years been be very cautious in implementing extensive external school evaluation systems. So far major efforts have been directed to school based evaluation programs focusing on empowerment and professionalisation of teachers and school leaders. Major control functions have been taken care of by other means of governing, eg. budgeting and through national school curricula. However, the national policy of school evaluation is gradually changing, influenced by societal demands on accountability, which are becoming more visible than ever before at the end of the twentieth century. This movement is challenging deep-rooted traditions in the Norwegian society, particularly those concerned with equality and equity in education.

References

Alfredsen A., Harsvik T. & Harvik J.A. (1997) *Bedre skoler gjennom vurdering. Erfaringer fra skolebasert vurdering,* Rapport no 2, UNIKOM, Universitetet i Tromsö

Birkemo A., Gröterud M., Hauge T.E., Knutsen A.E. & Nilsen B.(1994) *Laeringskvalitet i skolen,* Institutt for laererutdanning og skoleutvikling, Universitetet i Oslo

Birkemo A. (1996) *School Effectiveness,* Institute for Educational Research, University of Oslo, report no 5

Birkemo A., Bonesrönning H., Haug P., Langfeldt, Vislie L., Moen V. (1997) *From resource to result. A project plan,* University of Oslo, Institute for educational research

Blichfeldt J.F. et.al (1996) *Utdanning for alle. Evaluering av Reform -94,* Tano Aschehoug

Bonesrönning H. (1996) Student body composition and school performance: Evidence from Norway, *Education Economics,* 4/1, 11-31

Bonesrönning H. & Rattsö J. (1994) Efficiancy variation among the Norwegian high schools: Consequences of equalisation policy, *Economics of Education Review,* 13/4, 289-304

Bru E., Boyesen M., Munthe E. & Roland E.(1997) Perceived social support and emotional and musculosketal complaints among Norwegian 8th grade students, in Scandinavian Journal of Educational Research, forthcoming

Creemers B.P.M. & Reynolds D.(1997) Issues and implications of international effectiveness research, in *Journal of Educational Research* (forthcoming)

Elley W.B. (ed.) (1994) *The IEA Study of Reading Literacy: Achievement and Instruction in Thirty-Two School Systems,* Pergamon

Eilertsen T.V. (1994) *Klasserommet som laeringsarena,* Plan og praksis, KLARA-arbeidet i fem skoler, Rapport no 2, UNIKOM, University of Tromsö

Eilertsen T.V & Hansen L.H. (1993) *Klasserommet som laeringsarena,* Plan og profil. En analyse av fylkets og skolenes virksomhetsplaner, Rapport no 1, UNIKOM, University of Tromsö

Engen T.O., Kulbrandstad L.A. & Sand S. (1996) *Til keiserens hva keiserens er? Om minoritetselevenes utdanningsstrategier og skoleprestasjoner,* Oplandske Bokforlag

Friestad L.B.H. & Johnsen A.(1992) *Sammenlignbare data i grunnskolen: Sluttrapport*, Agderforskning, rapport no 100, Kristiansand
Fullan M. (1993) *Change forces. Probing Debths of Educational Reforms*, Falmer Press
Granheim M. & Lundgren U. (1990) *Steering by Goals and Evaluation in Norwegian Education*, LOS-paper no 8-90, Norges raad for anvendt samfunnsforskning
Granheim M., Kogan M., Lundgren U. (1990) *Evaluation as policymaking, Introducing Evaluation into a National Decentralised Educational System*, Jessica Kingsley Publishers
Grötan A. (1997) *Med vidvinkel og telelinse. Prosessorientert skrivepedagogikk i videregaende skole*, Hovedoppgave i nordidaktikk, Institutt for nordistikk og litteraturvitenskap/Institutt for laererutdanning og skoleutvikling, Universitetet i Oslo.
Gröterud M. & Nilsen B. (1997) *Tilrettelegging for god undervisning og laering*, (forthcoming report)
Hauge T.E. (1991) *Kompetanseutvikling i skolevurdering, Erfaringer med intern skolevurdering i grunnskolen*, Institutt for laererutdanning og skoleutvikling, Universitetet i Oslo
Hauge T.E.(1994) Skolen og elevenes laeringsutbytte. Sökelys pa norske forskningstradisjoner, i Birkemo A., Gröterud M., Hauge T.E., Knutsen A.E. & Nilsen B.: *Laeringskvalitet i skolen*, Institutt for laererutdanning og skoleutvikling, Universitetet i Oslo, 23-36
Hauge T.E. (1997a) *Laeringskvalitet og effektivitet i skolens undervisning*. En analyse av begreper og vurderingstradisjoner (Quality of learning and teaching effectiveness), Forthcoming ISERP publication, Department of Teacher Education and School Development, University of Oslo
Hauge T.E. (1997b) *Research on teachers and teacher education in Norway. Reflections on the understanding of teacher professionalism*, Paper presented at the 6th Norwegian National Conference in Educational Research, University of Oslo, May 1997. (Part of the paper is presented in a forthcoming volume of *Scandinavian Journal of Educational Research*, written in cooperation with T.Bergem, O. Björkqvist, I. Carlgren, S.E. Hansen.)
Helstad K. & Roe A. (1996) *'Om vi ikke bruker alt, saa bruker vi noe'. Prosessorientert skrivepedagogikk i ungdomsskolen*, Hovedoppgave i nordidaktikk, Institutt for nordistikk og litteraturvitenskap/Institutt for laererutdanning og skoleutvikling, Universitetet i Oslo.
Holmbo C. (1997) *'Je bruker itte IT', En rapport om informasjonsteknologi i norsk skole basert paa resultater fra TIMSS-undersökelsen*, report no 26, TIMSS, University of Oslo

Höien T., Lundberg I. & Tönnessen F.E. (1993) *Kor godt les norske barn?* Högskolen i Stavanger, Senter for leseforskning

Imsen G. (1996) *Mot ökt likestilling? Evaluering av grunnskolens arbeid for likestilling,* Report no 11, Norwegian University of Science and Technology, Department of Education *IT i norsk utdanning. Plan for 1996-99* (1996): Kirke-, utdannings- og forskningsdepartementet Jacobsen D.I., Johnsen A.& Robertson K. (1995): *Resultatvurdering i offentlig sektor,* Kommuneforlaget

KUF (1989) *OECD-vurdering av norsk utdanningspolitikk,* Kirke- og utdannings-, og forskningsdepartementet, Aschehoug

Kjaernsli & Lie (1996) *13-aaringers kunnskaper og holdninger i realfag i et internasjonalt perspektiv,* rapport no 23, TIMSS, Universitetet i Oslo

Klette K.(1994) *Skolekultur og endringsstrategier,* Dr. polit. Dissertation, Institute of educational research, University of Oslo.

Klette K. (1997) *Working Time Blues: On how Norwegian teachers experience restructuring in education,* Paper presented at the PACT Conference, Oslo, May 19-23, 1997

Kvalsund R. (1994) *Elevrelasjoner og urformell laering. Samanliknande kasusstudier av fadelte og fulldelte bygdeskoler,* Volda Laerarhögskule/Möreforsking Volda

Lie, Kjaernsli & Brekke (1997) *9-aringers kunnskaper og holdninger i realfag i et internasjonalt perspektiv,* rapport no 25, TIMSS, Universitetet i Oslo.

Lundberg I., Tönnessen F.E., Höien T. (1994) *Norsk leseundervisning i internasjonalt lys,* Högskolen i Stavanger, Senter for leseforskning

Lödding B. (1996) 'Jeg ville integrere meg' - aspekter ved minoritetssituasjonen for tospraklige elever, i Blichfeldt F. et.al: *Utdanning for alle? Evaluering av Reform 94.* Tano Aschehoug, 73-96

Lödding B. & Tornes K. (red)(1997) *Idealer og paradokser. Aspekter ved gjennomföringen av Reform 94,* Tano Aschehoug

Ministry of Education (1997) Nasjonalt vurderingssystem for grunnskolen. Forslag fra et utvalg. (Proposal to a national evaluation system for primary and lower secondary schools).

Monsen L. & Tiller T. (red)(1991) *Effektive skoler - skoleutvikling eller mer byrakrati,* Ad Notam

Mortimore P. (1993) School Effectiveness and Management of Effective Learning and Teaching, *School Effectiveness and School Improvement, 4,* 290-310

Nilsen S. (1993) *Undervisningstilpasning i grunnskolen - fra intensjoner til praksis,* ph.d. dissertation, University of Oslo, Department of special education

Norges Forskningsraad (1997) *Kompetanse, utdanning og verdiskaping.* *Programnotat,* Omradet for kultur og samfunn

Ogden T. (1995) *Kompetanse i kontekst, En studie av risiko og kompetanse hos 10- og 13-aringer,* Norwegian institute of child welfare research, report no 3

Olweus D. (1993) *Bullying at school: What we know and what we can do,* Blackwell

Reynolds D., Creemers B.P.M., Nesselrodt P.M., Schaffer E.C., Stringfield S., Teddlie C. (1994) *Advances in School Effectiveness Research and Practice.* Pergamon

Reynolds D., Teddlie C, Creemers B.P.M., Cheng Y.C., Dundas B., Green B. Epp J.R., Hauge T.E., Schaffer E.C., Stringfield S. (1994) School effectiveness research: A review of the international literature, in Reynolds D., Creemers B.P.M., Nesselrodt P.M., Schaffer E.C., Stringfield S., Teddlie C. : *Advances in School Effectiveness Research and Practice.* Pergamon, 25-51

Robertsen K. & Friestad L.B.H (1991) *Effektiviseringsmuligheter i grunnskolen,* Stiftelsen for samfunns- og naeringslivsforskning, Norges Handelshögskole, rapport no 27, Bergen

Roland E. (1993) *Sosiale avvik og aggresjon,* Senter for atferdsforskning, Högskolen i Stavanger

Sandberg N. & Vibe N. (1996) Betingelser for kompetanseoppnaelse: Hva hemmer og fremmer framgang i videregaende opplaering? I Blichfeldt et.al.: *Utdanning for alle? Evaluering av Reform -94,* TANO, 126-149

Schmidt et.al. (1996) *Characterising Pedagogical Flow,* An Investigation of Mathematics and Science Teaching in Six Countries, Luwer Academic Publishers

Schmidt W.H., McKnight C.S., Valverde G.A., Houang R.T., Wiley D.E. (1997) *Many Visions, Many Aims,* Volume 1. A Cross-National Inverstigation of Curricular Intentions in School Mathematics, Luwer Academic Publishers

Solheim R., Nygaard H.D., Aasved H. (1984) *Sökelys paa smaaskolealderen,* Bergensprosjektet II, Universitetsforlaget

Solstad K.J. (1994) *Equity at Risk? Schooling and change in Norway,* Statens utdanningskontor i Nordland

SSB (1997) *IT i skolen. Del 1 Tilstandsundersökelser i skolene.* Hovedresultater og dokumentasjon, SSB's Notater 97/42

St. meld. 37 (1990-91) *Om organisering og styring av utdanningssektoren,* Kirke-, utdannings- og forskningsdepartementet

St. meld. 24 (1993-94) *Om IT i utdanningen,* Kirke-, utdannings- og forskningsdepartementet

St. meld. 29 (1994-95) *Om prinsipper og retningslinjer for 10-aarig grunnskole - ny laereplan*, Kirke-, utdannings- og forskningsdepartementet
St. meld. 47 (*1995-96) Om elevvurdering, skolebasert vurdering og nasjonalt vurderingssystem*, Kirke-, utdannings-og forskningsdepartementet
Sörlie M-A.& Nordahl T. (1997): *Skole og samspillvansker*, Rapport NOVA: Barnevernets utviklingssenter, Oslo
Tönnessen F.E. (1995) *Leselyst og lesestoff*, Högskolen i Stavanger, Senter for leseforskning, Notat 1, 1995
Tönnessen F.E. (1996a) *Laering og lesing*, Högskolen i Stavanger, Senter for leseforskning, Notat 1, 1996
Tönnessen F.E. (1996b) *Linjer i barns lesing*, Högskolen i Stavanger, Senter for leseforskning, Notat 2, 1996
Underveis. Handbok i skolebasert vurdering (1994) Kirke-, utdannings- og forskningsdepartementet
Wichstrom L. (1993) *Hvem* sprang? Hvem sto igjen og sprang? Ungdomsskoleelevers skolemotivasjon, UNGforsk, Rapport 4/93
Aalvik T. (1994) *Skolebasert vurdering - et naerbilde*, Apostrof - skriftserie, Bislet Högskolesenter

SECTION TWO:
THE AMERICAS

11.

New directions for effectiveness and improvement in Canada

Larry Sackney

Introduction

When this report was being written, 120,000 teachers were on strike in Canada's largest province of Ontario. Teachers were striking because of major restructuring initiatives undertaken by the provincial government; in fact, most provinces have undertaken considerable restructuring initiatives during the past few years. Education is experiencing turbulence as it has never before. Reduction in the number of school districts, school closures, introduction of Charter schools, new curricula, establishment of parent councils, new teacher certification procedures, and decreased funding have all contributed to a turbulent environment in the education sector. The biggest changes relate to the centralisation of curricula, funding, and teacher and board autonomy. For example, Bill 160 passed by the Ontario legislature gives the Minister and Cabinet the power to decide student class sizes, teacher preparation time, the length of the instructional day and the number of teaching days, and instructional areas where a teaching certificate may not be necessary. Furthermore, the Ontario government is planning to reduce education expenditures by $800 million out of a $14 billion budget.

Although education is a provincial responsibility in Canada, many of the changes are similar because the various provinces face similar problems, and because the Council of Ministers of Education, Canada (CMEC) are collaborating more. For example, the four western education ministers and the two territories have jointly agreed to develop curricula and materials. A similar agreement has been reached by the Maritime provinces.

This report deals with national, provincial and research efforts that focus on school effectiveness and improvement. Because it is not possible to deal with all changes in the last few years, only a cursory overview is provided.

National initiatives

To date Canada does not have a national office of education, but the Federal government does have an impact on elementary and secondary education in a variety of ways. Presently many of these efforts are centred around issues of youth employment and training, aboriginal education, and the funding of research studies pertaining to youth. Being concerned with global competition, the Federal government sees the need for more and better trained youth particularly in the areas of science, mathematics and technology. For example, at present approximately 50,000 people with computer skills are required by the high tech industry. Furthermore, the highest unemployment rates are found among the 15-24 year olds in the nation.

In response to the above issues, the Federal government through the Innovations Program of Human Resources Development Canada sponsored a study of exemplary Canadian secondary schools organised by the Canadian Education Association (CEA). The two-and-a-half year project was the largest study ever done in Canada of successful practices in secondary schools and the dominant issues confronting them.

The schools in the study were chosen from a list of 260 nominations of outstanding secondary schools. In the end, 21 schools were chosen for a year long exploration of their meanings of success (Haughey, 1977). The study culminates with a report entitled: *Secondary Schools in Canada: The National Report of Exemplary Schools Project.* A complement and overview to the report is the video 'Searching for Exemplary Schools', filmed on location in several of the 21 exemplary schools.

The authors of the study concluded that what made these schools and educators successful was their sense of being special, their imagination and energy in responding to the more difficult issues, and their competence and dedication in engaging their students in the pursuit of important ideas, valuable skills, and human values (CEA, 1996). Other findings were: there was great diversity in practices among the schools; successful schools offered courses where students of differing abilities and interests had the possibility of succeeding; teacher norms and values and their reflection within the school community were important for success; the degree of caring exhibited; the extent to which schools connected with the wider community; and the extent to which schools gathered information about their performance and made adjustments from the feedback, were strong predictors of success (Haughey, 1997).

The report concluded that if high schools are to be more than 'prep schools' for post-secondary institutions, and if they are to avoid reproducing social hierarchies from one generation to the next, they must strengthen their commitment to quality of opportunity for all students. It urged more complete reporting of what secondary schools do and how well they do it. The report also called for better community links and for the schools to be more responsive to external demands. As well, it recommended that attention be given to the social goals of education and to their links with success in education, career, and personal life.

Provincial Initiatives

Amalgamation and governance changes

The trend in the various provinces has been to enlarge the local governing entities through amalgamation. Since the mid-1990s, provincial and territorial governments have enacted major changes to the arrangements for governing education. Discernible trends include reduction in the number of school boards, redefinition of school board powers, changed relationship between governance and financing, expanded governance arrangements for linguistic minorities, mandated parent councils, increased options for school choice, and the implementation of frameworks for integrating services to children and youth (CEA, 1996).

All provinces have reduced the number of governing district boards. Newfoundland has created ten uni- or inter-denominational boards from the previous 27 denominational ones. Nova Scotia has regrouped 22 boards into 7. Ontario passed legislation to reduce the existing 129 major boards to 66. Quebec has introduced legislation to restructure its current 156 school boards. Manitoba is reducing the number of school divisions from 75 to 57. Saskatchewan, after extensive public consultation, is the only province not mandating amalgamation, although the government is encouraging school boards to voluntarily amalgamate (CEA, 1996).

Early in 1997 school districts in New Brunswick were the first in Canada to be replaced with a parent-focused structure at the school, district and provincial levels. Every public school in the province will establish a School Parent Committee with more than 50% of those being elected parents who are not employees in the school. The role of the School Parent Committee is to advise the principal on matters that directly affect the student and to provide a communication link with parents. In each of the 18 districts, District Parent Advisory Councils comprising of parents from the School Parent Committees will be established to advise the superintendent on matters that directly affect the school system. Each District Parent Advisory Council will participate in the selection committees for hiring school principals, with veto power over hiring of teachers. At the provincial level, two provincial boards of education will exist composed of one parent representative from each district and three to five ex-officio representatives appointed by the Minister. The role of the boards will be to advise the Minister on educational and expenditure plans, curriculum and provincial achievement and standards of performance.

Framework for common curricula
The four Western provinces and two Territories have established a framework for the development of common curricula. The curricula framework are common guidelines to be used as a basis for provincial curriculum development. It is anticipated that the sharing of resources and materials will lead to lower curriculum costs and easier transition for students as they move from one province to another. The provincial departments are also moving to an 'evergreen curriculum' or what is called a paperless curriculum.

Indicators

It is becoming apparent that provinces are moving to some form of standardised testing and the production of provincial and national indicators reports. These will be used more frequently to rank students, teachers, schools, school boards and provinces.

The Province of New Brunswick, for example, has recently (1997) outlined its objectives for quality education:

- Education will be more sharply focused; greater concentration will be on areas of competence. Included is a focus on literacy, on core subjects, on more homework, on using technology as an important learning tool and on making more effective use of school time.
- Higher standards and expectations will help all students reach their full potential: by giving parents and teachers a clear picture of what a child should know and be able to do in each subject area and at each grade level.
- Greater accountability will be required from all those in the system: by demanding accountability and responsibility at all levels, informing parents of their child's achievement in clear, consistent and unambiguous language, finding new means to increase parental involvement in education, finding more effective means for dealing with highly disruptive students and to bring more order into schools.

(CEA, 1997)

Perhaps the most drastic move in the direction of accountability is that being carried out in the Province of Ontario. The establishment of the Office of Quality and Accountability is the most obvious move by provincial governments in this direction.

At the national level, the Council of Ministers of Education, Canada (CMEC) in January, 1995 released the results of the first national assessment of reading and writing of 13 year-old and 16 year-old students. The results showed, in general, students in each group achieved similar results in all provinces and territories. More recently, the results of the mathematics assessment has been completed and reported. In this case, the results showed that achievement results varied from province to province and that Quebec students outperformed students from other provinces.

Teacher certification

Most Canadian provinces have been looking at updating their teacher preparation and certification requirements to reflect current ideas of effective teaching. A number of provinces are in the midst of implementing reforms to improve and enhance the quality of teaching (CEA, 1997).

Alternative schools

Although the notion of alternative schools is not as prevalent as in the United States, the Province of Alberta passed legislation allowing for Charter schools. To date some nine charters have been granted mostly in the cities of Calgary and Edmonton, and other provinces are looking at similar legislation.

Year-round schools

A few school boards have taken up the year-round model of schooling, most of which are found in Western Canada. Calgary Public Schools opened its eleventh and twelfth year-round schools this year. British Columbia had commissioned a study on this model, but to date has not acted on the report (Shields & LaRocque, 1997).

Commissions

A number of provinces have released reports by education commissions. In Quebec, *The Report of the Commission for the Estates General on Education* was recently released calling for some significant changes to education. Some of the recommendations included:

- schools should link with partners outside of the education system.

- the province should identify priority learning areas and, for each, the desired level of student achievement.

- no student should be allowed to leave the education system without a qualification that allows him or her to enter the labour market.

(Estates General Report, 1996)

In Ontario, *The Ontario Royal Commission on Learning* has resulted in the province making a number of changes. As of September, 1996 all grade 3, 6, 9 and 11 students in the province are to be tested annually in reading, writing and mathematics. A new independent Education Quality and Accountability Office will conduct the testing in both English and French languages and report the results to the public. This new office, the first of its kind in North America, will also manage Ontario's participation in national and international tests. The Office will conduct research and develop educational accountability practices and gather data to help determine the effectiveness of the education system (information on student performance, dropout and graduation percentages, percentage of students entering college, incidence of violence and harassment and school board expenditures on instruction) (CEA, 1997).

Use of technology

All provinces are investing in computer technology as a means of improving learning. Not only has the number of computers in classrooms increased, but many provinces are networking computers and connecting to the Internet.

An example of increased technological usage is that of New Brunswick and Microsoft Canada. They have formed a partnership to set up an interactive 'virtual campus' using Microsoft-On-Line Institute to deliver education electronically. The Campus will give students from K-12 access to courses not available at their own school, and it will also help students to interact with other students around the world.

College of Teachers

Another pattern being developed in Canada is the establishment of a College of Teachers. The role of the College is to prescribe the standards for practice, accreditation, certification and professional practice. Presently, two provinces, British Columbia and Ontario have moved in this direction, and others are contemplating such an initiative.

Ontario, the most recent province to set up a College of Teachers, has established a framework for mandatory recertification of teachers every five years, accreditation of teacher training programs, and improved professional development for all teachers. The governing body of the College of Teachers includes teachers, parents, students, staff of faculties of education, school boards and ministry officials as well as representatives from the private sector.

Research

There has been considerable scholarly effort in the area of school effectiveness and school improvement. At OISE, Leithwood, Fullan and Hargreaves continue to work in this area. Leithwood currently has two books in press. The first book edited by Leithwood and Seashore-Louis is entitled *Organisational learning in schools* and is being published by Swets and Zeitlinger. The second book written by Leithwood and Steinbach, *Changing leadership for changing times*, is being published by the Open University Press. Leithwood and his colleagues have focused much of their research in the area of organisational learning. Their findings are that leadership is important in the development of a learning organisation.

Andy Hargreaves is the Director of the Centre for Educational Change. He and his colleagues are currently working on an improvement project with the Peel Board of Education on change frameworks in six secondary schools. In addition, the Centre has a number of other improvement projects. On the publication front, Andy has a number of books on the market. His recent books include: Hargreaves, A., & Ryan, J. (1996). *Schooling for change.* London: Falmer Press; Hargreaves, A. (1997). *Rethinking educational change with heart and mind.* ASCD Yearbook; Hargreaves, A., & Fullan, M. (1996). *What's worth fighting for in your school.* NY: Teachers College Press; Goodson, I., & Hargreaves, A. (Eds.) (1996). *Teachers professional lives.* London: Falmer Press; Adelman, N., Walking-Eagle, K., & Hargreaves, A. (Eds.) (1997). *Racing with the clock.* New York: Teacher College Press; Hargreaves, A., & Evans, R. (Eds.) (1997). *Beyond educational reform: Bringing teachers back in.* Milton Keynes: Open University Press.

Dennis Thiessen is involved with an Ohio colleague in a study to determine how twelve innovative Ohio secondary schools are being transformed into learning communities; a case study methodology is being used. Dennis is also involved with Professor Jean Rudduck from the United Kingdom in examining the role of students in improving schooling.

Numerous colleagues across Canada were involved in the CEA Exemplary Schools Project including Pat Renihan (University of Saskatchewan), Margaret Haughey (University of Alberta), Jane Gaskell (University of British Columbia), Claude Deblois (University of Laval), Norm Henchy (McGill University), and Dennis Theissen (University of Toronto). Some of the salient findings of this project were reported in the previous section and will not be further elaborated here.

In British Columbia, Carolyn Shields has been studying the improvement of schooling for First Nations in Utah and British Columbia. Carolyn has funding from the Muttart Foundation. As well, Shields and LaRocque have prepared a report on year-round schooling for the British Columbia Ministry.

At the University of Saskatchewan, Sackney, Hajnal and Walker are in the last phase of their study on the use of the effective schools research to make school improvements. Funded by the Social Sciences and Humanities Council of Canada (SSHRCC), the four-phased study attempts to examine the factors that contribute to successful institutionalisation of these improvement efforts.

Some of the results show that among the successful schools, leadership was widely shared, and specific structures were in place to facilitate shared decision-making. Teachers in successful schools felt more empowered and greater collaboration existed in those schools. In successful schools there was a clearer sense of purpose, more evidence of organisational learning, more trust, and a greater sense of professional community among the staff. Politics were more rampant in unsuccessful schools and individualism seemed to characterise their work. Other differences were noted between successful and unsuccessful schools, but the quality of relationships that existed in the schools were strong determinants of success (Hajnal, Walker & Sackney, 1998). A number of school improvement projects are also being conducted. As well, considerable researcher and practitioner research on teaching and learning is being created through the Stirling McDowell Foundation for Research into Teaching.

Conclusion

From this report it is evident that there is much activity in Canada directed at school effectiveness and improvement. At the national level, there is concern that Canadians are able to compete in the global economy. Consequently, the Federal government is interested in encouraging research and practices that result in improved outcomes in mathematics and the sciences. The high unemployment rate of youth has resulted in a search for ways of improving the retention and productivity of young people. The funding of the Exemplary Schools Project was an example of Federal concern about improving the retention of students in schools and thereby making them more marketable.

At the provincial levels, there has been increased centralisation of governance and decreased autonomy at the district and school levels, increased accountability measures, more attention devoted to teacher training and certification, use of achievement indicators and specified standards of achievement, and the establishment of school parent councils. The publication of provincial indicators reports, the School Achievement Indicators Program (SAIP), and the establishment of Education Quality and Accountability Office in Ontario are all attempts at enhanced achievement outcomes. The development of common curricula and the implementation of frameworks for integrating services to children and youth are designed to encourage a more holistic approach to schooling. The move to a more common curricula will result in cost efficiencies and increased ease of movement of students from province to province.

At the district levels, the increased emphasis on technology and improved instruction are designed to improve learning outcomes. Another recent activity has been the publication of district indicators reports and more attention to school improvement planning. Numerous school districts are engaging various stakeholder groups in a 'Futures Search' activity.

From a research perspective, there has been greater attention being paid to student learning outcomes; restructuring endeavours and their success; organisational learning; learning communities; successful change frameworks and greater emphasis to action research approaches.

These are interesting times in Canadian education. Governments are anxious to restructure the educational system as it exists today. Whether they will be successful in attaining their goals and improving the quality of education that today's youth receive is open to question.

Schools, for their part, are concerned with the resources available to deal with the diversity of youth, and the learning problems that they bring to school. Violence and abuse is perceived to have increased in schools and schools are being asked to grapple with more complex problems. The challenge is immense.

If we have learned anything from the effective schools and school improvement research it is that we need a multi-faceted and more holistic approach to the improvement of student achievement. What is required is the implementation of frameworks that integrate services for children and youth and that involves all stakeholders including students, parents, teachers, administrators, business and community. The problems are too complex for the school staff to solve on their own. We also need school staff to operate more as a learning community. At the heart of the learning process is the quality of the relationships that exist, for in the end, it may not be what marks the students attain, but how they feel about themselves and others.

References

Canadian Education Association. *Newsletters.* Various issues from 1995-1997.

Canadian Society for the Study of Education. (1997). SSHRCC funded research studies, 1993-1996. *CSSE News, 24* (1), 7-31.

Gaskell, J. (1995). *Successful secondary schools in Canada: The National report of exemplary schools project.* Toronto: CEA. Individual technical reports on the 21 case studies are available from CEA as well as the video.

Hajnal, V., Walker, K., & Sackney, L. (in press). Leadership, organisational learning, and selected factors related to the institutionalisation of school improvement initiatives. *The Alberta Journal of Educational Research.*

Haughey, M. (1997). Successful secondary schools in Canada: A report on the exemplary schools project. *The Canadian Adminstrator, 36* (5), 1-12. (Other issues were also consulted).

Saskatchewan Teachers' Federation. (1996). *Learning from practice.* Saskatoon: Author.

Shield, C., & LaRocque, L. (1997). Reflections on consultative decision-making: Challenging concepts of best practice in a provincial change initiative. *The Canadian Administrator, 36* (7), 1-9.

12.

Chilean educational reform: an opportunity to extend high achievement to all schools

Haroldo Quinteros

Background

Chile is a very centralised country. The main educational policies dictated by the government are compulsory for all schools. Private schools, however, are permitted some freedom to introduce minor organisational and curricular changes. Distinctive policies among state schools are virtually non-existent. However, any enquiry that is performed on Chilean Education in any of its aspects requires placing it in the proper historical perspective of the country.

The 1965 educational reform

The first effort made to improve education in the second half of this century happened in 1965. The government of President Frei (1964-1970) enacted a comprehensive educational reform (Barrios, 1997), which was reinforced and deepened by Salvador Allende's government until it was overthrown by a military coup in 1973. The reform consisted basically of:

- The extension of primary education until the eighth grade. In Chile, secondary education has never been compulsory; therefore the measure was very important because it extended visibly school coverage in the whole country.

- Massive training of new teachers. It was necessary to train thousands of new teachers rapidly, and to build more schools and classrooms for the purpose of serving two new grades. Although the goal to get 30 students per class in all state elementary schools was not achieved (neither has it until the present day), the problem of coverage was corrected in great measure.

- Fostering of pedagogic research and experiment. In 1966, the first state institution aiming at teacher-updating was founded ('Centro de Perfeccionamiento, de Investigación y Experimentación Pedagógica', Pedagogic Centre for Teacher Improvement, Pedagogic Research and Experiment, PC). The Pedagogic Centre has given technical support to teachers and schools ever since, and has been in operation until today. All curricular and methodological reforms have always originated in this institution.

Education under the military government

In the year 1973, a military coup ended the constitutional regime of the country, and the military government that came as a consequence of it decided to carry out a substantial reform of all institutions, including education (Ministerio de Educación, 1994).

The new government ruled the country until 1990, and enforced a new economic model, commonly known as 'neo-liberal', characterised, as it is well known, by a low public investment, and by the weak presence of the State in the financial and administrative dynamics of the country. In other words, the State became subsidiary. The following changes were produced in education:

Subsidiarity

Before the coup, the State dedicated 4.3% of the national income to Education; the military regime reduced it to 2.6% (Corporación de Promoción Universitaria, 1995), because the newly-born state intended to abandon its educational function and leave it in private hands. The government allowed any private person to set up a school or university and make them function as viable enterprises according to the market laws of offer and demand.

Before 1973, the private educational system, almost entirely self-financed, constituted 8% of all schools, a figure which has not changed yet; but during the military government, state-subsidised private schools developed spectacularly. Before 1973, they were a few Catholic schools, bout 1% of the whole system that obtained from the State only funds to pay part of the salary of the teachers. Now, they are 28% of the system, and the Government pays half of all school costs (UNESCO Regional Office for Education in Latin America and the Caribbean, 1993).

In other words, the State uses funds in order to finance these 'educational enterprises', which is precisely one of the causes for the poverty in which state education works today.

It is important to take into account that private investment in Education is very scarce; the State takes the heaviest burden: 93% of all funds invested on Education, whether private or state, come from the Government (Colegio de Profesores de Chile, 1997).

It is also important to note that the national budget for education did not increase during the military regime, and neither were there governmental policies destined to increase the number of teachers or schools over the ongoing growth of the population.

Decentralisation

The Ministry of Education concentrated on general curricular lines, but the educational process, according to the plan of the new regime, began to be administered by the municipalities of the country, then controlled by a mayor appointed by the government. The military government ordered them to sell as many schools as possible, but this measure could never be fully taken. The possibility of transferring schools to become the property of their teachers was seriously considered, but the idea could not be carried out either.

In brief, municipalities administer education, a fact which is amply rejected by the present government and the national teachers' union. The Constitution, passed in 1980, does not allow any changes. Described below is the situation for the four educational levels, preschool, primary, secondary and tertiary education under the military dictatorship:

Nursery schools

They have never been compulsory, and most of them are either totally private or state subsidised. It was not a relevant educational feature during the military government.

Primary schools

The major state investments in public education were done at the primary school system. The purpose of preferentially financing primary education aimed at raising production: with the labour force, in spite of being traditionally cheap, being adequately instructed with eight years of schooling.

Secondary schools

Before the coup, less than 10% of all schools were private; now half of Chilean high schools are. The majority of them have been state subsidised since the military founded a new educational order. A small percentage are extremely expensive for Chilean standards (fees of about $US 300-500 a month) and educate the upper classes (less than 1% of the population). Nearly all are located in Santiago, the capital, they are often bilingual and have connections with developed countries ('The Grange School', 'Santiago College', 'L' Alliance Française', 'La Scuola Italiana', 'Die Deutsche Schule', etc.)

Universities

State universities and institutes (traditionally oriented to professions) were not funded before the coup. The state dedicated 1.8% of the national income to higher education. The military regime reduced this figure to only 0.5%. Now all universities are funded, and they will continue to be so for a long time yet, since they are paid by law and neither will they share Educational Reform funds for the purpose of recovering their gratuitousness.

Outcomes of the first reform

President's Frei government (1964-1970) initiated important social reforms in the country. The most important changes in Chilean social life introduced by Frei were the Agrarian Reform and the Educational Reform. These changes were dramatically deepened under Salvador Allende's socialist government, which brought about a harsh response from Conservative forces, openly supported in their fight against Allende by the US government. Conservatives won the support of the Chilean Army and President Allende was overthrown in September 1973. After that, a military regime, headed by General Augusto Pinochet, ruled the country until 1990.

It is very interesting to note that the military regime performed a drastic involution in Chilean economy and social life. Frei, for instance, was the first to emphasise the need of strengthening state education. The neo-liberal economic scope recommended by the American so-called 'Chicago School of Economics' was applied to Education with two important measures: a hard cut on public expenditure, and the subsidiarity system.

The present educational reform

The present Educational Reform (ER) (Navarro, 1997), passed in 1996, started in 1997 and will last until the year 2001. Its main objective is to correct what has come to be known as the 'Chilean Educational Crisis' (Ministerio de Educación, 1994).

The starting point of the reform was the 'MECE' Plan -'Mejoramiento de la Equidad y Calidad de la Educación'- (Programme for the Improvement of Equity and Quality of Education, PIEQE) (Ministerio de Educación, 1992). It began in 1992 as an experiment and is now a part of the reform. A year before, the government had already ordered a study of the situation of state education, and it was evaluated as 'critical', mainly due to the following problems:

- overpopulated schools (a national average of about 40 children per class -the legal maximum is 45),

- material poverty in half of them,

- a big number of incomplete rural schools,

- obsolete methodologies,

- teachers without up-to-date training, and

- teachers so badly paid that they often work in two or three schools.

When the reform was announced, the President of the Republic, in his yearly message to the National Congress (May 1996), declared, in short, that the purpose of the reform was the gradual reassumption of the pedagogical function of the State. The main corrective measures for the reform - backed by an investment of around US$ 70 million - are the following:

Curricular reform

A number of reform activities have begun to take place, including:

- *Decentralisation.*
  The staff of schools may propose to the government their own curricula and new forms of school organisation. This is a revolutionary measure, aimed at eliminating a centralist and authoritative tradition.

- *New teaching methods.*
  With the purpose of raising student achievement, the reform hopes to end the traditional methods of class teaching and provide for the

introduction of new methodologies based on constructivist and active learning, with a lot of team and interactive work.

- *Extension of the class work period.*
  Schools (though not all of them yet) will have classes in the morning as well as in the afternoon, and with more teaching hours (Chile has about a third less class work than developed countries with about 800 class periods a year).

- *Construction of 20,000 additional classrooms across the country.*
  This must commence to reduce the quantity of students per class.

- *Strengthening the initial training of teachers and increasing teachers' salaries.*
  The old style of education (a central and bossy management, old curricula, poverty of schools, overpopulated classes), together with the low salary of teachers, and poor social support for the teaching profession are obviously discouraging, and Chilean young people who succeed in entering college are not really interested in following teaching as a career. Moreover, a few years after graduation, a great number of teachers abandon their profession and look for better paid jobs.
  In order to cope with these problems, the State will deliver the national universities - both state and private owned - a large amount of money (about 20% of all Education Reform funds) in order to foster the growth of the faculties of education. Scholarships will be granted to all young men and women who decide to pursue a teaching career throughout the country. As well, teacher salaries will increase. The first stage will be completed by the end of the Education Reform period, by 2001. It is stated that by then a newly graduated teacher will earn about US$ 700 a month, almost a 300% increase from 1990, when a new teacher earned about US$ 250.
  All these measures are meant, of course, to dignify the teaching career, to meet the deficit of teachers and to diminish the number of children per class. An approximate figure for the appropriate future class size has not yet been determined.

- *Programs for the updating of teachers.*
  The programs include scholarships at the Pedagogic Centre and national and foreign universities (mainly in USA and Europe), and stays abroad for a selected number of school teachers during the four years of the ER. The stays include school visits and various kinds of academic programs.

- *Recognition awards for the teaching profession.*

Pedagogic research and experiment

The universities and institutes that train teachers have always caught up with the theoretical advances achieved in world education. Traditionally, teachers have been trained in an adequate atmosphere of study and practice at actual schools and, after graduation, many of them have had the opportunity to update at the Pedagogic Centre.

Pedagogic research has always been financed by the state, mainly through the Pedagogic Centre. Its various departments constantly organise academic events with the attendance of teachers from all the country. The State grants scholarships to around five hundred primary and secondary teachers yearly. These events are also offered to teachers of the private sector for a modest fee. Experience, however, has shown that the presence of teachers of private schools has always been poor.

Something that is worthwhile noticing is the fact that schools of the social élite do not perform any type of research, but they carry out projects on proposals conceived at the Pedagogic Centre and abroad (particularly in developed countries). Private schools are controlled by the state in respect to very general curricular aspects, so they have the resources and a great freedom to innovate, which is not possible in state schools.

The government has emphatically declared that pedagogic research and experiment are decisive elements of the reform, since their aim is to shorten the distance between the achievement standards of private schools and those of the State. Research and Experiment are performed by two entities:

The Ministry of Education

The Ministry of Education undertakes educational research in a variety of ways:

- Through its Statistics departments. All educational statistical information is to be found here; all research on achievement undertaken in Chile is based on this kind of information. The Ministry has regional offices in which such data can be found.

- At the Pedagogic Centre. The PC has a number of experts dedicated to educational research exclusively. It also has dormitories for teacher-students who attend courses, with a good set of premises and apparatuses for experiment. Research and experiment on matters considered relevant are made with children of all school levels coming from nearby schools. However, despite the Government's offers and state financial support, the coverage of the system is not entirely satisfactory.

- At state schools, through the 'Grupos Profesionales de Trabajo' (Professional Working Groups, PWGs) (Ávalos, 1997). These groups appeared with the PIEQE (1992), now in force, though not in all schools. The PWGs are teacher-workshops that gather to study and discuss problems of pedagogical theory covering learning-teaching areas and specific subject matters. The school 'Unidad Técnico-pedagógica' (Technical-pedagogical Unit, TPU) is in charge of organising and coordinating the PWGs. Once the discussions finish, teachers 'experience' in their classrooms, and then discuss their experiences with their colleagues within the PWGs. The system has proved very efficient and motivating for teachers. The results of the studies are periodically sent to the Ministry by every TPU.

Teacher training universities:

There are twenty-six important Chilean universities, private and state out of a total of around sixty. They are the universities belonging to the 'Consejo de Rectores' ('Rectors' Council', supported by the Ministry of Education). Not all of them possess faculties of Education, but those that do can exhibit:

- Research work undertaken by students (papers and graduation theses), normally consisting of small research activities that often repeat themselves due to the lack of communication and coordination among universities. These works are always descriptive (a style imposed at universities during the military regime). They are, in fact, of poor theoretical meaning and have little impact on national education policies.

- Research undertaken by professors. All universities have an office that invites professors to participate in yearly research contests. The least funded research projects belong to the social sciences area, like education, due to the tendency to favour those related to farming, fishing, mining or industrial development, which, in fact, typifies research in developing countries.

At any rate, university researchers still tend to avoid going beyond description. The culture of interpreting facts ideologically and giving opinions or making proposals have not yet fully reappeared. Original research is also scarce, due to -among other factors- lack of resources, the difficulty to organise multidisciplinary research teams, the short terms given for the presentation of results, the virtual prohibition of error, and the poor concentration of professors in their research areas. College research, as an exclusive activity, is poor since in nearly all university professors are requested to perform three functions simultaneously: teaching, research, and social extension.

Relevant research and experiment

It may be inferred from the above concepts that:

- Research is only descriptive. Diagnosis works and proposals are scarce.

- Relevant experiment is based on the studies made by renowned foreign experts, whose proposals are adapted to Chilean reality. This seems to be a characteristic of underdeveloped and developing countries. For instance, two of the present 'rages', both at the Pedagogic Centre and the Professional Working Groups, are the 'constructive' paradigms, as set forth by Piaget and his followers in the field of Methodology, and Effective Schools -though not explicitly - insofar as school organisation is concerned.

The most relevant studies are performed on:

A new kind of school:

The fundamental proposals of the Effective Schools Movement (ESM) have become a 'school pattern' or 'school model' in Chile. As stated above, élite private schools, not strictly controlled by the state, have been able to perform some interesting experiments in the light of the ESM. The experiments have naturally increased the levels of their already good achievements, which, if compared with those of state schools, are bringing about serious social consequences that cannot be discussed here. These schools are now called 'colegios exitosos' (successful schools). Their marketing is based on the high scores obtained by their students in the national proficiency tests -the tests given in the 4th and 8th classes of primary education and the Chilean baccalaureate ('Prueba de Aptitud Académica', Academic Ability Test).

The ESM is obviously attractive to the Government, because, in the first place, the meaning given to the term 'equity' in the Educational Reform is equivalent to raising achievement in state schools to the average level of private schools. However, due to the poor knowledge of the ESM, many educators think that it is not applicable in Chile, due to its hypothetical global meaning (a new kind of school and teaching methods). For example, teachers of poor schools often argue that social factors (poverty, exclusion, drug addiction, etc.) will prevent the organisation of a school based on ESM in the aspect of a school 'ethos'. There is also another problem: effective schools are dynamic, free, democratic and ever-innovating, and Chilean education, as in all Latin America, has traditionally been centralised, authoritarian, and has tended to uniformity (even under the municipal regime, in the Chilean case).

Nevertheless, this situation is gradually changing. In some regions of Chile, for instance, municipalities have shown a more collaborative spirit: in the northern province of Iquique, from next March 1998, a plan (both rural and urban), sponsored by the Municipality and the regional office of the Ministry of Education, will be implemented on an ESM basis.

Teaching methods

A number of new methods of teaching children are being considered within the new education reform:

- 'Programas de Desarrollo de Habilidades Sociales' (Programs for the Development of Social Abilities, PDSA). The training of children from early childhood in group and interactive work is now considered of vital importance. A series of projects in the frame of the PDSA are being carried out in all nursery schools. One of their most interesting variants is the 'Programa Caracol' (the 'Snail' Program), (L'bano, 1994) being carried out in some schools; its objective is the training of children in the mother tongue, considered the most efficient means of communication and socialisation.

- Methods of Group Instruction. The PC has been working for many years on the group instruction methods suggested by Benjamin Bloom (1984), which, roughly speaking, are aimed at replacing tutorial work. It is one of the topics now discussed within the PWGs, for its incidence on individual achievement improvement and teachers' time saving.

- Kumon's Method for the Teaching of Mathematics (Ministerio de Educación, 1996). This method, invented in Japan, is based on a kind of didactic material, and, according to our information, is being applied in 33 countries. PC experts consider it particularly important because of the present low standards in achievement in Mathematics and natural sciences. It is also interesting because its constructivist and self-learning scopes, which are supposed to diminish lecturing.

Evaluation

The various internationally accepted forms of subject-matter evaluation have always been applied in Chilean schools. It is interesting to observe that from 1998, the Third International Mathematics and Science Study (TIMSS) (Arancibia y Undurraga, 1997) evaluation system will be applied in Chile. This system is sponsored by the IEA (International Evaluation of Education Achievement). Chile will participate with all 8th form students. The test will provide the Chilean government with information about Mathematics and Science achievement in comparison with nearly 50 countries. The preparation of children for these tests require skill in various interactive tecniques; thus the corresponding training of teachers is now being performed at the PC. The TIMSS test will continue to be applied if it proves its validity.

Conclusion

Although the two democratically elected governments were elected with an absolute majority (1990 and 1993), they have not been able to produce basic economic and social reforms in Chile, as the military government had passed a State Constitution in 1980, which includes a peculiar system of elections, that does not permit the government the parliamentary majority to carry out all its plans, including the destination of more funds to perform a definitively profound Educational Reform. Thus, a great deal of what is being done to improve Education comes from hard-working and imaginative teachers.

Future perspectives

In fact, the future of Chilean Education is promising. The following points may justify this assertion:

- Chile, in the first place, lives now in a democracy, whatever deficiencies it may still have. Now, unlike the years of the military regime, the free expression of all ideas is stimulated. As for Education, parents at their schools, social organisations and mass media can freely express themselves and participate in the process of reforms. It is also important to keep in mind that any schools may now work with their own curricula and organisational patterns, if they justify them to the Ministry of Education.
- It must be underlined again that the foundations of ER are the dignification of the teaching profession, and the State's reassumption of its educational function. The basic measures, all of them in force, are: improvement of teachers' salaries, training of new teachers, massive updating of teachers, curricular reform and construction of more classrooms and schools.
- Educational research and experiment is being stimulated and performed as perhaps never before in Chilean history. The formation of PWGs illustrates the massive participation of teachers in this respect.

- 'Last but not least', since the present educational changes are being carried out in an atmosphere of liberty, i.e. free from any kind of prejudice, the ESM has now a real possibility to develop in Chile.

References

Arancibia y Undurraga (1997) 'TIMSS: La Evaluación que viene', in Revista de Educación, Ministerio de Educación. Julio, de 1997.

Ávalos, Beatrice (1997) '*El MECE Media: Una Experiencia Innovadora*', Revista Foro Educacional, N° 1, 65. Ed. Universidad Católica Blas Cañas, 1997.

Barrios, Marciano (1997) *Reflexiones en torno a la reforma Educacional de 1965*, Revista Foro Educacional, N° 1, 49. Ed. Universidad Católica Blas Cañas, 1997.

Colegio de Profesores de Chile (Teachers' union) (1997) '*Chile Educa a Chile*' (A document issued at the union's 'First National Congress of Education', August 1997).

Corporación de Promoción Universitaria (1995) '*Situación y Pol'ticas de Gobierno en Materia de Educación Superior: el Aporte de la Corporación de Promoción Universitaria*'. Revista Estudios Sociales, N° 83, 1995.

L'bano, Luz (1994) '*Programa Caracol*', in Revista de Educación, Ministerio de Educación. October, 1994.

Ministerio de Educación (1992) '*MECE: Temas para los grupos de discusión*', September, 1992.

Ministerio de Educación (1994) Comité Técnico asesor del Diálogo Nacional sobre la Modernisación de la Educación Chilena designado por S.E. el Presidente de la República: '*Los desaf'os de la Educación Chilena frente al Siglo XXI*', Ministerio de Educación, September, 1994. This document is better known as '*Informe Brunner*'. A good summary of Education under the military is to be found in chapters 1 and 2.

Ministerio de Educación (1996) '*Método Kumon: El Poder de los Números*'. Revista de Educación, August, 1996.

Navarro, Iván (1997) '*Fundamentos de una Renovación Educativa*' Revista Foro Educacional, N° 2, 23. Ed. Universidad Católica Blas Cañas, 1997.

Unesco Regional Office for Education in Latin America and the Caribbean (1993) Ministerio Secretar'a General de Gobierno: '*Educación: la Llave Maestra del Desarrollo*', a booklet distributed in all schools in October, 1996. Another good description of Chilean primary education is to be found in Unesco's document 'Pre-school and basic Education in Latin America and in the Caribbean', Unesco Regional Office for Education in Latin America and the Caribbean, Santiago de Chile, March, 1993.

13.

Evolution and impact of effective schools research on school improvement in the United States of America

Janet Chrispeels and Gilbert Austin

Introduction

An overarching feature of the educational context in the United States is the extensive decentralisation of educational decision-making given to the 50 states and over 15,000 school districts managed by locally elected boards of education. The lack of a centralised system of education with a national curriculum and examinations makes it difficult to present a singular picture of effective schools research and practice. Describing a national perspective masks important state and local variations and initiatives. Therefore, this report does not pretend to capture the entirety of the phenomenon. Instead, it presents a brief history of school effectiveness research, describes the context of American schools, discusses the evolution of school improvement with that context and how school improvement has been impacted by effective schools research, and indicates some trends in effective schools and school improvement research and practice.

A brief history of school effectiveness and improvement research

The US is generally regarded as the initiator of what has come to be called effective schools research (ESR). Teddlie and Reynolds (in press) divide the ESR field into three strands: school effects research, effective schools research, and school improvement research. A quick review of some of the highlights of these three strands provides insights into the past, present, and future of school effectiveness research in the US.

School effects research

The Coleman Report, Equality of Educational Opportunity (1966), represents the earliest and most notable large scale school effects research. Prior to the time of this study people believed that schools were generally effective though there was some concern for equity. The function of educational research was largely to discover methods to fine-tune what was held to be basically sound. Curiously, at least some of the effect of Coleman's report was due to a misinterpretation of his findings. Coleman did not conclude that schools fail to make important contributions to student achievement. Rather, he concluded that schools promote and facilitate great amounts of learning. He also concluded that differences between schools in promoting unusual levels of achievement were not striking, and most of these differences were more readily explained by family background than by the characteristics of schools themselves. Other school effects studies (Averch et al., 1974; Jencks et al., 1972) confirmed these findings.

In the decade of the 1960s the federal government for the first time joined with state and local educational agencies to work on the task of educating *all* the children in the United States. With the election of Lyndon Johnson to the presidency, three important pieces of legislation were passed which affected the lives of young children. In 1964 Johnson signed into law the Economic Opportunity Act, which created the Office of Economic Opportunity (OEO). In November, 1964, under OEO, the first planning committee met and discussed launching the preschool program called Head Start. By the summer of 1965 Head Start was in operation nationwide. The passage of the Elementary and Secondary Education Act (ESEA) in 1965 represented another major breakthrough on the part of the federal government to help education address issues of equity; and it served as a vehicle for shaping educational policy in a decentralised system by linking financial incentives with policy regulations.

One of the most important features of these new educational efforts by the federal government was the idea of accountability, which continues today to influence state and national policy making. The late Senator Robert Kennedy had included in ESEA the stipulation that evaluations were to be mandatory. The Program Planning and Budgeting Systems, which emerged in the 1960s, enabled the secretaries of agencies such as the Department of Health, Education, and Welfare to ask many more penetrating questions than they had previously been able to ask. The studies and legislation reviewed here spurred the next phase of US educational research—effective schools research.

Effective schools research

The effective schools research drew on ideas advanced by Dyer (1966). He suggested that looking at the centre of a distribution of scores was of minimal value since it indicated only a mean or average level of performance. He encouraged research to look at 'outliers' (scores at either end of the distribution) and try to understand what caused these schools to be outside their anticipated level of performance. When predicting student performance, Dyer's model takes into account difficult-to-change socioeconomic status and student input-performance variables (eg., student home and community characteristics related to achievement) over which the school has little control. The most common method of applying Dyer's model is regression-residuals analysis whereby mean values of predictor variables are used to predict mean output achievement. Drawing on these ideas, the earliest effective schools research began by investigating outliers (Austin, 1978; California State Department of Education, 1977; Weber, 1971).

Another major difference between effective schools and the school effects research is the attention to the processes of schooling and their relationship to equity in outcomes. Researchers focused on the processes by investigating schools serving low income students that had achieved higher than expected results (Armor et al., 1976; Austin, 1978; Edmonds, 1978; Edmonds & Frederiksen, 1979; Lezotte & Bancroft, 1985) or by controlling for the economic background of pupils (Brookover et al., 1979; Brookover et al., 1978). Although these studies identified a wide variety of process and organisational variables related to differential outcomes for students, the most lasting and influential effect on US effective schools initiatives was the five-factor model identified by Edmonds (1979): strong instructional leadership from the principal, a focus on instruction, a safe and orderly school learning environment, high expectations, frequent monitoring and use of assessment data to guide improvement. Edmonds (1986: 95) stated:

> *My own work began in 1973. Initially it was an attempt to determine whether schools existed anywhere in the United States that did not have a familial effect. Was it possible to find schools with a significant low-income pupil population (or*

a homogeneously low-income pupil population) in which those
pupils were clearly demonstrating academic mastery? In this
work, mastery is defined as performance on standardised
measures of achievement.

This list of factors was later *expanded* to regularly include school-home
relations and opportunity to learn. As Teddlie and Reynolds (in press) point
out, the work by Brookover and his colleagues (1979) was also valuable in
identifying how students' sense of futility and academic self-concept are
affected by school climate and teacher expectations.

Although numerous case studies continued to identify these and other
effective school factors *in turn around* schools, the effective schools research
came under sharp criticism because of sampling biases and analysis strategies
(eg., Cuban, 1983, 1984; Firestone & Herriot, 1982; Good & Brophy, 1986;
Rowan, Bossert, & Dwyer, 1983). Purkey and Smith (1983), although
critical of the effective schools research, point out:

Having expressed our reservations about the available
research and writing on school effectiveness, we nevertheless
find a substantive case emerging from the literature. There is a
good deal of common sense to the notion that a school is more
likely to have relatively high reading or math scores if the staff
agree to emphasise those subjects, are serious and purposeful
about the task of teaching, expect students to learn, and create
a safe and comfortable environment in which students
accurately perceive the school's expectations for academic
success and come to share them.

Purkey and Smith (1983) proposed two sets of variables drawn from
effective schools research: organisational-structural and process variables.
The organisational-structural variables include: school site management,
instructional leadership, staff stability, curriculum articulation and
organisation, schoolwide staff development, parental involvement and
support, schoolwide recognition of academic success, maximised learning
time, and district support. The four process variables define the general
concept of school culture and climate: collaborative planning and collegial
relationships; sense of community; clear goals and high expectations; and
order and discipline. These variables can be considered as first generation
effective schools findings and are displayed in the first column of Table 1. A
more recent review of the school effectiveness literature by Levine and
Lezotte (1990) confirmed, reiterated, and expanded on many of these
variables.

Combining effectiveness and improvement studies

Since the mid 1980s, more sophisticated studies of school improvement and effectiveness moved from lists of variables and began to explore different contexts in which schools were effective, the relationship between school and district effectiveness, and change across time (Austin & Garber, 1985; Chrispeels & Pollack, 1990; Chrispeels, 1992; Hallinger & Murphy, 1982, 1986; Murphy, Peterson, & Hallinger, 1986; Teddlie, Stringfield, & Desselle, 1985, Teddlie & Stringfield, 1993). The 10-year study of effective and ineffective Louisiana schools by Teddlie and Stringfield (1993) contributed to the field through its longitudinal analysis and its examination of both school and classroom effects showing the relationship between effective schools and effective classrooms.

The field made important methodological advances at this time (Bryk et al., 1986; Bryk & Raudenbush, 1992; Willms & Raudenbush, 1989), and as Teddlie and Reynolds (in press: 18) point out, these advances led:

> *to more sophisticated research across all three strands of ESR. The foremost methodological advance ... was the development of multilevel mathematical models to more accurately assess the effects of all the units of analysis associated with schooling.*

Some of these studies have utilised the large national data sets generated by the *High School & Beyond Study* and the *National Educational Longitudinal Study* (NELS) to examine student achievement data in relation to a variety of teacher and school variables (Bryk, Lee, & Holland, 1993). Other studies have focused on smaller scale quantitative and qualitative studies (Austin & Garber, 1985; Chrispeels, 1992; Crowson & Boyd, 1993; Goertz et al., 1995; Lieberman, 1995; Louis & Miles, 1990; Marks & Louis, 1997; Murphy & Hallinger, 1993; Rosenholtz, 1989; Wehlage, 1992). The second column in Table 1 summarises the second generation of effective schools variables that emerged from these studies and compares them with first generation findings using the Purkey and Smith (1983) framework.

In spite of these methodological advances, by the late 1980s, effective schools research in the US was dismissed by most educational researchers in academia. However, as Cuban noted in Teddlie and Stringfield's *Schools Make a Difference* (1993: ix) 'had this study been available in the early 1980s...the trajectory of 'effective schools' research among academics might have been very different'. Since the mid-1980s few studies of school effectiveness have been conducted, in comparison to other countries (Scheerens & Boskers, 1997), but implementation and research on school improvement have continued. Many school improvement initiatives in fact have been informed and shaped by the early effective schools findings. Thus, in the US there has not been the dichotomy or distance between effective schools and school improvement research found in Britain (Reynolds et al., 1997). Particularly important has been the assumption that school improvement must move beyond single curricular or instructional practice innovations to whole school reform. Examining the federal, state, and local contextual features of US education illuminates how policy and governmental actions have influenced effective schools and improvement research and practice. The next section highlights key contextual components.

Table 1: Comparison of first and second generation school effectiveness variables

Organisational-Structural Characteristics	
First Generation	**Second Generation**
Site Management	*Site-Based Management*
• Autonomy for each school to improve its academic achievement	• Budget and instructional decision-making at school level through school improvement or governance teams
Leadership	*Team Leadership*
• Principal is key facilitator to initiate and maintain school effectiveness	• Principal works with teacher leaders to develop shared vision
	• Establishment of principals' academies and better assessment of principal skills through NASSP Assessment Centres
Staff Stability	*Staff Selection, Stability & Teaming*
• Keeping staff turnover low	• Site selection of staff to meet school curriculum goals.
	• Increased inter-grade and subject cooperation, joint planning.

Organisational-Structural Characteristics	
First Generation	**Second Generation**
Curriculum and Instruction • Clear objectives • Articulation across grade and subject, focused on basic skills • Learning styles • Teacher-centred and directed	*Alignment of Curriculum, Instruction and Assessment* • A seamless curriculum addressing basics and critical thinking • Multiple intelligences • New time arrangements; block scheduling • Learner-centred; teacher facilitated
Staff Development • School-based, focused on school goals and staff needs	*School-Identified Staff Development* • Long-term with follow-up and coaching • Develops not only content and knowledge skills, but also process and collaborative skills
Maximised Learning Time • Time on task focus • Increased portion of school day devoted to academic subjects	*Flexible Scheduling* • Level of learning held constant; time allowed to learn vary • Extend learning time in creative ways • Uses of technology

Organisational-Structural Characteristics	
First Generation	**Second Generation**
Widespread Recognition of Academic Success	*Inclusion of All Children in Regular School Classes*
• School honours academic success in many curriculum areas and for different groups of children	• Mainstreaming and detracking • Use of multiple strategies to achieve mastery by all students
Parent Involvement	*Parent/Community Participation*
• Parents need to be informed of school goals and student responsibilities	• Parents/community serve on improvement teams • Community resources tapped to support students/family needs

Process Characteristics	
First Generation of School Effectiveness Variables	**Second Generation of School Effectiveness Variables**
Collaborative Planning	*Shared Leadership*
• Teachers and administrators work together • Commonalty of goals	• Teachers assume a variety of leadership roles • Entire staff is involved in collaborative planning. and developing a shared vision • Greater involvement of parents/community in school governance.

Process Characteristics	
First Generation of School Effectiveness Variables	**Second Generation of School Effectiveness Variables**
Sense of Community • School creates a sense of community and reduces alienation and isolation	*Professional Learning Community* • Teachers as professionals • School as a learning community which maximises learning for students and adults. • Authentic school-home partnership built on trust and communication
Clear Goals and High Expectations • Goals focused around a few academic subjects	*Clear Goals and High Expectation* • Multiple goals of schools recognised, especially school to career transitions. • Greater diversity in student body requiring a broad array of responses while maintaining high expectations
Order and Discipline • Focus on discipline plans • Recognition for good behaviour	*Safe and Orderly Learning Environment* • Cooperative team learning • Faculty, students, community assume responsibility for safe school • Teaching tolerance and mediation skills

Context issues impacting research and practice

Federal level

Although the US federal government plays a minimal role compared to other countries where education is more centralised, 'it is an error historically to think of US schools as predominantly centralised or decentralised ... The web of interactive relationships is far too complex for that' (Tyack, in Crowson & Boyd, 1993). Federal policies, funding and dissemination activities have influenced school effectiveness and reform in a variety of ways: funding for disadvantaged students, dissemination of information, and through involvement in testing, and the creation of a national data base.

National funding and program mandates for disadvantaged pupils (Head Start, Follow-Through, Title 1, Chapter I and Title VII programs), illustrate the interactive web of relationships between federal, state and local levels and between research and practice. The Coleman Report, Equality of Educational Opportunity (1966), indicated the importance of family and socioeconomic conditions to schooling outcomes. Since SES was shown to be significant in explaining the achievement gap between poor and affluent students and between school differences, educational policy makers reasoned that compensatory programs were needed for disadvantaged students. Although the achievement of disadvantaged students improved, these programs did not close the gap. In some respects, compensatory programs were counter to school effectiveness goals because they reinforced the use of tracking and separation of students into curricular paths. Recent Title I program changes, however, reflect the application of school effectiveness research allowing schools to utilise the funds for whole school change and improvement.

The federal government also plays a role through disseminating information about effective programs, especially through its "What Works' series and the National Diffusion Network. Although this information helps to inform local educational agencies, it also reinforces a 'project or program' orientation to school improvement rather than systemic change efforts. Additionally, federal funding of regional educational laboratories represents another vehicle for researching and disseminating information about school effectiveness and improvement. The Mid-Continent Regional Educational and the Northwest Regional Laboratories were the first in the country to develop instruments and improvement programs using school effectiveness research. The Southwest and Central Educational Development Labs have also carried out major school improvement initiatives. These labs have formed a consortium, the School Change Collaborative, to ensure that their individual efforts have far-reaching effects through collaboration and sharing of the knowledge base. The Collaborative's current focus is on school self-study and the development of professional learning communities involving entire staffs. On the national level, other private non-profit groups distribute effective schools information and provide training such as the National Center for Effective Schools (now housed at Phi Delta Kappa), Center for School Effectiveness at Okemos, Michigan, and Center for the Social Organisation of Schools at Johns Hopkins University, to name a few.

Current federal initiatives include greater involvement in testing by funding and publishing comparison scores among states using the National Assessment of Educational Progress and continuing support for a national research data base, the National Educational Longitudinal Study (for a fuller discussion of national data sets, see Stringfield & Herman, 1996). These initiatives are directed and funded by the National Center for Education Statistics, a part of the US Department of Education. The federal government funds research on the development of national curriculum standards and the creation of a national test that would be tied to these standards. Although there is general public support for the development of curriculum standards, there is not the same level of support for a national test (Los Angeles Times, November 2, 1997). The present Commission of Education is a strong advocate for the development of a national test.

State level

Constitutional authority and responsibility for K-12 and higher education rests with the 50 state governments; however, much of this authority is delegated to local districts, except in the state of Hawaii, which operates as a unitary, centralised system. States vary in the level of funding they provide to local districts and in the level of control over curriculum and assessment. As states have been challenged in the courts over the inequities of funding, a significant trend in the US is the gradual shift away from reliance on local property or land taxes and the funding of education from other state revenues. California, for example, was one of the first states in which the inequalities of district funding was successfully challenged (Serrano vs. Priest, 1971) requiring the state to provide funds to ensure greater equalisation. This pattern has been repeated in many other states (Stringfield & Herman, 1996). The concern for greater equity in school funding arises from a recognition of the detrimental effects of inadequate inputs on children's educational opportunities (Kozol, 1991). Kozol's work has given rise to new efforts to assess and understand school effects in terms of inputs. A recent Education Week report (1997) rated states B- overall in equality of inputs, with inner cities and rural areas suffering the most.

As states assume greater responsibility for the funding of schools, they also exert increased authority in the areas of graduation standards, length of the school year, state curriculum frameworks, text book selection, and statewide assessment. Initiatives such as in Kentucky, Tennessee, South Carolina, California, Maryland, Massachusetts, Minnesota, and Vermont have led to the linking of state funding to the implementation of a variety of school reform initiatives including:

- the establishment of school councils composed of parents, teachers, administrators, other school staff, and at the secondary level, students and implementation of site-based management (eg., California, Florida, Massachusetts, South Carolina, Kentucky);

- funding for restructuring or establishing charter schools (eg., California, Massachusetts, Minnesota);

- the establishment of subject matter professional development programs for teachers and principals' academies (eg., California, Maryland, Vermont); and

- the reduction of class size in the primary grades (eg., Tennessee, California).

A critical area that deserves special discussion is efforts being made to address issues of leadership. The search for effective schools led educators to the works on transactional and transformational leadership by Burns (1978), Bass (1985) and Rost (1991). These writers, who explored the nature of relationships between leaders and followers, presented a definition of transformational leadership that is more in keeping with efforts to redefine the relationship between teachers and administrators perceived as needed in effective schools if fundamental changes are to occur. Leithwood, who also has conducted pioneering work in transformational and transactional leadership research, states that 'Transformational leadership evokes a more appropriate range of practice, it ought to subsume instructional leadership as the dominant image of school administration, at least during the 1990s' (Leithwood, 1992). The thrust of the current direction is that leadership that is transformational in nature will take a school to a higher level of success than the transactional style (Leithwood, 1992; Sergiovanni, 1987). Lambert et al. (1995) in *The Constructivist Leader* build on these works by stressing the importance of relationships to leadership. Change is often truncated because too little time is spent in dialogue to build relationships among administrators and teachers, teachers and students, school staff and families. School change these authors argue requires 'constructivist leadership...the reciprocal processes that enable participants in an educational community to construct meaning toward a common purpose of schooling' (Lambert et al., 1995: 52).

Maryland and California, among many, represent two states that are addressing principal and teacher professional development and leadership training needed for school reform. In Maryland, the implementation of the Principals' Academies and a Leadership in Educational Administration and Development (LEAD) Center represent examples of how training of future principals has evolved over the last two decades as new insights about school improvement and school effectiveness are available (Austin, 1989). Professional development offered in the late 1970s and 1980s concentrated on teaching principals the technical skills necessary to effectively perform on the job. Topics included instructional leadership, school management, reducing student disruption, and vocational and special education. Ten years later, in 1987, the University of Maryland and the Maryland State Department of Education received a federal grant for a six-year project to establish one of the many LEAD centres funded throughout the US. The program was built on the philosophy that principals could not lead or manage if they failed to keep abreast of current educational trends and practices. Although funding for the LEAD centres ended in 1993, by 1997 the Maryland Principal Association pressured the State Department of Education to reopen the Principals' Academy, once again confirming the importance of leadership to school change. The state also established a Commission on School-Based Administration to review the training, certification, and selection processes for principals.

On the west coast of the US, the content of the California School Leadership Academy's (CSLA) program, now in its 12th year, evolved similarly responding to new research on school improvement and acknowledgment that principals need to redefine their role as 'leader among leaders' who foster and develop the leadership of others—teachers, parents and students. Typical of this reconceptualisation of leadership, CSLA now offers professional development for school teams, recognising that principals cannot lead their schools alone through the complex processes of restructuring (California School Leadership Academy, 1995). The changes undertaken in professional development for principals reflect the second generation of effective schools research regarding instructional leadership (see column two in Table 1).

District and school level

A hallmark of the American educational context is the variability in size of school districts and schools. Centralisation and consolidation efforts have reduced the number of school districts considerably, but there are still small districts composed of one or two schools and serving 100 students or less. Most major cities in the US are served by large urban districts. The average elementary school ranges from 300 to 600, with class sizes of 26-30. Middle or junior high schools range from 300 to 1,500, and high schools typically range from 800 to 2,000, with a few serving as many as 4,000 students. Teachers in elementary schools typically teach all subjects in self-contained, grade-age specific classrooms; whereas most middle and high schools have subject matter specialists with students moving every 45-55 minutes to a new teacher. Many recent reform initiatives, however, are altering these regular patterns of schooling with the implementation of multi-grade classes, block scheduling, radically reduced class sizes in the primary grades, schools-within-schools that personalise large high schools, and team or interdisciplinary teaching. The vastness of the educational landscape makes it difficult to determine the extent of implementation of these reforms, and there are only a few emerging research studies showing the impact of these innovations (Elmore, Peterson, & McCarthey, 1996; Louis & Kruse, 1995; Wehlage, 1992) .

Regardless of size or configuration, an elected board, consisting of 5 to 9 members, governs most school districts, while a superintendent, chosen by the board of education, serves as CEO and manager. 'In a few districts, both the school board and the superintendent are appointed by other elected officials such as the local mayor' (Stringfield & Herman, 1996: 161). District boards of education set local educational standards and policies with regard to curriculum, assessing student progress, hiring and evaluation of school personnel, construction and maintenance of school facilities, attendance, discipline, homework policies, and the purchase of supplies and materials. Districts carry out these functions and responsibilities within guidelines established by state departments of education or legislative policy.

The organisational structure of most US school districts reflects a hierarchical bureaucratic model. Although teachers maintain considerable autonomy behind their closed classrooms doors, they typically have little influence on the development and implementation of policies that affect them and their students. As many states and districts implement Site Based Management (SBM) and initiate school restructuring, however, more teachers are participating in shared decision-making (a second generation school effectiveness variable in Table 1). Kentucky, for example, in its comprehensive education reform act in 1990 mandates increased teacher participation through the implementation of School-Based Decision-making (SBDM) in all schools by 1996. David (1992: 11), in a report on the first year of such implementation, found widespread confusion concerning participation expectations, but concludes that even this confusion provided convincing evidence that real change was occurring. Even as implementation has continued over time, many councils still are primarily involved in procedural issues such as schoolwide planning and internal organisational questions. Van Meter (1993: 23), in a study conducted at the mid-point of

Kentucky's SBDM implementation schedule, concludes that the nature and level of teacher participation in school decision-making varied widely, as 'within individual sites—in this case schools—[implementation] takes place in a somewhat unpredictable manner that is unique to each site and situation'. Kentucky's experience with SBM, has been confirmed in other research on shared decision-making. These findings raise questions about how SBM supports effective schools and impacts student learning (Malen, Ogawa, & Kranz, 1990; Weiss, Cambone, & Wyeth, 1992; Wohlstetter & Odden, 1994).

Five factors identified in the research that may impede SBM from increasing school effectiveness are:

• few SBM committees receive adequate training,

• SBM committees often get bogged down in management issues, leaving little time to address teaching and learning,

• teams do not collect or use data to guide their improvement efforts and set priorities,

• normal politics are allowed to operate keeping teams from focusing on improvement priorities, and

• few districts implementing SBM change their own hierarchical way of operating,

Thus, teachers may find their site decisions in conflict with centrally determined decisions. The tension between hierarchical district decision-making structures and shared decision-making at the site leaves the principal caught in the middle between conflicting authority structures, compounding the difficulty of implementing site level reforms (Harari, Strait, Rodarte, & Chrispeels, 1998). Several recent studies (Crowson & Boyd, 1993; Goertz et al., 1995; Marks & Louis, 1997; Robertson & Briggs, 1998; Smylie, Lazarus, & Brownlee-Conyers, 1996) indicate that teacher empowerment and SBM can impact student achievement, but the relation is likely to be indirect, and only in well-developed cases will SBM actually impact teacher instructional practices. One reason for the discouraging results of SBM in enhancing student learning is SBM in and of itself does not increase teacher's knowledge and skills. Teachers in many schools are ill-prepared to teach to the higher standards being set by the states. Education Week's review of American schools (1997) found that 30% to 40% of secondary teachers are teaching outside of their subject area. Elementary teachers also often lack knowledge needed to teach math, science or social studies. Others have found that teachers have adopted new instructional strategies advocated by reformers, such as cooperative groups, or hands-on learning activities, but they often lack the content/subject matter knowledge needed to effectively use these strategies (Elmore, et al., 1996). Elmore et al. (1996) in their case studies of restructuring schools did not find that the schools were restructuring or reculturing in ways that would ensure teachers developed a deep understanding of subject matter. Much work remains to be done to fully understand the indirect impact of teacher empowerment on school improvement and effectiveness and how school restructuring could be refocussed in ways that not only give teachers more say but also knowledge needed to be an effective teacher.

Evolution and impact of effective schools research on school improvement

One of the most interesting aspects of school effectiveness in the US has been the contrast between the limited and, in many respects, short-lived research on effective schools, and the extensive ongoing implementation of effective schools models by practitioners (Bullard & Taylor, 1994; Taylor, 1990; Teddlie & Reynolds, in press). Soon after Edmonds' (1979) work was published, the state departments of education in Connecticut, New York, and the Mid-Continent Educational Laboratory developed surveys to measure the existence of the effective schools factors. The Connecticut State Department of Education developed, tested and has used extensively the Connecticut School Effectiveness Questionnaire, copyrighted in 1981. Revised in 1989, it has been used since its inception to test teachers' judgments of the implementation of the correlates of the effective schools movement in Connecticut schools and elsewhere in the country. Similarly, the Northwest Lab launched its 'Onward to Excellence Program' in 1983-84. The San Diego County Office of Education soon followed with the publication of its survey instruments (1984) and a program implementation manual (Chrispeels & Meaney, 1989). Bamberg and Andrews (1989) at the University of Washington developed survey instruments and an intervention program to help Washington schools. On the east coast, efforts were underway to understand school effectiveness in rural schools (Meyers, 1989). Suburban schools in upstate New York (Sudlow, 1984) and in Florida and South Carolina the departments of education developed reform efforts based on an effective schools model. More recently, Kentucky has integrated the effective schools process into its statewide reform initiative. By 1989, the US General Accounting Office found that 4 out of every 10 school districts in almost every state had undertaken some type of school effectiveness program. This leads to the question: Why did so many schools and school districts adopt with fervour and conviction an improvement approach that researchers found to be so flawed?

Four basic reasons may explain the zeal with which the effective schools movement grew well beyond its research base. First, the research studies of effective schools gave principals and teachers hope that there was something they could do to help inner city urban children be successful in school. Second, the effective schools model challenged educators to look at their school as a whole system with complex, interrelated parts. Reforms of the previous decades generally focused on classroom innovations or new curricula and benefits often were short-lived because of the failure to link classroom innovations to organisational structures. Third, the effective schools factors made sense to educators (and in some ways served as the slogan of the day). The factors gave focus and direction to improvement efforts, especially when the school collected and used student achievement data to drive its improvement efforts. Fourth, schools that systematically paid attention to the factors, especially the alignment of curriculum and instruction with state assessments, were able to show gains in student achievement — a powerful political motivator.

School effectiveness initiatives have been eclipsed in the last ten years by calls for restructuring and systemic reforms. The reforms undertaken in such states as Kentucky, California, Michigan, and Vermont evolved from centralising, top-down strategies to raise standards. According to Goertz, Floden, and O'Day (1995), systemic reforms differed from comprehensive reforms of the early 1980s, first, by focusing on improving achievement for all students (a major goal of earlier school effectiveness reforms, but neglected by some in the standards raising era), and second, by attempting to bring greater coherence and congruence among policies (eg., adopting curriculum frameworks, providing staff development to support the frameworks, and developing new statewide assessment systems aligned with the curriculum, Chrispeels, 1997; Fuhrman, 1993).

These states and others have also supported 'bottom-up' efforts to restructure and redistribute governing authority (Goertz, Floden, & O'Day, 1995; Evertson & Murphy, 1992). Some restructuring includes the adoption of reform programs affiliated with a founder or developer, for example, Accelerated Schools with Henry Levin, the School Development Model with James Comer, the Coalition for Essential Schools with Ted Sizer, Success for All with Robert Slavin, Outcome-based Education with William Spady, the Quality School with William Glasser, and the ATLAS Communities developed by Howard Gardner, James Comer, Ted Sizer and Janet Whitla (Block, Everson, & Guskey, 1995; Stringfield, Datnow, Herman & Berkeley, 1997). Unlike more generic and 'home-grown' effective schools programs, which represent an amalgam of many people's efforts, these newer initiatives generally present a program that schools can follow, and they have developed specific training that must be attended before the program is implemented.

Programs such as the Coalition for Essential Schools or Accelerated Schools provide guidance, but the school community is urged to engage in a process of *reinventing* itself.   Other programs such as *Success for All*, are more prescriptive. Proponents of these programs argue that classroom teachers and school administrators do not have time to 'reinvent the wheel' and need to utilise best practices developed and tested by others to speed the reform process (Scheerens & Bosker, 1997). If the designs, however, do not match the state accountability system, it is uncertain if teachers will fully implement the components of the program needed to achieve its purported outcomes (Smith et al., 1997).

In the next section we examine five major strands in school effectiveness and improvement research, which have evolved from the past decade's implementation of restructuring and reform.

Future trends in school effectiveness and improvement

We believe these strands need to be addressed if we are to advance the school effectiveness knowledge base and school practices in the 21st century. Examination of these strands, among others, will help to define the third generation of school effectiveness. They are:

- the relationship between district and school effectiveness;
- the link between classroom and schoolwide effectiveness;
- the relationship between teacher professionalisation, empowerment, and student learning;
- the impact of decentralisation, choice, and charter school movements on equity and school effectiveness; and
- the development of valid and reliable assessment systems that accurately and authentically measure not only what students know but also reflect growth and improvement.

Relationships between district and school effectiveness

There is a growing recognition in both the research and practice communities that successful restructuring cannot be compartmentalised. As Crowson and Boyd (1993: 29) point out, 'there is yet little sense (in depth and in detail) as to how an urban school district should be effectively 'backward mapped' from the core technology toward a coherent system of service-to and support-of school site improvement'. Similarly, Fullan's (1993) admonition that school reform needs leadership at the school site to initiate bottom-up improvements and district execution of top-down reform leaves many questions about the 'how' of co-development of both school and district. Particularly important is the need to investigate how school, district, and state can coordinate restructuring initiatives to address issues of teaching and learning.

Linking classroom and schoolwide effectiveness

The US has a strong foundation of classroom level research (Brophy, 1989; Brophy & Good, 1986; Marshall, 1992; Weade & Evertson, 1988), some of which shows how difficult it is to translate state-initiated changes in curriculum to the classroom (Marsh & Odden 1991; Peterson, 1990). This body of research, however, has generally existed side-by-side with effective schools research and few connections have been made between the class and school level. As discussed above, Teddlie and Stringfield (1983), Stringfield, Teddlie and Suarez (1985) and Teddlie, Kirby and Stringfield (1989) were the first to conduct sophisticated studies showing the link between effective schools and effective classrooms. However, we believe that research is needed to investigate the complex process of how teachers and students create classroom cultures and communities that define opportunities for learning for all students (Santa Barbara Classroom Discourse Group, 1992), and how these classroom communities relate to the broader school organisation and culture. This research agenda is suggested given findings that show 30% of the differences in student learning are within school variations (Scheerens & Bosker, 1996).

The relationship between teacher professionalisation, empowerment, and student learning

Recent trends in school improvement practice and research have centred on the topic of teacher professionalisation and empowerment (Darling-Hammond & Goodwin, 1993; Lieberman, Saxl, & Miles, 1988; Little, 1990; Louis & Kruse, 1995). School effects studies, both qualitative and quantitative (Chrispeels, 1992; Rosenholtz, 1989; Stringfield & Teddlie, 1993) show that schoolwide organisational factors affect teachers, which in turn, influences the impact they have on their students. These effects, although small, explain only 10% of the variance in school outcomes and indicate that the working climate for the adults in the school should not be ignored. Important work by Marks and Louis (1997: 245) show that 'overall, empowerment appears to be an important but not sufficient condition of obtaining real changes in teachers' ways of working and their instructional practices...'. They found the impact of empowering teachers on student learning, however, to be indirectly linked through the school's organisation for instruction. This work lays a foundation for continuing to explore more fully how these indirect processes work to enhance student learning.

Although important insights have been gained about effective professional development (Griffin, 1983; Guskey, 1986; Lieberman & Miller, 1979; Joyce & Showers, 1988), there is still debate on its design and delivery. Researchers and practitioners differ on whether professional development should focus on the individual teacher and classroom needs or be targeted to more general, systemic and organisational issues; whether it should be school based and teacher driven or draw on the expertise of others outside the system; and whether it should address small and incremental or large scale change (Guskey & Huberman, 1995). Little (1993) has outlined six principles of professional development that she believes will support systemic change, but little research has been done to investigate the types of professional development that will enhance school effectiveness and improvement, especially effectiveness that results from increased teacher knowledge. A study of California School Leadership Teams showed that providing professional development, especially in the use of research and school data, was a strong predictor that teams were more likely to focus on teaching and learning (Chrispeels, Brown, & Castillo, 1997). Linking the work of the leadership teams to student achievement, however, is problematic, especially in the absence of appropriate and comparable measures of student achievement.

The work on teacher professionalisation has recently been addressed in *What Matters Most: Teaching for America's Future* (National Commission on Teaching and America's Future, 1996). The two major emphases in the book are (1) increasing teachers' access to knowledge to meet the demands they face and (2) redesigning schools so they can better support serious teaching and learning. Yet, we see too little attention being paid to developing teachers subject matter and pedagogical knowledge and its impact on effective schools.

Impact of decentralisation, choice and charter schools on equity and school effectiveness

Equity issues are an essential component of school effectiveness, yet, given the difficulty of obtaining disaggregated student outcomes, socioeconomic status, and prior achievement data, many studies fail to accurately account for who benefits from various school improvement initiatives. It is likely that public and political pressure will continue to push for increased decentralisation in the US. School-based management and the establishment of charter and other schools of choice need deliberate, consistent, and pervasive strategies to ensure equity if the reforms are to be for all students. We suggest two important research agenda arise from this theme:

- understanding how autonomous charter or schools of choice impact equality of inputs and outputs; and
- exploring the political contexts that support or constrain school effectiveness.

This latter topic is especially important given the finding that the loudest protests about school reform come from upper middle class parents, whose children are doing well in the system and who feel their children may lose a competitive edge if overall effectiveness is improved (Farkas, 1993).

The development of valid and reliable assessment systems

Closely related to the equity issue is the need to accurately assess student learning. The development of valid and reliable instruments to assess effectiveness along a variety of dimensions remains illusive. Very few states have comprehensive systems of assessment that are closely aligned with school curricula. Efforts are under way in many states to develop an array of assessment tasks, but reliability issues continue to plague these new systems (Chrispeels, 1997; Goertz et al., 1995). As assessment systems have moved away from traditional standardised tests, small but well-organised segments of the public have protested, and in the case of California were successful in derailing the state's new assessment system (Chrispeels, 1997). There remain critical research and policy questions for the next generation of effective schools research. What are fair and authentic systems of assessing student progress that are acceptable to the public and serve the interests of politicians, citizens and students? How can we know whether school improvement is adding value to students? One groundbreaking work in the field is being conducted by the Connecticut State Department of Education; it is a whole series of new assessment tasks to measure school effectiveness.

Concluding thoughts

The five strands outlined above are likely to dominate the research, policy, and practice agendas for the decade to come. The challenge is to gain an understanding of the interrelationships among the strands. As research proceeds along these lines, there is the possibility of weaving together these strands to generate a more grounded and comprehensive theoretical framework of school effectiveness and improvement. The value of theory building is that it can clarify the complexity and dynamics of systemic reforms that lead to effective schools. This may move us toward 'explanatory mechanisms which in their turn will be examined for their usefulness in explaining school effectiveness phenomena' (Scheerens & Bosker, 1997: 266). As Scheerens and Bosker go on to point out, theory building can be a means of expanding and improving the knowledge base and can help to focus more on future research, vis-a-vis the broadness of concepts and complexity of possibly interesting relationships; to obtain, by means of more theory-driven research, results that are easier to interpret; to discover factors and critical relationships that can be used as levers for school improvement. (1997: 266.) Research in these areas will produce empirical findings and hopefully theory that will lead to a third generation of school effectiveness research and practice.

Acknowledgments

We wish to thank Sam Stringfield and Rebecca Herman for allowing us to draw from their original Country Report 'Assessment of the State of School Effectiveness Research in the United States of America' which appeared in *School Effectiveness and Improvement*, 7(2), 159-180, 1996; and Charles Teddlie for sharing his recent review of school effects and school effectiveness research in the United States, 'An Introduction to School Effectiveness Research,' in Teddlie, C. & Reynolds, D. (in press) *The International Handbook of School Effectiveness Research*, London: Falmer. Thank you also to Kathleen J. Martin for editorial assistance.

References

Armor, D., Conry-Oseguera, P., Cox, M., King, N., McDonnell, L., Pascal, A., Pauly, E., & Zellman, G. (1976). *Analysis of the school preferred reading program in selected Los Angeles minority schools*. Santa Monica, CA: Rand Corporation.

Austin, G. R. (1978). *Process evaluation: A comprehensive study of outliers*. Baltimore, MD: Maryland State Department of Education. (ERIC Document Reproduction Services No. ED 160-644.

Austin, G. R. (1989). *Lead center evaluation, year two*. Baltimore, MD: Center for Educational Research and Development, University of Maryland Baltimore County.

Austin, G. R. & Garber, H. (1985). *Research on exemplary schools.* Orlando: Academic Press.

Averch, H. A., Carroll, S. J., Donaldson, T. S., Kiesling, H. J., & Pincus, J. (1974). *How effective is schooling? A critical review of research.* Englewood Cliffs, NJ: Educational Technology Publications.

Bamburg, J. E. & Andrews, R. L. (1989, March). *Putting effective schools research to work: The process of change and the role of the principal.* Paper presented at the annual meeting of the American Educational Research Association, San Francisco, CA.

Bass, B. M. (1985). *Leadership and performance beyond expectations.* New York: The Free Press.

Block, J. H., Everson, S. T., & Guskey, T. R. (1995). *School improvement programs: A handbook for educational leaders.* New York: Scholastic.

Brookover, W. B., Beady, C., Flood, P., Schweitzer, J., & Wisenbaker, J. (1979). *Schools, social systems and student achievement: Schools can make a difference.* New York: Praeger.

Brookover, W. B., Schweitzer, J. H., Schneider, J. M., Beady, C. H., Flood, P. K.,& Wisenbaker, J. M. (1978). Elementary school social climate and school achievement. *American Educational Research Journal,* 15, 301-318.

Brophy, J. (Ed.). (1989). *Advances in research on teaching* (Vol. 1). Greenwich, CT: JAI Press.

Brophy, J. & Good. T. (1986). Teacher behaviour and student achievement. In M. Wittrock (Ed.). *Handbook of research on teaching* (3rd. ed. 328-375). New York: Macmillan.

Bryk, A. S. Lee, V., & Holland, P. (1993). *Catholic schools and the common good.* Cambridge, MA: Harvard University Press.

Bryk, A. S. & Raudenbush, S. W. (1992). *Hierarchical linear models.* Newbury Park, CA: Sage.

Bryk, A. S., Raudenbush, S. W., Seltzer, J., & Congdon, R. T. (1986). *An introduction to HLM: Computer program and user's guide.* Chicago IL: University of Chicago, Department of Education.

Bullard, P. & Taylor, B. O. (1994). *Keepers of the dream. The triumph of effective schools.* Chicago: Excelsior!

Burns, J. M. (1978). *Leadership.* New York: Harper and Row.

California State Department of Education (1977). *California school effectiveness study: The first year 1974-75.* Sacramento, CA: Author.

California School Leadership Academy. (January, 1995). *School Leadership Team: An infrastructure strategy to support school change.* Hayward, CA: Author.

Chrispeels, J. H. (1997). Educational policy implementation in a shifting political climate: The California experience. *American Educational Research Journal, 34*(3), 453-481.

Chrispeels, J. H. (1992). *Purposeful restructuring: Creating a climate of achievement and learning in elementary schools.* London: Falmer.

Chrispeels, J.H., Brown, J. H. & Castillo, S. (1997, March). *School Leadership Teams: Factors that influence their effectiveness in bringing about school change.* Paper presented at the annual meeting of the American Educational Research Association, Chicago, IL.

Chrispeels, J. H. & Meaney, D. (1985). *Building effective schools: Assessing, planning, implementing.* San Diego, CA: San Diego County Office of Education.

Chrispeels, J. H., & Pollack, S. (1990). Equity schools and equity districts.. In B. Creemers, T. Peters, & D. Reynolds (Eds.). *School effectiveness and school improvement,* 295-308. Amsterdam: Swets & Zeitlinger.

Clark, T. A. & McCarthy, D. P. (1983). School improvement in New York City: The evolution of a project. *Educational Researcher, 12*(4), 17-24..

Crowson, R. L. & Boyd, W L. (October, 1993). *Implications of restructuring and site-level decentralisation upon district-level leadership.* Urbana-Champaign, IL: National Center for School Leadership, University of Illinois.

Cuban, L. (1983). Effective schools: A friendly but cautionary note. *Phi Delta Kappan, 9,* 695-96.

Cuban, L. (1984). Transforming the frog into a prince: Effective schools research, policy, and practice at the district level. *Harvard Educational Review, 54*(2), 129-151.

Darling-Hammond, L., & Goodwin, A. L. (1993). Progress towards professionalism in teaching. In G. Cawelti (Ed.), *Challenges and achievements of American education: The 1993 ASCD yearbook,* 19-52. Alexandria, VA: Association for Supervision and Curriculum Development.

David, J. L. (1989). Synthesis of research on school-based management. *Educational Leadership, 46*(8), 45-53.

Dyer, H. S. (1966). The Pennsylvania Plan. *Science Education, 50,* 242-248.

Elmore, R. F., Peterson, P. L. & McCarthey, S. J. (1996). *Restructuring in the classroom: Teaching, learning, & school organisation.* San Francisco, CA: : Jossey-Bass.

Edmonds, R. R. (1986). Characteristics of effective schools. In E. Neisser (Ed.), *The achievement of minority children,* 93-104. Hillsdale, NJ: Erlbaum.

Edmonds, R. R. (1979). Effective schools for the urban poor. *Educational Leadership*, 37, 15-27.

Edmonds, R. R., & Frederiksen, J. R. (1978). *Search for effective schools: The identification and analysis of city schools that are instructionally effective for poor children.* ERIC Document Reproduction Service No. ED 170 396).

Education Week (1997). *Quality Counts: A report card on the condition of public education in the 50 states.* Washington, DC: Author.

Evertson, C. M. & Murphy, J (1992). Beginning with the classroom: Implications for redesigning schools. In H. H. Marshall (Ed.). *Redefinifig Student learning: Roots of educational change*, 293-320. Norwood, NJ: Ablex Publishing.

Farkas, S. (1993). *Divided within, besieged without: The politics of education in four American school districts.* New York: The Kettering Foundation.

Firestone, W. A., & Herriott, R. (1982). Prescriptions for effective elementary schools don't fit secondary schools. *Educational Leadership*, 40(12), 51-52.

Fullan, M. B. (1993), Coordinating school and district development in restructuring. In J. Murphy and P. Hallinger (Eds.), *Restructuring schooling: Learning from ongoing efforts*, 43-164. Newbury Park, CA: Corwin Press.

Fuhrman, S. H. (Ed.). (1993). Designing coherent education policy: Improving the system. San Francisco, CA: Jossey-Bass.

Goertz, M. E., Floden, R. E., & O'Day, J. (1995). *Studies of Education Reform: Systemic Reform: Vol me 1: Findings and Conclusions.* (CPRE Research Report Series Report #335A) New Brunswick, NJ: Consortium for Policy Research in Education.

Good, T. & L. & Brophy, J. E. (1986). School effects. In M. C. Wittrock (Ed.). *Third handbook of research on teaching*, 570-602. New York: Macmillan.

Griffin, G. A. (Ed.). (1983). Staff development:. *Eighty-second yearbook of the National Society for the Study of Education.* Chicago: University of Chicago Press.

Guskey, T. R. (1986). Staff development and the process of teacher change. *Educational Researcher*, 15(5), 5-12.

Guskey, T. R., & Huberman, M. (Eds.). (1995). *Professional Development in Education: New Paradigms & Practices.* New York: Teachers College Press.

Hallinger, P., & Murphy, J. (1982). The superintendent's role in promoting instructional leadership. *Administrator's Notebook*, 30(6), 1-4.

Hallinger, P., & Murphy, J. (1986). The social context of effective schools. *American Journal of Education*, 94(328-355.

Harari, I, Strait, C., Rodarte, M. & Chrispeels, J. H. (1998). *Factors leading to role conflict and role ambiguity in a school leadership team.* Paper presented at the Annual Meeting of the American Educational Research Association, San Diego, CA.

Jencks, C. S., Smith, J., Ackland, H., Bane, M. J., Cohn, D., Gintis, H., Heyns, B., & Michelson, S. (1972). *Inequality: A reassessment of the effect of family and schooling in America.* New York: Basic Books.

Joyce, B. & Showers, B. (1988). *Student achievement through staff development.* New York: Longman.

Kozol, J.(1991). *Savage inequalities: Children in America's schools.* New York: Harper Perennial.

Lambert, L., Walker, D., Zimmerman, D. P., Cooper, J. E., Lambert, M. D., Gardner, M. E., Slack, P. J. F. (1995). *The constructivist leader.* New York: Teachers College Press

Leithwood, K. (1992). The move toward transformational leadership. *Educational Leadership*, 49(5), 8-12.

Levine, D. U. & Lezotte L. W. (1990). *Unusually effective schools: A review and analysis of research and practice.* Madison WI: National Center for Effective Schools Research and Development

Lezotte, L. W., & Bancroft, B. A. (1985). Growing use of the effective schools model for school improvement. *Educational Leadership*, 42(6), 23-27.

Lieberman, A. (1995). *The work of restrcturing schools: Building from the ground up.* New York: Teachers College Press.

Lieberman, A., & Miller, L. (1979). *Staff developmet: New demands, new realities, new perspectives.* New York: TeachersCollegePress.

Lieberman, A., Saxl, E. R., & Miles, M. B. (1988). Teacher leadership: Ideology and practice. In A. Lieberman (Ed.), *Building a professional culture in schools*, 148-166. New York: Teachers College Press.

Little, J. W. (1990). The persistence of privacy: Autonomy and initiative in teachers' professional relations. *Teachers College Record*, 91, 509-536.

Little, J. W. (1993). Teachers professional development in a climate of educational reform. *Educational Evaluation and Policy Analysis*, 15(2),129-151.

Los Angeles Times. (November 27, 1997), 27.

Louis, K. S., Kruse, S. D. & Associates. (1995). *Professionalism and Community: Perspectives on reforming urban schools.* Thousand Oaks, CA: Corwin.

Louis, K. S. & Miles, M. (1990). *Improving the urban high school: What works and why.* New York: Teacher's College Press.

Malen, B., Ogawa, R. T., & Kranz, J. (1990). What do we know about school-based management? A Case study of the literature: A call for research. In W. H. Clune and J. F. Witte (Eds.). *Choice and control in American education.* Vol. 2. New York: Falmer Press.

Marks, H. M. & Louis, K. S. (1997). Does teacher empowerment affect the classroom? The implications of teacher empowerment for instructional practice and student academic performance. *Educational Evaluation and Policy Analysis*, 19(3), 245-275.

Marsh, D. D., & Odden, A. R. (1991). Implementation of the California mathematics and science curriculum frameworks. In A. R. Odden (Ed.), *Education policy implementation*, 219-239. New York: State University of New York.

Marshall, H. H. (1992). *Redefining student learning: Roots of educational change.* Norwood, NJ: Ablex Publishing.

Meyers, H. W. (1989, January). *Rural education school improvement strategies: Improving leadership and organisational structure.* Paper presented at the Second Annual Meeting of the International Congress for School Effectiveness, Rotterdam, The Netherlands.

Murphy, J. & Hallinger, P. (1993). *Restructuring schooling: Learning from ongoing efforts.* Thousand Oaks, CA: Corwin

Murphy, J. Peterson, K. D., & Hallinger, P. (1986). The administrative control of principals in effective school districts: The supervision and function. *The Urban Review*, 18 (3), 149-175.

National Commission on Teaching and America's Future. (1996). *What matters most: Teaching for America's Future.* New York: Author.

Northwest Regional Educational Laboratory (1984). *Onward to Excellence: Making schools more effective.* Portland, OR: Author.

Peterson, P. L. The California study of elementary mathematics. *Educational Evaluation and Policy Analysis*, 12(3), 257-262.

Purkey, S. C., & Smith, M. S. (1983). Effective schools: A review. *Elementary School Journal*, 83, 427-452.

Reynolds, D. Sammons, P., Stoll, L, Barber, M. & Hillman, J. (1997). School effectiveness and school improvement in the United Kingdom. In A. Harris, N. Bennett & M. Preedy, eds. *Organisational effectiveness and improvement in education*, 124-137. Philadelphia: Open University.

Robertson, P. J., & Briggs, K. L. (1998). Improving schools through school-based management: An examination of the process of change. *School Effectivenss and School Improvement*, 9(1), 28-57.

Rosenholtz, S. (1989). *Teachers' workplace: The social organisation of schools.* New York: Longman.

Rost, J. C. (1991). *Leadership for the twenty-first century.* New York: Praeger.

Rowan, B., Bossert, S. T., & Dwyer, D. C. (1983). Research on effective schools: A cautionary note. *Educational Researcher, 12*(4) 24-31.

Scheerens, J. & Bosker, R. (1997). *The foundations of educational effectiveness.* New York: Pergamon.

Sergiovanni, T. (1987). *The Principalship.* Newton, MA: Allyn and Bacon, Inc.

Serrano vs. Priest, 96 Cal. Reporter. 601, 487 P. 2d 1241, 5 Cal. 3d 584 (1971).

Smith, L J., Maxwell, S., Lowther, D., Hacker, D., Bol, L. & Nunnery, J. (1997). Activities in schools and programs experiencing the most, and least, early implementation success. *School Effectiveness and School Improvement, 8*(1), 12550.

Smylie, M. A., Lazarus, V., Brownlee-Conyers, J. (1996). Instructional Outcomes of School-Based Participative Decision-making. *Educational Evaluation and Policy Analysis, 18*(3), 181-198.

Stringfield, S., Datnow, A., Herman, R, & Berkeley, C. (1997); Introduction to the Memphis restructuring Initiative. *School Effectiveness and School Improvement, 8*(1), 3-35.

Stringfield, S. & Herman, R. (1996). Assessment of the state of school effectiveness research in the United States of America. *School Effectiveness and School Improvement, 7*(2),159-180.

Stringfield, S., Teddlie, C., & Suarez, S. (1985). Classroom interaction in effective and ineffective schools: Preliminary results from phase III of the Louisiana School Effectiveness Study. *Journal of Classroom Interaction, 20*(2), 31-37.

Sudlow, R. E. (1984). *Conducting an effective schools program.* Spencerport, NY: Spencerport Central Schools.

Taylor, B. 0. (Ed.). (1990). *Case studies in effective schools research.* Madison, WI: National Center for Effective Schools Research & Development, University of Wisconsin-Madison.

Teddlie, C., Kirby, P. C., & Stringfield, S. (1989). Effective versus ineffective schools: Observable differences in the classroom. *American Journal of Education, 97*(3), 221-236.

Teddlie, C. & Reynolds, D. (in press). The international handbook of school effectiveness research. London: Falmer.

Teddlie, C. & Stringfield, S. (1993). *Schools make a difference: Lessons learned from a 10-year study of school effects.* New York: Teachers College.

Teddlie, C., Stringfield, S. & Desselle, S. (1985). Methods, history, selected findings and recommendations from the Louisiana school effectiveness study, 1980-85. *Journal of Classroom Interaction, 20*(2), 22-30.

Van Meter, E. (1993). *School-based decision-making: Lessons from Kentucky's statewide SBDM mandate.* Unpublished manuscript. University of Kentucky. Lexington.

Weade, R. & Evertson, C. M. (1988). The construction of lessons in effective and less effective classrooms. *Teaching and Teacher Education,* (3),189-213.

Weber, G. (1971). *Inner city children can be taught to read: Four successful schools.* Washington, DC: Council for Basic Education.

Wehlage, G. (1992). Restructuring urban schools: The new futures experiment. *American Educational Research Journal, 29,* 51-93.

Weiss, C. H., Cambone, J., & Wyeth, A. (1992). Trouble in paradise: Teacher conflicts in shared decision-making. *Educational Administration Quarterly, 28,* 350-367.

Willms, J. D., & Raudenbush, S. W. (1989. A longitudinal hierarchical linear model for estimating school effects and their stability. *Journal of Educational Measurement,* 26(3), 209-232.

Wohlstetter P, & Odden, A. (1994). Rethinking school-based management policy and research. *Education Administration Quarterly, 28,* 529-49.

SECTION THREE:
ASIA AND THE PACIFIC

14.

Through systemic reform to improved learning outcomes for students: the Australian experience

Peter Cuttance and Peter Hill

Introduction

School effectiveness has been debated by academics for many years within Australia, but it is only in recent times that findings from empirical research have been published and that school effectiveness has captured the attention of education policy makers. Similarly, there has been a long history of school improvement initiatives in Australian schools, but these have tended to be ad hoc, localised and short term, and it is only now that systems are beginning to confront the need to design and implement theoretically-based, improvement processes for all schools.

The general direction of school reform in Australia has been in line with world-wide trends (Caldwell, 1993; Caldwell and Spinks, 1992) and has involved:

- allowing parents more choice in which school their child attends;
- devolving decision-making about operational matters to the local school level;
- centralising decision-making about the curriculum and about standards of student achievement at key stages of schooling;

- implementing evidence-based accountability arrangements to drive improvement and change; and

- focusing less on inputs and more on student outcomes and strategies for improving the quality of teaching and learning in classrooms.

Most of the effort to date has been concerned largely with the first four of the above and in establishing the preconditions for improved educational outcomes for students. Over the past year or so, the focus has begun to shift to the fourth and most important element of the reform agenda: penetrating the classroom door and improving the quality of teaching and learning. This is an issue that has been avoided for several decades in Australia in favour of a focus on inputs to the educational process, on curriculum issues and on understanding contexts of learning.

Among those responsible for implementing reforms in school systems in Australia, there is an unprecedented interest in developing ways of measuring the effectiveness of schools. Indeed, the capacity to do so is increasingly seen as the most critical component of initiatives aimed at improving student outcomes and empowering schools to be more responsive to community expectations. There is an acute awareness of the power of data to drive change and of the importance of putting in place evidence-based improvement processes.

The focus on student learning outcomes has been nowhere more evident than in the area of curriculum. Agreement has been reached across all Australian States and Territories that the curriculum should encompass eight key learning areas (the Arts, English, Health and Physical Education, Languages other than English, Mathematics, Science, Studies of Society and the Environment, and Technology). While different States and Territories may define them somewhat differently, student learning outcomes for each key learning area have been specified and systems are increasingly expecting that all schools will seek to achieve these outcomes.

The development of outcome statements for each of the eight key learning areas has contributed to a considerable expansion of time devoted to the visual and performing arts, languages other than English, and health and physical education, especially in the primary school. In addition, there has been an equally strong emphasis on generic curricular experiences including the new information technologies and vocational education, especially in secondary schools, and co-curricular experiences such as school camps, excursions, drama productions, musical activities, exchanges, and so on. The measurement of school effectiveness in so far as the full range of curricular provision is problematic and measurement of effectiveness tends to be confined to the use of indicators of provision, access and to instances of excellence and success that have been documented.

Alongside the trend towards devolution of decision-making and a focus on student learning outcomes, there has been an increasing emphasis on strong accountability processes based on performance of students in core curriculum areas, particularly literacy and numeracy. This has been evident in the adoption of population testing programs and in the implementation of reporting, accountability and review processes that look to evidence regarding the relative performance of schools in terms of student achievement in the core curriculum. The evaluation of the effectiveness of schools in terms of student performance in the core curriculum has generally been resisted by schools and by teacher unions but this has not prevented some systems from using both raw and adjusted or 'value-added' indicators of performance and making available to schools their results, alongside results for all schools and/or for schools serving similar populations of students.

Being a federal system, policies and practices vary from system to system among the six states and two territories comprising the Australian Commonwealth. At the same time, the involvement of the Federal (Commonwealth) government in school education and regular meetings of federal and state/territory ministers for education (constituted as the Ministerial Council on Employment, Education, Training and Youth Affairs) ensure that there is a vigorous national agenda of reform and a considerable convergence of policies among education systems.

This paper presents examples from the various states and territories of current school reforms. The examples are discussed in three main sections:

- Systemic reform initiatives, encompassing the decentralisation of operational decision-making and the centralisation of curriculum and learning standards.
- School accountability and improvement initiatives.
- Learning focused initiatives, those focused directly improving learning outcomes for students.

The report concludes with a commentary on the various initiatives under way and on the status and direction of school effectiveness and school improvement in Australia.

Systemic reform initiatives

Most Australian states and territories have over the last decade moved to make schools more self-managing, though the extent of self-management varies. Northern Territory schools, which have become increasingly self-managed since the early 1980s, are responsible for curriculum delivery, student assessment, staff recruitment and development, financial planning and program evaluation. This self-management operates within a framework set by the Department of Education.

Tasmania, a more recent adopter of self-managing schools as government policy, is currently implementing the government's *Directions for Education* statement which gives schools more authority, more control over funds and more flexibility to make their own decisions, but with responsibility for achieving mandatory learning outcomes in specified curriculum areas.

Like the above two systems, Western Australian schools now have considerable scope for local decision-making, with plans to progressively extend local decision-making to human resources administration. Schools now have the flexibility to provide education to their students in a way which best suits local conditions and student learning goals. State schools, however, operate within the parameters of a centrally established Curriculum Framework and Student Outcome Statements.

The most far reaching systemic reforms in Australia at the moment, however, are those that are being implemented in Victoria and those planned for implementation in Queensland. The Victorian *Schools of the Future* initiative, which commenced implementation in 1992, and the Queensland *Leading Schools* reform, for which implementation has just commenced, both grapple with a re-negotiation of the role of and relationships between schools, their communities and educational bureaucracies. Both reform initiatives are predicated on allowing schools greater discretion over operational decision-making, particularly in relation to school budgets. Conversely, the recognition of governments' interest in establishing and maintaining educational standards has resulted in the strengthening of a centralised curriculum and educational standards function. To put it in another way, the reforms under discussion involve education systems maintaining a firm hand on setting the goals of schooling, but with schools and their communities having greater decision-making authority over the processes and the allocation of resources for achieving those goals.

The *Schools of the Future* reform of public education in Victoria has decentralisation as a key feature. With 1700 schools, Victoria is the largest system of public education anywhere to have decentralised as much as 90% of its budget to the school site level. Victoria has gone further than other states in including the payment of staff within the devolved functions. The allocation of resources to Victorian public schools reflects a systematic effort to match learning needs at different stages of schooling through the School Global Budget Research Project (Education Committee 1995, 1997).

A school charter, an agreement between the school and its local community on the one hand and the school and the Department of Education on the other, provides schools with focus and direction. Each charter has a life of three years and sets out important agreements about the nature of the school and its priorities.

A curriculum and standards framework covering all levels in primary and secondary schools is the key centralising component of the 'Schools of the Future' initiative, balancing the devolution of operations. The monitoring of standards is through tests in key subject areas at two levels of primary school and through public examinations and assessment at the end of Year 12 (the final year of schooling). Further, trials of assessment tests are being conducted for Year 7, the first year of secondary schooling. An accountability system based around annual reports and triennial reviews, to be discussed later, is an additional feature of the reforms which also include a new professional career structure for teachers.

The next step in self management in Victoria is evident in recently enacted legislation entitled the *Education (Self Governing Schools) Act.* This will allow schools to request additional powers from the minister for education to employ their own staff, negotiate conditions locally, and enter into partnerships with other schools, colleges and other bodies. While only a few schools are expected to take advantage of this legislation initially, it is expected that it will introduce further contestability and diversity into the public education system.

Queensland is the most recent Australian state to introduce school-based management, and is in a position of being able to take advantage of the comprehensive reforms of other systems of education, in Australia and internationally, over the past two decades. The *Leading Schools* initiative, planned for implementation in 1998, builds upon the substantial research into school-based management that is now available.

Specifically, the *Leading Schools* initiative is based upon a four dimensional approach to school-based management which emanates from significant American research into successfully restructured schools (Newmann & Wehlage, 1995). The four dimensions are:

- the creation of structural foundations, namely a school council, a clear educational vision which has the support of the total school community and frameworks for managing resources;

- the development of participatory school community practices emanating from the vision.

- the restructuring of school operations (eg., timetables, organisation of classes, volunteer participation, uses of technology, etc.) specifically to enable the educational vision to be addressed, and

- the generation of processes of 'authentic pedagogy' which reflect the school's vision and build upon educational research into effective learning and teaching.

In common with Victoria, the Queensland reforms entail a re-negotiation of roles and relationships among schools, their communities and education bureaucracies. The emerging implications of these changes are described below.

The role of the principal is seen as considerably less pervasive than that which characterises most approaches to school-based management. In the Queensland approach, 'teacher leadership' is a very important factor, particularly in dimensions three and four.

The role of school councils is seen as critically important in dimension one (in the establishment of the school's vision and resources and accountability plans).

The role of support systems has been changed, with the Queensland Department of Education being re-named 'Education Queensland' and re-organised into thirty-six school districts whose task it will be to oversee the development and approval of systemic strategic plans for all schools and to provide school-specific support services.

The four-dimensional framework for school-based management adopted in Queensland represents a significant departure from most existing models which have tended to place most emphasis on the first three dimensions of change. The structuring of educational reforms in Queensland around an educational vision has a parallel in Victoria where attention is now shifting to achieving high standards for all students within the *Schools of the Future* framework.

In this respect, there are similarities with the agenda in Britain under the Blair Labour Government, with its White Paper on *Excellence in Schools* calling for a focus on 'standards not structures' and achieving a 'balance of pressure and support' (Secretary of State for Education and Employment, 1997). The view that *Schools of the Future*, as implemented thus far in Victoria, may be a necessary but insufficient measure to achieve lasting school reform has been expressed by Caldwell and Hayward (1998) in their recently-published book on the *Schools of the Future* reforms.

The process and outcomes of the Victorian *Schools of the Future* reforms have been systematically monitored from the outset. Recent reports provide evidence of an impact on student learning, with a model that illustrates a number of direct and indirect effects of key elements of the reform. School principals have indicated they would not wish to return to arrangements pre-*Schools of the Future* (Co-operative Research Project, 1997). The Queensland *Leading Schools* initiative will be evaluated systematically by an external agency that will assess the impact of the initiative on student learning outcomes.

School accountability AND improvement

Reforms which devolve operational decision-making to schools within a centralised curriculum and standards framework logically imply the need for a complementary accountability and improvement process to account for the use of public funds and the achievement of Government policies.

The State of Victoria, as noted above, has implemented a comprehensive accountability framework for government schools as part of its *Schools of the Future* reforms. The framework incorporates a three year school performance plan (the school charter), an annual public report on performance and a triennial school review. The school review includes a school self assessment and a verification of that self assessment by an independent educational evaluator. The review process results in a public report that incorporates performance directions to be included in the school's next three year charter.

Key performance measures used in the accountability framework and in the school review include standards of student learning and benchmarks for measures of parent satisfaction, staff perceptions of morale and goal congruence, student post-school destinations to higher education, work or training and rates of student and staff absence.

The Victorian Department of Education's Office of Review uses the data contained in school annual reports to 'benchmark' performance. The benchmarks are actual performance standards achieved by schools and are presented so that a given school can compare its performance with that of 'like' schools according to the socio-economic and English language speaking status of its student population. The 'benchmarks', cover each of the performance measures in the accountability framework and are used in school reviews as criteria for assessing school performance.

There are a number of similarities between the New South Wales (NSW) and Victorian models of school accountability and reporting, as well as significant differences. Like Victoria, the NSW model, which commenced in the second half of 1997, involves an annual school self evaluation and independent verification.

In Victoria, where the education system is highly devolved and outsourcing is a central tenet of government policy, the verification aspect of the review is conducted by ten external agencies under contract to the Office of Review. The contracts include a performance review component to ensure the quality of the process. In New South Wales, which has one of the more centralised school systems in Australia, a departmental officer assesses the accuracy of the school self-evaluation and subsequent annual school report.

The annual reports in NSW are produced by the principal in collaboration with staff, parents, students and the school's self-evaluation committee. The reports draw on a range of empirical evidence, including the results of external examinations, and observations to provide the required substance and validation.   There is a standardised format for the report to ensure a systematic account of the school's achievements and areas for development. This is to enable schools to identify priorities and direct attention and resources to specific aspects of performance. Schools' test results, however, are not reported publicly in a way that allows parents to directly compare the effectiveness and performance of individual schools.

In contrast, school reviews in Victoria present data on student learning outcomes and compare the school's performance with that of other schools catering to similar populations of students. Hence, the reports take account of students' prior background characteristics in evaluating the relative effectiveness of individual schools.

The Victorian Department of Education is developing an extended strategic school improvement framework to support schools in achieving improved performance. The framework will emphasise the development of organisational competencies and capacities to improve school performance. A number of different approaches are being developed to provide support for underachieving schools in need of renewal.

The Victorian school improvement framework combines three connected elements:

- *Evaluation and diagnosis*

  A combination of data from triennial reviews, school annual reports and visits to schools from senior department personnel will be used to identify individual schools that are experiencing difficulties and target support for school improvement.

- *Policy*

  Policy issues revolve around the range of possible and appropriate strategies for intervention to support individual schools, in particular, those schools which are experiencing difficulty in improving their performance. Strategies are tailored to the needs of individual schools and aim to build the capacity to develop school ownership of new directions and solutions.

- *Support*

  The key issue relates to the partnerships between internal and external agencies in supporting school improvement.   External agencies, including universities, will provide support through research and development projects that build knowledge and expertise in school improvement, professional development, and consultancy support over an extended period for individual schools. A key element of this approach is the development of a range of interventions designed for schools requiring support for core activities, such as literacy and the appropriate application of learning technologies.

In NSW, development directions are identified in school annual reports. Unlike Victoria, where the improvement framework is being implemented, the nature of the framework for implementing the NSW improvement strategy is yet to be developed, though there are plans for school and district resources to be allocated on the basis of priorities and needs identified in annual school reports. Additional components proposed for the NSW school accountability and improvement strategy are targeted in-depth school reviews and a program of systemic monitoring and reporting.

Victoria and New South Wales are just two of the Australian states that are implementing relatively new school accountability and improvement strategies. Both territories, the Australian Capital Territory and the Northern Territory, as well as the states of South Australia, Tasmania and Western Australia have accountability and improvement programs which include some type of review with an annual reporting component.

Where there is substantial variation across Australian school systems is in the processes for validating school performance reviews, particularly where reviews contain a significant self-assessment component. In Victoria the validation and review process is carried out by independent agencies contracted to the government, operating on the basis of a model similar to that of financial auditors in the business sector. However in most other systems in Australia this part of the process is undertaken by the school system's own administrators.

The fundamental issue in this context is the type of assurance offered by different approaches. Quality assurance that is entirely dependent upon the organisation itself can be described as a form of self-assurance. Quality assurance as it is understood in the literature requires that a second party (customer, purchaser) or a third party independent of both producer/supplier and customer/purchaser provide certification that the organisation's practices, operating systems and outcomes meet particular standards. The standards are normally established by government and industry bodies that have no vested interests in any particular organisations in the industry.

New South Wales schools have their self-evaluation validated by an external officer who does not have a line management role in relation to the school. In Western Australia where schools also engage in self-evaluation, the process is validated by District Directors who are responsible for the functioning of schools in their District. In South Australia the validation is external and independent, but undertaken each year for only a sample of schools. Both Australian territories, the Australian Capital Territory and the Northern Territory, have accountability programs which do not include independent validation.

In the Australian Capital Territory (ACT) government schools undertake an internal review every five years. Schools review their operations and programs according to the goals and priorities of the Department's Education Plan and their own vision for the future. The review involves, amongst other things, the administration and analysis of standard questionnaires to all parents, staff and students (from Years 5-12). All sections of the school community, parents, staff and students - are encouraged to participate.

Based on their review findings each school formulates a development plan to improve school effectiveness. The key outcome of this quality assurance process is a report that provides educational direction for the school. Each school is required to report annually to the Department of Education on the implementation of the school development plan which is monitored by the Directors of Schools.

In the Northern Territory schools are required to develop school improvement action plans on a triennial basis and to provide their community and the Department of Education with an annual report giving a clear picture of the school and its achievements.

South Australian schools undertake a self-evaluation and produce an annual report. South Australia is also planning to conduct developmental reviews of schools to address specific issues or needs. Schools designated for a developmental review may be identified on the basis of their annual report, data provided by the District Superintendent, special circumstances, or the system's analysis of student achievement information.

In most Australian school systems there is a program of testing to monitor literacy standards in Years 3 and 5. In most cases the results of these tests are also used by schools and education authorities for development purposes. With rare exceptions, there is no public reporting of school performance on the basis of these tests and little public scrutiny of system performance on these tests.

Learning-focused initiatives

Two areas of learning are receiving particular attention at the moment in Australia - literacy and learning technologies. 'Middle schooling', though not a learning area, is also an area of innovation and reform.

Literacy

While literacy is an ongoing issue, it has assumed particular prominence in recent years as evidence has accumulated from various state and national surveys and full cohort testing programs regarding levels of the performance of students and of groups of students. The results point to a very large gap in the performance levels of high and low achieving students in any given cohort of students and to the relatively higher performance of girls and the lower performance of students from low socio-economic backgrounds, Aboriginal and Torres Strait Islander students, and students from non-English speaking backgrounds (Ministerial Council on Employment, Education, Training and Youth Affairs and Curriculum Corporation, 1996).

The lack of comparability in the data collected by states and territories as part of their literacy testing and assessment programs has prompted substantial cooperation aimed at setting national goals and agreeing to a national approach to reporting student performance in terms of a common set of standards. Gaining agreement on such matters is difficult, largely due to the involvement of two levels of government in education, namely state and federal. In March 1997, Ministers for Education nevertheless agreed to the goal that 'every child commencing school from 1998 will achieve a minimum acceptable literacy and numeracy standard within four years'. They also endorsed a national strategy for meeting this goal, although many of the details remain to be worked out.

In September 1997, a national survey attempted to estimate the proportions of Year 3 and 5 students above and below a draft set of 'benchmark' standards that are expected to form the basis for monitoring progress towards meeting the national literacy goal (Australian Council for Educational Research, 1997; Management Committee for the National School English Literacy Survey, 1997). A special report prepared for the Federal Minister (Australian Council for Educational Research, 1997) estimated that about 30 percent of Year 3 and 5 students were performing below the 'benchmark' standard in reading and writing, suggesting that meeting the national goal will present significant challenges in the years ahead.

Systems have begun to take seriously the kinds of support required by schools and teachers in significantly improving literacy standards and in closing the achievement gap revealed by testing and assessment programs. In some States, notably Queensland, New South Wales and Victoria, considerable emphasis has been placed on systemic implementation of *Reading Recovery* as a one-to-one intervention program (Clay, 1993). In others, considerable resources have been devoted to professional development programs for teachers and the production of resource packages for schools, including, for example, Western Australia's *First Steps* and Victoria's *Keys to Life* materials.

In the case of Victoria's *Keys to Life* materials, these have been informed by substantial research and development into a whole-school approach to improving literacy outcomes. This research, carried out as the Early Literacy Research Project (ELRP) is continuing in Victoria, Australia, as a joint initiative of the Victorian Department of Education and The University of Melbourne. The aim of the ELRP has been to maximise the literacy achievements of 'at risk' students in the early years of schooling (ages 5-8). A description of the ELRP and the results of an initial evaluation of the first year of implementation are summarised in Crevola & Hill (in press). The effect sizes for participating schools are in excess of 0.6 of a standard deviation across ten measures of literacy progress used in the research.

The ELRP has drawn attention to the power and potential of adopting a comprehensive, whole-school, design approach to school improvement. The design used in the ELRP was influenced by the *Success for All* design of Slavin and colleagues (Slavin, Madden, Dolan, Wasik, Ross, Smith, & Dianda, 1996; Slavin, Madden, Karweit, Livermon, & Dolan, 1990). The details, however, reflect local input and the considerable investment that systems in Australia have made to approaches to teaching early literacy pioneered in New Zealand (Department of Education, New Zealand, 1985).

Learning technologies

Learning technologies is currently a priority for most Australian education systems. Over the next three years each school in Tasmania will acquire a computer for every five students, accompanying software programs and network links to the rest of the world. Permanent and some part time teachers will be provided with a laptop computer.

The Northern Territory, Western Australia and New South Wales are also in the early stages of implementing major information technology initiatives, each with specific goals for the use of computers in teaching and learning and enabling access to the internet.

Victoria's *Classrooms of the Future* project typifies this current interest in learning technology in schools. This project had its origins in a 1992 government working party which investigated current and future uses of technologies in school education. The working party concerned itself with issues such as effective teaching and learning, the uses of technology in improving student learning, and the change and support required to enable new ways of learning. The subsequent report (Government of Victoria, 1994) has led to significant advances in the way computers and other learning technologies are being used to improve student learning and change teaching practices in Victorian schools.

One of the biggest influences on the adoption of the use of new learning technologies to improve student learning in Victorian schools has been the US-based *Apple Classrooms of Tomorrow* (ACOT) project. Teachers and students in ACOT project schools have had routine access to computers and other learning technologies which are used as tools in the normal teaching and learning process.

Lessons from the ACOT project (summarised in a report on the first ten years of the project; ACOT, 1995) have been incorporated in the Victorian *Navigator Schools* project. Four primary and three secondary *Navigator Schools* are currently developing and refining new teaching approaches and administrative practices and disseminating their experiences to other schools.

The Middle Years of Schooling project

The national group of schools whose work is represented in the *Middle Years of Schooling Project* have been part of a research group sponsored by the National Schools Network and the Australian Curriculum Studies Association and funded by the Commonwealth Government. This project continues a tradition of school-school and school-university partnerships for the purposes of collaborative inquiry

In the schools taking part in this project, there are a wide range of definitions and practices of integrated curriculum, sometimes even within the one school. There was no single approach towards middle schooling, nor towards integrated curriculum across these schools, although there have been clear shared principles about what counts as important in the curriculum and how this might best be organised to facilitate improved student learning outcomes. The understanding of what constitutes the 'middle years' varies across States: it can refer to Years 5-6, Years 5-7, Years 5-8, Years 7-8, Years 8-9, or Years 7-10.

The diversity among the schools has been an important resource for those participating, and also demonstrates the flexibility of the concept and practices of middle schooling at this point in Australian curriculum history. Each of the schools need to pay attention to their own institutional history and resources, expectations of community and staffing profile in order to develop an approach to curriculum change.

The schools can be seen as different along a number of dimensions. For the purposes of learning from these schools, it is important to know that they include:

- newly established schools which have started with a different, more integrated approach to curriculum and school organisation;
- schools where the middle-years is a distinct organisational feature, separate from the rest of the school's effort;
- schools where the initiative has had a longer term, systematic and ripple effect across the whole school; and
- schools where the project represents some years of ongoing work while for others this material is related to one semester's initiative.

Commentary

In many ways, the direction and pace of school reform in Australia mirrors that in other countries and reflects the convergence of thinking that can be observed on matters of educational policy across the world. It is also very evident that the school effectiveness and improvement movement has had a major impact on Australian education at the policy level. This is reflected in the significant numbers of academics and senior officers from Australian education systems that attend ICSEI annual conferences and in the frequency with which researchers with international reputations in the field have been invited to Australia to address significant forums. Concepts and understandings emanating from the field of school effectiveness and improvement have taken root in a broader climate of reform in which schools are being given greater responsibility for day-to-day operational decision-making within a framework of system-level standards and accountability for student learning.

In many ways, policy remains ahead of the research evidence regarding the effectiveness of various reform measures. While efforts have been made to put in place large-scale evaluations of systemic reform initiatives, it is difficult to mount tightly-controlled studies that unequivocally establish the extent to which changes have impacted positively on student learning. The challenge is for researchers to develop creative approaches embedding research into systemic reform programs and to bring about a closer alignment of research and policy.

A more significant challenge is to ensure that knowledge about school effectiveness and improvement is internalised and acted upon at the school level and at the level of teachers in classrooms. In a general environment of pessimism about the status of teaching and low morale within the teaching profession, such knowledge has the power to inspire and motivate when it is embedded in initiatives and professional development experiences that connect in positive ways with classroom teaching. In the final analysis, school effectiveness and improvement involves identifying and working with those things that make schools better places for teachers as well as for students. In the Australian setting, the school effectiveness and improvement movement therefore has much to contribute, not only to improving the quality of education in schools, but also addressing the problem of the declining status of the teaching profession. For these reasons, it can be expected that Australian educators will continue to maintain an active participation in the international school effectiveness and improvement movement.

Acknowledgments

A number of individuals and school system personnel contributed the material on which this report is based, including: Steve Buckley, Brian Caldwell, Frank Crowther, Gerry Cullen, Tim Doe, Bill Griffiths John Harris, Neville Highett, Phil Holmes-Smith, Harry Payne and Judyth Sachs. Shirley Stokes drafted the sections of the report based on the material provided by the persons noted above. Any errors and omissions in the interpretation of the material provided are, however, solely the responsibility of the authors.

References

Apple Classrooms of Tomorrow (ACOT). (1995). *Changing the Conversation About Teaching, Learning & Technology: A Report on 10 Years of ACOT Research.* San Francisco: Apple Inc.

Australian Council for Educational Research. (1997). *Literacy standards in Australia.* Canberra: Commonwealth of Australia. (Minister's Report).

Caldwell, B. J. (1993). *Decentralising the Management of Australia's Schools.* Melbourne: National Industry Education Forum.

Caldwell, B. J. and Hayward, D. K. (1997). *The Future of Schools: Lessons from the Reform of Public Education,* London: Falmer Press.

Caldwell, B. J. and Spinks, J. M. (1992). *Leading the Self-Managing School.* London and New York: The Falmer Press.

Clay, M. M. (1993). *Reading Recovery: A guidebook for teachers in training.* Auckland, New Zealand: Heinemann Education.

Cooperative Research Project (1997). *Still More Work to be Done But ... No Turning Back.* Report of the Cooperative Research Project on Leading Victoria's Schools of the Future. Melbourne: The Department of School Education.

Crevola, C. A., & Hill, P. W. (In press). Initial evaluation of a whole-school approach to prevention and intervention in early literacy. *Journal of Education for Students Placed at Risk.*

Department of Education, New Zealand (1985). *Reading in junior classes.* Wellington, New Zealand: Ministry of Education.

Education Committee (1995). *The School Global Budget in Victoria: Matching Resources to Student Learning Needs, Interim Report of the Education Committee.* Melbourne: Department of School Education.

Education Committee (1997) *The School Global Budget in Victoria: Matching Resources to Student Learning Needs, Final Report of the Education Committee.* Melbourne: Department of School Education.

Government of Victoria (1994). *Victorian Government Working Party on the Use of Technology as an Education and Communications Facility in Schools: Technologies for Enhanced Learning - Current and Future Use of Technologies in School Education.* Victoria: The Department of School Education.

Management Committee for the National School English Literacy Survey (1997). *Mapping literacy achievement: Results of the 1996 National School English Literacy Survey. Incorporating a report on the Survey principles, procedures and findings* by Geoffrey N Masters and Margaret Forster, ACER. Canberra: Commonwealth of Australia. (Main report).

Ministerial Council on Employment, Education, Training and Youth Affairs and Curriculum Corporation. (1996). *National report on schooling in Australia 1995.* Carlton, Victoria: Curriculum Corporation.

Newmann, F. and Wehlage, G. (1995). *Successful School Restructuring. A Report to the Public and Educators by the Center on Organisation and Restructuring of Schools.* Madison: Wisconsin Center for Educational Research.

Secretary of State for Education and Employment (UK) (1997). *Excellence in Schools.* White Paper presented to Parliament by the Secretary of State for Education and Employment, July, London: Her Majesty's Stationery Office.

Slavin, R. E., Madden, N. A., Dolan, L. J., Wasik, B. A., Ross, S. M., Smith, L. J., & Dianda, M. (1996). Success for All: A summary of research. *Journal of Education for Students Placed at Risk, 1.*

Slavin, R. E., Madden, N. A., Karweit, N. L., Livermon, B. J., & Dolan, L. (1990). Success for All: First-year outcomes of a comprehensive plan for reforming urban education. *American Educational Research Journal, 27,* 255-278.

15.

The development of effective secondary schools in Hong Kong: a case report

Wong Kam Cheung

Introduction

In Hong Kong, there has recently been a public outcry on falling standards in education in general and on students' English language ability in particular. Amid this outcry came the publicised result of the Third International Mathematics and Science Study (TIMSS) in junior secondary in which Hong Kong came fourth after Singapore, South Korea and Japan in Mathematics among 36 countries (Law, 1996). These seemingly paradoxical events speak well of the dilemma that Hong Kong faces in the educational arena even after Hong Kong has become the Special Administrative Region of China since July 1, 1997. The concern for quality in education has been an ongoing issue and has prompted the Education Commission published its latest Report on *Quality School Education*.

In a broad brush, this paper will introduce the development of effective schools[1] in Hong Kong and other related issues.

Effective schools: the Hong Kong perspective

Effective schools existed long before the effective school research occurred in place in late 70s in the West. These schools were the result of the historical and cultural development of different areas. Effective schools may share a number of similar characteristics (Purkey, et al, 1983; Mortimore, 1992: Levin, et al, 1993), but the making of these schools is unique and is embedded in each school's own culture and environment.

The initial phase

In Hong Kong early effective schools were the creation of government policy. Unlike most other activities in Hong Kong where the policy of minimum-intervention was applied, the Government was heavily committed to the provision and regulation of the education system in Hong Kong since the 1960s. Indeed the minute bureaucratic surveillance of regulations has earned the Education Department the reputation of 'over-administration' (Llewellyn, et al, 1982), a description still relevant today.

The Hong Kong Government, like many other Governments in the world, has gone through stages of providing education to the children of Hong Kong. In the early period when the Hong Kong economy was in its infant stage (i.e. from 1950 to 1960), the focus was to provide primary education for every child. The number of secondary schools, particularly Government and government-funded schools (which were referred to later as public sector schools), was limited. Entry to these schools was determined by a public examination, first through a Joint Primary Six Examination, and then, from 1962, through a Secondary School Entrance Examination (SSEE). The SSEE, similar to the 11+ examination in UK in the 60s, tested primary school graduates' achievements in Chinese language, English language and Mathematics. The SSEE was a high-stakes examination[2]. Allocation to the public sector secondary schools was strictly based on the combined results of these three subjects. Those who 'failed' the examination ended up either in the private schools which were flourishing in those years but were lower in standard in both facilities and teacher qualifications[3] or in the labour market.

From 1962 to 1978, before SSEA was replaced by another mechanism of Secondary School Places Allocation (SSPA), it shaped the pattern of secondary schools in Hong Kong. In the 1960s, less than 20% of the primary graduate population had a chance to enter these schools. This is an important factor to be reckoned with when the concept of effective schools is considered for Hong Kong.

In the early years, this policy of allowing only a small number of academically capable young people to enter public sector secondary schools was a result of limited resources and considered inevitable. It has, perhaps unintentionally, created two phenomena. First, it established a meritocratic school system that was congruent with traditional Chinese values[4]. Some highly effective secondary schools (the early elitist schools), as measured by the Hong Kong Certificate of Education Examination (HKCEE) results at age 17+, were created. These schools were largely grammar schools in nature and consisted of the early government schools and religious schools run by church denominations such as Roman Catholic and Anglican[5]. Second, the presence of the high ability students in these schools made school management an easy task and gave the public the impression that the public sector secondary schools were well run and organised. The small number of highly effective schools was visible in the local scene. Their 'success' helped to sustain their attractiveness to many parents and students, even though some of them dropped in teaching and other standards over the years.

No doubt, if measured against the criteria for effective schools established in the West (Edmonds, 1979; Purkey et al, 1983; Mortimore, et al, 1988; Stoll et al, 1992), these effective schools could easily satisfy many of the conditions and, in particular, the following:

- an orderly and disciplined environment,
- focus on learning,
- close monitoring of tests and examinations, and
- instructional leadership.

There are two distinct features of these early effective schools which one finds consonant in all East Asian societies. The first is the emphasis on basic skills in education. All these schools are, without exception, grammar schools that lay great emphasis on traditional academic subjects such as languages, mathematics, science and social science subjects, like history and geography. It is a commonly held belief in this part of the world that children must learn and master the basics before they can become more effective in learning other things[6].

The other feature is the acceptance of examinations, particularly public examinations, as a fair means of assessing standard and quality. As the earliest civilisation to use public examinations, and the emphasis of its culture being self-cultivation and a sense of equality, many Chinese are internalised to accept examinations as both necessary and fair. It is perhaps not surprising that the Hong Kong education system is known for its examination pressure. Even today, a child must pass through two to three public examination hurdles before he/she can reach university.

Students in these effective schools were highly self-motivated. Part of this self-motivation was nurtured by schools, a phenomenon consistent with the findings in the West (Rutter et al, 1979; Mortimore et al, 1988; Teddlie, et al, 1993; Levin, et al, 1993). But the major part was believed to be related to cultural, societal and particularly family expectation and influence, referred to by different writers as 'Confucian-heritage cultures' (Biggs, 1996) or 'Confucian hypothesis' (Tu, 1996). The impact of societal culture on effective schools in the East Asian context is an issue that deserves attention.

The intermediate phase

This pattern of schooling remained largely the same even after SSPA was initiated to replace SSEA in 1978, the same year as 9-year free and compulsory education for all was introduced. It is still functioning. There are a few special features of the SSPA:

- Unlike SSEA, the SSPA is only loosely-coupled with the primary school curricula (in the jargon of the Government documents, the SSPA was curriculum-related, not bound). This was intended to lighten the pressure on the necessity to prepare for the tests. Hence, the SSPA adopted the format of an aptitude test (officially known as Academic Aptitude Test) which consists of a verbal reasoning (VR) and a numerical reasoning (NR). The combined results of the two tests are used to scale the internal examinations of the students.

- Continuous internal assessment was another characteristic of SSPA to lighten the pressure of the one-off public examination.

- After the SSPA, the primary school graduates are grouped into five ability bands of equal size. The Band 1 students are given priority to select schools first, followed by Band 2 students and so on and the Band 5 students choose last.

- The SSPA then allocates students on a district basis (a total of 18 districts were created). New effective schools began to emerge in the districts alongside the old effective schools as a result of this.

Despite all the changes, the SSPA continues to remain a high-stakes examination (Wong, 1996). The introduction of 9-year free and compulsory education has not altered the need for public 'examination'. It has changed only the examination content, making it less dependent on the school curriculum. After 1979, the battle for a subsidised secondary school place gave way to the fight for a place in a 'better quality' secondary school. Hence the pattern of high ability students being concentrated in a small number of schools remains. At the other end of the scale, there are schools that accept mostly Band 5 students and are nicknamed 'Band 5' schools.

In the new effective schools, the students were equally, if not more, self-motivated. Despite all the changes, the criteria for measuring up to effective schools remained largely unchanged.

It became clear that the ability to attract more Band 1 or 2 students would greatly enhance the status of the schools. Finding ways to attract high band students became the major concern of all schools in the new system. Marketing strategies were employed to attract the attention of both parents and students. Ironically, some schools spent so much effort in the strategies that the strive for effective schools status became a strive for effective students.

The concern for quality

Although new effective schools have been created since the expansion of secondary school education in the 70s they are, after all, a minority. The majority of the new schools in the new towns must settle with students with a lower banding. What made the situation worse was that in order to remain attractive to parents and students, the majority of the new schools followed the example of the elitist schools to adopt a grammar school curriculum and English as the teaching medium. This has created a serious problem of mismatch between the needs of the students in mass education and the curriculum content[7].

Government initiatives

Now that the quantitative objectives have largely been achieved, the attention of the Government and the community has shifted to the qualitative issues of education. The Government has always expressed concern for the quality of schooling and has been very keen to promote school improvement. The recent initiatives include the publication of the *School Management Initiative* (SMI): Setting the framework for quality in Hong Kong Schools in 1991 and the *Target Oriented Curriculum* (TOC) in 1993. The former relied on a school-based management framework as the key for reform and has attracted over 200 primary and secondary schools (Wong, 1991; 1993) while the latter touched on key elements of curriculum, especially the form of assessment and the teaching styles of teachers (Morris, 1996).

The latest attention of the Government was geared towards a holistic approach to the quality in education. The Education Commission released its Report No 7: *Quality School Education in October*, 1997. The Report:

- advocates the use of performance indicators and encourages schools to set up goals and objectives;

- introduces the quality assurance mechanism to measure schools;

- allows school to use school funds more flexibly;

- proposes a more coherent pre-service and in-service training for teachers; and

- sets up the new Quality Education Fund (QEF) to assist schools to achieve outstanding performance.

The Government is determined to set the agenda for school improvement in the coming decades. In October 1997, the Chief Executive Officer announced in his maiden policy speech that a huge sum of five billion dollars was set aside for the Quality Education Fund.

Some inconsistencies

However, there is concern that in its endeavour for quality education, the Education Department may repeat the 'over-administration' errors they made in the 70s and 80s.

Partly due to a continuous criticism from the education community that its inspections were piecemeal and ineffective, and partly as a response to the quality appeal of the Commission Report No 7, the Advisory Inspectorate Division of the Education Department intends to carry out week-long 'whole school' inspections of schools. They gathered information on performance indicators from Scotland and Australia, learned the experience from OFSTED in UK and compiled the 'Performance Indicators for Secondary Schools' monograph. As the contents of the monograph reveal, the inspection will focus on the areas of Management & Organisation, Teaching and Learning, Support for Students, School Ethos and Attainment and Achievement. The strategy of management by objective (MB), which builds on the rationality of clear objectives followed by planning and actions, was largely adopted. The intention of the Inspectorate is to have every single school in Hong Kong fully inspected even though in the existing resources they can only visit a school once every three to four years.

As spelled out in the monograph, the demand on records of documentation (serving as indicators) in term of school policies and procedures, records of meetings of all kinds, teachers' handbook to classroom teaching and learning are massive. While it is a good thing to make school accountable, when it is applied indiscriminately to all schools in Hong Kong, problems will be created.

The first is the stress put on schools. Experience elsewhere (Ouston *et al,* 1996) showed that full inspection is a stressful experience for the school to endure but the experiences were not necessary useful. The experience in UK shows that while there were some positive responses, chiefly from those whose own Development Plan overlapped with the Action Plan of the inspection, the rest, particularly classroom teachers, were less positive and even rather demoralised by the process (Ouston et al, 1996; Brimblecombe, et al, 1996).

Another issue associated with inspection is the promotion of 'good practices', which is also the aim of the local Advisory Inspectorate. The nature of the debate is whether the inspection will present a required model, a preferred model or accept a range of alternatives (Maw, 1996). In the UK there is the Handbook for Inspection of Schools to guide and control the day-to-day practice of inspection. Although the Handbook is ambivalent on the issue of 'good practices', the inspectors are admonished not to bring their own preferences to influence the process of the inspection (Maw, 1996:26-27).

In Hong Kong the inspection is less transparent and open. The fact that the inspection is carried out by the Advisory Inspectorate from the Education Department reinforces the impression that it is a top-down measure to control schools. They are not regarded as collaborators who assist the schools to take their development plans forward. Furthermore, the local culture of respecting leadership would make the local schools interpret the detailed requirements in the inspection manual as a preferred model for schooling. If this happens, it will not only contravene the spirit of the *School Management Initiative*, a school-based management model that the Education Department has pushed very hard since 1991, it will also stifle the variation of schooling in Hong Kong.

Another inconsistency which has arisen through massive negative responses is the compulsory enforcement of a particular teaching medium for all secondary schools. Since 1990, after the publication of the Education Commission Report No 4. the Government accepted the policy that the majority of secondary school students in Hong Kong should learn in their mother tongue. Since 1994, the Education Department has been sending advice to schools on the ability of their students and has pledged that the Government would take tough action in those schools that did not follow the advice on the teaching medium. Eager to attend to its bureaucratic regulations, in late 1997, the Government announced a list of 100 secondary schools (14 more schools were included after appeal - see note 5) which were allowed to use English as the medium of instruction. The remaining 350 or so schools were permitted only to use the Chinese language. Although the public has been dissatisfied with the present situation where the majority of secondary schools chose English as the teaching medium and tolerated the use of Cantonese (mixed codes) in classrooms, few would expect a drastic decision from the Education Department for a quick solution. The artificial division of schools on the medium of instruction will further consolidate the English medium schools in their elitist school status.

In its enthusiasm to adhere to bureaucratic surveillance on this issue, the Education Department has neglected its previous position on school-based management, which they had also advocated with equal zeal among schools. This seems to be a catch twenty-two situation but it does not mean that there is no alternative. At least in the full inspection of schools some other ways of implementing these issues can be worked out.

For example, instead of making inspection for all schools, a situation the Advisory Inspectorate could not fully cope with, the Inspectorate could make a better use of its limited resources for the needy schools. Inspection could be made compulsory only to those schools that have performed poorly over the years and need intervention anyway. It would not be difficult for the Inspectorate to identify these schools and the concern for poor standards gives the Inspectorate a legitimate reason for intervention. Concentrating on the schools that need support will not only drastically reduce the number of schools to be inspected to a manageable size, but will give the Inspectorate more time to offer effective assistance. Moreover, the inspection manual could be employed as a useful framework for the poorer performing schools to change.

The inspection for the rest of schools could be made optional or through invitation. The idea of invitation is to promote good models. Set in the spirit of choice, the promotion of 'good practices' will carry a different tone. The message could be taken up voluntarily and a genuine collaborative spirit could be achieved.

Shift of influence on education policy

Under the local environment and with the heavy commitments of the Government in education, it is natural that most of the agenda of initiatives was originated by the Government. The schools were largely reactive to the changes. However, individuals from schools could exert influence on change through membership of the advisory committees of the Government. Thus far, the main advisory body of the Government on Education is the Education Commission and Board of Education. The Legislative Council, the membership of which was also appointed by the Government until the 1980s, could also have impact on education. During the years of development, there is a clear shift of influence from the traditional elitist schools to the members of the new Subsidised Schools Council.

For a long time, the membership in the Board of Education, the Legislative Council, and Education Commission was drawn mainly from the Grant Schools Council. Individual members of the Council and the Council itself provided educational leadership and had exerted great influence in early policies in education. This situation began to change after the introduction of free and compulsory education and the further expansion of the senior secondary and matriculation education in the late 1970s. The increasingly larger number of new aided secondary schools of the Subsidised Schools Council was a force to be reckoned with.

Being new, there were more school members from the Subsidised Schools Council who were dynamic and ready to engage in innovation. As such they were more ready to involve themselves in the new and diverse program to meet the need of mass education initiated by the Government. The promotion of Chinese, rather than English as the teaching medium in schools was one example. Thus it made political sense that the Government should absorb more people from these new schools into their advisory network[8]. This shift of influence from the old elitist schools to the new ones began in the 1980s. Today, the policy decision bodies in education are largely served by members from new schools and the influence of the old elitist schools, both as individuals and as a group, has became peripheral.

Individual effort aside, the single most concerted action for school improvement from schools is still the *Towards Better Schools Movement*. The Movement was founded in 1992 by a group of school heads from largely the new schools (and a few government schools). Since its beginning, the Movement had assistance from the Education Department by providing secretariat and funding support until 1997. The Movement adopts self-renewal strategies, organises regular public seminars and conducts in-house workshops for the sharing of good practice. The members of the Movement have recently exposed themselves to international gatherings such as the ICSEI conference and through other international experience and research on effective schools.

Research work on effective schools

Systematic studies on effective schools in Hong Kong originated with Cheng Yin Cheong's work in the late 1980s. He has published quite substantially on effectiveness and related areas. More recent work includes two Research Grant Council (RGC) studies; one released recently by Leslie Lo and his colleagues from the Chinese University (Lo, et al, 1997) and a more ambitious on-going one by Wong Kam-Cheung which involves a whole cohort of students in the analysis and includes the examination of time as a factor.

However, thus far, all studies on effective schools in Hong Kong rely heavily on the Western theoretical framework as a model and using psychometric analysis. While it is important to borrow experiences from overseas and employ quantitative methodology to establish the scene, there is a lack of in-depth understanding of the factors leading to effectiveness, both at the societal and school levels. Recently at the societal level, Cheng Kai Ming called attention to the neglected dimension of cultural comparison

(Cheng, 1995). Cheng and Wong (1996) published a paper to establish the cultural framework for effective schools studies.

An example of the cultural factor which is quite unique in East Asian societies like Hong Kong, Taiwan, Korea, Japan and Singapore is the parental influence and expectation on children expressing itself in the massive scale of private tuition. A recent study showed that around 35% of the primary 5 to 6 students had private tuition (Wong, 1996). The figure for secondary schools could be higher. Although family influence has always been recognised as crucial in the study of effective schools, what makes private tuition such an important factor is its direct influence on the attainment of students measured by public examination. It is not known how much variance could be explained by private tuition where teaching to the test is the order of the day, nor whether could this be measured. Any effective schools research in Hong Kong, and indeed in this part of this world, that ignores this factor will be incomplete.

Another example of the cultural influence is leadership. Effective schools research attaches a great deal of importance to school leadership. It is not sure whether the research agenda on leadership should be the same in the East and West. Much of the recent emphasis on leadership in the West is on transformational leaders and their ability in empowering teachers (Leithwood et al, 1996) through participatory decision-making. While it is important to recognise the transformational leaders and empowerment, it is less certain whether participatory decision-making is the necessary research agenda in the local scene. Under the influence of the Chinese pragmatism, it could very well be the case that the concern of the local teachers is to get things done in schools in an orderly manner. School principals who provide leadership to satisfy these needs of the teachers will command their respect. Similarly role modelling is considered important in both teaching and management in the local culture. Principals who set themselves up as role models in the schools carry a lot of weight through their leadership. All these considerations would ask for a different research agenda to be pursued rather than using similar questionnaires to those developed in the West.

At the school level, a missing factor in the effective schools research so far is the understanding of the inside processes of individual effective schools - the holistic knowledge of a school as a complex organisation and the dynamic interplay of behaviour among different members of the school. As argued earlier in the paper, the Hong Kong schools have a number of unique features which are not found in many schools in the West. Grouping of students according to their ability is one such characteristic. Grouping of students is done at two levels. The first is through SSPA where students of different abilities are grouped into different schools. Effective schools in Hong Kong, both old and new, are thus created.

The second difference is the common practice of streaming inside secondary schools. Almost all Hong Kong schools, including both new and old effective schools, practice some form of academic streaming. In an initial study on school effects, it was discovered in boys' schools, that students who took arts performed extremely poorly in the HKCEE as compared with their counterparts in other type of schools (Wong, 1993). It was discovered that in the local boys' schools, students are streamed into Science and Arts subjects after Secondary 4 (age of 16). The Science stream enjoyed a high status and only those students who failed to gain a place in the Science stream were forced to take up Arts subjects. As a consequence the students who take the Arts stream suffered from low esteem which greatly affected their public examination performance. We are aware the effects of a school is not uniform, but the effective schools studies so far have not been able to tease out these local factors for further analysis.

In order to address these local factors at both societal and school levels, it is necessary to recognise the fact that culture does matter in schooling and there are genuine differences between schooling in the East and West. Fortunately there are now more researchers who are prepared to see these differences. It is hoped that, both in theory and in practice, more findings will be published in the near future to inform us about the making of effective schools in Hong Kong.

Notes

1 In this paper effective schools are referred broadly to those schools which have achieved outstanding performance chiefly in public examinations. This consideration is consistent with both the literature and the local concern. Whether this definition is too narrow or desirable will not be discussed in this paper.

2 In 1970, out of 80099 primary 6 students, only 16428 (20.5%) were assigned a place in the public secondary secondary schools.

3 For example, according to Education Department Half-yearly Statistics Summary , in 1971, there were only 97 public sector secondary day schools with 70,861 enrolment but there were 304 private schools and their enrolment stood at 243,698. As a comparison in 1978, the respective figures for public sector and private secondary schools were 199 and 216, an increase of over 100% for the public sector schools.

4 These values refer to 'the government leadership, competitive education, a disciplined work force, principles of equality and self-reliance, and self-

cultivation' (Tu, 1996: p2). One could of course argue that it was the cultural milieu which had conditioned the choice of the options making them consistent with its value.

5   These church schools are members of the Grant Schools Council and there are twenty two of them. Grant Schools Council is different from the later Subsidised Schools Council which was established in the early 70s with over 400 members. For historical reasons, although there is no difference between the two groups of schools in government funding, Grant Schools Council is considered in general to be still more prestigious. One recent example is that in the compulsory regrouping of schools into English and Chinese medium of instruction based largely on students' ability, only 114 schools, out of 450, were allowed to use the English medium and all the 22 Grant Schools are in the list.

6   Howard Gardner in his book 'To Open Minds' recorded his trip in the mid 1980s to study creativity teaching. He was very much impressed by the performances of some gifted children in the mastery in music, painting, calligraphy and other arts forms but was critical of the emphasis placed in the teaching of basics. He thought that this would stifle the creation of individual children. One afternoon in his hotel lobby, his four year old son Benjamin was playing with the key (it was a large key) in front of the key box. In the side of the box there was a key hole in the shape of a key and Benjamin was finding ways to put the key in. A waitress passed by and saw this. She stepped forward, held the hand of Benjamin and guided him to put the key through the key hole into the box. Howard was not impressed by this. Later in the day he brought this subject up with his hosts. He emphasised that in US, they would simply let the child play with the key until he found out the way to put the key back. 'But Professor,' his host replied, 'there is only one way to put the key into the key hole.' The perception provides the difference in the education of the young between the East and the West.

7   For those who are familiar with the Hong Kong situation know that Hong Kong is basically a monolingual society where Cantonese is the dominant dialect. Using English as the main teaching and learning medium has created a lot of difficulty for both teachers and students.

8   There is of course the influence of the Professional Teachers' Union and other teacher bodies to be considered. Since they are not the focus of the paper their role will not be discussed here

References:

Biggs, J. (1996). Western misperceptions of the Confucian-heritage learning culture, in Watkins, D.A. & Biggs, J.B. (eds), *The Chinese Learner*, CERC & ACER, Hong Kong: 45-68.

Brimblecombe, N., Ormston, M., & Shaw, M. (1996). Teachers' perceptions of inspection, in Ouston, J., Earley, P., & Fidler (eds*). OFSTED Inspections: The Early Experience*, London, David Fulton Publishers: 126-134.

Cheng, K. M. (1995). The neglect dimension: Cultural comparison in Educational Administration, in Wong, K.C. et al (eds*). Educational Leadership and Change: An International Perspective*, Hong Kong University Press: 87-102.

Cheng, K.M. & Wong, K.C. (1996). School effectiveness in East Asia: concepts, origins and implications, *Journal of Educational Administration, 34*, N 5; 32-49.

Edmonds, R.R. (1979). Effective Schools for the Urban Poor. *Educational Leadership, 37*, 15-24

Education and Manpower Branch and Education Department, (1991). *The School Management Initiative: Setting the framework for quality in Hong Kong Schools*, Hong Kong Government.

Education Commission, (1997). *Quality School Education*, Hong Kong Government.

Education Department, (1998). Perfomance Indicators for Secondary Schools (first edition), Education Department, Hong Kong (unpublished monograph).

Law, N. (ed.) (1996). *Science and Mathematics Achievements at the Junior Secondary Level in Hong Kong: A Summary Report for Hong Kong in the TIMSS*. Faculty of Education, University of Hong Kong.

Leithwood, K., Tomlison, D. & Genge, M. (1996). Transformational school Leadership, in Leithwood. K., Chapman, J., Corson, D., Hallinger, P. & Hart, A. (eds) Inter*national Handbook of Educational Leadership and Administration*, Boston, Kluwer Academic Publishers.

Levin, H.M. & Lockheed, M. E. (eds) (1993). *Effective Schooling in Developing Countries*, Falmer Press, London.

Llewellyn, J., Hancock, G., Kirst, M., & Roeloffs, K. (1982). *A Perspective on Eduction in Hong Kong: Report by a visiting panel*, Hong Kong Government.

Lo, L. N. K. et al. (1997). *A survey of the effectiveness of Hong Kong secondary school system*. The Chinese University of Hong Kong.

Maw, J. (1996). The Handbook for the Inspection of Schools: Models, outcomes and effects, in Ouston, J., Earley, P., & Fidler (eds*). OFSTED*

Inspections: The Early Experience, London, David fulton Publishers: 22-32.

Morris, P. et al (1997). *Target Oriented Curriculum Evaluation Project, Interim Report*, INSTEP, University of Hong Kong.

Mortimore, P. (1992). Issues in school effectiveness, in Reynolds, D. and Cuttance, P (eds) *School Effectiveness Research Policy and Practice*, London: Cassell.

Mortimore, P., Sammons, P., Stoll, L., Lewis, D. and Ecob. R. (1988). *School Matters: The Junior Years*, Wells: Open Books.

Ouston, J., Earley, P., & Fidler, B., (1996). Secondary schools' responses to OFSTED: Improvement through inspection? in Ouston, J., Earley, P., & Fidler (eds*). OFSTED Inspections: The Early Experience*, London, David Fulton Publishers: 111-125.

Ouston, J., Earley, P., & Fidler, B., (eds) (1996). *OFSTED Inspections: The Early Experience*, London, David Fulton Publishers.

Purkey, S.C. and Smith, M.S. (1983). Effective schools: a review, *Elementary School Journal*, 83, 427-52.

Rutter, M., Maughan, B., Mortimore, P., & Ouston, J., with Smith, A. (1979*). Fifteen thousand hours: Secondary schools and their effect on children*, Cambridge, M.A.: Harvard University Press.

Stoll, L. & Fink, D. (1992). Effective school change: the Halton approach, *School Effectiveness and School Improvement*, 3 (1), 19-41.

Teddlie, C. & Stringfield, S. (1993). *Schools make a difference: Lessons learned from a 10-year study of school effects.* New York: Teachers College.

Tu, W. (1996). *Confucian Traditions in East Asian Modernity*, Harvard University Press, Boston.

Wong, K.C. (1991) School Management Initiative - the initiate response, *New Horizons*, 32, 271-32

Wong, K.C. (1993). School-based Management, School Effectiveness and the School Management Initiative: Different? How Different?, in A. Tsui and I. Johnson (eds) *Teacher Education and Development*, Education Paper 19, Faculty of Education, University of Hong Kong: 45-58.

Wong, K.C. et al (1996). *Research on Aims, Objective, Targets, Enforcement of 9-year Compulsory Education and the Assessment and Allocation System Vol 2*, Board of Education, Hong Kong.

16.

School effectiveness and school improvement in Malaysia

Rahimah Haji Ahmad, Zulkifli Abdul Manaf and Shahril Marzuki

Introduction

Malaysia was formed in 1963 when the Federation of Malaya (which gained independence from the British in 1957), amalgamated with Singapore and the then newly independent states of Sabah and Sarawak. However, in 1965, Singapore left the federation to be on its own.

The population of Malaysia, about 20 million people, consists of more than thirty ethnic groups and subgroups, of which 61 percent are bumiputeras or 'sons of the soil', 30 per cent Chinese and nine percent Indians and others. Of the bumiputeras, 50 percent are Malays, while the other 11 percent consist of indigenous peoples such as the Ibans, Kadazans, Muruts, Kenyahs, Dayaks, Bidayuhs, and Muruts in Sabah and Sarawak, and a smaller number of Semais and Jakuns in Peninsula Malaysia.

The national language and the medium of instruction in schools is Malay or Bahasa Melayu, otherwise known officially as Bahasa Malaysia, literally translated as the Malaysian Language. The official religion is Islam, but government policy ensures that there is complete freedom of worship among her people. After independence, the government policy adopted has ensured that there is a harmonious relationship among her people, political stability and continued economic growth. Since 1987, Malaysia has recorded an annual growth rate of 8-9 percent.

The Malaysian system of education

The education system has, since independence, explicitly been identified as the main instrument for national unity and development, with an emphasis on human resource development. It was realised on the eve of independence, that the system of education, which was structured along ethnic and cultural lines under the British colonial government, only reinforced the pluralistic nature of the society, and did nothing towards building a unified nation. The education system then was made up of:

- English schools, modelled on the English grammar schools,

- Malay schools, structurally similar to the English schools but with curriculum suited to the local Malays,

- Chinese schools set up by the Chinese community with curriculum, textbooks and teachers imported from China,

- Tamil schools in rubber estates, to cater for Indians who were mostly rubber tappers, and

- the Malay community also had informal religious schools, oriented towards the Middle East, with an emphasis on Arabic and reading the Quran.

Education in Malaysia is a federal matter. It is now a centrally administered national system, with a common curriculum, common textbooks and common examination system. It can be described as a 6-3-2-2 system, which consists of six years of elementary (primary) education, three years of lower secondary, two years of upper secondary and a further two years of post-secondary or pre-university education. Children start school at the age of seven, as pre-school education is not part of the formal school system. Most children however, have some form of optional pre-school education that is available to most of the population.

While the medium of instruction in public schools is Bahasa Malaysia, English is taught as a very important second language from year one. At the same time, the system allows for the former Chinese and Tamil elementary schools, specifically Sekolah Rendah Jenis Kebangsaan (Cina) and Sekolah Rendah Kebangsaan (Tamil), or National Type Primary School (Chinese) and National Type Primary School (Tamil), to continue using Chinese and Tamil as the medium of instruction. Bahasa Malaysia and English are taught as subjects.

At the end of every stage, students sit for a common public examination, namely: the Ujian Pencapaian Sekolah Rendah (UPSR) or Elementary School Assessment Examination at the end of year six, the Penilaian Menengah

Rendah (PMR) or the Lower Secondary Assessment, after three years of lower secondary and finally the Sijil Pelajaran Malaysia or the Malaysian Certificate of Education at the end of upper secondary school. The latter is equivalent to, and modelled on the O-levels. For those wishing to prepare themselves for tertiary education another two years in pre-university classes will lead them to the Sijil Tinggi Persekolahan Malaysia, or Malaysian Higher Certificate of Education, which is equivalent to the A-levels. By tradition, there has always been a strong emphasis on examinations. Technical and vocational education is provided at the upper secondary level, as part of the national education system.

The overriding objectives of the Malaysian education system as alluded to earlier, are:

- national unity through a unified national system with Bahasa Malaysia as the medium of instruction based on common content curriculum and textbooks, and
- human resource development with an emphasis on individual human development with Malaysian values, to prepare citizenry for the next millennium.

The national philosophy of education is stated thus :

Education in Malaysia is an ongoing effort towards further developing the potential of individuals in a holistic and integrated manner, so as to produce individuals who are intellectually, spiritually, emotionally and physically balanced and harmonious, based on a firm belief in and devotion to God. Such an effort is designed to produce Malaysia citizens who are knowledgeable and competent, who possess high moral standards and who are responsible and capable of achieving a high level of personal well-being as well as being able to contribute to the harmony and betterment of the family, the society and the nation at large.

(Ministry of Education, 1993)

The emphasis on values education is manifested by making Islamic Education and Moral Education compulsory for the Muslims and non-Muslims respectively, and the adoption of the philosophy of values across the curriculum.

Beginning in the early 1980's, the Malaysian education system has been undergoing reforms, mainly through revamping the curriculum. The new

Primary School Curriculum, otherwise known as Kurikulum Baru Sekolah
Rendah (KBSR), was first introduced in 1983, followed by the Integrated
Secondary School Curriculum or Kurikulum Bersepadu Sekolah Menengah
(KBSM) in 1988. In 1996, a new Education Act was adopted, which is an
amendment of the 1966 Education Act, taking into consideration current
developments in education and world developments in general, and the rising
importance of private education in Malaysia as an alternative for parents, and
the demand for ensuring quality education for all.

Private school education largely complements the public schools. They are
required by law (now explicitly stated in the new Education Act, 1996), to
follow the national curriculum and prepare students for the common public
examinations. During the early decades after independence, public
examinations also acted as a sifting process, and students who failed in the
public examinations, were not promoted, and sometimes forced to leave
school. Private schools then were for students who failed in the public school
system, giving them another chance to sit for the examination, and continue
their education. With the present educational policy that ensures eleven years
of schooling for all, private schools take on another role that of giving parents
an alternative to the public school. Many are now claiming to give better
education by having better facilities. They must abide by the national
philosophy and follow the same curriculum and prepare students for the same
examinations, and the medium of instruction at the secondary level, must be
in Bahasa Malaysia.

School effectiveness and improvement research in Malaysia

In Malaysia, whether schooling makes a difference to the general public has
never been an issue of public debate. The traditional view is that schooling is
considered very important and education is viewed as a vehicle for upward
mobility in society. As such good schools have always been highly regarded.
The general population seems to concur in their beliefs that good schools are
basically 'high achieving', measured by overall student performance in public
examinations. This is because traditionally, those performing well in public
examinations have a better chance of pursuing higher education or have better
employment opportunities. Student performance is also associated with
student discipline and school culture. These schools are usually well known,
and they strive very hard to maintain their tradition and school culture in
order to continue to be recognised as such by the public. Traditionally good
schools are located in cities or big towns where facilities are superior to those
found in the rural areas.

Educational research literature in Malaysia, has always centred around
learning and teaching and student achievement, mostly measured by test

scores, or on variables which correlate with student achievement. As such in a broad sense literature on student achievement is in a way related to school effectiveness as good teaching and learning is considered a factor of effective schools. On the other hand, there is some literature which focuses on school outputs or clearly allude to school effectiveness, while still others specifically focus on the study of school effectiveness and improvement. The latter, however are far more recent phenomena since the concept of school effectiveness is a fairly new in Malaysia.

There has been research activities related to school effectiveness and school improvement in Malaysia since the early eighties. This was stirred by the need to assess the implementation and effectiveness of the then new elementary school curriculum. These have concentrated on variables such as leadership styles, school climate and some other variables related to effective schools such as teacher job satisfaction, student discipline and most of all, student achievement. In addition to that, it has been recognised that the principal plays an important role in determining good schools. Thus many research reports and conference papers have focused on the characteristics of principals that have made some schools more effective than others.

Research on school effectiveness and school improvement *per se* is still lacking. The problem lies in the theoretical framework. There has been no agreed upon standard definition of what is school effectiveness, and the holistic concept of school effectiveness is fairly new. Nevertheless there has been some research activities that focus on the internal processes that occur within the schools which researchers believe have some effect on the school output, mostly measured by student achievement. The Malaysian effective school literature focusing on this is a mixture of empirical studies conducted by masters and doctoral students from institutions of higher learning both local and abroad, research teams from the universities, and the Ministry of Education. In addition to that there are papers and concept papers from individuals from all levels, be it from the school level, Ministry of Education, or the university, which are based on observations, hunches, beliefs and philosophy on what effective schools ought to be, rather than on empirical research. It is observed that the writings are deeply influenced by the findings from the effective school literature generated by researchers from other parts of the world eg., U.S.A, Britain and Australia. The methodology used in school effectiveness and school improvement research in Malaysia varies from quantitative to qualitative approaches. Sometimes a picture of both is found in the analysis of data.

The following description of Malaysian studies is not meant to be an exhaustive account but rather an illustrative summary of this kind of work. This paper will not include studies which focus on factors which affect student achievement (which is abundant), except when they are stated as studies relating to school effectiveness. Studies on principal leadership are also excluded when they are not seen in the context of school effectiveness.

Earlier studies, which can be considered as studies on school effectiveness, centre on leadership of the principal and the study of school climate and student achievement. The earliest known study was a doctoral dissertation (Rahimah, 1981) which assessed the relationship of leadership style and school climate in elementary schools. It was found that leadership style which emphasised human relations and task completion, was associated with a positive school climate which in turn have a positive effect on student academic performance. Razali (1990) used the same climate measures to explore school climate and its relationship with leadership style, teacher job satisfaction and student discipline. He found that an open school climate is associated with a strong leadership style. These are positively correlated with teacher job satisfaction. In this study it was also found that an open school climate is mostly found in medium sized schools.

Another study on effective rural secondary schools in Malaysia (Abdul Karim, 1989) found that there were twelve institutional characteristics which differentiated effective and less effective schools. These can be grouped into:

- principal factors, specifically:
  (i)   principal's leadership skill,
  (ii)   principal's role perception,
  (iii)   principal's years of experience.

- teacher factors, specifically:
  (i)   teacher expectation of students,
  (ii)   teacher attitude toward students,
  (iii)   teacher's regard for their school, teacher perception of government mandates, reports and directives,
  (iv)   teacher satisfaction with students.

- teaching and learning processes, specifically:
  (i)   effective use of school resources,
  (ii)   number of employed improvement strategies, student self discipline, and

- parental involvement in the school.

Taken as a whole, these factors reflect school climate and leadership. According to Abdul Karim (1989) this study demonstrated the utility of the Dimensional Model as a conceptual framework for analysing Malaysian schools. The framework could also be transformed into a planning paradigm for improving schools. In the same year, the Ministry of Education (1989) published a report on the climate of effective and ineffective schools in peninsula Malaysia, which described similar factors.

An ongoing research on effective schools using school climate as proxy was started in 1994, with reports published in 1995, 1996 and 1997 (Zulkifli, Rahimah & Lee, 1995; Rahimah & Zulkifli, 1996a, 1996b, 1997a, 1997b, 1997c). A profile of effective and less effective secondary schools in Malaysia was developed (Rahimah & Zulkifli, 1996a). Among the characteristics of effective schools are climate of good interpersonal relationship, greater evidence of teaching and learning, democratic administration (open door policy) and better physical facilities for teaching and learning. The study postulated that effective schools have a different school climate as compared to the less effective schools, and the results of t-tests on the sub-scale scores of the school climate profile supported this hypothesis.

Indirectly the findings demonstrated the reliability and construct validity of the school climate instrument (Zulkifli, Rahimah, & Lee, 1995). A further study has defined some of the major characteristics of principals from effective schools and how these principals play a very important role in determining school effectiveness (Rahimah & Zulkifli, 1996b, 1997b). The latter studies were based on further visitations and data collection through re-administration of the same instrument, observations and interviews with the principals, selected teachers and students. Basically, the studies used the process model of school effectiveness as described by Cheng (1996a, 1996b). The School Climate Profile that was used in the research has desirable psychometric properties (Zulkifli, Rahimah & Lee, 1995). Rahimah and Zulkifli (1997a, 1997b) indicated the usefulness of the School Climate measures as an indicator of school effectiveness, and the characteristics of the principals of effective schools.

At the same time, a case study on the school culture of unusually effective secondary schools conducted by the Ministry of Education identified certain characteristics of effective schools (Ministry of Education, 1996). These include principal leadership, social climate, curriculum implementation, and physical surroundings. The factors described are similar to those used by the Rahimah and Zulkifli (1996a) profile. This study added on another factors, that of parental involvement in the school.

Effective schools were found to have principals who emphasised on mission and vision for the schools. These were manifested in clearly stated philosophy, aims, objectives, vision, mission and school motto, each of which were explicitly made known to every member of the school community. Principals also plan out various programs towards realising the vision and mission of the schools. The principals in these effective schools were highly committed in their work and strive to make the school attain the vision and mission, and encourage the inculcation of high quality work ethics and accountability among the staff. The administration is more inclined towards a democratic system, involving all staff. There was empowerment given to the staff so that school administration was not disrupted even during his absence.

With regards to climate and social environment, it was found that the school climate was conducive for teaching and learning, clearly emphasising on the teaching and learning of basic skills, and student performance. Teacher expectation of student performance was high, and there was also a clear policy of monitoring and evaluation of student progress.

In terms of physical surroundings, the whole school, including classrooms, office and school grounds, are clean and well kept. The school is also felt to be a safe place, and free from major discipline problems. The whole school community feel that the school was like their second home.

With regards to teaching and learning, the curriculum was well implemented. Teachers and students take teaching and learning seriously. They make extra efforts preparing students for the public national examinations. Special programs are often designed to prepare students for the examinations, both in terms of mastery of content as well as in the techniques of answering examination questions. Furthermore, they arrange for motivational talks to prepare students to be emotionally prepared to face the examinations. Remedial programs and additional classes were conducted to ensure better understanding of the class materials.

The Parent-Teacher Association (PTA) plays an important supportive role in the school. The principals in these effective schools relate very well with and the community at large. The most recent study to date, (Shahril, 1997) used Edmonds' (1979) five-factor model of school effectiveness, to investigate whether the model holds true in the Malaysian context. This appears to be the most comprehensive study on effective schools, with a sample of 1052 elementary school teachers from 68 elementary schools nation wide. The results show that the major factors such as strong effective principal leadership, positive school climate, high expectations of student achievement, frequency of evaluation seems to prevail. The study identified a new factor pertinent to the Malaysian context, that is function of a strong parent-teacher association in determining school effectiveness, which supports the Ministry of Education study above.

In addition to the research mentioned, there is an increasing amount of literature, which debates the issue and outline characteristics of effective schools, particularly in the decade of the 1990's. In the paper entitled, 'The excellent manager: Towards a dynamic school culture', Rahimah (1988) focused on the role of the principal as the main force in effective schools. There are papers published by the Ministry of Education, (Ministry of

Education, 1989, 1996), individuals representing the Ministry of Education, (Abdul Shukor, 1996), and the Inspectorate of Schools (Mohd Arif, 1995), and principals (Hamedah, 1996). There is a book written on leadership and effective schools in Malaysia (Hussein, 1993). In addition, seminar activities seem to focus on the same issues. Most seminars would have sessions devoted to effective schools and quality of schooling. Two seminars were organised by the Ministry of Education in 1995 specifically to discuss effective schools, in terms of concept and the ideal school for Malaysia. In addition various other colloquiums and seminars as well as workshops were held at all levels.

In all these, various issues were raised and debated. They were mostly based on beliefs, observations and philosophy of the writers, reflecting on the mood in the country in line with what is explicitly stated in the National Philosophy of Education (Ministry of Education, Malaysia, 1993). This forum forms a strong basis for the challenge to be faced by the Ministry of Education in coping with education demands of current times.

This furore reflects the commitment of the Malaysian society and the Ministry of Education in coping with educational issues and education of the future citizenry, as manifested in what a school should be to achieve the Malaysian vision for the society in the next millennium. It is apparent that interest has focused on different and various kinds of criteria, which can be associated with effective schools, other than the traditional reliance on the element of student achievement, as measured by student performance in examinations. As such, more current literature on effective schools centre around variables or characteristics of effective schools or what are the characteristics of so-called effective schools, which differentiate them from the others. Characteristically, effective schools are more and more looked at holistically, and the recognition that there are many facets of an effective school. This is in line with the Malaysian educational philosophy, that education is human development, specifically the development wholesome individuals with values pertinent to the Malaysian society equipped to face the next millennium. Criteria being taken into consideration now include conforming to society's norm, excellence in athletics, excellence in co-curricular activities, and employability of its product (if it is a vocational school).

Numerous variables that are believed to contribute to the effectiveness of the schools have been identified. Among these variables are school climate, principal leadership, parental involvement and the Parent Teacher Association, teacher expectation of students performance, teacher attitude toward students, teacher empowerment, and curriculum implementation. Teaching and learning continue to be important variables, because they are perceived positively by both parents and students. It is pertinent to mention here that these variables have been well studied, and appear in Malaysian literature constantly, in studies related to all fields in education and teacher education.

The Ministry of Education has taken the lead in specifying the criteria to be used to judge good schools, and has formulated guidelines and specifications of what a model school should be, encompassing characteristics of an ideal school for Malaysia.

As a move for nation-wide school improvement, the Ministry has introduced a strategy to reward and recognise schools, which demonstrate excellence, annually. Schools, which are found to meet the highest criteria as identified in the guidelines, will be recognised as the school of the year.

Since school effectiveness can be viewed from several perspectives the Ministry recognises there can be several types of effective schools, depending on where is their main strength. To date four categories are identified. They are Effective Schools (Sekolah Berkesan), Model Schools (sekolah contoh), Vision Schools (Sekolah Wawasan), and Excellent Schools (Sekolah Cemerlang). This will also ensure that more schools are given recognition, and an implicit acknowledgment that effective schools are manifested in different ways, each of which is no more important than the other. For all the categories, overall academic performance is still an important factor. Each category emphasises different aspects of the effective school, such as input and product, product only, process and product. The main theme is to excel in whatever aspects identified and measured, while at the same time maintaining academic excellence. Descriptions of the different categories of schools are as follows:

Effective schools

Effective schools resemble schools as envisioned by Edmonds (1979). The same five variables ranging from strong, effective leadership to safe and conducive climate are the basis for evaluation. However the variables are further delineated into two broad categories of Social Organisation, and Curriculum and Instruction. Under Social Organisation, the factors considered are:

- school climate and discipline,
- clear academic goals and social actions,
- high academic expectations,
- teacher commitment,
- guidance for students (pastoral care),
- incentive and rewards,

- leadership and administration,
- community support, and
- effective communication.

Under Curriculum and Instruction the factors are:

- curriculum leadership and instruction,
- high academic learning time,
- regular monitoring of homework,
- a well-balanced curriculum,
- variability and effective instructional strategies used by teachers,
- opportunities to increase accountability among students, and
- systematic evaluation.

National model schools

Model schools are those which are considered to be excellent in all aspects, almost an ideal school. Criteria used are based on the following characteristics: principal leadership, teacher attitude, student attitude, curriculum, Co-curriculum, discipline, school climate and culture, resource centre, and the school's contribution to society.

This prestigious award is announced every year on Teachers Day, which is celebrated on May 16 every year. Each year schools are awarded in this category, one each to rural primary, rural secondary, urban primary and urban secondary school.

Vision schools

The concept paper describing this category of schools was first tabled in 1995 at the third National Education Convention on Educational Management. A visionary school is a school that provides a conducive environment, which encourages teachers, students and society to work together to achieve the goals of education at the school level, as envisioned by our National Vision (Vision 2020), National Vision for Education and the National Education Philosophy.

Excellence in education is the major aim of visionary school, with an emphasis on human development of the individual student. Excellence is looked at in a more global and integrated way taking into account all the elements in the school environment that influence the growth and development of the student. The criteria used is the results produced by the school, based on both academic results as well as the students who are graduates of the schools. Excellence of the school programs are based on four aspects, specifically curriculum programs, co-curriculum programs, personality of the students, and school culture which encompass solidarity, management style and leadership, caring service, empowerment, monitoring system, knowledge area, caring school and culture of excellence.

Excellent schools

The main criteria for schools of excellence seems to be focused on the school as a quality organisation based on quality principles and zero defect, heavily biased towards administration and management. The Ministry of Education is still finalising the specific criteria. Among the criteria identified, for excellent schools (Berita Harian, 1995) are:

- the attainment of zero defect in all aspects especially in terms of discipline among teachers, students, and school support staff,
- excellence in student academic achievement,
- quality involvement in the co-curricular (extra-mural) activities,
- creative and innovative teaching and learning process and administration,
- cleanliness and cheerful environment,
- active involvement and valuable contribution by members of the school in community work,
- high percentage of students pursuing higher education,
- good interpersonal relationships among school citizens,
- efficient management of school finance,
- esprit de corps and dedication among management, teachers and support staff, and
- strong leadership.

Conclusion

Beginning in the 1980's, school reform in Malaysia was directed towards making the school as the main instrument for citizenship development. The then new curriculum for elementary and secondary schools, has as the main focus, to produce all round individuals, well balanced in all aspects of the intellect, emotion, physical well being, and spiritual. The goals of the curriculum are well reflected by the subjects taught in the schools. The major thrust in the curriculum is to ensure that all the aspects taken into consideration, and treated holistically. School effectiveness is then measured in terms of the attainment of these objectives. Hence the move for school improvement measures manifested in the organisation of competition for national awards in the various categories described above.

At the same time current changes in technology, and the advent of information technology including computer technology, computers find its way to the schools. Beginning with the introduction of computer clubs to ensure computer literacy, computer literacy subjects came to be included in the curriculum. Computers in education have won the heart of the Ministry of Education. In 1993, sixty schools throughout the country were selected for the CIE pilot project. Although the implementation of the Computer in Education (CIE) project had its share of problems and obstacles, sceptics and laggards, its impact and potential application in education is greatly felt by educators.

Together with the inception of the Multimedia Super Corridor (MSC) in 1997 the infusion of multimedia Internet into the classroom seems unavoidable. There will be a multimedia university and the Ministry of Education (1997) mooted the idea of Smart schools. It is planned that by the year 1999 the first 85 schools will operate under the smart schools concept. All schools will be smart schools by the year 2010.

This will have an impact on the way we view effective schools. The variables on which effectiveness is measured will accommodate these changes. School effectiveness will have to take into account efficient management of limited resources, new skills and new demands as well as the accommodation of modern technology in the curriculum.

In the future the concept of effective schools must be thought of using a new paradigm where students are the active learners in the classroom. Since students will be the active learners under the guidance of the teachers, the evaluation of teaching and learning processes have to change accordingly.

Teaching, learning and school administration will be computerised. Teachers will function as facilitators only and will have more time for more individualised interaction with students who need special attention. Parents, teachers and the whole school community will be linked via Local Area Network (LAN) and Wide Area Network (WAN). It is expected the role of multimedia in teaching, learning and communication will be increased and future research in effective schools will have to take into consideration this issue.

The concept of effective schools and school improvement may have to be modified somewhat to cater for changing times and new development in educational technology. For example, while the country is going through a period of economic unrest and uncertainty some educational plans have to be put on the back burner for a while. As much as we would like to see the full steam implementation of the Smart Schools project, the economic situation is forcing its implementation at a much smaller scale with some modifications to suit the shrinking budget. Probably one model that we can use to assess a school's effectiveness is its resilience to stand up and continue its goal achievement despite the difficulties faced. We can call it the resilience model. This is based on our reflection that in the past, there were schools, which continue to succeed in their goal achievement despite shortcomings and less than ideal infrastructure. This is in comparison to other comparable schools where despite the presence of enabling factors, the schools still fail to achieve its targets. It must have been the resilience factor that underlies their environment.

Another observation in the effective and improving schools of Malaysia is the support of the Parent Teacher Association (PTA). However, in schools where the PTAs are active and supportive in terms of monetary and parental involvement, the key variable is the principal. The better principals that significantly impact the schools are perceived as a 'go getter'. He or she does not wait for directives to make things happen. They will manage the school using the school staff as a team. In other words, principal leadership tends to foster positive school climate and learning environment. This will in turn accelerate the attainment of school goals and objectives, which in many instances are used as a benchmark for school effectiveness and school improvement.

In Malaysia, even though the principals are predominantly male, there is an increasing trend of female principals. This is especially true in the urban areas. Culturally, the Malaysian society would like to have the male gender to head the school organisation but the increasing of number of capable female teachers in the school makes it increasingly difficult to ignore them. The public is concerned with increasing discipline problems among school children in recent years. One of the factors cited as a possible cause is the decreasing proportion of male teachers in the system. It is noted that in there is a very high inverse correlation between school effectiveness and the incidence of disciplinary problems. Even though the Education Ministry is trying very hard to lure men into teaching it is not very successful because the male enrolment in the various teacher-training programs is steadily declining. This is probably due to the public attitude towards the profession. It is not regarded as a noble profession any more. It is usually the last resort vocational choice among graduates. Furthermore the salary is not competitive as compared to other vocations that may require the same time span or even less for training to be on the job. To make matters worse, even the better-qualified women are also shying from the teaching profession because they have other better opportunities in the work force. We need better-qualified personnel to fill the void in years to come. In order to have effective schools, we need effective teachers who are more academically qualified.

The establishment of the Institut Aminuddin Baki (Aminuddin Baki Institute) by the Ministry of Education (Ministry of Education, Malaysia, 1995) is specifically to ensure excellence in the educational management of the country. This will be achieved through a series of concerted efforts via collaboration with the local and foreign universities.

Some cultural issues that make the Malaysian educational scene a little unique need to be addressed here. These include the following:

- The issue of values education. Religious and Moral education is taught in schools. Values education, (Islamic Education for the Muslims and Moral Education for the non-Muslims) is compulsory in the Malaysian schools, the philosophy of values across the curriculum – meaning that all teachers are expected to integrate the teaching of values in their subjects.

- The objective is to create a Malaysian citizenry who is resilient, innovative, and pro-active, and a well-rounded person. ie., - a modern Malaysian society able to cope with modern 'demands', but not forgetting the basic values suitable to Malaysia. This is in line with the National Education Policy (Wan Mohd Zahid, 1993; Abu Bakar Nordin, 1994).

- Second mode of entry into the institution of higher learning. This will give the citizens another chance to enter tertiary education, which will be otherwise almost impossible under the traditional conditions. This is made possible through distance education.

- The upgrading of the teaching certificates for teachers. Beginning with the July 1996 intake, graduates of the thirty-two teacher-training colleges will be awarded the Malaysian Teaching Diploma.

- The oldest teacher training college is upgraded to a university status. Thus we see the birth of the Universiti Perguruan Sultan Idris (Sultan Idris Teaching University)

- Greater emphasis on science, mathematics and technology in the school curriculum. This is in line with the attainment of the 2020 vision to make Malaysia an industrial nation by the year 2020.

These among other things will help make education in Malaysia an instrument to achieve national solidarity. Continuous effort in school effectiveness and school improvement by educators and researchers is another contribution towards this end.

References

Abdul Karim B. Mohd. Nor. (1989). Characteristics of Effective Rural Secondary Schools in Malaysia. Doctoral Dissertation, University of Wisconsin, Madison, USA.

Abu Bakar Nordin (Ed.). (1994). *Reformasi pendidikan dalam menghadapi cabaran 2020.* (Educational reforms in handling the 2020 challenge]. Kuala Lumpur: Nurin Enterprise.

Abdul Shukor Abdullah. (1996). 'Membina sekolah yang berkesan: Pengurusan setempat, empowerment, dan kepimpinan sebagai inisiatif polisi.' [Development of effective schools: Site management, empowerment, and leadership as policy initiative]. Paper presented at the 2nd Effective Schools Seminar, 14-16 November 1996, Institut Aminuddin Baki, Ministry of Education, Malaysia, Genting Highlands, Malaysia.

Berita Harian (1995). *Sekolah Cemerlang* [Excellent Schools]. Ruangan Pendidikan, 27 March 1995.

Cheng, Y.C. (1996a). *The pursuit of school effectiveness.* Hong Kong: Hong Kong Institute of Education.

Cheng, Y. C. (1996b). *School effectiveness & school-based management: A mechanism for development.* London: The Falmer Press.

Edmonds, R. R. (1979). Effective schools for the urban poor. *Educational Leadership, 37,* 15-24.

Hamedah Wok Awang. (1996). 'Mewujudkan sekolah efektif melalui konsep rantaian tindak balas'. [Creating effective schools through the reaction chain concept]. Paper presented at the 2nd Effective Schools Seminar, 14-16 November 1996, Institut Aminuddin Baki, Ministry of Education, Malaysia, Genting Highlands, Malaysia.

Hussein Mahmood. (1993). *Kepimpinan dan Keberkesanan Sekolah.* [Leadership and School Effectiveness]. Kuala Lumpur: Dewan Bahasa dan Pustaka.

Information Malaysia Yearbook (1995). Kuala Lumpur: Berita Publishing Company.

Jayasankaran, S and Hiebert, M. (1997), Malaysian dilemmas, *Far Eastern Economic Review* , September 4th, 1997, pp18-20.

Ministry of Education Malaysia. (1989). 'Kajian keberkesanan sekolah: Mengkaji iklim di beberapa buah sekolah menengah yang berkesan dan tidak berkesan di semenanjong Malaysia.' [School effectiveness study: Studying the climate of selected effective and ineffective schools in peninsular Malaysia]. A research report submitted to the Educational Planning and Research Division, Ministry of Education, Malaysia.

Ministry of Education Malaysia (1995). *Annual Report.*

Ministry of Education, Malaysia (1996). 'Effective Secondary School Culture Case Study: A Preliminary Report'. Paper presented at the National Educational Research Seminar, Perdana Hotel, Kota Bharu, Kelantan, Malaysia, 18-21 December 1996

Ministry of Education, Malaysia (1997). *Smart Schools. A report from the Smart Schools Task Force*, Educational Planning and Research Division, Ministry of Education, Malaysia.

Mohd Arif Bin Osman. (1995). 'Ciri-ciri sekolah berprestasi tinggi dan rendah.' [Characteristics of high and low performing schools]. Paper presented at the 2nd Regional and School Educational Administration Colloquium. Faculty of Education, University of Malaya, 16th September 1995.

Rahimah Haji Ahmad. (1981). The relationship between and among leadership style, school climate and student achievement in the elementary school principalship in the Federal Territory of Kuala Lumpur, Malaysia. Doctoral Dissertation, University of Southern California, Los Angeles, USA.

Rahimah Haji Ahmad. (1988). 'The excellent manager: Towards a dynamic school culture'. Paper presented at the 10th Convention of ASEAN Council of Teachers. Theme: Towards Excellence in Schools, Penang, Malaysia, 11-14 December 1988.

Rahimah Haji Ahmad, & Zulkifli A. Manaf. (1996a). 'The dynamics of principal leadership in school climate'. Paper presented at the eighth Regional/ International Conference of the Commonwealth Council on Educational Administration (CCEA), Kuala Lumpur, Malaysia, 19-14 August 1996.

Rahimah Haji Ahmad & Zulkifli A. Manaf (1996b). Towards developing a Profile of Effective and Less Effective Schools. *Jurnal Pendidikan, 17*, 51-64.

Rahimah Haji Ahmad & Zulkifli A. Manaf (1996c). The School Climate and Supervisory Practices for Promoting Instructional Improvement. A case study. A Research Report submitted to Mbf Education Group.

Rahimah Haji Ahmad & Zulkifli A. Manaf (1997a). 'Characteristics of Effective and Less Effective Schools in Rural and Urban Settings: A Case Study from Malaysia.' Paper presented at the 10th International Congress for School Effectiveness and Improvement, (ICSEI), Theme: A world of World Class Schools, January 5-8, 1997, Peabody Hotel, Memphis, Tennessee, USA

Rahimah Haji Ahmad & Zulkifli A. Manaf (1997b). 'The Role of Principals Leadership in Determining School Effectiveness'. Paper presented at the 10th International Congress for School Effectiveness and Improvement,

(ICSEI), Theme: A world of World Class Schools, January 5-8, 1997, Peabody Hotel, Memphis, Tennessee, USA.

Rahimah Haji Ahmad & Norani Mohd Salleh (1997), *State-of-the-Art Report on Bullying/School violence in Malaysia* , Report submitted to Unesco, Paris, February 1997.

Ramaiah, A. L. (1995). *Penyelidikan Keberkesanan Sekolah: Masalah Konsepsi dan Metodologi.* [School Effectiveness Research: Problems of Concept and Methodology]. A monograph. Kuala Lumpur: Faculty of Education, University of Malaya.

Razali Bin Othman. (1990). Satu kajian mengenai iklim sekolah menengah di daerah Temerluh. [A study of school climate in a secondary school in the Temerluh district]. Unpublished M. Ed Thesis, Faculty of Education, University of Malaya

Shahril Marzuki (1997). Kajian sekolah berkesan di Malaysia: Model lima faktor. [Effective schools study in Malaysia: The five-factor model]. Doctoral dissertation. Universiti Kebangsaan Malaysia, Bangi, Selangor, Malaysia.

Zulkifli A. Manaf, Rahimah Haji Ahmad, & Lee Ong Kim (1995). 'An Evaluation of the School Climate Profile Instrument'. Paper presented at the 2nd Asia Pacific Conference on Educational Assessment and Research. September 4-8, 1995, Empress Hotel, Chiang Mai, Thailand.

Zulkifli A. Manaf, & Rahimah Haji Ahmad. (1997a). 'The school climate as an indicator of school effectiveness.' Paper presented at the 11th National Teacher Education Conference, 4-6 April 1997, Universiti Putra Malaysia, Serdang, Selangor, Malaysia.

Zulkifli A. Manaf, & Rahimah Haji Ahmad. (1997b). 'The characteristics of principals of effective schools'. Paper presented at the 11th National Teacher Education Conference, 4-6 April 1997, Universiti Putra Malaysia, Serdang, Selangor, Malaysia.

Zulkifli A. Manaf, & Rahimah Haji Ahmad. (1997c). 'The learning environment and supervision practices in a private school'. Paper presented at the third Asia Pacific Conference on Educational Assessment and Research, 5-8 September 1997, Manila, Philippines.

17.

School effectiveness and school improvement in New Zealand

Peter Ramsay with Adrianne Affleck

The context

New Zealand is a small nation state within the British Commonwealth, lying to the east of Australia in the South Pacific. It has a population of 3.6 million people and is multi-ethnic in composition. Successive migrations have joined the indigenous Maori since the 18th Century. Exploitative groups like the whalers, traders and sealers, were the first white population on the scene. They were followed by the missionaries who arrived in the 1820s and set about converting Maori to Christianity. The first group in the field were Anglican, closely followed by Wesleyan and Roman Catholic. Systematic white settlement began in the 1840s under the leadership of Edmund Gibbon Wakefield. The first sailing ships established settlements in Nelson, New Plymouth, Canterbury and Dunedin. It is interesting to note that the intention from the outset was for the ships to contain a cross-section of social class from Britain.

The discovery of gold in the South Island led to a fresh wave of settlement and brought a significant number of Chinese into New Zealand. Labour demands followed and there has been considerable in-migration, mostly from Europe, but also via a chain mechanism from Asia. More recently Pacific Islanders have arrived in considerable numbers until now when Auckland is often referred to as the largest Polynesian city in the world. New Zealand has also accepted refugees from a range of nations including Hungary, Cambodia and Vietnam. With the freeing up of migration laws new citizens have arrived from Asia, usually well qualified and affluent. The major countries concerned here are Japan, Korea, and to a lesser extent, Taiwan. New Zealand, therefore, is multicultural, but two groups, white Caucasian (Pakeha) and Maori form over 80 per cent of the total population.

The school population reflects the above, but it is worth noting that uneven distribution of population means that in some areas Maori predominates (eg. the East Coast of the North Island), while in others Pacific Islanders are the majority group (eg. in Southern Auckland). By the standards of most overseas nations the school population is small in numbers. In 1996 there were 678,000 children and young adults enrolled in primary and secondary schools, serviced by 39,000 teachers. A feature of the New Zealand system is the high number of small sized schools - in the primary sector for example 65 per cent of schools have four teachers or less. Multicultural teaching is therefore common-place in this country.

The original form of Pakeha government in New Zealand was provincially based, but driven by the smallness of the country and the size of the population, as well as considerable inequalities between gold-rich Otago and other provinces, the system became highly centralised. The first efforts at school improvement and effectiveness were, therefore, central in nature. An advisory service was developed which was to be at the heart of in-service teacher education. This service went from strength to strength and, focussing for the most part on new curriculum development, provided most of the basis for school and teacher improvement. There has, however, been considerable criticism of this system, and indeed this present writer is on record as stating that it was 'haphazard, non-systematic, and those who needed it the least got it the most' (see Ramsay 1994, for a full account). The Advisory Service reached its peak in the 1970s when 235 advisers served teachers length and breadth of New Zealand. There is no research on the effectiveness of the Advisory Service, but informal evidence suggests that they had a considerable impact, particularly in rural areas where they were often viewed by teachers as a life-line.

Policy

In recent years New Zealand education has undergone major reform. The first wave of reform began in 1987 with the establishment of a task force to recommend changes in school administration. This came at a time when the public sector, generally speaking, were in the throes of change from public service organisations to state-owned enterprises reformulated along business lines. Corporatisation was common place, and selling-off of public assets (eg telecommunications, railways) was occurring. These changes were driven by market notions derived largely from American economist Milton Friedman

(1962). In the education sector the NZ Treasury's briefing papers to the incoming Labour government in 1987 mooted minimal state intervention in education, and if it was to occur it was argued that it should be targeted, at specific groups where maximum benefits for expenditure would be achieved (for example, Maori).

This was the setting which the taskforce worked in. In the event their recommendations were contrary to many of Treasury's suggestions, especially in the area of state funding. However, the taskforce did set in motion, *inter alia*, comprehensive devolution of many responsibilities earlier performed by central authorities (see Ramsay, 1992, and below for a fuller account). In 1989 a new Education Act put these recommendations into legislation. The new legislation and the new conditions for Boards of Trustees created conditions for considerable research and developmental work in school development which is described below. In the 1990s a second wave of reform has occurred in the area of school curriculum. Again, this has provoked considerable research in the area of teacher and school-based development. I turn now to an account of research of school effectiveness and improvement in NZ which will conclude with an account of the impact of the reforms just described.

Research

No in-depth studies of school improvement and education were undertaken in New Zealand until the late 1970s. Working in underprivileged schools in the southern suburbs of Auckland, Ramsay and his colleagues (1982) undertook what Reynolds (1994), writing from an international perspective, referred to as 'a pioneering study in the field'. This study found that schools which had very similar histories and ethnic and socio-economic structures appeared to have markedly different success rates. In order to investigate this further the researchers selected eight schools which were matched as closely as possible for composition and makeup in pairs. The researchers then spent 15 months observing within the schools endeavouring to explain why one group of schools did so much better in terms of educational outcomes than the other group of schools. It is interesting to note that the study was conducted simultaneously with the seminal work of Rutter and his colleagues (1979) in the United Kingdom. It is even more interesting to note that most of the results were similar. Both studies emphasised *inter alia* such factors as the leadership role of the principal, the development of shared goals, tight knit support mechanisms within the schools, a camaraderie amongst teaching staff and a cooperative environment. There were, however, two important differences which reflect the tensions which have existed in the research in New Zealand ever since.

First, while Ramsay and his colleagues found significant differences in terms of differential cross-school attainment in areas like reading and mathematics, they did not entirely put this down to the tight organisational structures and visions outlined above. Indeed, they emphasised some important aspects relating to the nature of knowledge being utilised in the schools. They pointed to the fact that the effective schools had changed the official curriculum considerably, taking on board the interests of mainly working class Polynesian students within schools. They noted the very real efforts to emphasise aspects of knowledge pertinent to the particular cultures. They cited examples of teachers rewriting text books in a language form understood by the students which was then used as a starting point to move forward into conventional English. Quite simply, where Rutter and his colleagues took the curriculum for granted it appeared in this instance that the teachers were making considerable efforts to alter the curriculum according to their perceptions of students' interests and needs.

The second major difference related to social class. While this factor was held constant in both studies, Ramsay and his colleagues were working in the most underprivileged district in New Zealand. In their conclusions they were careful to note that even though they found significant differences between the groups of schools, they also found that none of the schools in their district reached even the average levels of attainment for the rest of New Zealand schools. They concluded therefore that despite their findings of the influence of school, family background and class were highly significant variables in affecting outcomes.

Reynolds (1994) has noted that there have been no follow up qualitative studies in New Zealand. He is absolutely correct as New Zealand sociologists became preoccupied with replication of some of the well-known school effects studies from overseas which commenced with Coleman in 1996. First in the field in this area were Lauder and Hughes, who reported their findings in 1990. This study focussed on 20 Christchurch secondary schools. The researchers were interested in comparing pupil success in the school examination system and occupational destination on leaving school with a range of variables. They controlled for socio-economic status and academic ability and then investigated the relationship between school outcomes and school type and school socio-economic status mix. Their findings were very interesting. As one would expect they found a huge difference in attainment from school to school. When they controlled for gender, social class and the measured ability of the children on entry to school, the raw differences lessened by 45%, but the differences were still statistically different. This led them to suggest that the type of school attended made a difference as far as children within the schools were concerned. However, the researchers took a further step and asked to what extent the differences in outcome according to school type could be explained by the variables of gender, social class and ability mix. In other words, did the school composition have an effect on children's performance within the schools? Here they came to the conclusion that school mix rather than school type had a significant influence on school outcomes. Moreover they stated:

And while we cannot directly test for variables such as the quality of school organisation or staff, one implication to be drawn from [the results] is that the difference that remains between the most and least 'successful' schools does in some way reflect school variables of this kind. (Lauder and Hughes, 1990: 49)

The researchers then grouped their schools according to their mean socio-economic status and ran regressions in order to see if they could answer the question of the extent that social class mix of schools relates to the performance of particular kinds of students. A highly significant result emerged from this analysis. Lauder and Hughes showed that pupils of equal low ability typically leave the most privileged schools with five School Certificate passes while those from the least privileged schools leave without any qualifications at all. Quite justifiably the researchers stated that such a difference cannot be treated lightly. Following on from this they turned to their final question which was: 'Does the social class mix of a school have an impact on the subsequent destinations of its students over and above that predicted by examination success?'. Here they found that for low school achievers the kind of school attended made relatively little difference to the subsequent destination. However, they also found that high achieving pupils from high socio-economic status schools had a considerable advantage over high achieving students from low socio-economic status schools.

The policy implications of changing the social mix of schools in order to advantage lower socio-economic status pupils is to say the least, significant. Lauder and Hughes' (1990) study is therefore very important, drawing the attention of researchers and policy makers in New Zealand for the first time to the importance of socio-economic status mix in New Zealand schools.

The question of school mix has been pursued in recent years by Martin Thrupp (1996, 1997). Thrupp's work is of extreme importance, as not only does it go some way to resolving the dispute surrounding school mix, but is also the only significant qualitative study since that of Ramsay and his colleagues in the 1970s. Thrupp worked in four schools of different social class composition. He identified a group of working class students, whom he termed 'ordinary kids' in each of the schools and used multiple data sources to gain a view of the processes to which these ordinary kids were being exposed. The depth of his analysis is remarkable. He provided considerable evidence to suggest a relationship between school mix and the aspirations and achievement of the ordinary kids. It was suggested that there may be a rubbing off effect of mixing with higher socio-economic status, which seemed to be of benefit to some of the ordinary kids in his sample. However, Thrupp himself demonstrates that he is a careful academic when he states:

> *The preceding discussion has suggested a number of organisational and management differences among the schools which might plausibly explain a school mix effect. But it must be stressed that what is discussed here represents only part of the study. The instructional finding suggested that Tui College teachers were generally less qualified, less motivated and less able to help the ordinary kids because they taught classes which were less compliant and less able to cope independently than those at the middle class schools. Moreover the ordinary kids at Tui College were exposed to less demanding lessons, texts and other teaching resources. As well, the reference group findings pointed to the ordinary kids at Tui College mixing mainly with working class students who typically had a narrower range of curriculum-relevant experiences, less regular school attendance, lower academic goals, and lower socio-economic status occupational aspirations/expectations than the mainly middle class friends and associates of the ordinary kids at middle class schools. 'Alienated' student sub-cultures were also a feature of Tui College's social landscape in which several of the ordinary kids became involved: this was not the case at many of the middle class schools where these groups were much smaller. Overall it is hard to see how years of exposure to these kinds of differences would not have led to reduced achievement for the ordinary kids at Tui College compared to the middle class schools.*

(Thrupp, 1996: 382)

Thrupp then argues a convincing case for policies which address the effect of school mix. He concludes by stating that the key contribution of his study was that it provides a detailed picture of 'how middle class families wittingly or unwittingly gain advantage in education by educating their children in segregated, and therefore inherently unequal schools. In doing so [the study] provides further evidence for the market as a class strategy.' (Thrupp, 1996: 386)

Taken together, the work of Thrupp, Lauder and Hughes represents a very important contribution to the effect of school mix on individual children's attainment at schools. Three other studies are, however, of equal importance when one considers how effective schools have been in New Zealand. Two of these studies are the outcomes of projects at Massey University, Palmerston North, directed by Harker and Nash. The first of these studies is known as the Access and Opportunity in Education Project. This project is reported in two phases - phase one by Nash, Harker and Charters (1990) and phase two by Nash, Harker and Durie (1991). The full research was brought together in a book by Nash in 1993. The study was based on a random sample of households with children aged five to 15 living in them. In all 1397 families and 3354 children were involved. The researchers used an interview schedule which was designed to obtain quantifiable information 'about the fundamental and effective resources of class-located families' (Nash, Harker and Charters, 1990: ii). They operated on the understanding that families would endeavour to utilise their resources (financial, cultural/intellectual and social) in the interests of maintaining or possibly improving their family's social standing in the present and succeeding generations. Their resources were referred to in their phase one report as financial, cultural and social capital and an attempt was made in this phase of the project to assess the importance of those variables using empirical analysis. An interesting early finding was that analysis revealed that only literate culture made a substantial contribution to the reading performance of the children in the study, while conventional sociological variables such as socio-economic status were significantly but not strongly associated with reading performance. A further very interesting study was that a comparison of the mean scores of older siblings and younger siblings revealed that the mean difference between social class groups on reading comprehension increased as the children grew older. This led the authors to conclude that social class appeared to have a cumulative effect. They pointed out that the mean scores of working class students declined particularly sharply and it seems that Maori ethnicity for these children acts to multiply the effect of social class (Nash, Harker and Charters, 1990; iii). The researchers were though, careful to point out that there was a great deal of variability within families and they conclude that 'while literate resources are important (one of the highest correlations with reading performance is with number of books owned), many children from homes with little literate cultural capital do well in the educational system' (Nash, Harker and Charters, 1990; iv). In phase two of the project the researchers analysed detailed interviews with parents. Overall they confirmed the thesis 'that class position provides family with resources which enable them to make differential use of formally equal educational provision [and that] is actually the fundamental cause of social differences in educational access and opportunity'.

The authors of this study were heavily influenced by the writings of French sociologist Pierre Bourdieu (Bourdieu and Passeron, 1977). His notion of cultural capital acquired in middle class and upper class homes securing an advantage for these children in these families, is at the heart of the study. It is interesting to ascertain that this phenomenon is apparent in a relatively new nation like New Zealand where class privilege is only just beginning to be understood. For this reason alone the work of the Massey educational sociologists is extraordinarily important and deserves prominence in the educational literature.

Their second study, Progress at Schools, is equally important. The study focussed on school effectiveness as it related to academic outcomes and considered it in terms of what Willms and Rudenbush (1989) referred to as Type A and Type B effects. The Type A effect raised the following question: 'Giving average background characteristics, how well would a student perform in any particular school' while the Type B effect raised the question: 'Given similar student populations, are some schools more effective in achieving specified results than others?' (Harker and Nash, 1996; 146). Harker and Nash used a cohort of 5393 students attending 37 schools from throughout New Zealand and they considered their School Certificate marks in English, Mathematics and Science. There are a number of extremely interesting results reported in this study. Firstly, the researchers found that the achievement differences between the various groups of students in the schools are much the same in all schools. Put in another way this could suggest 'that Maori, Pacific Island and working students are equally disadvantaged at all schools' (Harker and Nash, 1996: 153). In the analysis that follows Harker and Nash showed quite clearly that Type A effects are demonstrable in New Zealand schools and in their words are in some cases quite substantial differences. They also, along with Thrupp (1996) and the earlier studies of Lauder and Hughes (1990), argued that compositional and contextual factors which they interpreted as the existence of a peer group effect, may result in a critical mass of high ability students from high socio-economic status families which would affect the performance of all students who attended such a school. Along with the other researchers they emphasised the possibility of school mix affecting the performance of all students within the school. Harker and Nash then went on to investigate the Type B effect which provides a much fairer estimation 'of the impact schools are having on their pupils after taking into account the different pupil populations that each school has' (Harker and Nash 1996: 162). Here they found that differences in the school population was the greatest factor in determining the academic outcomes of schools, thus concurring with other New Zealand research and much of the overseas literature. I also found, though, that some schools were achieving well what would be expected of them given their composition. They pointed to the need for qualitative research which would investigate the dynamics of these succeeding schools. Indeed, this is to be part of a further report on how schools are achieving these rates of success (Harker and Nash, 1996: 166).

One further project worth mentioning is an ongoing study referred to as the Smithfield Project. The investigation (divided into three phases which began in 1992 and which is due for completion in 1998) focuses on the new market forces and parental choice. Initial findings show that parents tend to choose schools based on myth, ie. school reputation, rather than actual ability. Their final report is likely to be both provocative and challenging (Lauder, Hughes, Watson et al, 1995).

The foregoing represents a summary of the major studies in the area, albeit by no means a complete account. The over-riding weakness in New Zealand studies is that noted from Harker and Nash - that is the dearth of qualitative studies in the field. This is not to say that there has not been some important quantitative work. For example, Jones's study of girls in an inner city secondary schools in Auckland is of considerable importance, almost being the New Zealand version of Willis's seminal British study. Martin Keely's study at Auckland Grammar School on the interactions of boys at that school and their typifying of children into various groups, is also an interesting study. However, neither of these researchers would claim to be within the school effectiveness and improvement movement - Ramsay and his colleagues' study almost stands alone in this respect, although the very significant contribution of Thrupp has been noted above. The present writer can merely reiterate Harker and Nash yet again. Studies which investigate the dynamics of schools, particularly of succeeding schools, are needed desperately in New Zealand.

One might also comment that while not underestimating the need to provide quantitative detailing of school effect, that such studies have almost outlived their usefulness. Study after study has demonstrated that schools alone cannot compensate for society. Translating that kind of research into appropriate policy decision-making has not yet been achieved here or elsewhere. Bridging the gap between research and policy is therefore an important step which some researchers seem to be pleased to ignore.

The research described thus far has not had any major impact on what goes on in schools and nor, as I have just commented, does it appear to have any major impact on national policy development. I turn now to an account of research in a rather different area which has stemmed largely from deliberate government intervention.

Government interventions

Like most states of its nature, New Zealand has a long history of successive governments endeavouring to initiate school reform in order to achieve a variety of goals ranging from equality of opportunity to the more modern market-driven goals of relating schooling to the economy. New Zealand has had more than its share of major reports and successive endeavours to invoke change. Here I will restrict my account to three major reforms which have taken place in the past decade and to demonstrate the kinds of research and development programs which have arisen from them.

As noted above during 1986 the government embarked on a major project which endeavoured to review the school curriculum in New Zealand. It was an extremely comprehensive exercise involving a large number of people in meetings, responding to questionnaires and being interviewed by a range of researchers. In 1987 a report was prepared by a group of people selected by the then Department of Education, which represented a far-reaching departure from some well-established existing practices. There were very many recommendations and in the budget statement of 1988 the then Labour government set aside over a million dollars in order to investigate the feasibility of some of the recommendations of the Curriculum Review Committee. The upshot of this was a dual project which became known as the Curriculum Review Experimental Study. This was a very interesting project which had two arms to it. One was centred in the Department of Education, led by a senior curriculum officer, Helen Shaw, and which aimed to trial some of the new procedures in clusters of schools throughout New Zealand. The second arm was an independent research team centred at The University of Waikato.

The second major report on education in the 1980s came from the task force which was set up to review educational administration, usually referred to as the Picot Committee. Their recommendations were dramatic and most, albeit not all (see Ramsay 1992), went into the Education Act and the amendments which followed in 1989 and 1991. The main thrust of the reforms was to localise educational control. It should be noted from the outset, though, that many operations continued to remain at the centre, especially in the area of the development of the curriculum and the payment of teachers salaries and conditions of service. However, the newly established boards of trustees were placed in the position of rapid learning as were many school principals who had had their powers extended and changed, especially in the primary school area, quite considerably. In the area of school improvement, the National Administrative Guidelines (NAGS) required the boards of trustees and the principal to appraise staff regularly and to provide appropriate staff development. They were also required to put in place quality control systems. The need for training of staff was evident and the government's response was to make many millions of dollars available for specific contracts which were simultaneously to trial materials and to train individuals. Some of these contracts were quite specific. For example, a project known as Achieving Charter and Curriculum Objectives (ACCO) helped schools develop strategic plans in much the same way as the Curriculum Review Research in Schools Project (CRRISP) had before it.

Following the administrative reforms a new wave of developments followed in the curriculum area. The curriculum was thoroughly overhauled and in order to implement it in schools the Ministry of Education again resorted to contracting groups and individual consultants to help schools come to grips with the new knowledge and ideas. Typical of these projects was that conducted by Ramsay and his colleagues in a cluster of 18 schools in the Waikato area. Once again the research and development model was utilised and schools were asked four specific questions. The first was, 'Where are you at?' and was designed to commence self-review. The second, 'Where do you want to get to?' aimed to put the schools in a situation of preparing a five-year strategic plan. The third question, 'How are you going to get there?' focussed the schools on the kinds of intermediary goals required and the processes needed to implement them. Finally, the question, 'How will you know when you get there?' was posed, thus creating conditions for evaluation and for a feedback loop. Much of this process was predicated on the well-known change theories developed by researchers such as Fullan (1993) and Deal (1990).

The rapidity of the changes noted above and their dramatic nature also spawned the development of material designed to help boards of trustees and principals cope with the new requirements. Some of this material such as a principals' manual was developed under the auspices of the Ministry of Education, whereas others in the area of school leadership came from either private consultants or from people working in the tertiary institutions (see for example, Cardno 1990, Strachan and Robertson 1998).

Two other areas are worthy of mention under this section of government interventions. One of the recommendations of the Picot Committee was the establishment of an Education Review Office (ERO). This office was charged with the function of both reviewing and auditing schools on a regular basis. Their operations include an efficiency audit, which is designed to see that appropriate systems are in place in the school, followed by an effectiveness review which is designed to see whether the schools are achieving the goals established in their own charters as well as ensuring that appropriate learning programs are in place. The work of the office has met with a mixed reaction. Some principals and teachers claim that the reviews have been very positive and very helpful, whereas others have found the visits to be something of a 'commando raid', with the claim that the officers are seeking to find the negative rather than the positive. Certainly it appears that in recent times - probably due to a marked reduction in the personnel now employed within the Education Review Office - the function seems to have moved more to an audit than a review. Moreover, they seem to be unappreciative of school composition and in some ways may well have annexed the reports on school effectiveness for right-wing purposes. For example, in a recent report on schools in Otara, Ramsay and his colleagues' pioneering work was cited to demonstrate that schools can make a difference. However, as Thrupp (1997) quite properly points out the report ignores the fact noted earlier that Ramsay and his colleagues were careful to comment on the success rate of the schools compared to the national average. It almost appeared as if ERO in their report wished to wash out social class as an issue at all. Nonetheless a form of monitoring is both valuable and helpful if properly directed. The review office is currently under review itself and the green paper points the way to more effective procedures.

The second project is known as the *National Education Monitoring Project* (NEMP). Government funded, its task has been to monitor achievement longitudinally in order to ascertain movement and achievement rates. A great deal of time and energy and money has been expended on the development of appropriate check lists which will realise sound data for longitudinal comparisons. It is using a form of light sampling to achieve these goals and is not intended to be the kind of measuring agency publishing league tables as is the case of the United Kingdom. This project is viewed by most teachers as being very valuable as it will provide information which will allow them to realistically assess the progress of students in their care.

The educational and curriculum reforms have been monitored by two projects - *Monitoring Today's Schools*, carried out at The University of Waikato (Mitchell et al, 1995), and through the NZ Council for Educational Research (Wylie 1992). Both of these studies provided interesting data, although it should be noted that both have the weakness of being self-report only - no observational work was carried out by either group. Nor were either of these projects able to measure the impact of the reforms on children's attainment, as no baseline material was available for them. This is where the national education monitoring project will have a role to play.

Conclusions - where now?

There are three major points which may be drawn by way of conclusion in an assessment of where the school effectiveness and improvement movement needs to go in New Zealand. First, there remains a need for in-depth qualitative studies, preferably longitudinal and ethnographic, of successful schools in New Zealand. In carrying out this survey it was disturbing to find that since Ramsay and his colleagues (1982) study in the late 1970s, the only in-depth study has been that of Martin Thrupp (1996, 1997). There has been some peripheral work carried out on behalf of the organisation for Economic and Cooperative Development in the area of teacher quality by Ramsay (1994), but it could hardly be held to be within the genre of school effectiveness and school improvement. It is encouraging to note that Harker and Nash (1996) do have a qualitative section in their progress at schools project. It is to be hoped that this study may throw more light on the dynamics and complexities of successful schools.

Despite the need for qualitative studies, we still must be mindful of the fact that the school effect appears to explain between eight and 15 percent of the variants (see for example Reynolds 1994, Hopkins 1990). There is no question that schools cannot compensate completely for society (Mortimer, 1991). Sociologists and other researchers in the area of school effectiveness must therefore continue to press a case for social justice and must be vigilant to not allow their research to be appropriated by the New Right in order to wash out the effects of social class and family background (Mac an Ghail 1996; Tomlinson 1997). At a time when the gap between rich and poor people is widening in New Zealand and simultaneously the gap between rich and poor schools increases (Gordon, 1993), there is a need for governments to be reminded of the need to provide compensatory measures for any children who may be disadvantaged through no fault of their own.

Related to this is the third point which was identified when discussing the early research in the field. There still seems to be a lack of attention to the content of the school curriculum. Indeed, it is rather ironic to discover that researchers who in earlier times have cavilled against the nature of assessment and testing in New Zealand schools (for example, Nash 1993) are using standard forms of examination as the independent variable. These examinations can hardly be claimed to be either culture or class-free. In fairness to these researchers, they do acknowledge this point, but nonetheless they continue to use the School Certificate examination, for example, as the measuring stick for success at schools. There is a long-held point of view with which the present writer concurs, that the dominant elite will seek to control knowledge and to have their knowledge transmitted in the school curriculum (see Bourdieu and Passeron, 1977; Apple, 1982, Giroux, 1983). It is perhaps expecting too much for a complete recognition of the value of working class and/or Maori knowledge in New Zealand schools. It is encouraging to note, though, that Maori themselves are developing a system which will keep alive their culture and their language, that is, Maori immersion schools. The results of this bold experiment will be interesting, as for the first time dominant forms of knowledge have been significantly altered. Sociologists will need to keep unpopular notions of the dominant elite controlling the school through the curriculum before policy-makers and politicians. There may be, probably a long way in the future, a pricking of social consciences and a marked change in what is valued as knowledge in the schools.

References

Apple, M. (1982), *Education and Power* Boston: Routledge and Kegan Paul.

Bourdieu, P. and Passeron, J. (1977), *Reproduction in Education, Society and Culture*. London: Sage.

Cardno, Carol (1990), *Collaborative Management in New Zealand Schools* Auckland, New Zealand: Longman Paul.

Coleman, J. et al (1966), 'Equality of Educational Opportunity', cited in *School-based management and school effectiveness*, C. Dimmock (ed), London: Routledge, pp185-200.

Crooks, T. and Flockton, L. (1996), *NEMP; National Educational Monitoring Project* Dunedin, New Zealand: University of Otago.

Deal, T.E. (1990), 'Reforming Reform', *Educational Leadership* 47(8) 6-12.

Friedman, M. (1962) *Capitalism and Freedom* Chicago, University of Chicago Press.

Fullan, Michael (1993), *Changing Forces: Probing the depths of educational reform* London: The Falmer Press

Giroux, H. (1983), *Critical Theory and Educational Practice* Victoria: Deakin University.

Gordon, L. (1993), *Rich and Poor Schools in New Zealand* A paper presented to the Association for Research in Education. Hamilton.

Harker, Richard and Nash, Roy (1996), Academic Outcomes and School Effectiveness: Type 'A' and Type 'B' effects. *New Zealand Journal of Educational Studies*, 31(2), pp143-170.

Hopkins, D. (1990), 'The international school improvement project (ISIP) and effective schooling: Towards a synthesis', cited in School-based management and school effectiveness, C. Dimmock (ed) London: Routledge, 185-200.

Lauder, Hugh and Hughes, David (1990), 'Social Inequalities and Differences in School Outcomes', *New Zealand Journal of Educational Studies*, 25(1), 37-60.

Lauder, Hugh, Hughes, David, Watson, Sue, et al (1995), *Trading in futures: The Nature of Choice in Educational Markets in New Zealand: The Smithfield Project. Phase One.* Ministry of Education.

Mac an Ghail, M. (1996), 'Sociology of education, state schooling and social class: beyond critiques of New Right hegemony', *British Journal of the Sociology of Education*, 17(2).

Mitchell, David, et al. (1993), *Hear our voices: Final Report of Monitoring Todays Schools*. Hamilton, New Zealand: University of Waikato.

Mortimer, P., (1991), 'School effectiveness research: Which way at the crossroads', cited in *School-based management and school effectiveness* C Dimmock (ed), London: Routledge, 185-200.

Nash, Roy (1993), *Succeeding Generations: Family Resources and Access to Education in New Zealand*. Auckland: Oxford University Press.

Nash, Roy, Harker, Richard and Charters, Helen (1990), *Access and opportunity in education: first phase report*. Palmerston North, New Zealand: Massey University, Education Department.

Nash, Roy, Harker, Richard and Durie, Arohia (1991), *Access and opportunity in education: phase two; Interviews with parents*. Palmerston North, New Zealand: Massey University, Educational Research and Development Centre.

Ramsay, P., Sneddon, D.G., Grenfell, J. and Ford, I. (1983), 'Successful and Unsuccessful Schools: A study in South Auckland', *Australia and New Zealand Journal of Sociology* 19 (2), 272-304.

Ramsay, Peter (1992), Picot - Four years on: The Reforms of Education Administration *New Zealand Principal* 7(2), 8-17.

Ramsay, Peter, et al (1993), *Developing Partnerships: Collaboration between teachers and parents*, Wellington, New Zealand: Ministry of Education.

Ramsay, Peter (1994), 'Continuing Education of teachers in New Zealand', *Unicorn* 20(4) 25-36.

Reynolds, D. (1994), 'Linking school effectiveness knowledge and school improvement practice', in *School-based management and school effectiveness* C. Dimmock (ed) Auckland: Routledge, 185-200.

Robertson, Jan (1991), *ACCO: Achieving Charter Curriculum Objectives: A teacher development program using a school development strategy* Hamilton, New Zealand: University of Waikato.

Rutter, M. Maughan, B., Mortimore, P. and Ouston, J. (1979), *Fifteen Thousand Hours: Secondary schools and their effects on children* cited in School-based management and school effectiveness, C. Dimmock (ed) London: Routledge, 185-200.

Strachan, Jane and Robertson, Jan (1993), Developing appraisal processes in schools. *Education Today* June, 16-18.

Thrupp, Martin P. (1996), The Education Review Office and South Auckland Schools: A case of Ideology and Analysis? *New Zealand Annual Review of Education* 6, 51-70.

Thrupp, Martin P. (1997), School mix and the outcomes of Educational Quasi-Markets in *Education Policy in New Zealand: the 1990's and beyond* Mark Olssen and Kay Morris Mathews (eds). Palmerston North, New Zealand: Dunmore Press, 372-390.

Tomlinson, Sally (1997), '*Sociological Perspectives on Failing Schools*, paper presented at International Sociology of Education Conference on Education Policy, Social Justice and Change. University of Sheffield, UK.

Wylie, C. (1992), *The Impact of Tomorrow's Schools on Primary and Intermediates*. Wellington: NZCER.

18.

Improving the effectiveness of schools in Pacific Island countries: a regional approach to teacher development

Tony Townsend and Asenaca Vakaotia

Background

This report covers eleven Pacific Island nations ranging in population from nearly a million (Fiji) to just a few thousand (Niue). Despite the inexorable onset of the outside world, complete with McDonald's, take-away pizza stores and video recorders, the Pacific Island community still displays a grace and caring for each other that many of us in the west seem to have lost. They wish to improve their education system in order to improve the lives of their people, not specifically to make them more competitive. Their story deserves to be told.

Have you ever wondered what the notion of school effectiveness means in places where not everybody goes to school in the first place? Where more than fifty percent of the teachers have not been formally trained? Where if they were fully trained the government could not afford to pay them because populations are counted in the thousands rather than the millions? Where any major financial difficulty at government level might see a fifty percent pay cut for teachers overnight, and perhaps an exodus of many of that country's teachers to other countries? Where literacy and numeracy are seen to be important, but where many students leave school at grade six and return to a rural, isolated and subsistence lifestyle where a knowledge of agriculture or making clothes might be the basic skills required? Where, for many people, the only education they receive is from village elders? Given some of these circumstances, perhaps the notion of raising test scores by a few points might be seen as not having the level of significance that some western politicians might suggest. Perhaps the notion of children as humans might be more significant than children as mini-economic units.

And yet, there are many countries where some or most of the circumstances listed above are still in existence, but have high hopes for their children and for the education system that helps to develop them. So this report into school improvement efforts is a little different to others you might read in this book. It contains little research into what specific factors might improve a school's performance, yet it draws on the knowledge gained from other countries and others' efforts. It will provide an insight into how smaller nations, with support from some of the bigger ones, try to instil into children a love of learning and an understanding of how to live. This paper focuses on a program to raise the educational capability of these countries. Specifically, it looks at the BELS program, which saw the training of 74,843 parents and 2,483 teachers in 280 schools in 1995/96. BELS stands for Basic Education and Life Skills, a regional program funded by UNDP, UNESCO, UNICEF and AusAID, which aims to strengthen primary eduction in the 11 participating countries: Cook Islands, Fiji, Kiribati, Marshall Islands, Niue, Solomon Islands, Tokelau, Tonga, Tuvalu, Vanuatu and Western Samoa.

The Countries

Fiji

Fiji has a population of around 750,000. Its formal education system features a strong partnership between Government and non-government organisations. The system ranges from pre-school to primary, secondary and tertiary education and encompasses technical and vocational education, and special education for the handicapped. There are 695 primary schools of which about a third offer education from Classes 1-6. The rest offer additional classes 7-8 which are equivalent to Forms 1-2. The class 1-8 roll in 1993 was 147,558 while that of secondary schools (Forms 1-7) was 65,538. Intake at Class 1 level was about 21,000 children. The education budget is around 58 million dollars, which is 22.4% of all government expenditure.

There is universal access to primary education with about 90% of the children completing the 6 years of primary education. In Fiji about 58% of primary and 48% secondary schools are rural or island schools. Most schools in Fiji are managed by non-government bodies. These include different religious groups (eg. Christians, Hindus and Muslims), and committees comprising members of the local communities. The Ministry operates only 2% of primary schools (14 out of 695), 8% of the secondary schools (12 out of 145), 8% of vocational and technical schools and 2 of the 4 teacher training institutions. Religious groups run 22% of the primary and 39% of the secondary schools while local communities run 75% of the primary and 51% of the secondary schools. However, teachers are paid by the Government.

The current primary curriculum offers literacy in Mathematics, English, Fijian, Hindi, Urdu and Rotuman. Health Science is taught as a subject from Class 1 to Class 8. Environmental Education is taught across the curriculum at all levels and is integrated into Elementary Science, Health Science, Social Science and School Gardening, and relevant aspects of it are found in the languages, Arts and Craft, Physical Education, Music and Mathematics. Integrated Science is taught through Elementary Science from Class 1 to Class 6, and Basic Science in Classes 7 and 8. A policy on the compulsory learning of Fijian by all non-Fijian students, and Hindi by Fijian students is in place. Trialing of the curriculum began in 1996.

The Fiji Ministry is presently revising the primary school curriculum. The revision is aimed in particular at improving the quality of education offered in literacy, health, environment, science and technology and moral education. The revision is also looking at alternative ways of assessment, especially the ones used by teachers in the classroom. A 10-year plan is already underway beginning from 1992. By 2000 it is hoped to have the revision of all 13 subjects from Class 1 to Class 8, and from Form 1 to Form 4 completed.

Apart from the usual in-school tests and examinations, Fiji has 2 national means of assessment at primary level:

- two national examinations, Fiji Intermediate Entrance Examination at Class 6 and the Fiji Eighth Year Examination at Class 8 levels
- Standardised Tests of Achievement for Fiji (STAF).

The STAF, prepared by the Ministry, is used as a test instrument by teachers at Class 5 level to determine the level of students' achievement after 5 years of education. It enables teachers to take any action required before the pupils sit the FIEE at Class 6 level. Fiji also participated in the use of the Pacific Islands Literacy Level (PILL) Test in 1993. PILL has been developed by the basic Education and Life Skills (BELS) Project, to which we will shortly return. It is an assessment instrument administered to pupils at the end of their 4th year in schools to find out the state of 'health' of the education system with the basic aim of helping both teachers and pupils.

The Solomon Islands

Solomon Islands is a nation of some 350,000 people most of whom inhabit the six main islands of Guadalcanal, Malaita, San Cristobal, Santa Ysabel, Choseul and New Georgia. The population is predominantly Melanesian, which according to the 1995 National Census comprised 93% with the remainder of Polynesian, Micronesian, Chinese and European origin. These people speak some eighty different languages and come from very different and contrasting social and geographical locations, ranging from very remote mountain villages to tiny coral islands throughout the ten provinces. The people have different and distinct customs and traditional practices.

The picture that emerges from this portrays a complex society where diversity and separateness feature predominantly. Education therefore had come to play a major unifying role in a country of hundreds of islands and diversity. The current education system and that of the primary sector during the missionary days of education administration brought together students of different islands and cultural background.

Primary Education

The Solomon Islands primary education is of seven years duration. Children enter preparatory class at 6 years of age and later sit for the Solomon Islands Secondary Entrance Examination at the age of twelve. Primary Education is administered and run by Education Authorities on behalf of the Government.

There are currently eighteen Education Authorities and 529 Primary Schools. Education Authorities are responsible for the maintenance of those schools which they have established and in respect of which they are registered as an Education Authority under the Education Act.

Although primary schools are administered by various authorities the control of education is held by the Government which:

- Sets National Primary Education policy guidelines.
- Conducts school inspections
- Controls the National Curriculum.
- Controls National Examination and Selection for Secondary and Tertiary Education.
- Provides funding for schools and Teachers Salaries.

There are 2228 Primary School Teachers in the 539 primary schools. Of these 589 (26%) are untrained and 1639 (77%) trained. The untrained teacher recruitment is necessary as local teacher training cannot yet satisfy teacher demand. Most untrained teachers are Solomon Islands School Certificate holders who will later on take the Teacher Training examination for enrolment. Approximately 853 (33%) of all primary school teachers are females. There are 73,120 primary school students. Of these 40,087 are males and 33,039 are females. About 75% of children in any age cohort commence schooling and around 85% of these complete grade 5, but for girls, the participation rate is lower - around 40%. The education budget is around 4 million dollars, which is 14.1% of all government expenditure.

Secondary Education

All primary school children reading Class 6 and wishing to proceed to Secondary School must sit the Solomon Islands Secondary Entrance Examination. This is a Selection Examination, administered annually in August to all Class 6 pupils. The examination consists of English, Mathematics and a General Paper Comprising of Science, Health and Community Studies and Social Studies.

Forty percent of the pupils sitting in any one year proceed to secondary school. About 10% of those not selected are allowed to repeat class 6 while the rest terminate their formal education at this stage. While Rural Training Centres cater for some of these pupils a great number will have to return to their villages. Due to this great number of 'drop-outs'/push-outs', critics view the examination as an 'Education Murder'. However, in the present circumstances this is the only fair and objective way selecting those pupils who will benefit from secondary education. While the examination is used for selection, there is no pass/fail concept in the examination. Besides the pupils' examinations marks, other factors come to play in determining how many pupils proceed to secondary school. These include both financial and administrative factors.

Pupils are either selected to National Secondary Schools or Provincial Secondary Schools. National Secondary Schools enrol pupils from form 1 to Form 5/6 while Provincial Secondary Schools cater for students to Form 3 level.

The Government, under the Third World Bank Project, is building 5 new Secondary Schools and upgrading existing schools in an attempt to remedy the drop-out problem. Other Education Authorities opened 8 Junior Secondary Schools in 1995 and 5 more will open in 1996. This will allow more primary school children to acquire Secondary Education.

A report prepared for the USP strategic planning seminar in Honiara by the Permanent Secretary lists a series of national goals for the coming years:

- moving towards universal access to a full nine years of basic education;
- providing equal opportunity for girls;
- enhancing the quality of basic education through teacher training and provision of textbooks;
- expanding literacy;
- increasing form 6 output;
- establishing senior vocational schools.

He makes a point that is equally applicable to many of the Pacific Island countries, and perhaps carries a message for some western countries as well (Sikua, 1997: 1)

> *Although the country is endowed with natural resources, the competent use of these resources for creation of national wealth is constrained, among other things, by deficiency of human creativity. In modern times, human creativity is enhanced by improving the quality of the human population, and this, generally, is the goal of national development. It is perceived that the most important resource available to the nation is its human population and the direction and pace of national development depends ultimately on the development of this human resource. Improving the quality of the human resource through education and training of manpower is largely a national responsibility led by the initiative of the Government.*

Western Samoa

Primary Education covers an eight-year cycle divided into two three-year sections: lower primary (Years 1 to 3), middle primary (Years to 6) and upper primary (Years 7 and 8) often referred to as the intermediate level.

A total of 160 primary schools are located throughout Western Samoa - 142 government, 16 mission and two private - with an overall enrolment of approximately 38,000 representing an estimated 93-94 per cent of primary school-age (5 to 11 years) children. The 142 government schools served around 31,000 students and employed 1300 teachers. There were 22 junior secondary schools with a population of around 5500 students and 250 teachers and three senior secondary schools with 1640 students and 77 teachers. The education budget is around 14 million dollars, which is 15.8% of all government expenditure.

Although virtually all children spend some time in primary school, the drop-out rate is about 15 percent. Under the Education Amendment Act 1991-1992, all children between the ages of 5 and 14 years, or until completion of Year 8 (normally at the age of about 12 or 13), are required to attend school unless exempted by the Director of Education. However, 139 of the primary schools, catering for over 26,000 students, were rural schools where such rules were difficult to police.

Most primary schools are staffed by teachers who are Western Samoa Teachers College-trained; approximately 75 percent are women. The overall primary teacher-student ratio is about 1:27. The eight-year primary cycle culminates in the Year 8 National Exam covering Samoan, English, mathematics, science and social studies. Except for Samoan, examinations are conducted in English. The main function of the examination is to rank students for selection into secondary schools. A further function is the monitoring of achievement of curriculum objectives.

A number of projects designed to improve the quality of education are currently underway. The Teacher Education Quality Improvement Project (TEQIP), funded by AusAID, provides in-service training for practising primary teachers and is now in its third year of operation. The Educational Policy and Planning Development Project has seen the appointment of a policy adviser and the In-School Population Education Project aimed to develop a science unit that focused on 'My Natural World Around Me' and is into its fourth year of operation. As well, the BELS program, commenced operations in Samoa in 1993.

Vanuatu

At independence in 1980 the government decided to maintain both English and French as official languages. This also meant two systems of education with separate curricula. It was later decided that a unified curriculum was desirable as a means of bringing the people closer together and to ensure that all students enjoyed a common curriculum which could give them equal opportunities in secondary and tertiary education and in the employment market.

A recent but important development has been the establishment of kindergartens throughout the country, a result of the people's desire to improve the education of their children. UNICEF was instrumental in the training and funding of pre-school advisers. While not being a part of the primary system, kindergartens have proved important in the general preparation of 4-year olds for entry into class 1. The medium of instruction depends a lot on the locality and could be the vernacular, English, French or Bislama (the local language).

Primary education in Vanuatu is not compulsory. The system provides six (6) years of primary education. At the end of primary school (class 6) students sit for the national Senior Primary Examination/Diploma de Fiji d'Etude Primaire - a selection exercise for the few places available in the secondary schools. Around two-thirds of children in any age cohort attend school and only 60% of these remain by grade 5. The education budget is around $900,000, which is 19.2% of all government expenditure.

The restructuring of the Ministry of Education created a Basic Education Department responsible for schools in Years 1-10 and for curriculum examinations and teacher training. Government also agreed to create 12 new year seven (7) classes in the 6 provinces in 1996, allowing more students to enter secondary schools. This move will reduce the primary school dropout rate while providing better opportunities for more students.

Tonga

Primary Education has been compulsory since 1962. The 1974 Education Act requires that every child between the ages of 6 and 14 living within reach of a Government Primary School shall attend that school, unless he/she has completed six years of primary education. There are 105 Government Primary Schools and 11 Mission Schools in the Kingdom. Total number of teachers (Government/Mission) - 719. Total number of pupils (Government/Mission) - 16,540. The education budget is around 1.35 million dollars, which is 13.3% of all government expenditure.

The Secondary Schools Entrance Examination is the National Examination at the end of Class 6. The examination consists of one-hour papers in English, Mathematics, Tongan and Environmental Science. The marks from the four papers are standardised and, when aggregated, produce a national rank order of all candidates which is then used by the Ministry and other education authorities as the principal means of allocating students to their preferred secondary schools.

Marshall Islands

Marshall Islands pre-history is virtually unknown. European contact with the archipelagos began in the early 16th century when the first Spanish explorers sailed across the Pacific; however, continuous contact did not occur until the third decade of the 19th century. Germany bought the Marshall Islands from Spain in 1899, and they were mandated to Japan in 1920 by the League of Nations. Under United Nations Security Council Authority, from 1947 the Marshall Islands were part of the US Trust Territory of the Pacific Islands. The Compact of Free Association process of negotiating self-government began in 1979, but was protracted by issues and problems associated with US responsibilities for defence, the use of the missile-testing range of Kwajalein, settlement of compensation claims for nuclear testing, and economic aid agreements. Although a Compact of Free Association was signed in 1982, it did not come into full effect until 1986, when the United National Trusteeship finally concluded. The trusteeship was formally terminated by the United Nations Security Council in 1990. The Republic of the Marshall Islands (RMI) became a full member of the United Nations in September 1991

The Republic of the Marshall Islands (RMI), not unlike other widely dispersed island countries in Micronesia, consists of a double chain of either atolls or coral islands in the Central Pacific Ocean. The Marshall Islands consist of 29 atolls and 5 coral islands and 870 reefs. The two island chains are approximately 208 kilometres apart and run northwest to southeast. The total land area is approximately 171 square kilometres, scattered over some two million square kilometres of ocean. The total population (1988 census) is 43,3890 with a projection of 56,000 by the year 2001.

Government Objectives and Priorities

The Republic of the Marshall Islands regards education as the most important means of development. Its education policy seeks to provide Marshallese, regardless of age or sex, with the opportunity to develop themselves to the best of their ability. Once constitutional government was established in 1979, the President appointed a thirty member Marshall Islands Task Force on Education, noting that: 'There is concern about our current education system in the Marshall Islands. Education of our children is of paramount importance to our developing nation and it is vital at this time that the future direction of our efforts in this area be clearly charted.' The Task Force was charged with making recommendations on a wide range of issues regarding the status of education and its future direction. This first significant and implementable report for the Marshall Islands educational system, entitled Education for Self-Reliance, was submitted to the President in 1981.

The primary recommendation was for the Marshall Islands to adopt the principle of Education for Self-Reliance as the nation's guiding philosophy of education. This recommendation addressed the primary question confronting every government. 'Education for What?' The recommended philosophy was further translated into more specific recommendations for what the educational system should deliver and how the educational system should function. The 1981 Task Force's recommendations were generally not implemented; they were virtually ignored and the Ministry of Education continued to drift without clear goals. Ten years later a reconstituted group was appointed by Cabinet and convened by the Minister of Education to evaluate progress, review recommendations, and to update or suggest new recommendations.

The second Task Force on Education (1989) presented a serious and frank submission to Cabinet, entitled Report of the Second Task Force on Education. It found that the education system was not producing the skilled and educated labour force needed to satisfy national development goals nor was it adequately preparing the younger generation to cope with rapid social change. The management and structure of the education system was found to have serious shortcomings and failures. Education needed to be revitalised, reoriented, and realistically financed in order to fulfil its responsibility to the Marshallese to produce well-educated and self-reliant citizens. To start the improvement of education, the Task Force presented eight recommendations; these were designed to guide and complement and comprehensive master planning effort that was soon to be conducted by the US based Academy for Educational Development (AED) under contract to the Ministry of Education (MOE).

The School System

Education is considered the most important means through which national development can be accelerated, and it has always received considerable attention within traditional Marshallese society. Even in the days when there were no secondary schools, promising Marshallese students were sent to the Marianas and Phonpei or Chuuk to obtain secondary education and training. Formal educational programming has been associated with the Marshall Islands since the late 1850s. Educational expansion continued throughout the 1970s and to 1979 when the Marshall Islands became self-governing. With the implementation of the Compact of Free Association in 1986, US federal education program funds began a step-down, leading to their eventual elimination.

The Marshall Islands education system is patterned after that of the United States. The elementary schools are from Grades one to eight with secondary schools covering Grades nine to twelve. Schools, including both public and private, are in session from September to June. Private schools serve a substantial percentage of the population and they receive financial support from government. Compulsory education is from age six through fourteen or completion of eighth grade. A high school entrance examination is administered to all eighth graders to determine the 300 students who will be admitted to the public high school each year.

The Pre-Elementary School Level
This level is not provided for in the Republic of the Marshall Islands, although there is a Marshall Islands Head Start Program serving 1200 five year olds. The program operates from 35 centres with 63 classrooms, 89 teachers and aides. There are several components including health and nutrition, social service activities, education and special needs. Each Center has a parent organisation. Some private pre-schools operates in major centres.

The Elementary School Level
Elementary school attendance is compulsory. Under the Education Act (1991), the Government is: 'to provide a thorough and efficient system of education, to provide all children in the Republic, regardless of socioeconomic status, handicap, or geographical location, the educational opportunity that will prepare them to develop into self-reliant individuals and to function socially, politically and economically in society.' In the school year 1994-1995, there was a total enrolment of 13,335 elementary school students in both public and private schools. Enrolment is up by over 1550 students since 1991-1992. A total of 76 public elementary schools (vis-a-vis 27 private) accounts for about 73 percent of the elementary school enrolment. The lowest national coverage for elementary level students has been estimated by the Asian Development Bank (ADB) at 78 per cent in 1992; this means that there were around 3000 children aged 6 to 14 who did not attend school. Reports suggest that the participation rate has been declining recently and that there are very limited alternative education opportunities for out-of-school youth.

As of 1995-1996, the total number of eighth graders were 1,077. A slight increase from the 1994-95. Of this number, 300 students entered the two public secondary schools based on performance and competence in the national examination. The total number of 13,393 for 1995-1996 has greatly increased from 9,531 students in 1994-1995. RMI has also had an increase in the numbers of secondary teachers from 348 in 1994-1995 up to 485 in 1995-1996.

The hard core data from the Pacific Islands Literacy Level (PILL) which was administered to 5th graders, showed an overwhelming majority, attending both public and private schools performed poorly. The PILL test results and solutions to remedy this situation must be seen within the wider context of our reality, past and present.

Cook Islands
The Cook Islands comprises 15 islands scattered over 2 million square kilometres of ocean. The total population of the Cook Islands is 18,551 of

which 10,981 (59%) live on the main island of Rarotonga. The remaining population live on 12 of the other 14 islands.

Tourism is the main industry in the Cook islands although black pearl farming is currently being developed in the Northern Group atolls of Manihiki and Penrhyn and is believed to have the potential to become a major source of revenue for the country in the near future.

In 1992, over 50,000 tourists visited the Cook Islands. A high percentage of the population on Rarotonga, both men and women, are fully employed with mostly occupations associated with the tourist trade. However, employment opportunities in the Outer Islands are far more limited with most people dependent on a more traditional lifestyle. Planting, fishing and weaving are more evident.

Primary Education is compulsory in the Cook Islands for children between the ages of 5 & 16. In total, there are 25 Government Primary Schools, 6 Mission schools and 2 Private Pre-schools. Most Government Primary schools have a Pre-school attached to them and are also Government funded. There are 3,433 Primary students altogether with 169 Primary Trained Teachers.

In the Secondary Sector, there are 6 Government Secondary Schools and 3 Mission owned. There is a total of 2,095 secondary students and 180 secondary trained teachers. In total, there are 5,528 students and 349 teachers in the Cook Islands. The annual education budget is around 3 million dollars or around 17% of total government expenditure. The recent financial troubles for the Cook Islands government brought about an overnight 50% cut in the salary of all public servants, including teachers. Many teachers resigned and went to New Zealand to teach (all Cook islanders are New Zealand citizens), leaving the education system in disarray.

All secondary students sit for the Cook Islands Certificate with those who qualify moving on to the New Zealand Certificate, Sixth and Seventh Form Certificate, Tertiary Education is continued overseas.

Tuvalu

Tuvalu has nine islands with a total population of about 10,000. Each island has its own primary school owned by the island council. An additional primary school is run by the Seventh Day Adventist Church (SDA) at the capital, Funafuti.

About 2000 pupils attend primary schools with the La Perouse Primary school in Funafuti having between 650 and 700 pupils. Pupils enter school in the year in which they turn six. Government established 73 teaching posts for teachers to teach in the nine Island Council schools and the approved teacher-pupil ratio is 1: 25. In addition, about 70% of primary school teachers are females and the majority of them were trained in Fiji. The annual education budget is around 850,000 dollars or around 16% of total government expenditure.

Due to the isolation of the islands from each other, the only means of reaching them is by boat, which usually visits once or twice a month. This is one of the reasons why professional development of teachers is difficult.

Tokelau

Tokelau is a New Zealand self-governing territory with a population under 2000. Formerly called Union Islands, the country consists of three main atolls: Atafu, Nukunono and Fakaofo. Most who live in Tokelau have very rudimentary knowledge of English as a second language. Tokelau is used in the schools, where the literacy rate is 94%.. Most of the population are fishermen with some agriculturalists: coconut, taro, breadfruit, banana, arrowroot. Christianity and traditional religions are practised.

Each of the three main atolls runs a government school commencing at Year 1 and continuing to Year 12, with one National Form 5 (Year 12) attached to one of the schools. Students are promoted automatically from one class to the next. At present, there are two national examinations given throughout the education system. One is the recently introduced Pacific Island Literacy Level (PILL) Test, which is given at the end of Year 4 and the other is the Form 5 National Exam. Screening does not exist until Form 5 level where top students are selected for scholarship awards overseas. There are 24 teachers for approximately 550 children in Tokelau schools. The annual education budget is around 630,000 dollars.

Niue

With a total population of just over 2000 people and just two schools, the Niuen education system must be close to the smallest in the world. Education is compulsory from 5 -14 years and is free of charge at both early childhood and primary levels, with just nominal charges at the intermediate and secondary levels.

The Mission Statement for the Education Department on Niue is: To provide and maintain a quality education service thereby contributing to the human resource training needs of the government, the skills, the needs of the Niue population and the subsequent fulfilment of the National Goals. There are 18 teachers including the principal and 332 children in Niue Primary School, the only primary school in the country and a further 300 children and 25 teachers at the only secondary school. A representative of each of the thirteen villages forms the school committee (PTA). The education budget on Niue is 750,000 dollars, around 16% of the government's total expenditure.

The Niue Education system was reviewed in 1987 by Niueans for Niueans and was implemented in 1989. It looked at:

- the quality of education
- the needs and interest of the children
- the continual development and support of bilingualism (vernacular/English)

The following changes took place. ECE/Pre-school education was placed under the Education Department umbrella. It caters for 3-4 year olds. One officer and mother - helpers (voluntary) serve 4 centres. Each centre opens one day per week. Children are transported to and from these centres from their respective villages. This was an end and the beginning of an era. Seven village primary schools and the monolingual school were closed and primary education was centralised at a national school at Alofi, Niue Primary School. The school provides compulsory education from Classes 1-6 and for the first time a unit for special needs children (5) was included. (In 1993 the unit was transferred to Niue High School). Children travel to and from school on contracted buses.

The 1996-97 Education Plan argued that 'education is at the core of our nation's efforts to achieve economic and social progress'. It went on '... it prepares students not only for academic success but also for life in general...' A series of goals were proposed, including:

- the highest standards of achievement;
- equality of educational opportunity for all;
- development of knowledge, understanding and skills...to compete successfully in the modern ever-changing world;
- a broad education through a balanced curriculum;
- excellence achieved through the establishment of clear learning objectives, monitoring student progress, performance against those objectives and programs to meet individual needs;
- access to a nationally and internationally recognised qualifications system.

It can be seen from some of these goals that the school effectiveness message has reached even the smallest of school systems.

Kiribati

The Republic of Kiribati is an island group in the Western Pacific Ocean, consisting of an archipelago of low-lying coral atolls surrounded by extensive reefs. Kiribati became independent on July 12, 1979, and is a parliamentary democracy. The capital of Kiribati is Tarawa. Kiribati includes three administrative units, sixteen atolls of the former Gilbert Islands; eight atolls of the former Line Islands; and eight atolls of the former Phoenix Islands. Kiribati has few natural resources and its economy is very small. The islands are not self sufficient in food. There are 85 schools, and 537 teachers for approximately 15,000 students in the Kiribati primary school system and 7.4% of its Gross National Product is spent on education. At the time of writing, little information about the education system has been collected.

The BELS project

BELS is owned and implemented by the 11 participating countries in collaboration with the donors, executing agency (University of the South Pacific) and the Progamme staff. The Program began in 1993 and was executed by UNESCO during its first phase. Execution was transferred to the University of the South Pacific in July 1995 and the Program is now being managed by the University's Institute of Education.

As Singh (1997: 2) points out:

the BELS Program Document (1993) highlighted a number of problems in primary education from a regional perspective:

- *The grossly inadequate number of well-trained teachers, particularly in outer islands.*

- *The high costs of traditional in-service training.*

- *The difficulty of providing sustained follow up activities following training.*

- *The low status of teachers and their morale.*

- *The lack of planning, management and evaluation skills in Senior Ministry Officers.*

- *The low reading standards in primary schools.*

- *The inadequate supply and distribution of reading materials for schools.*

- *The lack of balance and relevance in curricula.*

- *The inadequate school-community linkages.*

• *The lack of capacity within Ministries to collect data and manage information systems.*

(BELS Program Document, 1993:6)

What are BELS' immediate objectives?

The Program's immediate objectives can be grouped into four broad areas:

• inservice education of teachers
• community involvement in education
• educational planning and management; and
• curriculum development in agricultural education.

The program has a program implementation and appraisal module (module D) with three professional development-focused modules, each with a number of specific initiatives, as indicated below:

Module A (Primary and Literacy Education)
• Primary Teacher Inservice Training
• Literacy Education
• Community Support for Education
• National Headteachers' Training Network

Module B (Education System Planning and Management
• Educational Management Information Systems
• Assessment Data for Educational Management
• National Planning/Examinations Unit

Module C (Curriculum Innovations for Life Skills)
• National Initiatives- Curriculum Reform
• Curriculum Development - Agricultural Education
• National Curriculum Development Units

Module D (Program Implementation and Appraisal)

To provide a more detailed understanding of the program, one module, PALE, will be described in more detail. PALE is the Primary and Literacy

Education component of the broader BELS program. It contains three initiatives:

- Classroom Skills
- Community Support for Education
- Literacy Education

It also incorporates the National Headteachers' Training Network.

The objective of the PALE program is to provide training for all headteachers, teachers and parents in aspects of each of these modules. For the classroom skills component, the regional objectives were to provide training for 35 national resource people, 200 national trainers, 1500 headteachers and 5000 teachers which would strengthen the curricular, pedagogical, diagnostic and evaluative capabilities of teachers within classrooms.

For the literacy education component, the regional objectives were to provide training for 30 national resource people, 120 national trainers, to enhance the capacity of teacher training colleges in the teaching of literacy and to establish 30 model schools where sound literacy programs took place, and where other headteachers, teachers and teacher trainees could visit. This would involve the training of 30 teachers in model classrooms.

For the community support for education component, the regional objectives were to provide training for 200 national trainers, advisers and facilitators, 1500 headteachers and 5000 teachers and to work with these people to establish processes whereby parents could become partners in the education of their children.

The program uses the cascade model of professional development, where the specific training of a few people cascades into the eventual training of all. The model included:

- Sub-regional training for national resource persons (NRPs)
- NRPs prepare training materials and train Provincial or District Trainers (TRS)
- TRS prepare training materials and train Headteachers and School Trainers
- Headteachers and School Trainers prepare training materials and train teachers
- Teachers implement the material by using the ideas/methods in their teaching and in working with parents.

What has BELS achieved so far?

BELS is a comprehensive program and has involved a large number of national administrative and professional personnel in its activities. It is on target for achieving its objectives and has provided opportunities to about:

- 2500 teachers to participate in in-service education on classroom skills, literacy education and community support for education;

- 75,000 parents to participate in discussions on community involvement in education;

- 30 educational administrators to implement an information system using computers to capture and use educational data,

- 30 educational personnel in defining, measuring and monitoring standards in basic literacy and numeracy through Pacific Islands Literacy Levels [PILL] tests; and

- 11 curriculum development officers in the participating countries to review and develop materials in Agricultural Education.

It is firmly believed that one of the best ways of ensuring continuity of ideas is to introduce them into the teacher training curriculum in the region. With this in mind, this package, comprising the South Pacific Literacy Education Course (SPLEC), Training Units on Assessment and on Community Support for Education have been compiled. In the case of the Community Support for Education component a book (Townsend and Elder, 1998) aimed at helping principals and teachers to improve parent and community support for education, financially, socially and academically has been published and distributed to all 3500 schools in the region. These areas integrate easily with the existing pre-service curriculum in the teacher training colleges for primary teachers in the region and it is hoped that lecturers and students will find them interesting and professionally challenging.

Assessment of the program

Gurmit Singh, one of the people actively involved in the development and implementation of the program, suggested that the cascade model, in itself, was not as useful as other forms of professional development. He argued (Singh, 1997: 8):

> *In retrospect and notwithstanding variations necessitated by contextual factors, it does seem that in order for the cascade*

model to work, a clear understanding of its strengths and weaknesses ought to be appreciated by all those collaborating and discussed thoroughly at the very beginning of a project. This should lead to an initial appraisal as to whether the basic requirements for implementing the model can be met or not at both levels, regional and national. Such an appraisal could also lead to putting in place the basic requirements if there is a gap and putting in place mechanisms for sustaining the conditions during the implementation phase.

He identified (Singh, 1997: 8): a number of conditions that needed to be in place:

At the regional level

● Quality project staff

● Rigorous Training of the National Resource Persons

● Maximum consultations with participating countries

and at the national level

● Selection and retention of the best available trainers as National Resource Persons

● Recognition of the status of the National Resource Person

● Status of the training program in terms of national training priorities

● Rigorous implementation of the agreed monitoring and reporting procedures

● Periodic formative evaluation involving the National Resource Persons

● Recognition of the role of the school-based training leader (HT or a selected member of the staff)

He concluded (Singh, 1997: 8):

The numerous points at which the chain of communication and implementation can break down, makes it necessary to maintain a) quality and b) rigour in all aspects of the training. The model has obviously a high potential for slippage and hence it is sometimes described rather negatively as the 'trickle-down' training model.

There is also a desire among the teacher educators to promote professional development of teachers which is more in line with the principles of teacher education espoused internationally (Educational Innovation, 1996:5). The suggestions cover the following:

- increasing teachers' input and control over aspects of their work such as curriculum, teaching methods, assessment and resources,

- promoting team-work in order to improve upon the traditionally isolated nature of teachers' work, where separated most of the time from other colleagues, teachers experience limited interaction, collective reflection and planning, and

- promoting independent learning both in children through a variety of teaching approaches and resources and in teachers through a mix of formal in-service education and school-based, teacher-led initiatives.

Conclusion

The BELS program indicates that the search for improved effectiveness in schools is not the province of the wealthy, developed countries. Although the impact of the BELS program might take some time to show up, it has already increased awareness by people in the Pacific of many of the issues equally applicable in developed and developing countries, the importance of literacy, the need for strong home-school partnerships, the need to incorporate the available resources (both human and technological) in the best possible way to improve the educational outcomes for the child. What the Pacific nations might also be telling the rest of the world, however, is we should value many and varied outcomes of schooling, not just the ones that are easily measured.

References

UNESCO (1996) *Educational Innovation*, No 88 Paris: UNESCO

Esera, T (1996) 1993 *Annual Report for the Department of Education*, Western Samoa Department of Education.

Siakimotu, A. (1996) *Department of Education Departmental Plan 1996-97*, Government of Niue

Sikua, D. (1997) *Education and Human Resources development Needs for Solomon Islands: 1997-2006*. A paper presented at the USP Strategic Planning Seminar, Honiara, February.

Singh, G. (1997) 'Regional Collaboration in In-Service Education for Primary Teachers in Pacific Island Countries'. A paper presented at the Oxford International Conference on Education and Development, Oxford, September.

Townsend, T & Elder, H. (1998) *Community and Parent Support for Schools*, University of the South Pacific, Suva, Fiji

Vakaotia, A. & Lumelume, S. (1998) 'Effective teachers create effective schools: A Pacific Focus'. A paper presented at the 11th ICSEI Conference, Manchester, January.

SECTION FOUR:
THE MIDDLE EAST AND AFRICA

19.

School effectiveness in Israel: the Arab sector

Ass'ad Shibli

Background

The Arab population which stayed in Israel after the state's establishment, was mostly rural, and lacked access to education services. During the next two decades educational services were expanded to include groups in the community that had been left out of the circle of educational services previously: mainly girls and rural settlements. As a result, a sharp decline in the rate of illiteracy and a parallel increase in the average years of education occurred from 1948 onwards. The number of students in the state-Arab educational system was multiplied almost by 20 times between 1948 and 1990 (from 12,000 to 220,000) while the Arab population in Israel grew only 5 times.

Although the teaching profession in the Arab society consisted mostly of men, considerable reductions in the number of unqualified teachers occurred from 70% of the total number of teachers in the early 1950s to about 15% of the 10,000 teachers who are currently working in Arab-state schools.

These changes are related to developments in three social areas:

- In the national-collective area: following the government's policy of expropriation of Arab land, ownership of land ceased to be of economic value. This policy has caused an increased nationalisation of the concept of education, a resource that cannot be expropriated, and a major tool in the Arab society's struggle over its continued existence as a defined collective.

- In the stratified area: the accessibility of various social groups to education services is closely related to the growth in an Arab-bourgeois class, whose status is not based on land ownership but on the ability to apply services based on professionalism. However, the problem of absorbing and integrating Arab academics in the general Israeli society is continuing.

- At the local-communal area: expanding educational services to various social classes has decreased the salience of ascriptive factors in the individual's social mobility, but, at the same time has moved social struggles between various sections into the school. On the other hand the existing gaps between the Arab state system and the Jewish one in the field of budgeting educational services, led to increased communal activities, financed by independent sources and voluntary activities, mainly in those areas which are neglected by the formal educational authorities.

(Mazawi, 1997).

In 1997 the Arab sector in Israel had 249,000 students, about 63% of them (158,000) in primary education, about 16% (40,000) in secondary schools, about 18% (44,900) in high school and about 2% (5,700) in special education. In comparison with the Jewish sector the proportion of Arab students in primary education is quite high (63% in comparison with 54% in the Jewish sector), but is lower in post-primary education (18% in comparison with 36% in the Jewish sector).

The Arab Israeli citizens are entitled to all civil rights, including the right of equal participation in the education system and rewards for education success (achievements and diplomacy). In theory, the laws and rules of the education system apply equally to Arabs and Jews, although, in practice, two education systems operate in parallel in Israel, one for the Arabs and the other for Jews

Despite this declared equality, evidence and research findings indicate the existence of differences in resource allocation for these two systems, and at the same time, different levels in the *learning outputs* of Jewish and Arab students (Al-Haj, 1996). The entry of Arabs into the labour market is also limited, in comparison with Jewish citizens.

The special conditions of the Arab minority in Israel prevent the incorporation of the Arabs into the Jewish labour market, including the governmental-public administration, which services the whole population. The Arab labour market is also limited because of the lower technological level of the traditional Arab sector (Nahon, 1990).

The Structure of the Israeli education system

The State of Israel provides public compulsory education to all children from the age of five to sixteen. In 1949, the Knesset passed the law of compulsory education which stated that 'the government is responsible for providing compulsory free education for ages five to thirteen'. In 1968, the government added one compulsory free year (grade 9), and in 1979, another year was added (grade 10). At the same time, the law of free high school education was passed. Elementary education in Israel, as well as most of the high-school education, is public. By the effect of the compulsory education law, the Ministry of Education and Culture grants recognition to schools, but has also the authority to determine their contents of study. The Ministry of Education authorises teachers, supervises their work, gives diplomas to the graduates of various stages of study, and is also responsible for funding most costs.

Despite the universalistic spirit of the compulsory education law, the education system is characterised by internal division. The compulsory education law of 1953 recognised three types of Jewish schools: non-religious schools (state schools); religious schools (state-religious schools); and ultra-religious schools (independent education). The law stated that each of these types of schools will have its own administration within the Ministry of Education and Culture.

There is almost a complete separation between the different kinds of Jewish schools, and the Arab schools. This separation is based on the mutual agreement of both parties on separation for the sake of cultural preservation (religion, language, culture), and was strengthened by the communal separation between Arabs and Jews. Although both systems draw their contents and resources from the same laws and regulations, and from the same central authority, which is the Ministry of Education and Culture, every system has its own administration, organisational and implementation teams.

The separation was accepted by the Israeli Arabs with favour, since it allowed Arab children to be educated and study in an education system that is suitable to the atmosphere in which they live. Thus, a special kind of harmony was created between the two basic education frameworks: the family and the school. This separation could contribute a great deal to the preservation of the culture and language for each side, on the one hand, and to educate for respect toward other, different people (Al-Haj, 1996).

Today things are seen in a different light. Among other things, hostility and strangeness between Jews and Arabs were created because of the separation and resulting ignorance about the other's culture. The separation forced the Ministry of Education officials to prepare special curricula for Arabs in Arabic. This was another problematic area, because of the quality and level of Arab textbooks. It is clear today that there is a gap in the quality and level of services that each system receives, and this has a direct effect on the level of the pupils and the level of services provided by each system. Substantial evidence points to the low level of achievements in the Arab system in comparison with the Jewish one. This situation is a direct result of unequal distribution of resources between the Arab and Jewish systems, inequality of budgets and trained and professional personnel to work in the Arab schools (Bashi, 1995). This gap is one of the reasons for the higher rate of dropout in the Arab sector, not to mention the fact that some of the children do not attend school at all, and the fact that the dropout percentage of Arab girls is twice as much as in the Jewish sector (Al-Haj, 1995).

Another reason for the discrepancy between the two systems is the different starting point of each system. While the Jewish sector had a reasonable starting point, the Arab education system lagged behind, due to the flight of the Arab intelligentsia to the Arab countries (Al-Haj, 1996).

The separation continues also in high school. Most Arab high schools provide education at a low level. The teaching level of mathematics, English and Hebrew is low and is characterised by mechanical learning, lack of laboratories and services and a few learning alternatives (for example, assignments instead of matriculation exam) (Al-Haj, 1996).

While elementary and high school education is separate for Jews and Arabs, higher education is uniform. Any student who is eligible to a full matriculation certificate, is entitled to register to university. Actually, there is fierce competition over admittance into university due to the difficult terms presented by the universities; four units in math and English with high grades, a good grade in Hebrew and mastery in this language. These are very difficult conditions for the Arab students, whose matriculation certificates do not meet the requirements.

It is important to note in this context the low academic achievements of Arab pupils in Israel in comparison with other Arab youth in other countries, and especially in some Arab countries.

To summarise, there is a vast gap in the quality of the Arab and Jewish education systems. This great inequality is mainly the result of unequal distribution of resources, difficult social conditions and atmosphere in the Arab sector, inferior starting point of the Arab education system and lack of alternative education settings, mainly special education schools. These conditions have a direct influence on the inferior level of education in the Arab sector.

The history of school effectiveness and improvement

An effective school is a school whose teachers cause their students to attain higher achievements than expected on the basis of their origin and social background. The concept of the effective school gained popularity during the late 60's, when the heated debate revolved around the question: 'Is school really capable of affecting students' achievements?' The prevailing assumption was that most of the variance between schools originates from differences in school inputs. Students from deteriorated schools of the inner city attained lower grades in achievement tests than those who attended well managed suburban schools, whose teachers had more experience (Hurn, 1990).

The most striking research that gave birth to the notion of the effective school was Coleman's report on the 'Equality of Educational Opportunity', published on 3rd July 1966. One of the major conclusions of this article was that

Schools have a marginal influence on student's achievements. These achievements depend, first and foremost, on the personal background and general social environment of the student. This lack of independent influence means that inequality, which is dictated by the children's home, neighbourhood and peers, continues and eventually leads to the same inequality which they encounter as adults. Equal opportunity means strong influence of the school on the student, which does not depend on the close environment of the student. Such influence does not exist in American schools

(Coleman and Campbell, 1966).

Coleman and Campbell (1966) stated that the variance in scholastic achievements is rooted chiefly in the variance of the background variables of the student's home, the 'cultural capital' of the student's family, and, to a smaller degree, in the school input, and classroom variables, such as the average ability of the class students.

Coleman's conclusion about the role and future of the school was considered most pessimistic. Jencks (1972) supported this outlook by concluding that the only predictor of student's success at school is home background, and the work of the staff has almost no effect on the academic achievements of students (Jencks, 1972).

This approach undermined the status of the school in the eyes of American society. In the second half of the 60's and early 70's, voices were heard that questioned the advisability of investment in education. The conclusions of many policy makers, mainly in the US and other Western countries was that education budgets and programs to promote underprivileged children should be cut down, and directed instead toward the adult population. Gaps will be closed by themselves, or, people will have to accept the constant existence of gaps among ethnic groups.

Educators, however, found it difficult to accept these findings. The logical assumption was that better schools will educate better students, and if poor children will attend better schools the gap between their achievements and those of other students will narrow. This line of reasoning presented a challenge to both researchers and educators. Indeed, from the 70s onwards, research on the subject of school influence focused on new directions. Methodological arguments were raised against the research methods and empirical findings that indicated school effectiveness did exist led eventually to the conception of the movement for school effectiveness (Bashi and Shesh, 1989). The methodological arguments were:

that the conclusion about the small effect of school variables resulted from studying the least effective school variables.   Due to the prevailing approach those studies concentrated on inputs, such as salaries, teachers, building conditions, number of books in school library, and variety of study subjects - that is, on resources related to budget, manpower and equipment.

(Friedman, Horowitz and Shaliv, 1988).

The importance of these factors is unquestionable, but more important is the question of how these resources are put to use within educational practice. In other words, the resources in their 'crude' form, are less important than the processes of teaching and learning (Cohen, 1982), which characterise the school as an organisation (Brookover, 1979), variables of school environment and the relation between the school and the environment (Rutter, 1983). The principal goal of the school effectiveness movement was to consider the factors that effect student achievements by using specific research methods that examine what the student learns at school.

The first step in establishing the movement for school effectiveness was taken with the replacement of the statistical research method - that tests predetermined hypotheses on representative samples, the prospective method - with the retrospective method that attempts to detect schools in which student achievements are higher or lower than expected, and analyses the details that distinguish these two kinds of schools (Chen, 1993).

Weber (1971) tried to demonstrate that Coleman and Jensen were mistaken in their claim that low achievements of poor children result from their inability or home background. He identified four schools in the inner city, where students had achieved very high grades in reading and argued that the identification of the particular properties of these schools in comparison with those of regular schools will provide an explanation to the unusual great success in teaching reading. The following characteristics were identified in all four schools:

- Strong principalship. The principal sets the school's atmosphere, participates in selecting teaching methods and distributes resources.
- Schools have set high expectations from their students.
- The importance of reading was emphasised.
- The progress of each student was monitored by administrating tests all-year round.

Indeed, these findings confirmed his argument that, relative to the students' background, some schools attain unexpectedly high achievements. The need for educators to prove that schools do have an effect on students' achievements led eventually to the establishment of the movement called school effectiveness.

School effectiveness in Israel

The movement for school effectiveness did not skip over Israel. Many efforts were invested during the years to improve and make Israeli schools more effective. One of the famous projects in this field during the last decade was the project of 'Kiriat Mal'achi, Sderot', or the so-called 'Bashi Project'. The aim of this project was to turn nine schools in the development towns of Kiriat Mal'achi and Sderot into effective schools, and to increase the level of academic and education achievements of the students according to the model and principles of school effectiveness. The project lasted three years, and included 2500 students and about 150 teachers from state and state-religious schools. The project emphasised academic achievements, and therefore new methods of measurement had to be invented in order to measure the pre-set levels of achievements. The follow-up study was conducted at two levels, criterion tests (minimum-basic tests) and standardised tests. The first type measured mastery of basic skills, which is, in the opinion of the project operators, a precondition to any higher learning. The second type evaluated normative products. Standard tests, which included comprehension and arithmetic, were administered to the first, second, fourth and sixth grades before and after the project.

Minimum tests

Minimum tests were administered for the first time by the end of the first year of the project. Students who failed in 10% of the questions or more were defined as failing. According to this definition, 50-70% of the students failed in each of the classes that took the tests. From this stage on, these minimum tests served as 'tools' for teachers and instructors. The results were analysed diagnostically for each student and formed an important tool for differential work. The student's level was measured every six weeks, using objective tests, with exchanging teachers between classes. No doubt, this method puts the teacher under constant scrutiny.

At first, principals and teachers were reluctant to take part in the project. Their objection was anticipated and understood, since it demanded far-reaching changes in the working methods of principals and teachers. Moreover, principals and teachers were subject to constant criticisms on the achievement level of their students. Gradually, they realised that the heavy investment of three years in the project was fruitful, and the results were positive from the perspective of the project's operators.

Professor Bashi summarised the project by saying:

> ...before the beginning of the project, the achievements of the elementary students in both towns were 3% lower than the national average. Today, three years after the project, it seems that in some of the cases the achievements of the students who participated in the project are higher with 1-3% than those of other students in Israel.

(*Yediot Ahronot,* 20 January 1990)

Other results of the project were marked decrease of violence and decreased absence of teachers and students from school.

In spite of that, the resistance towards school effectiveness grew among senior educators in Israel. For example, Professor Micha Chen, who headed the education department in Tel-Aviv University, stated that 'In no other place in the world was found any scientific support to the heart-warming assumptions that the school effectiveness movement spreads, namely, it is not true that gaps can be narrowed quickly. Bashi's reports are unreliable' (*Yediot Ahronot,* February 1990).

The ex-chairman of the Pedagogical Secretariat, Mr David Por, criticised school effectiveness. At the Van-Leer Convention, held in 1984 he stated that 'School effectiveness focuses on achievements, on academic study, because reading and arithmetic achievements are measurable. This is a narrow and minimalistic measurement. We have already seen rote learning of facts, but not actual learning. This is a very instrumental approach'. Another argument against school effectiveness was that 'good students are neglected and the focus is only on the weak'.

The spread of school effectiveness

Despite the financial hardships that the state of Israel faces, the widening of the movement for school effectiveness was approved by the Ministry of Education. The Ministry of Education planned that during 1990, about a hundred schools will adopt the model of school effectiveness, but in reality, only 25 schools worked according to this model, because of the fundamental differences between the experimental and the distribution stages.

Mordechai Peled, the former general-manager of the Education Ministry argued that,

> because of the special circumstances of the 'Bashi Project', it will remain a one-time event, which could not be replicated, and certainly not introduced with identical terms into the general education system. The State of Israel does not possess these resources today, and it is unlikely that the situation will change in the future.

(Peled, 1989)

Several unsuccessful attempts were made by the Ministry of Education and Culture, during the 1980's and 1990's. However, efforts to increase school effectiveness and autonomy were accelerated with the establishment of a steering committee for school-based management and the publication of its recommendations, in August 1993. The committee recommended that schools should be managed as a closed finance economy, based on a 'student basket' budget. Other recommendations concerned school activities, including an overt, egalitarian and differential budget that takes the needs of underprivileged children into consideration. The school will be able to plan its educational objectives, to set clear goals, to build a curriculum based on its needs and will receive feedback by flexible exploitation of the budget. The committee stated that the inspector's role will focus on counselling, support, assistance and guidance of the school regarding the needs and means to achieve its goals.

These recommendations are in compliance with current perceptions of self-management. This perception is based on two points:

- decentralisation of authority;
- responsibility and sharing.

That is, to transfer authority from the centre to the school and develop the school as an accountable organisation that is committed to the results.

The preparation stage to create the Israeli model of self-management began in the second half of 1995 school year. Nine schools participated in the experimental stage. Thirty-four schools joined the self-management project in the 1997 school year. In addition, a contract, signed by the Ministry of Education and Culture, the Ministry of Finance and Jerusalem Municipality will add eighteen schools to the project this year. All schools in Jerusalem will join in gradually in the future (Havinsky, 1997).

Technological education in the Arab sector of Israel

The goals of technological education are to create a source for the professional manpower infrastructure for the economic and industrial systems and to serve as a tool to prevent students from leaving school and to keep them in a learning framework until the end of the twelfth grade. These goals are especially significant for education in the Arab sector, both because in that sector there is not enough developed, established industry which can provide the youth with the tools to become integrated into the various economic and industrial systems, and also because the percentage of those who leave school is high. Many of the students who leave school look for jobs in the unskilled labour market, usually close to home.

Technological education began to develop in the Jewish sector in the 1960s, and for some years it has attracted about 50% of all the students in post-elementary education. In the Arab sector however, the percentage of students in technological education is much lower. This difference is related to the fact that for many years Arab society gave preference to academic education. In the second half of the 1980s the situation began to change, and the development of technological education is accelerating. The approach of Arab society to technological education improved, and at the same time there was a change in the attitude of the Ministry of Education which led to the opening of prestigious technological trends in the schools (Al-Haj: 74).

Table 1: The percentage of learners in technological education in the Arab sector

Year	Percent of Learners
1975	10%
1980	12%
1985	18%
1990	19%

The Arab sector, which until recently was based on a variety of traditional pursuits, and been undergoing modernisation in the last few years. This requires the education system to develop the technological education framework so that its graduates will initiate and develop the fields of business, trades and industry in the Arab settlements. Stressing the practical value of technological education can also help in that students will prefer it over academic education, which leads to further studies at the university level in the fields of liberal arts and social sciences, fields which leave university graduates with little opportunity for employment. This situation creates frustration and increases pressure in Arab society.

Presently there is a need to develop frameworks which will aid in accelerating industrial development in the Arab settlements, and which will take into consideration the demographic uniqueness of the Arab sector. In 1985, the Fund for the Development of Technological Education was founded by a group of Arab educators and heads of local authorities. Its goal was to encourage professional education in Arab high schools to bridge the gap between the Arab and Jewish sectors. The founders of the fund collected contributions from the Arab local authorities and received a token contribution from the Ministry of Education and from the Minister's office for Arab affairs. The money was earmarked primarily for the purchase of equipment and for the organisation of teacher training in technological subjects. (The Fund for Developing Technological Education, 1986). The fund had no significant influence, but its existence was an additional sign of the effort the Arab population's willingness to take an active part in the advancing of technological education in the high schools. Other active funds, such as the Hans Zeidel Fund, invests large sums in the purchase of equipment and in in-service training courses for teachers in Israel and abroad. However, achievements in the field of technological education are far from satisfactory. In 1988-9 only 17% of the students in the Arab schools studied in technological trends, as opposed to 48% in the Jewish schools (Al-Haj, 1996: 75).

A suggestion for increasing effectiveness and developing technological education in the Arab sector

The Department of Science and Technology of the Ministry of Education formulated a program whose goal was to raise the level of technological education and to adapt it to the new needs of Israel's economy in general and the Arab sector in particular. The intention was to double the number of students in the technological field and to increase the number of trends and to adapt them to the demands of the market. In the past, the principal trends in the Arab sector were carpentry, metal work, auto mechanics and sewing. Authorisation for fifteen new trends was given:

* electricity-electronics with specialisation in electronic systems,
* computerisation and control systems,
* art and design trends,
* tourism,
* office management,
* computerised book-keeping,
* architecture and
* construction.

A significant factor which seriously delayed the development of technological education in the Arab sector was the lack of suitable resources for the acquisition of modern equipment and the building of modern workshops. In the Arab sector a respectable share of the development of technological education was taken by the public educational networks (ORT, Amit, Amal), which were aided by overseas contributions, while there was only a small amount of activity in the Arab sector. There were no organised bodies supporting the local Arab authorities in the development of technological education. In recent years, there has been an increase in the number of schools receiving financial aid for buying equipment. According to the proposed program of the Department for Technological Education, it will be possible to find the budget for purchasing the necessary basic equipment for operating the program with the participation of the local authorities or the proprietary organisations of the schools, according to the 'shekel for shekel' principle.

To achieve the goals of technological education in the Arab sector, the Department for Technological Education proposes the following changes in the educational format of the schools additional non-standard educational frameworks, opening educational frameworks for modular training, adding new fields and the improvement of the existing ones, and the support of a system of training and inspection in the Arab sector. The realisation of the program for the development of technological education in the Arab sector will aid its graduates to become better integrated into the Israeli economy.

Conclusion

One of the main issues of education is the link between education and social change. Is education a factor of modernisation or a factor of conservation? Does education serve the whole community or the dominant group? Parsons (1959) and others claim that a school is an agent of social change. Other scholars, such as Friere (1985) believe in the 'conflict approach' which claims that education is a means of social control, that the dominant group uses it as an efficient tool to control cultural and socio-economical resources.

In spite of the declared policy, that Israeli Arabs are entitled to all civil rights, they are still discriminated against in all aspects and fields of the Israeli life, particularly in the education field where they should be equal to the Jewish sector. There should be positive discrimination. It is noteworthy to mention the fact that the Israeli establishment has never seriously considered the Arab education system. The only policy is always 'No Policy' and this is very typical of policies for the Arab citizen. Later on, the Israeli establishment adopted the 'Laissez faire' policy. This policy caused a lot of trouble among the Arabs, mainly by encouraging a deteriorating attitude toward the Israeli policy.

In the first phase of the establishment of the country (1948-66), the Army Regime in the Arab sector of the Israeli establishment embraced the mandatory policy to keep the 'status quo'. To some extent the Israelis practised this policy in different ways. After cancelling the Army Regime by the end of the 1970s, the second phase policy was 'Laissez Faire'. This caused a lot of damage to the whole system. It even acted to widen the gap between the two systems. In the third phase, from the beginning of the 1980s onwards, the debate has heightened between the Ministry and the Arab population. Even some circles of the Jewish community have joined the struggle by the Arabs for a better education. On the personal level, it is clear that the Arab minority has undergone drastic modernisation, but on the collective level they are marginalised due to the limited resources and opportunities.

It is clear that Arabs relate to education as a means of strengthening their position while the Israeli establishment conceives education as a means of social control. They perceive it as an adaptive system to control the whole society and to establish interactive ways that do not endanger their existence. The dominant group has never related to education as a means to develop minorities, or as a social agent which promotes change. The paradoxical attitudes of each side have caused a lot of misunderstandings and damage to the education system.

The partial citizenship of the Arab minority in Israel is an outcome of the complicated situation of the state of Israel as a Jewish state, and its security problems. The Arabs in Israel live in two circles of conflict, the first one as a minority within a Jewish majority, and the second as a majority in the Middle East. The Arabs feel themselves citizens of Israel but at the same time feel themselves alienated in their country. This alienation may cause a state of defensiveness, in which they find excuses to accuse the establishment for their own problems and faults.

The segregation of the two systems gives the dominant group the right to control and conserve the Arab system. The Arab Department within the Ministry of Education and Culture was always chaired by a Jewish employee until 1987, and from then onwards it was decentralised. This process even heightened the problem because resources were distributed with caution. The actual purpose of this process was to calm down the Arabs' feelings of frustration. The Ministry could systematically control the Arab system by controlling the curricula in order to channel their culture towards the taste of the dominant group. To neutralise and reduce the external effects of detested education, the Ministry started to introduce gradual changes in the Arab curriculum, especially in the Arabic language curriculum, in order to keep the balance. However, these changes did not respond to the rapid developments in Arab education, and the new versions of the curriculum in the Arabic language, were paradoxical. On the one hand, national and religious awakening occurred and, on the other hand, loyalty to the state of Israel was imposed.

Two forces, external and internal, affect the Arab school system. The external forces are represented by the central authority, which is the Ministry of Education, and the internal forces are in the Arab community, its culture and its genetic determinism, that is to say, the Arab mentality of bringing up new generations. It is said that education starts at home, but to tell the truth, some of the Arab homes are not mature enough to give appropriate education to their children, mostly due to the fact that their homes are subject to different influences, particularly the differences in socio-economic positions.

A further factor is the situation in Arab teacher community. Although the community is young, it already seems burned out, due to all the forces that affect it. Teachers have to cope with all the external and internal forces that determine their performance, including authoritative policies, students with socio-economic backgrounds and limited parent cooperation.

To conclude, despite the dark situation, there is light in the end of the tunnel. It is undoubted that the Arab education system has undergone rapid developments but this is not enough. There should be further changes, with an emphasis on more cooperation between the authority and the Arab sector.

I do believe that the coming years will be more productive. A focus on school effectiveness and school improvement will take on different forms which will, in the end, help to mend the situation in the Arab community.

References

Al-Haj, M. (1996) *Education among Arabs in Israel: Control and Social Changes* Jerusalem: Folershiemer Institute for Policy Research and the Hebrew University.

Al-Haj, M. (1995) 'Currents of change and preservation in the educational system', in Landaw, J. (Ed) *The Arab Citizens in Israel toward the 21st Century.* Jerusalem: Sikuy.

Al-Haj, M. (1994) *The Arab Education System in Israel.* Jerusalem: Hebrew University.

Bashi, J. (1995) 'The Arab education system in Israel: Suggestions to develop' in Landaw, J. (Ed) *The Arab Citizens in Israel toward the 21st Century.* Jerusalem: Sikuy.

Bashi, J. & Shesh, Z. (1989) *Yeul Batei Sefer - Bein Teoria Lema'ase Dfus Hita'arvut Vetozotav (School effectiveness - between theory and practice: Intervention pattern and its results)* Jerusalem: Van Leer Institute.

Brookover, J.B. & Lezotte, W. (1979) *Changes in school characteristics coincident with changes in student achievement.* East Lansing: Michigan State University.

Chen, M. (1993) *Beit Hasefer Haeffectivi Vehakita Hateterogenit (School effectiveness and class heterogeneity)* Tel Aviv: Tel Aviv University

Cohen, M. (1982) Effective schools: Accumulating research findings' in *American Education.*

Coleman, J.S. & Campbell, Y. L. (1966) *Equality of educational opportunity* Washington, D.C.: US Government Printing Office.

Friedman, Y, Horowitz, P. & Shaliv, R. (1988) *Efectiviut, tarbut veaklim shel batei sefer (Effectiveness, culture and school climate)* Jerusalem: Henrietta Sald Institute.

Havinsky, A (1997) 'School-based management: Implementation in Israel'. *Bamatnasim, 227,* p 8.

Hurn, C. (1990) *Ighalot hachinuch habeit sifri ve'efsharuyotav (The limitations and possibilities of school education)* Jerusalem: Academon.

Jencks, C. S. et al (1972) *Inequality: A reassessment of the effect of family and schooling in America* New York: Basic Books.

Nahon, I. (1990) 'Education and occupation among Israeli Arabs' in *Compilation of Social Studies,* Tel Aviv: The Sociologic Association.

Peled, M (1989) 'Hinuch Tachliti Nusach Israel (Instrumental education, Israeli style)', in *Hed-Hachinuch* July, 1989.

Weber, G. (1971) Inner city children can be taught to read: Four successful schools. (Occasional Paper No 18. Washington D.C.: Council for Basic Education.

Yediot Achronot, 20 January, 1990

Yediot Achronot, February, 1990

20.

School effectiveness, equity and quality: the challenge of improving the performance of South African schools

Father Smangaliso Mkhatshwa

It is a great honour for me to contribute to this book, happening as it does, on the eve of the 21st century. As a young and vibrant democracy, my country South Africa is facing new challenges, and education is the cornerstone of the reconstruction and development of our country. This chapter serves to illustrate some of the features of these changes and report some of the challenges we face.

In recent times I have considered with deep interest and gratitude the very valuable input of the various perspectives on school effectiveness. A common thread that runs through most of the school effectiveness activity, is either an explicit or tacit acceptance of the social systems of their countries. Scholars from the developing and developed countries are, without exception, primarily concerned with reforming educational practices based on value systems that seem to be taken for granted.

At the risk of oversimplifying a complex situation, we in South Africa are approaching the expressed concern of reaching out to all learners from a different perspective. Our new government embarked on a program of fundamental social transformation. In line with this national project, the South African Ministry of Education is in the process of transforming and restructuring the whole system of human resource development. We believe

that the education system, based on apartheid principles, was radically
flawed, immoral, inefficient and pedagogically unsound. Some of the best
educational policies have been produced since 1994. For us the most critical
challenge facing us now is how best to implement these enlightened policies in
our schools and other institutions of learning. We have had to uproot the old
system before we could start constructing a new way of providing education.
Hence our interest in the progress being made in school effectiveness and
school improvement research. Any education system is a reflection of the
social system in which it is embedded.

Let me begin my chapter with a brief comment on the legacy of apartheid
education; I'll then address a number of pointers from research on school
effectiveness, equity and quality in the South African context; and I'll
conclude by outlining some of the key education policy initiatives we are
currently developing.

Transforming the legacy of apartheid

It is now nearly four years since the first democratic elections in South Africa
brought to power the government which I am part of. We are nearly at the
point of our second election, and the task of transformation is just beginning.
As a state in transition after massive political restructuring, South Africa is
faced with the need to develop – and finance – education policies to bring
both equity and human resource development. Since assuming power in 1994,
the African National Congress-led government has been faced with the
enormous task of transforming the legacy of apartheid education. Only by
tackling this legacy can we begin to work for effectiveness, equity and quality
in our schools. The apartheid education system is notorious for legalising
deep racial inequalities. Perhaps less frequently highlighted are the entrenched
inequalities of class, gender and region. These inequalities are proving
difficult to eliminate and will take far longer than many people at first
anticipated.

With regard to schools, part of our legacy is that during the last 20 years
of apartheid, a large number of black schools ceased to function, particularly
secondary schools in urban townships. Two decades of almost continuous
protest in rejection of Bantu Education generated a culture of opposition and
resistance in schools. This combined with the poverty, material deprivation
and disruption of communities characteristic of apartheid, resulted in what
has been widely termed the 'breakdown of teaching and learning' in many -
though not all - of these schools. One of the major difficulties facing post-
apartheid education departments is to reverse these patterns of school
breakdown. While educational contestation was part of the broader social

movements that finally won over apartheid, this meant that schools became battlegrounds in that civil war, and boycotts, disruptions, challenges to established authority and endemic violence prevailed in many of the schools. The institutional life of schools, profoundly disrupted, has proved difficult to repair in the post-apartheid period. The establishment of legitimate state authority has not, of itself, reversed this breakdown. And the task of taking over government and changing it in a climate of fiscal restraint has proved to be an overwhelming task for the newly reorganised education departments.

The South African educational system continues to be punctuated by the racially skewed distribution of educational resources. The teachers best qualified under apartheid still are generally white, and still continue to teach in white suburban schools. Since teaching costs account for almost 90% of the educational budget, spending remains skewed in favour of white suburban schools. This is so despite our ongoing efforts to redistribute teachers across and within provincial boundaries. In addition, although pupil to teacher ratios are moving toward equity, they remain favourable in white suburban and black township schools to the disadvantage of black rural ones. Recently appointed teachers who occupy newly created management posts such as head of department and deputy principal at black township and rural schools lack the experience of their white, coloured and Indian colleagues who have generally occupied similar posts for many years and even decades. Management capacity to understand and explore the challenge of the best use of available resources is growing but limited in the majority of our schools.

Administrative posts, so vital for achieving a smooth running learning organisation is still skewed in favour of white suburban schools, and is likely to remain so since parents at these schools are able to raise significant resources to retain such posts and staff.

Governing bodies of white suburban schools have traditionally exercised greater powers over schools. As late as the early 1990s, they were handed ownership of school properties, including land and buildings, by the exiting National Party government. This situation does not compare favourably with that in Black, Coloured and Indian schools whose parent bodies were nothing more than extensions and rubber-stamps of the apartheid educational bureaucracy. Re-motivating the adult population to become educational partners in governance and dedicated parents and clients of the learning system is vital for placing school effectiveness on the agenda for the majority of our schools.

Despite our best efforts thus far, children from disadvantaged, poor and unemployed South African parents continue to attend overcrowded, poorly resourced schools with unmotivated and poorer qualified teachers and with limited management ability and experience. We regard all these problems as challenges to the tackled head on. And that is precisely the agenda of my government.

What can we, in South Africa, learn from other countries as we tackle the task of regenerating our schools? What are some of the key points in research on school effectiveness and school improvement that may inform the new education departments in our efforts to achieve for effectiveness, equity and quality in our schools? I'll turn now to some pointers for the international and South African research and experience.

Pointers from research on school effectiveness and improvement

I'm sure that many readers know more about the literature and debates on school effectiveness and school improvement than I do. Rather than attempt to rehearse these debates, I'll simply make a few key points – truisms, perhaps - from international research that I think have relevance to the South African context.

First, I take it for granted that all definitions of 'effectiveness', 'equity' and 'quality' are value-laden, and that any research into these issues reflects the strengths and weaknesses of the epistemological basis. In the South African context, the values for which we are striving in education are enshrined in our new Constitution and Bill of Rights. These affirm a culture of fundamental human rights - including the right to basic education, and to equal access to education. They also outlaw discrimination on the grounds of race, gender, religion, language and sexual preference. This is not say that complex terms such as 'equity' are thereby sewn up. Rather, it is to recognise that these contested terms are given effect in particular value contexts, and to make explicit the value context of the new South Africa. The struggle is to give effect to these values in the daily lives of schools.

Second, I take it for granted that lists of characteristics so beloved of effective schools research may be illuminating but sometimes misleading. It is far easier to identify desirable features of schools than it is to change schools. Schools are complex institutions, not compilations of discrete features, and changing schools is a complex and often lengthy process.

Third, I take it for granted that understanding concepts like 'school effectiveness', 'equity' and 'quality' - however these are defined - requires an understanding of macro social processes, of patterns of inequality and possibilities for intervention. In other words, these concepts can only be understood in their specific contexts. The challenge is to link macro social perspectives with the micro perspectives of individual schools.

Turning more specifically to research on school effectiveness and school improvement in the South African context, I'd like to mention two studies which locate us in the broader debates. The first is a study of school breakdown, and the second, a study of school resilience.

First, the study of school breakdown. A pilot project, which was carried out by the Committee for the Culture of Learning and Teaching (CCOLT) which was instituted in 1994 by the Member of the Executive Council for Education in the Gauteng Province, confirmed the following endemic problems (See de Clercq, Morgan & Christie, 1995; Chisholm & Vally, 1996, Christie, forthcoming).

:

- poor physical and social facilities which impacted negatively on teaching and learning;
- organisational problems including weak and unaccountable leadership, administrative dysfunction (for example timetabling difficulties), and inadequate disciplinary and grievance procedures;
- poor relationships with surrounding communities; and
- poor communication and interactions with education departments.

Yet school breakdown does not fully capture the picture of what has been happening in South African Schools. The second study I'd like to mention is a complementary project to the CCOLT study. In a qualitative study of 32 schools nationally, research was carried out to investigate the dynamics of predominantly black schools that were operating well under the same difficult circumstances that had overwhelmed neighbouring schools. (Christie & Potterton with others, 1997).

Cautioning against the 'list approach' to school effectiveness, the study identified a number of interlacing, dynamic features of schools that succeeded against the odds. These were:

- a focus on learning and teaching as the central activities of the school;
- flexible and purposive leadership;
- a safe and organisationally functioning institutional environment;
- consistent disciplinary practices anchored in educational purposes and personal interaction;
- a culture of concern within the school;
- crucially, a sense of agency and responsibility at school level;
- functioning, though not always close, relationships with their surrounding communities, and

- support from external sources close to the school (a church, non-governmental organisation, or tribal authority).

I'm sure you'll recognise that these features are much in accord with other qualitative studies into school effectiveness. What is important about the study is its contribution to building a local South African knowledge on these issues.

What then are the policies being drawn up by the new government in South Africa, and how do these relate to the debates and research findings on school effectiveness and school improvement? In the third and final part of my chapter, I'd like to report some of the policy challenges facing the South African government, and some of the policy initiatives that we have set in motion.

State policies for school change

Under the new Constitution, the National Department of Education is given the responsibility for framing policies for norms and standards for the country as a whole, while the nine Provincial Education Departments have the task of running the country's schools and changing them.

Since assuming power in 1994, the National Department of Education has concentrated on drawing up legal and regulatory policy frameworks for Education, often developed through task teams and feasibility studies. These framework policies include:

- the establishment of the South African Qualifications Authority which was a first significant step in providing an instrument for linking education and training through learning and qualifications pathways, recognising learning gained through experience and prior non-formal, non-accredited learning, and for providing a mechanism for lifelong learning development.

- New regulations for school governance, including the establishment of elected governing bodies for all schools;

- an outcomes-based curriculum framework, Curriculum 2005, to be progressively implemented in schools;

- the establishment of a management development network for schools with particular emphasis on human resources and financial management. This initiative was preceded by a thorough investigation into current management capacity to take on the challenges of an education management policy which placed emphasis upon partnership education. A report conducted by the Department of Public Service and Administration published in 1997 also drew attention to the problems of management capacity in the newly created provincial administrations and isolated education, health and welfare as the most troubling areas.

- Planning the phased introduction of a national strategy on teacher development. This plan was preceded by investigation into effective teaching in large classes, effective teaching in multi-grade classes, effective teaching in multilingual classes, and whole school development. The plan is also supported by classroom-based research to improve effectiveness in terms of the residual and the new curriculum, and institutional change and capacity building. It includes a recovery program in Mathematics, Sciences, Technology and Engineering, and targets in its first phase black learners who have underachieved in their matriculation examinations in Maths and Science. In its second phase the program takes successful learners through a Maths, Sciences, Engineering and Technology Primary or Secondary teachers diploma program and places them in public schools.

- the establishment of norms for class sizes, on the basis of which the smaller class sizes of historically white schools and the larger classes of historically black schools may be brought to more equitable norms for all;

- the completion of a survey of the National School and College Register of Needs which will go a long way in assisting provinces to re-plan and re-prioritise their budgets to address the shortages in basic educational facilities; and

- an area close to my own heart - the launch of a national Campaign for restoring the culture of Learning, Teaching and Service (COLTS), which is also being developed into provincial campaigns. This campaign is vital for the achievement of our educational transformation agenda, and draws on a wide range of social partners outside of the state. The campaign seeks to achieve and operationalise common understandings of excellence in schools, identify problems and challenges to effective learning and teaching, develop strategies to improve educational delivery in all nine provinces.

However, I am all too aware that frameworks for school reform do not themselves guarantee outcomes. I am constantly reminded that national educational departments have limited influence in changing what happens inside classrooms. What is critical are the activities and processes that take place within and around schools. Whether policy makers approach the change agenda through systemic reform or school-by-school, evidence is that changes at the classroom level are hard to achieve.

Another point which I am keenly aware of is that the difficulties in the implementation of policies should not be underestimated. There is always the danger, in the South African context, that the policies we are formulating may be more easily picked up by the more privileged schools. Targeting the poorest of the poor schools is not easy, and we cannot assume that simply formulating framework policies will achieve our goals of equity and development at the school level. Quality is delivered at the level of the school and classroom, and it is difficult for state policies to work at this level.

One of the major difficulties in state-led reform initiatives is that education systems operate through many levels. Policies formulated at national and provincial levels pass through levels of the bureaucracy in education departments, to the complex contexts of schools. Sustaining a reform thrust through these levels is often impossible. Top-down policies are more likely to succeed if they are accompanied by strategies for bottom-up involvement. However, it is not simply a matter of planning for policies to reach through layers of implementers. Mandating quality of teaching and learning in classrooms cannot be done even by the best organised of policy makers. Hence the need for partnerships involving all key players - viz: educators, learners, community representatives, the private sector, and of course, the education authorities.

Underpinning the government's problems towards redressing imbalances in education is the inadequate national budget. To address this issue the government has developed the first Medium Term Expenditure Framework. Its policy statement, among others, projects the total level of resources that will be available and analyses the trade-off and choices confronting the nation in addressing its reconstruction and development priorities. The new national budgetary process will do away with many weaknesses impeding optimal utilisation of our budget to the benefit of our education and human resource development.

Having acknowledged that, I'd like to bring this chapter to a close around a more positive note by referring again to the COLTS campaign and what I think is possible to strive for from the position of Deputy Minister of Education. While recognising the limitations of state reform policies, it is important also to recognise what they can achieve and will succeed in doing so. I do believe that one of the things that state policies may well be able to do is to provide leadership in setting a moral and political framework for improving teaching and learning at school level.

In the next section I will mention three key points which I believe can be achieved through this campaign.

The importance of teaching and learning

One of the most important task of the COLTS campaign is to build a new vision for quality schooling as part of the government's intellectual and moral leadership in education. It is critically important that the focus stays on teaching and learning.

This focus on teaching and learning is able then to be the basis for other school related interventions. For example, policies for school governance may be related to the need for providing a stable context for teaching and learning in which parents and the community have a role to play. School management development may be similarly related to the importance of providing an organisational basis for teaching and learning. A campaign for school discipline may build upon the importance of legitimate and accountable authority relations for teaching and learning. A campaign against sexual harassment and assault in schools may be anchored in moral principles of human rights and the importance of a safe and peaceful environment for learning and teaching.

I believe that encouraging a moral as well as political dimension to education policy is an important task in the regeneration of education in South Africa. Without this enriched discourse, policies risk an instrumentalism (Clarke, Reed and Lodge 1998) which is not likely to regenerate schools as places of education.

Building legitimate discipline and authority

Another important task in building quality schools in South Africa is to negotiate legitimate authority relations within the education system. As I mentioned earlier, authority under apartheid broke down in many schools, and without this, it is difficult for schools to function well. Again, it is important to build an enriched discourse, which goes beyond rules and regulations. It needs to relate to the moral and political values of the new order - values such as democracy, transparency, accountability and mutual respect.

Teacher and student organisations, religious, political and worker organisations have pledged their support for the COLTS Campaign. The challenge is how to harness and sustain the energy of these players.

A crucial task is drawing up codes of conduct for those involved in schools. Again, and I stress this, it is important that codes of conduct are anchored in the moral dimensions of education, rather than simply in rules. It is also important that schools themselves develop and take ownership of policies for legitimate authority and discipline. But in many cases they will only be able to do this if the National Department of Education and provincial departments negotiate system-level agreements with major stakeholders.

Building a sense of agency and responsibility

Finally, while there are important steps for national and provincial education departments to take, it is crucial for their interventions to work from the basis that schools themselves need to take at least partial ownership of problems and work towards their resolution. At the same time as recognising that certain problems cannot be resolved at the individual school level, it is nonetheless important to challenge assumptions that schools can do little for themselves. In particular, it is important to work against assumptions that interventions from outside – particularly the government - will free them from their problems. Any interventions by departments need to based on the principle that each school has resources within it than can be developed to change small if not big things within the school. The task, then, is to help schools to identify the sorts of things they are able to tackle for themselves, and encourage them to take responsibility for doing so. Experience locally and internationally suggests that school development planning could be used to build participation and co-operation in formulating school vision, goals and plans of action (see Dalin, 1994; Davidoff *et al,* 1995; Dimmock C, 1995; Education Support Project, 1995; Fullan, 1991, 1993; Hargreaves & Hopkins, 1991; Hopkins, 1991; Marsh, 1998, Whittaker, 1993).

Conclusion

The agenda for educational transformation in South Africa is massive and complex, and achieving school effectiveness, equity and quality will be no simple task. The opportunity to be part of this international forum on school effectiveness and improvement is greatly welcomed by me personally and as a representative of my country. I look forward to vigorous debate in the days and years ahead.

References

Chisholm L & Vally S (1996) *The Culture of Learning and Teaching in Gauteng Schools: Report of the Committee on the Culture of Learning and Teaching.* Johannesburg, Education Policy Unit, University of the Witwatersrand.

Chisholm L & Fuller B (1996) Remember people's education? Shifting alliances, state-building and South Africa's narrowing policy agenda. *Journal of Education Policy, 11* (6), pp. 693-716.

Christie P & Potterton M with French A, Cress K, Lanzerotti L, & Butler D (1997) 'School Development in South Africa: a research project to investigate strategic interventions for quality improvement in South African schools': Report prepared for Stichting Porticus, Holland.

Christie, P. (1997) 'Stability against the odds: resilient schools in South Africa.' Paper at the Oxford International Conference on Education and Geopolitical Change, Oxford, 11-18 September.

Christie, P. (1997) 'NQF: History and Identity'. Paper presented at CEPD/EPU Conference on The RDP and NQF, Johannesburg, 15-16 August.

Christie, P. (Forthcoming) Schools as (Dis)organizations: the breakdown of the culture of learning and teaching in South African schools. *Cambridge Journal of Education.*

Clarke, P., Reed, J and Lodge, C. (1998). School improvement: from instrumentalism to sustainability. Paper presented at ICSEI '98 Manchester. ICSEI '98 Proceedings compliled by Clarke, P. on CDRom University of Manchester.

Dalin, P. & Associates (1994) *How Schools Improve: An international Report.* London, Cassell.

Darling-Hammond, L. (1994) *Professional Development Schools: schools for developing a profession.* New York, Teachers College Press.

Davidoff, S., Kaplan, A. & Lazarus, S (1995) Organisation Development: An Argument for South African Schools. In G Kruss & H Jacklin (Eds.) *Realising Change: Education Policy Research.* Cape Town, Kenton Education Association.

de Clercq F, Morgan B & Christie P (1995) Report of the Sebokeng CCOLT Team. Unpublished report submitted to the Gauteng Committee for the Culture of Learning and Teaching, Johannesburg.

de Clercq, F. (1996) *Policy interventions and power shifts: a case study of South Africa's macro education policies.* University of the Witwatersrand, unpublished mimeograph.

Dimmock, C. (1995) Reconceptualizing Restructuring for School Effectiveness and School Improvement, *International Journal of Educational Reform, 4* (3), pp. 285-300

Education Support Project (1995) *School Change, School Based Inset and Education Reconstruction: Report of the "Matlafalang" School Based Inset Programme 1993-1994.* Johannesburg, Education Support Project.

Elmore, R. (1979/80) Backward Mapping: Implementation Research and Policy Decisions. *Political Science Quarterly, 94* (4), pp. 601-616.

Elmore, R. & Associates (1990) *Restructuring Schools: The Next Generation of Education Reform.* San Francisco & Oxford, Jossey-Bass.

Elmore, R. (1995) Structural Reform and Educational Practice. *Educational Researcher, 24* (9), pp. 23-26.

Elmore, R. (1996) Getting to Scale with Good Educational Practice. *Harvard Educational Review, 66* (1), pp. 1-26.

Fuhrman, S. (1995) Introduction: Recent Research on Education Reform. *Educational Researcher, 24* (9), pp. 4-5.

Fullan, M. with Stiegelbauer, S. (1991) *The New Meaning of Educational Change.* New York, Teachers College Press.

Fullan, M.(1993) *Change Forces: Probing the Depths of Educational Reform.* London, New York & Philadelphia, The Falmer Press.

Fuller, B. (1991) *Growing-up Modern: The Western State Builds Third-World Schools.* New York & London, Routledge.

Hargreaves, A. (1994) *Changing Teachers, Changing Times.* New York, Teachers College Press.

Heneveld, W. (1994) *Planning and Monitoring the Quality of Primary Education in Sub-Saharan Africa.* Washington D C, The World Bank.

Heneveld, W.& Craig, H. (1996) *Schools Count: World Bank Project Designs and the Quality of Primary Education in Sub-Saharan Africa.* Washington D C, The World Bank.

Hopkins, D. (Ed.) (1987) *Improving the Quality of Schooling.* New York, London & Philadelphia, The Falmer Press.

Hopkins, D.(1991) Changing School Culture Through Development Planning. In S Riddel & S Brown (Eds.) *School Effectiveness Research: Its Messages for School Improvement.* Edinburgh, HMSO.

Levin, H. & Lockheed, M. (Eds.) (1994) *Effective Schools in Developing Countries.* London & Washington, Falmer Press.

Lightfoot, S. L. (1983) *The Good High School: Portraits of Character and Culture.* New York, Basic Books.

Marsh, C (1988) *Spotlight on School Improvement.* Sydney, Allen & Unwin.

Reynolds, D., Hopkins, D., & Stoll, L (1993) Linking School Effectiveness Knowledge and School Improvement Practice: towards a synergy. *School Effectiveness and School Improvement, 4* (1), pp. 37-58.

Rondinelli D., Middleton, J. & Verspoor, A. (1990) *Planning Educational Reforms in Developing Countries: The Contingency Approach.* Durham & London, Duke University Press.

Stoll, L., & Fink, D. (1996) *Changing our Schools: Linking School Effectiveness and School Improvement.* Buckingham, Open University Press.

Vaillant, G. (1993) *The Wisdom of the Ego.* Cambridge Mass. & London, Harvard University Press.

Wang, M. & Iglesias, A. (1996) Building on Existing Structures: An Outreach Strategy for Improving the Capacity for Education in the Inner Cities. *Education Policy, 10* (2), pp. 273-296.

Whitaker, P. (1993) *Managing Change in Schools.* Buckingham & Philadelphia, Open University Press.

21.

Third Millennium Schools: prospects and problems for school effectiveness and school improvement

Tony Townsend, Paul Clarke and Mel Ainscow

The chapters in this book, which outline the developments, and the conditions under which those developments have taken place, from countries around the world, have clearly demonstrated how far school effectiveness research and school improvement developments have come since the early work of Weber (1971) and Edmonds (1978, 1979a, 1979b, 1981) in the United States and Reynolds (1976) and Rutter and colleagues (1979) in the United Kingdom. In less than twenty five years, the school effectiveness movement with its focus on results has joined forces with the school improvement movement with its accent on the process. As Smink concluded (1993:1) 'both approaches need the other to successfully modernize the system.'

It is obvious that the school effects research has been used, by school systems and by governments all over the world, as a strategy to identify new ways to promote achievement for *all* children. The school improvement focus has contributed, in no small way, to the world wide phenomenon called school restructuring, which, in almost every case, has seen substantial devolution of many aspects of school management to the school itself.

Hill and Cuttance (chapter 14) argue that the past decade has seen policy driving research rather than the other way around. They suggest that 'policy remains ahead of research evidence regarding the various reform measures'. Whereas early school effectiveness research has been accused of being

incestuous in that a few studies were often repeated and that subsequent meta-
analyses then became part of the 'evidence', we could now argue that the
school effectiveness research has been adopted by some education systems to
implement their own agenda. For instance, the argument that many effective
schools show high degrees of autonomous decision-making has been turned
around by some education systems to promote the argument that
decentralisation of decision-making to the school level will make *all* schools
more effective. The strength of that link has never been finally tested.

If nothing else the claim that schools can make a difference is no longer in
dispute. As Reynolds has argued, the school effectiveness research has had
the positive effect of 'helping to destroy the belief that schools can do nothing
to change the society around them...and...the myth that the influence of family
background is so strong on children's development that they are unable to be
affected by school' (Reynolds, 1994:2). But he also argues that it has had the
negative effect of 'creating a widespread, popular view that schools do not
just make a difference, but that they make all the difference' (Reynolds,
1994:4). It is perhaps this issue, rather than anything else, that needs to be
kept in mind when we consider the future of school effectiveness and
improvement.

The chapters in this book identify a diversity of critical issues, a diversity
of policy responses and a diversity of practical applications, all of which are
aimed at improving the effectiveness of schooling. However, many questions
about school effectiveness remain unresolved. As Rosenholtz (1989:1-2)
points out, 'the most interesting questions in this area are not at all
methodological, they are conceptual'. One of the key areas yet to be fully
elaborated upon relates to how school effectiveness is defined. Many
definitions have been proposed, but none have found universal acceptance.
Chapman (1992) identified school effectiveness as one of what Gaillie (1964)
called 'essentially contested concepts'. Since there will be a number of
different perspectives of the goals of education in general, and of the role
school plays in the fulfilment of those goals then, necessarily, the perspectives
of what makes a school effective will vary as well.

The current state of school effectiveness and improvement research

At the end of the eleventh International Congress for School Effectiveness and
Improvement, in Manchester, England, an analysis of the current state and
future of school effectiveness and school improvement research was
undertaken. Creemers *et al* (1998: 122-128) identified the following foci of
current school effectiveness research:

- The development of a different range of outcome measures to measure school effects in social and affective areas as well as in the cognitive domain.

- The issue of how to present 'effect size' and how to show the relevance of the various levels (eg class, school) of the educational system.

- The conceptualisation and measurement of processes at the various levels and the factors associated with effectiveness of them.

- The identification of the factors and variables that contribute to effectiveness and the differences between countries for these variables.

- The development of theoretical models that explain the differences in educational outcomes between students, classes, schools and contexts.

- Progress in the development of research methodology, particularly in the use of qualitative methodology, to provide an in-depth analysis of effectiveness.

They also (Creemers *et al* 1998: 128-129) identified the current foci of school improvement research:

- Changes that schools make to move from a 'less effective' to a 'more effective' or from a 'more effective' to a 'less effective' status.

- The development of implementation strategies and the adaptation of conventional strategies of school improvement to become increasingly based on effectiveness knowledge.

- The analysis of macro level policy techniques and strategies for change, such as teacher empowerment, teacher professionalisation, school based management and decentralisation.

- Inclusion of financial aspects of improvement, recognising the need for cost effectiveness and efficiencies of strategies and procedures.

- A focus upon the reliability or fidelity of program implementation, when schools are required to implement organisational and curricular changes reliably, rather than invent their own.

- Material on school culture and the 'ownership' paradigm and whether these improvements can change educational outcomes;

- A recent emphasis on teaching and learning recognising the need for concentration on the learning level as well as other levels of the school.

Issues for the future

The chapters in this book identify a series of issues (some currently of interest and others that are emerging) that need to be considered as we move into the new millennium, and many of these issues are international in scope. Those listed below might provide some specific examples of future research efforts that might be carried out, within educational systems, within countries and across countries:

- The relationship between school and system effectiveness and improvement
- The links between school and classroom effectiveness
- The relationship between increased teacher empowerment and professionalism and improved student learning
- The impact of reform or decentralisation activities on equity and effectiveness
- Developing reliable, valid and relevant assessment systems/issues of accountability
- A consideration of the impact of social change on schools, school systems and student outcomes
- The impact of technology on teaching and learning and its relationship to improved student outcomes
- The use of the need for 'national economic development' or other 'government priorities' as a prime motive for changes in curriculum at a national or systemic level (eg the focus on literacy) and the impact this has on equity and effectiveness issues.
- Turning knowledge of school effectiveness and improvement research into improved school practices.
- Reassessment of what it means to be an effective school. Are decisions about effectiveness based purely on academic achievement, or should we consider issues such as socialisation, student health, democratic values, citizenship, culture, and the like.
- Principal empowerment and leadership development as a means towards more effective schools.
- The relationship between levels of school funding and student outcomes (The decentralisation process has had an impact on funding levels for schools).

- The impact of international projects (eg TIMSS, IEA, ISERP) on decisions made about education.

- The relationship between empowerment and involvement of parents and the broader community and school effectiveness.

Each of these factors could provide a wealth of research and development activity in the next decade. However, perhaps the most obvious result that comes from a careful reading of the chapters in this book is that schools are still at the front end of monumental change, and that this is after two decades that have seen more changes in the way in which schools are structured and operated than had occurred in the previous hundred and fifty years put together. But it is almost certain that further change is on the way and it is within this larger framework that future school effectiveness and improvement developments will operate.

The bigger picture

It is almost as if the advent of the third millennium has brought with it the need to reconstruct our view of the purpose of, and even the need for, schools. It may well be that the focus of school effectiveness and school improvement in the next decade may move from some of the more specific issues such as those listed above, to a more general consideration of schooling as such.

The last two decades have seen huge changes in the way in which schools are managed and structured. Every school system considered in this book has undergone substantial alterations to both form and function, with the dominant trend being a decentralisation to the school level of some processes previously undertaken centrally, but within strong systemic control of curriculum and accountability frameworks. In many countries, it might be argued that the balance has gone too far towards the school and that school systems have given away their responsibilities to ensure that all students have access to the resources and curriculum they need to succeed. In many cases internationally, governments have opted to 'steer' (telling schools what they have to achieve) through curriculum and accountability frameworks rather than 'row' (doing the job of 'running' the schools). The result of this decision has been self-managing or self-governing public schools.

Early instances of self-management came in the early 1970s from Dade county in Florida and from Canada, where the Edmonton School District pioneered many of the features of self-managing schools seen today. Then in the late 1980s and early 1990s a plethora of schools systems around the world moved in the same direction. First, in 1988, we saw the United Kingdom with its *Education Reform Act* producing Grant Maintained (GM) and Locally Managed (LM) Schools, and New Zealand, which adapted the Canadian model as a means for developing a national system of self-managing schools called *Schools of Tomorrow*.

In the 1990s we have seen the United States with its charter school movement, Hong Kong with its *Self Managing Initiative*, Malaysia with *Education 2010*, and various Australian states adopting new strategies for school management; Western Australia (*Better Schools*, 1987), New South Wales (*Schools Renewal*, 1989), Victoria (*Schools of the Future*, 1993), Tasmania (*Directions for Education*, 1996) and Queensland (*Leading Schools*, 1997). It becomes obvious from the names used by many of the systems developing such programs that the emphasis was on changing schools for the better, leaving the undeniable conclusion that schools were not serving the community as well as they once were.

As Mkhatshwa argues in chapter 20, the balance of what governments and school systems are expected to do and what schools themselves are expected to do is starting to shift. What needs to happen is a fine tuning of that balance to ensure that appropriate contributions are made at both levels.

It may now be useful to spend a little time considering the ways in which schools have started to change and perhaps to predict where those changes might lead over the next twenty years or so. Despite the difficulty of predicting the future, (for instance, would anyone fifteen years ago have predicted schools would have access to global information of unlimited amounts instantaneously – i.e., the Internet, or have predicted the Asian economic crash, the end of the cold war, Bosnia?), the turn of the century has always been a time of reflection, so the turn of the millennium makes it an even more appropriate time to consider the future, to plan an education system that responds to it.

Let's consider 2010, the year children currently in the first year of school will emerge into the workforce, if they complete twelve years of school. What sorts of skills, attitudes and understandings will be necessary for survival in the global economic community, and what changes do we have to make to education in order to get there?

What will the world be like in the year 2010? The simple answer is, we don't know. So how can predict what will be the circumstances in terms of education nearly fifteen years away? We might predict that if current trends in technology and the globalisation of the economy continue that the world will probably need people that are highly skilled, highly knowledgable and independent, but interactive, thinkers. The world will need people who are able to make decisions, to enable them to adapt to new work, or new techniques, or to be entrepreneurial, when changes in work require changes in the workforce. Perhaps we need to add the desire to operate within a community, rather than as a series of separate units. This suggests people will want to work and make decisions in concert with one another and it encourages society to do the same.

We could perhaps construct a list of what we might call Third Millennium skills. Perhaps the following list might serve as a starting point:

- Literacy and Numeracy
- Technological Capabilities
- Communication Skills & Exchange of Ideas
- Awareness and Appreciation of Cultures
- Vision and Open Mindedness
- Development Capabilities & Entrepreneurship
- Critical Thinking Skills and Adaptability
- Teamwork and Community Service
- Awareness of one's choices
- Commitment to Personal & Community Growth
- Leadership capabilities

Our next step would be to consider how schools might be reconstructed to enable these skills to be developed. Townsend (1998: 246) suggested: 'perhaps what we need to do is to turn the clock back a little, to wonder what we might do if schools did not now currently exist.'

Beare (1997: 1) posed a question of a similar kind:

If, as an educational planner, you were presented with a greenfields site on which a new town or suburb was to be built to accommodate dwellings for approximately 22,000 people, what schools or educational buildings would you offer the developer?

He argued that there are some things that you would not have, including:

- the egg-crate classrooms and long corridors;
- the notion of set class groups based on age-grade structures;
- the division of the school day into standard slabs of time;
- the linear curriculum parceled into step-by-step gradations;

- the parceling of human knowledge into pre-determined boxes called 'subjects';
- the division of staff by subject specialisation;
- the allocation of most school tasks to the person called 'teacher';
- the assumption that learning takes place in a place called 'school';
- the artificial walls that barricade school from home and community;
- the notion of a stand-alone school isolated from other schools;
- the notion of a school system bounded by a locality such as a state or even country;
- the limitation of 'formal schooling' to twelve years and between the ages of five and eighteen.

(adapted from Beare, 1997: 2-4)

If we accept the arguments about what schools in the future should not be, we have some indication of the task facing school communities, school leaders, teachers and parents on the one hand, and governments and educational policy makers, on the other. Given some of these arguments, we might have to accept that schools of the third millennium might have to be totally different to those we have now.

Second Millennium and Third Millennium schools

Recent conferences in Australia threw up a range of opinions about the future of schools, from '...the formal education system could be said to be in its last throes' (Spender: 1997:1) to '... the most probable state of schools in 2007 is that they will be much the same as they are now' (White, 1997:1). Probably neither is right, but if we look at some of the reasons why this debate is now occurring, coincidentally at the end of the second millennium, they can probably be narrowed down to two main factors.

First, the rapid advance of technology has meant that the ways in which we used to learn may now have been supplanted by mechanisms that we can no longer control. Now teachers are no longer in charge of the content of learning, except for around 15 per cent of students' lives. For the rest of the time things such as the Internet can provide immediate content of any kind, which the student can draw on to support, or supplant, their formal learning. Second, the advent of the global economy and global communications has meant that no country, except perhaps the poorest that do not have the means of access, can work in isolation. There are now many means of comparing what we do with other countries, both economically and educationally, and since we now assume that the two are inextricably linked, to perform well at one means you need to perform well at the other. Otero (1998) characterises these two factors as 'rapid pervasive change' and 'increasing global interconnectedness'.

What these two factors suggest is that schools have been caught up in changes not of their making, but changes that they nevertheless have to respond to. With this in mind, we might argue that schools need to be transformed, and rapidly, if they are to once again be seen as a community resource rather than, which seems to be the case in many countries at the moment, as a drain on community resources. What we need to do is to move schools from second millennium institutions to third millennium institutions. To do this we need to consider the characteristics of schools as they are and as they might be in the third millennium.

Listed below are a series of features that, we could argue, characterise schools as they are now, or at least were in the recent past, before the current wave of reform hit. We have called these characteristics of second millennium schools. Next to these features, we have listed those that we think will be the new features, those that might be in place in as little as twenty or thirty years. We have called these characteristics of third millennium schools.

It is likely that some, or even many, schools have started the process of moving from second to third millennium characteristics, but for each instance, we believe that all schools will need to display the third millennium characteristics listed, either through the process of individual schools changing their culture and programs, or by it being forced on them, by governments or economic circumstances.

Second Millennium Schools	Third Millennium Schools
Schools provide formal education programs which students must attend for a certain minimum amount of time.	People have access to learning 24 hours a day 365 days a year through a variety of sources, some of which will be schools.
Schools offer a broad range of curriculum to prepare students for many varied life situations.	Schools offer a narrow curriculum focusing on literacy, numeracy, and generic technological and vocational skills.
Teachers are employed to 'know'. The learner fits in with the teacher.	Teachers are employed to match teaching to the needs of the learner.

Second Millennium Schools	Third Millennium Schools
Schools are communities of learners, where individuals are helped to reach their potential.	Schools are learning communities where everyone (students, teachers, parents, administrators) is both a learner and a teacher, depending on the circumstances.
The information to be learned is graded in a specific way and is learned a particular order. Everyone gets a similar content, with only limited differentiation based on interest.	Information is accessed according to the learner's capability and interest. The information will vary greatly after basic skills are learned.
Schools are still much the same in form and function as they were when they were first developed.	Schools as we know them have been dramatically altered in form and function, or have been replaced.
Schools have limited, or no, interactions with those who will employ their students or the people from the community in which the school resides.	Communities will be responsible for the education of both students and adults. Business and industry will be actively involved in school developments.
Schools are successful if they fit their students into a range of possible futures from immediate employment as factory hands and unskilled workers to tertiary education for training as professionals.	Schools will only be successful if *all* students have the skills required to work within, and adapt to, a rapidly changing employment, social and economic climate.
Formal education institutions are protected from the 'market'.	Formal education institutions are subject to 'market' forces.

If we look at what we consider to be the current and future characteristics of schools, we can also see that there is some underlying thinking that generates these features. The table below provides some attempt at identifying what characterises recent thinking about education, particularly in the west, together with how that thinking might need to change to promote third millennium education.

Second Millennium Thinking	Third Millennium Thinking
Important learning can only occur in formal learning facilities.	People can learn things from many sources.
Everyone must learn a common 'core' of content.	Everyone must understand the learning process and have basic learning skills.
The learning process is controlled by the teacher. What is to be taught, when it should be taught and how it should be taught are all be determined by a professional person.	The learning process is controlled by the learner. What is to be taught, when it should be taught and how it should be taught will all be determined by the learner.
Education and learning are individual activities. Success is based on how well learners learn as individuals.	Education and learning are highly interactive activities. Success is based on how well learners work together as a team.
Formal education prepares people for life.	Formal education is the basis for lifelong learning.
The terms 'education' and 'school' mean almost the same thing.	'School' is only one of a multitude of steps in the education journey.
Once you leave formal education, you enter the 'real world'.	Formal education provides a range of interactions between learners and the world of business, commerce and politics.
The more formal qualifications you have the more successful you will be.	The more capability and adaptability you have the more successful you will be.
Basic education is funded by government.	Basic education is funded by both government and private sources.

Using the current and future thinking about education, we could argue, pretty categorically, that the changes that schools have had to endure in the past decade or so will be nothing compared to what will happen in the next twenty or so years.

If this is the case we need to adapt current attitudes, and perhaps some of the practices, in education. American demographer, Harold Hodkinson (1990), has demonstrated that for every dollar spent at the front end of a person's life (on education) there is a savings of up to six to eight dollars with decreased later problems related to poverty, crime and poor health. A strong and well supported education system leads to a strong and capable society.

Educators around the world are starting to understand that, even within the school system, there seem to be two critical pressure points. The first is the early years of a child's education and the second has come to be known as the middle school years.

It is at kindergarten and the first couple of years of school that the first seeds of literacy and social interaction are planted. If they are not watered and fertilised well by the time the child is eight, the eventual fruit will either be withered or non-existent. Researchers ranging from Peter Hill at Melbourne University to Peter Mortimore at the University of London to Bob Slavin at Johns Hopkins in America have indicated the need for substantial focus, effort and adult time to be allocated to these early attempts to make all children literate. It is in the first three or four years of school that low student-teacher ratios, a strongly focused curriculum and active intervention for students who start to fall behind is necessary. This may mean that class sizes are higher for the rest of the primary school years.

It may also mean that we have to spend considerable effort and money on encouraging parents to play an active role in the literacy process. Just like riding a bike, the more you read, the better you get. Home libraries and parents who spend time reading with their children are just as critical as good teaching is in the first place. We need to find ways to encourage parents who may have struggled to read themselves to get involved in this process. The Basic Education and Life Skills program (chapter 18) in the Pacific, and the manual *Community and Parent Support for Schools* (Townsend and Elder, 1998) may provide education systems in the west with some strategies for developing this feature.

The second pressure point for education comes in the middle school, at the time when people are deciding whether they will leave at the legal age or will stay on to complete school. This has been a problem as long as education has been compulsory. A Scottish study in the 1890s showed that the group most likely to cause discipline problems were boys just below the legal leaving age who had decided they would be leaving. A hundred years later, nothing has changed.

Not surprisingly, this group are generally the students who had early trouble with literacy, students who have struggled to come to terms with education, have experienced failure and feel that education has nothing to offer them. Michael Barber (1996: 72-82) calls them the disappeared, the disaffected and the disappointed. So again, spending money in the early years is critical to the health of the system as a whole. Governments in many parts of the world are starting to focus on these critical stages of learning and are providing additional resources for literacy and numeracy in the early years.

But these resources are being allocated at a time of diminishing resources in general, particularly in the west, which means even more pressure is being placed on public schools to cope with the demands. Simultaneously, the acceptance of choice and the market as being the mechanism that will drive improvement, seems instead to have widened the gap. As MacBeath indicates in chapter 4, the more decentralised the system, the greater the difference between the best and worst performing students.

What it means to be an effective school, given some of the scenarios we have painted, suggests that the next twenty years of research may be even more interesting than that we have identified in this book. It will be a journey worth taking.

References

Barber, M. (1996) *The Learning Game*, London: Victor Gollanncz.

Beare, H. (1997) Designing a break-the-mould school for the future. A paper presented at the virtual conference of the Australian Council for Educational Administration, Hawthorn.

Chapman, J.D. (1992) 'Making Substance the Leading Edge of Executive Work: Towards a More Integrated Approach for Understanding Leadership, School Based Decision-making and School Effectiveness' in Dimmock, C. (Ed) *Leadership, School Based Decision-making and School Effectiveness*, London, Routledge.

Creemers, B., Reynolds, D., Chrispeels, J., Mortimore, P,. Murphy, J., Stringfield, S., Stoll, L. and Townsend, T. (1998) 'The future of school effectiveness and improvement' in *School Effectiveness and School Improvement, (9)* 2, pp. 125-134.

Edmonds, R. (1978) 'A Discussion of the Literature and Issues Related to Effective Schooling.' A paper presented to National Conference on Urban Education, CEMREL, St Louis, USA.

Edmonds, R. (1979a) 'Effective Schools for the Urban Poor', *Educational Leadership*, 37 (1), 15-27.

Edmonds, R. (1979b) 'Some Schools Work and More Can', *Social Policy*, 9 (4), 28-32.

Edmonds, R. (1981) 'Making Public Schools Effective', *Social Policy*, 12(4), 56-60.

Gaillie, W.B. (1964) 'Essentially Contested Concepts' in Gaillie, W.B., *Philosophy and Historical Understanding*, London, Chalto and Windus.

Hodkinson, H.L. (1990) 'The Same Client: The Demographics of Education and Service Delivery Systems.' A paper presented at the Annual

Conference of the National Community Education Association Convention, San Antonio, December, 1990.

Otero, G. (1998) 'Promoting Global Awareness in the Classroom.' Occasional Paper, Melbourne: Independent Association of Registered Teachers of Victoria.

Reynolds, D. (1976) 'The Delinquent School' in Woods, P. (Ed), *The Process of Schooling*, London: Routledge.

Reynolds, D. (1994) The Effective School. A revised version of an Inaugural Lecture. University of Newcastle upon Tyne, October.

Rosenholtz, S.J. (1989) *Teachers Workplace: The Social Organization of Schools*, New York, Longman.

Rutter, M., Maughan, B., Mortimore, P. & Ouston, J. (1979) *Fifteen Thousand Hours: Secondary Schools and Effects on Children*, Boston, Harvard University Press.

Smink, G. (1991) 'The Cardiff Conference, ICSEI 1991', *Network News International*, 1(3), 2-6.

Spender, D. (1997) From the factory system to portfolio living: Access, equity and self promotion in the 21st century. A keynote paper presented at the annual conference of the Australian Council for Educational Administration, Canberra.

Townsend, Tony (1998) 'The Primary School of the Future: Third World or Third Millennium?' in Townsend, Tony (Ed) *Primary School in Changing Times: The Australian Experience*, London and New York, Routledge.

Townsend, Tony and Elder, Henry (1998) *Community and Parent Support for Schools*, Suva, Fiji, University of the South Pacific.

Weber, G. (1971) *Inner City Children Can Be Taught to Read: Four Successful Schools*, Washington, D.C.: Council for Basic Education.

White, R. (1997) Schools in 2007. A paper presented at the virtual conference of the Australian Council for Educational Administration, Hawthorn.

Appendix A

A Comparison of School Systems

Country	Primary and Secondary Schools			Vocational Education	Tertiary
	Schools	Students	Teachers	Students	Students
United Kingdom	28,169	8,585,000	454,000	586,000	470,500
Belarus	4,900	1,628,500	122,700	126,400	178,000
Cyprus	490	119,000	7,300	4,100	7,800
France	41,656	4,065,000	218,100	Note 1	1,700,800
Netherlands	10,186	2,303,000	188,500	499,000	419,200
Norway	4,096	707,000	58,000	Note 1	172,500
Canada	16,231	5,365,000	301,000	Note 1	921,500
Chile	8,338	2,085,000	79,000	262,000	316,000
USA	85,393	51,000,000	2,970,000	Note 1	14,210,000
Australia	9,679	3,100,000	200,100	990,000	604,200
Hong Kong	860	468,000	19,500	48,500	76,500
Malaysia	6,968	2,719,000	135,000	41,000	136,000
New Zealand	2,742	671,000	37,000	107,000	104,500
Pacific	2,343	534,000	59,500	203,700	169,000
Israel	2,682	1,119,000	87,000	123,000	91,500
South Africa	22,260	11,783,000	350,000	140,500	505,500

Note 1:   Vocational education students are included within the primary/secondary numbers

Appendix B

The Authors

Adrienne Affleck is a Research Assistant in the Department of Education Studies at the University of Waikato in Hamilton, New Zealand.

Professor Mel Ainscow is Dean of the Research and Graduate School, University of Manchester

Professor Gilbert Austin works at the University of Maryland in Baltimore, USA.

Professor Janet Chrispeels works in the Department of Education at the University of California, Santa Barbara, USA

Dr Paul Clarke works at the School of Education, University of Manchester

Professor Peter Cuttance is the Head of the School of Educational Psychology, Measurement and Technology at the University of Sydney in Sydney, Australia.

Dr Peter Daly works in the Department of Education at the Queen's University in Belfast, Ireland

Dympna Devine works in the Education Department of the Faculty of Arts at University College in Dublin, Ireland.

Professor Trond Eiliv Hauge works in the Department of Teacher Education and School Development at the University of Oslo in Oslo, Norway.

Professor Peter Hill is the Associate Dean and Executive Director of the Centre for Applied research in Education, at the Institute of Education at the University of Melbourne in Melbourne, Australia.

Dr Leonidas Kyriakides works at the Pedagogical Institute in Nicosia, Cyprus.

Professor Haroldo Quinteros works at the Arturo Prat University in Iquique, Chile and is currently on leave at Tübingen University in Germany.

Professor John MacBeath is the Director of the Quality in Education Centre at the University of Strathclyde in Glasgow, Scotland.

Dr Charil Marzuki works in the Department of Educational Development, Faculty of Education at the University of Malaya in Kuala Lumpur, Malaysia.

Denis Meurat works at the Institut Universitaire de Formation des Maitrs (IUFM) de Bretagne, Rennes, France.

Father Smangaliso Mkhatshwa is the Deputy Minister of Education in the South African Government.

Professor Haji Ahmad Rahimah is Dean of the Faculty of Education at the University of Malaya in Kuala Lumpur, Malaysia.

Dr Peter Ramsay works in the Department of Education Studies at the University of Waikato in Hamilton, New Zealand.

Professor David Reynolds is the Director of the Newcastle Educational Effectiveness and Improvement Centre in the Faculty of education at the University of Newcastle upon Tyne, in England.

Professor Kathryn Riley is Director of the Centre for Educational Management at Roehampton Institute, University of Surrey, London, England.

Professor Larry Sackney works in the Department of Educational Administration at the University of Saskatchewan, Saskatoon, Saskatchewan, Canada.

Professor Jaap Scheerens is the Director of OCTO in the Faculty of Educational Science and Technology at the University of Twente, Enschede, the Netherlands.

Ass'ad Shibli is the Director of the Shibli Comprehensive School in Israel.

Dr Louise Stoll is Co-ordinating Director of the International School Effectiveness and Improvement Centre (ISEIC) at the Institute of Education in the University of London, England

Professor Desmond Swan works in the Education Department of the Faculty of Arts at University College in Dublin, Ireland.

Associate Professor Tony Townsend works in the Faculty of Education at Monash University in Melbourne, Australia.

Asenaca Vakaotia is the Coordinator of the Community Support for Education component of the Basic Education and Literary Skills program based at the Institute of Education at the University of the South Pacific in Suva, Fiji.

Associate Professor Wong Kam Cheung is Head of the Department of Education at the University of Hong Kong.

Professor Iouri Zagoumennov is Director of the Belarus Educational Centre for Leadership Development in Minsk, Belarus.

Associate Professor Manaf Abdul Zulkifli works in the Department of Pedagogy and Educational Psychology, Faculty of Education at the University of Malaya in Kuala Lumpur, Malaysia.

Index